GREAT FRENCH PAINTINGS FROM THE CLARK

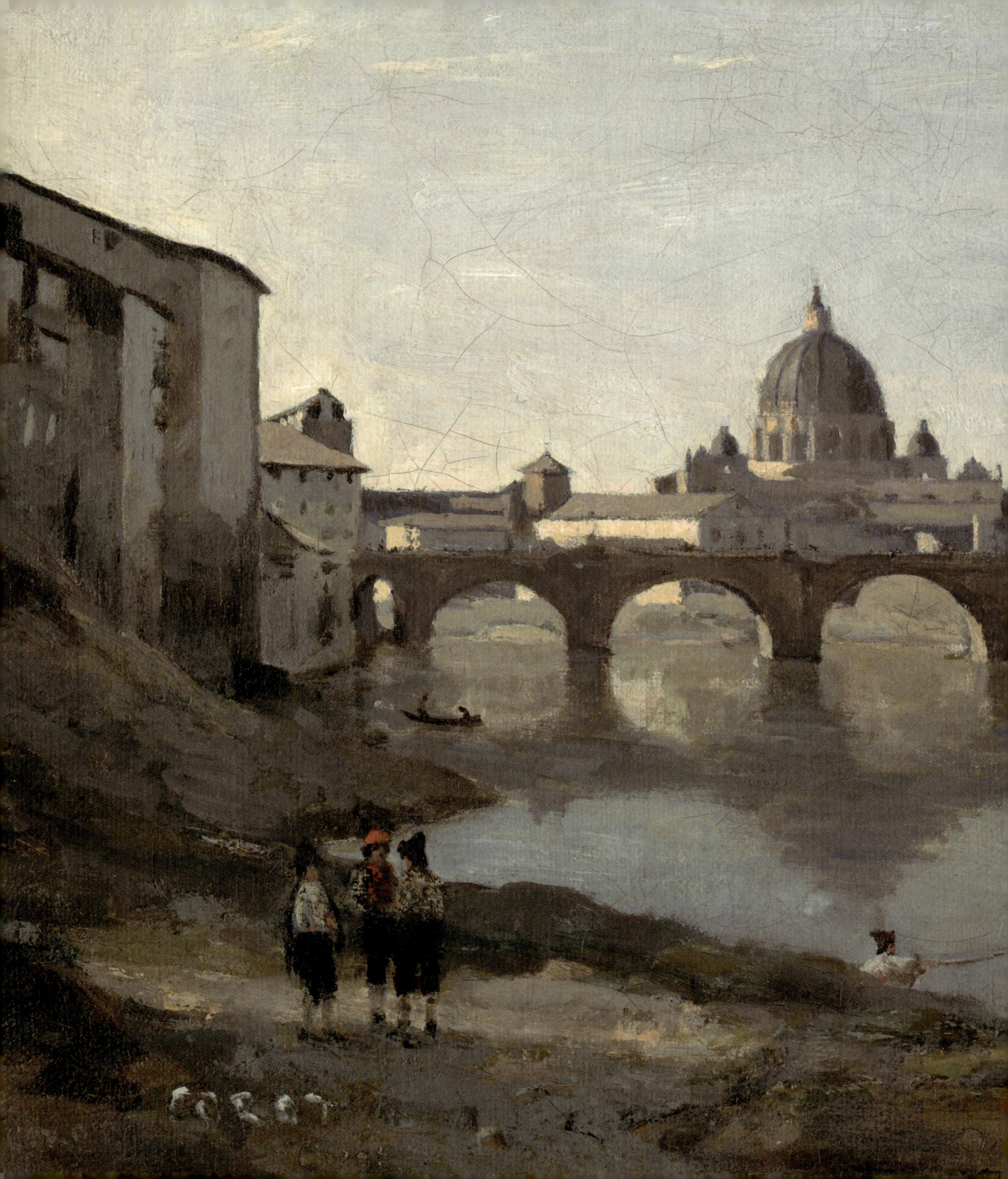

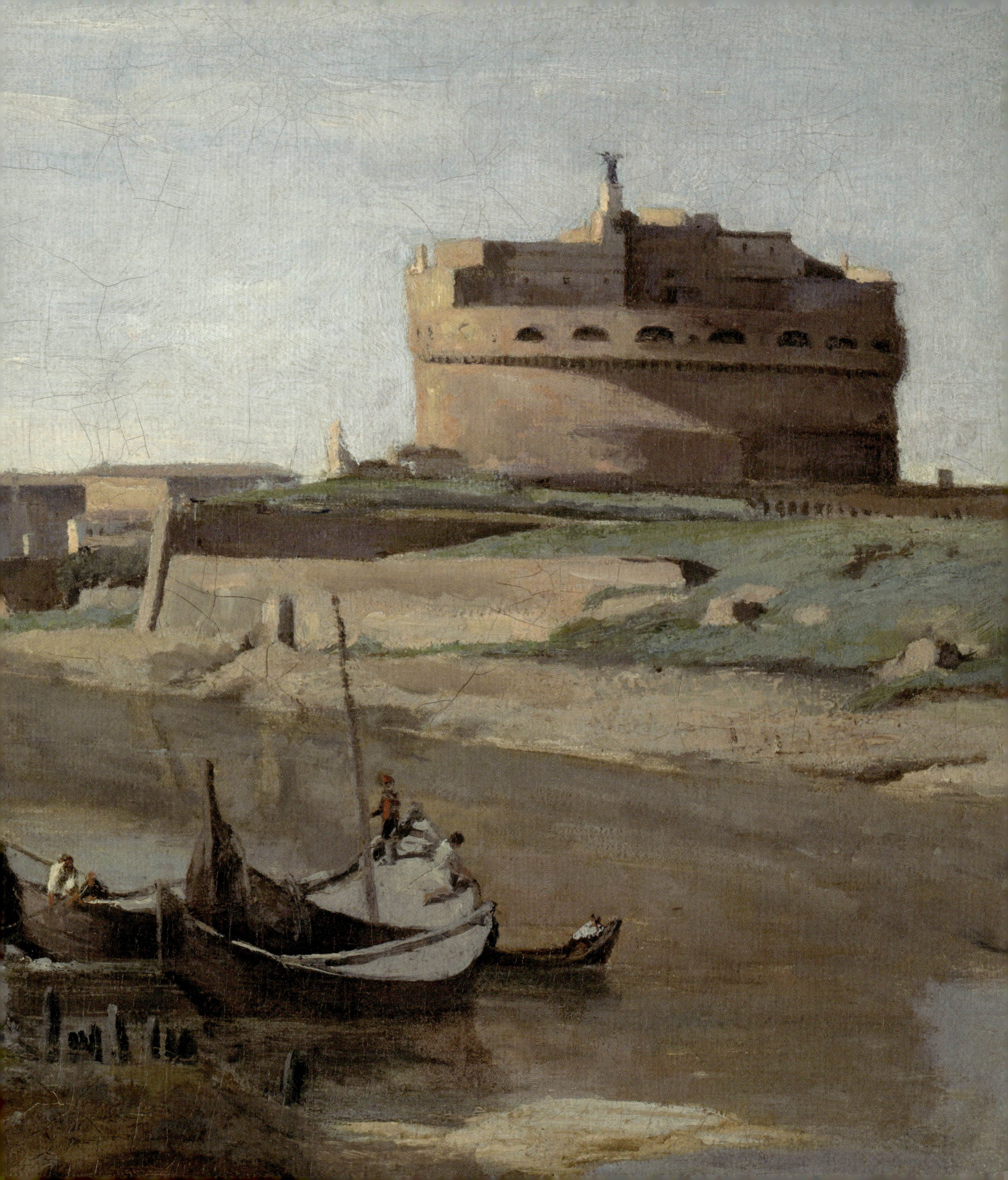

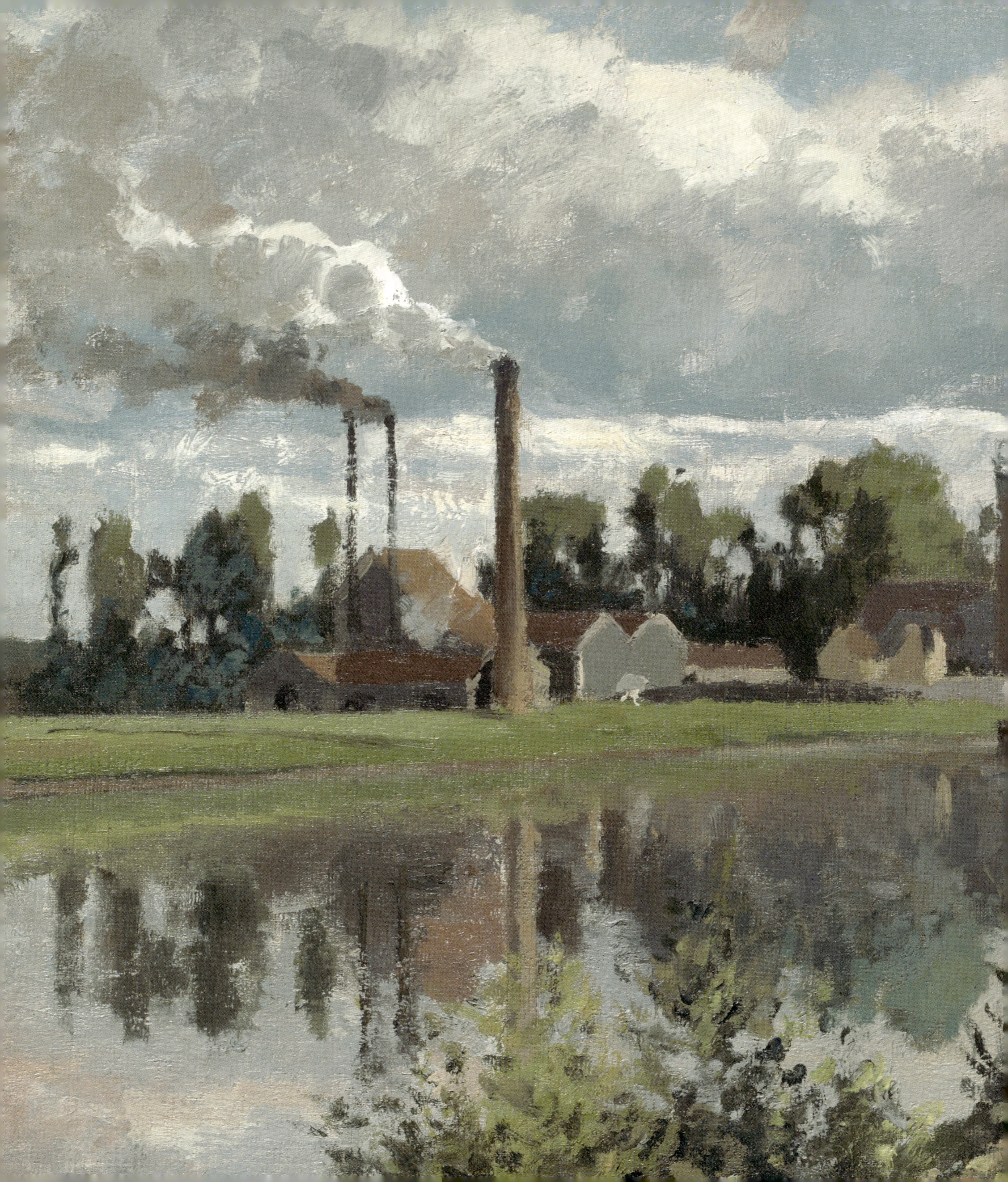

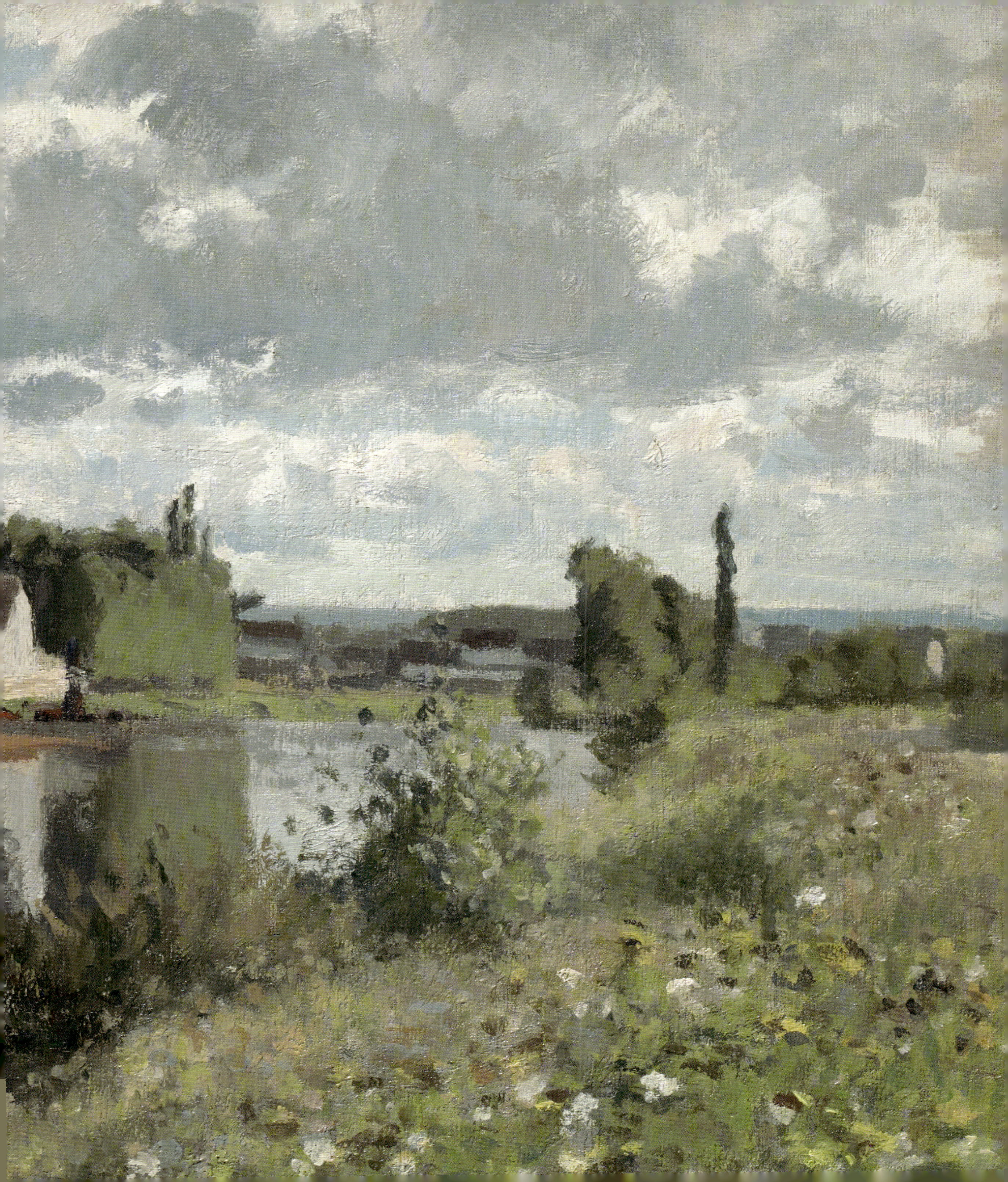

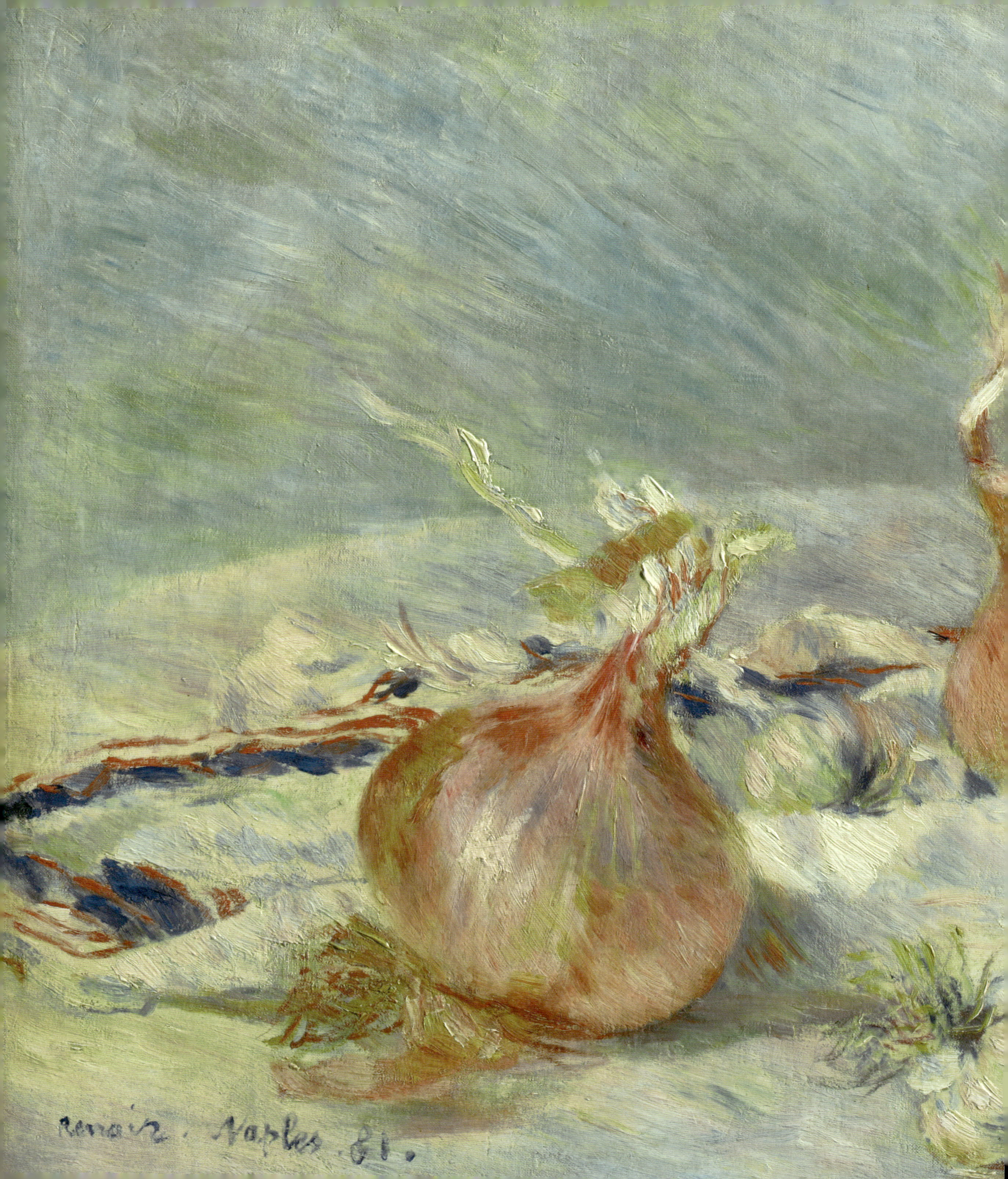
Renoir. Naples 81.

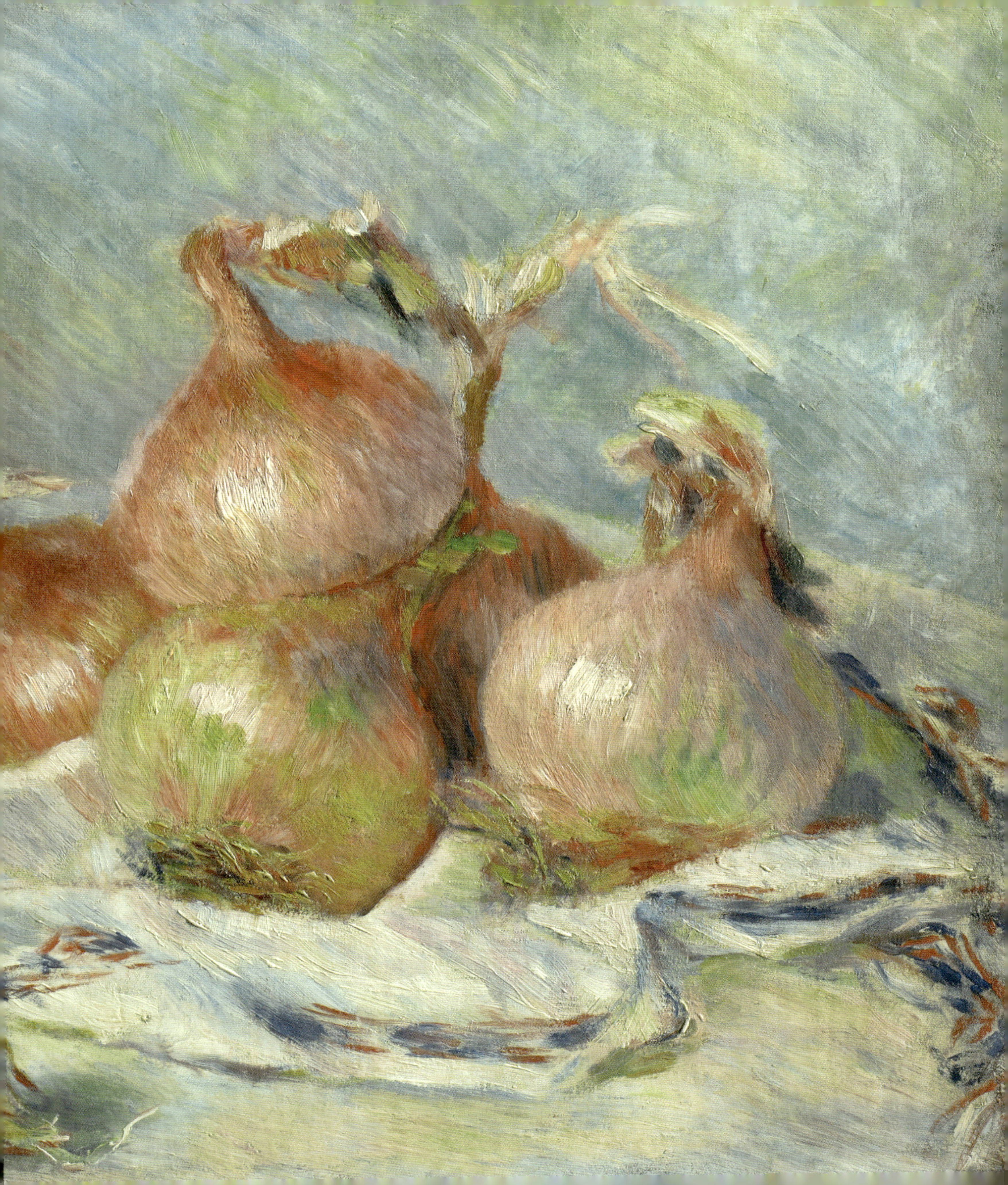

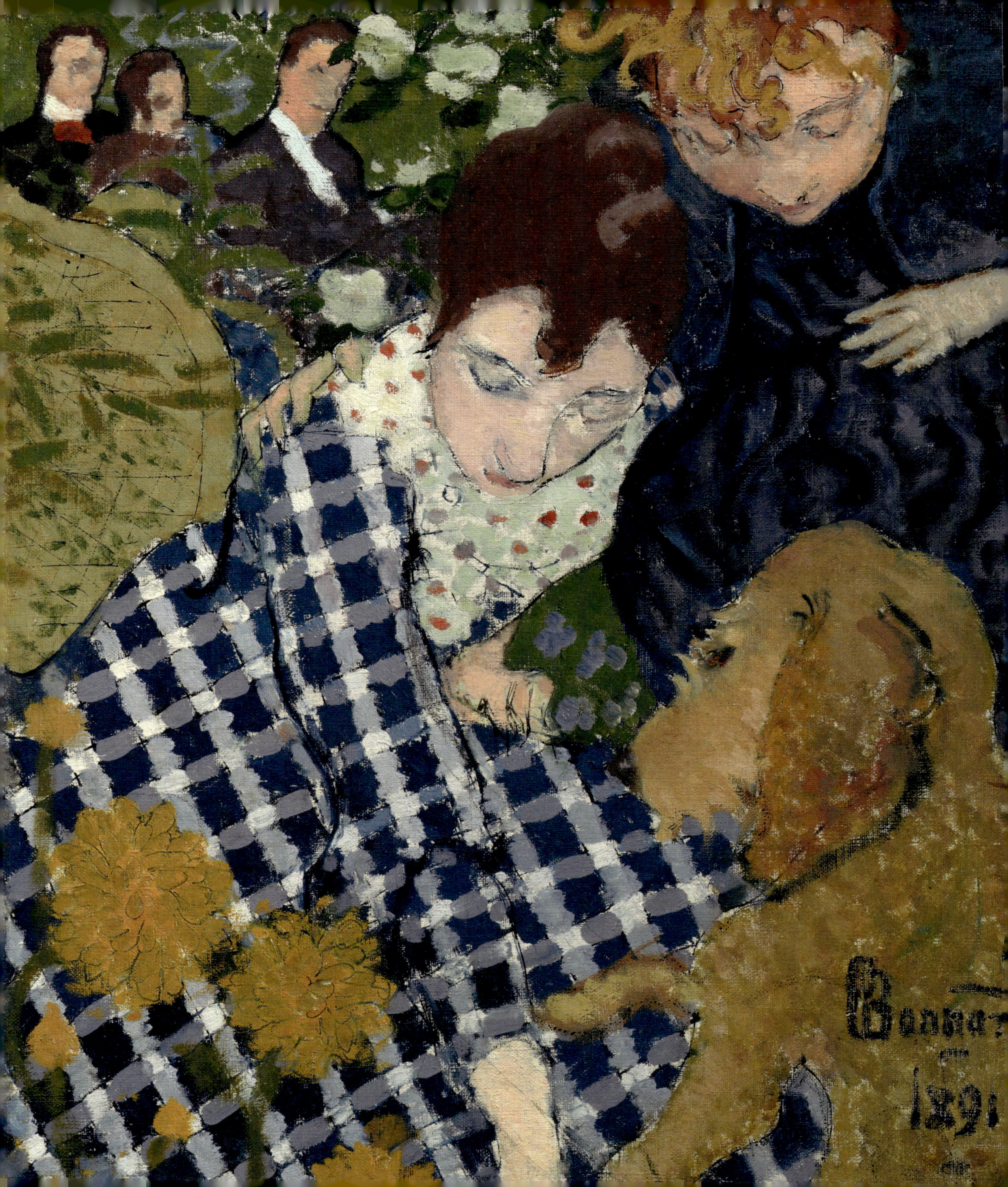

GREAT FRENCH PAINTINGS FROM THE CLARK

Barbizon through Impressionism

Essays by James A. Ganz and Richard R. Brettell

STERLING AND FRANCINE CLARK ART INSTITUTE
WILLIAMSTOWN, MASSACHUSETTS

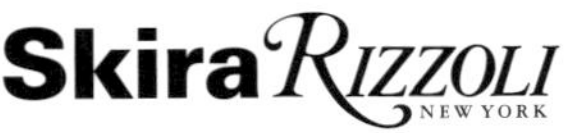

First published in the United States of America in 2011 by

Skira Rizzoli Publications, Inc.
300 Park Avenue South
New York, NY 10010
www.rizzoliusa.com

AND

Sterling and Francine Clark Art Institute
225 South Street
Williamstown, MA 01267
www.clarkart.edu

2011 2012 2013 2014 / 10 9 8 7 6 5 4 3 2 1

Library of Congress Catalog Control Number: 2010940960

ISBN: 978-0-8478-3553-9 (Skira Rizzoli hardcover)
ISBN: 978-0-931102-93-6 (Clark hardcover)
ISBN: 978-0-931102-91-2 (Clark paperback)

Printed and bound in Italy

AT SKIRA RIZZOLI:

Margaret Rennolds Chace
Associate Publisher

Julie Di Filippo, Marian Appellof
Editors

AT THE CLARK:

Curtis R. Scott
Director of Publishing and Information Resources

Katherine Pasco Frisina
Production Editor

Dan Cohen
Special Projects Editor

Designed by Rita Jules, Miko McGinty, Inc.
Index by Kathleen M. Friello

On the front cover: Edgar Degas, *Dancers in the Classroom* (detail of cat. 36); On the back cover: Camille Pissarro, *The River Oise near Pontoise* (detail of cat. 23)

Details:
Pages ii–iii: Camille Corot, *Castel Sant'Angelo, Rome* (cat. 1)
Pages iv–v: Camille Pissarro, *The River Oise near Pontoise* (cat. 23)
Pages vi–vii: Pierre-Auguste Renoir, *Onions* (cat. 61)
Page viii: Pierre Bonnard, *Woman with a Dog* (cat. 72)
Page xiv: Claude Monet, *Seascape: Storm* (cat. 10)
Page 2: Pierre-Auguste Renoir, *Portrait of Madame Monet* (cat. 49)
Page 28: Berthe Morisot, *The Bath* (cat. 69)
Pages 46–47: Pierre-Auguste Renoir, *Sunset* (cat. 58)
Pages 54–55: Camille Corot, *Road by the Water* (cat. 3)
Pages 64–65: Théodore Rousseau, *Farm in the Landes* (cat. 7)
Pages 80–81: Claude Monet, *Tulip Fields at Sassenheim, near Leiden* (cat. 14)
Pages 98–99: Camille Pissarro, *Road: Rain Effect* (cat. 22)
Pages 116–17: Édouard Manet, *Interior at Arcachon* (cat. 30)
Pages 132–33: Edgar Degas, *Before the Race* (cat. 37)
Pages 140–41: Jean-Léon Gérôme, *The Snake Charmer* (cat. 40)
Pages 154–55: James Tissot, *Chrysanthemums* (cat. 46)
Pages 166–67: Pierre-Auguste Renoir, *Bridge at Chatou* (cat. 51)
Pages 186–87: Pierre-Auguste Renoir, *Bay of Naples, Evening* (cat. 60)
Pages 198–99: Pierre-Auguste Renoir, *Apples in a Dish* (cat. 65)
Pages 216–17: Paul Gauguin, *Young Christian Girl* (cat. 73)

CONTENTS

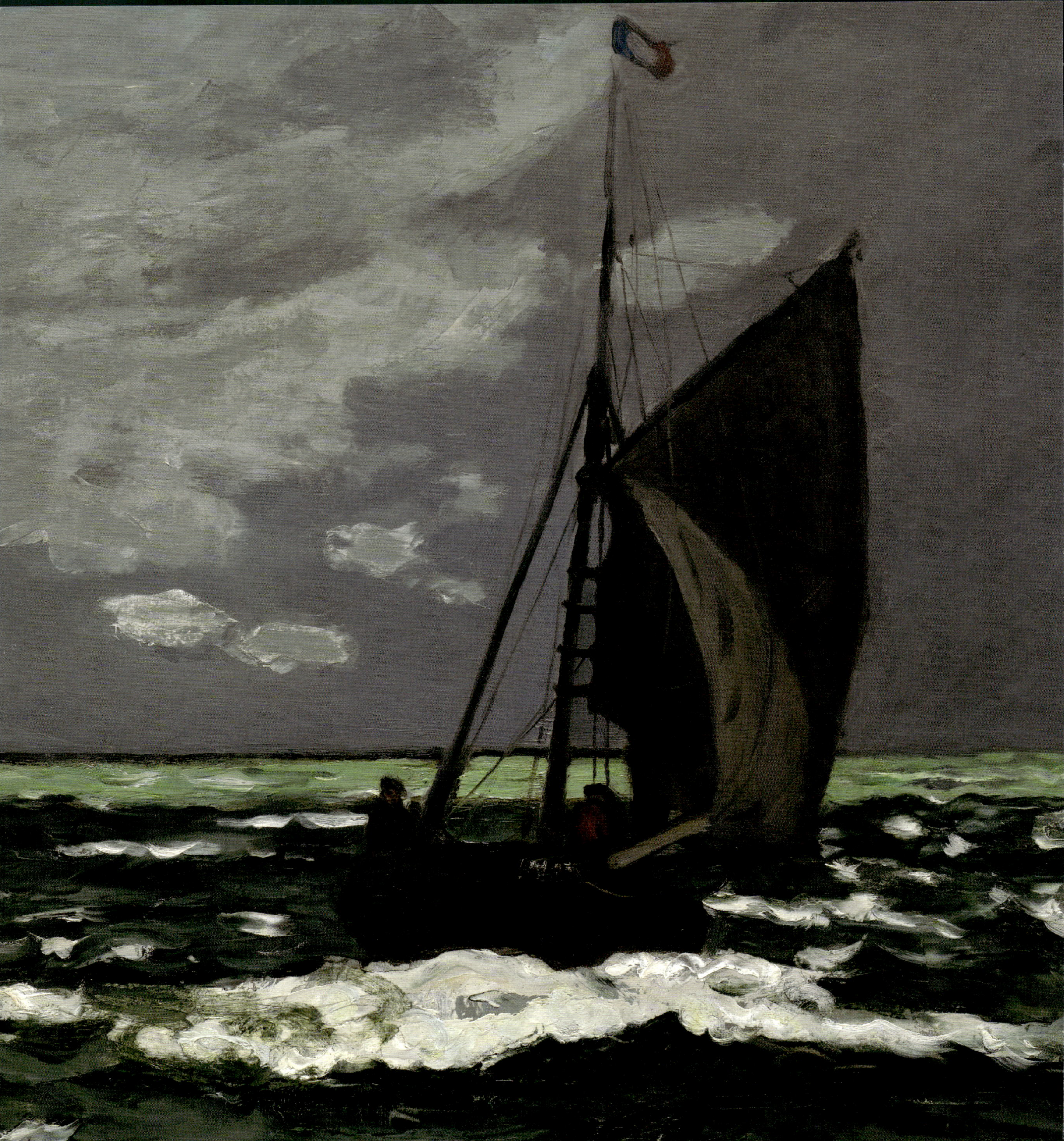

FOREWORD

The Clark is one of the few institutions in the world with a dual mission as both an art museum and a center for research and higher education in the visual arts. Its collections and distinctive exhibitions are well known. From its 140-acre woodland campus in the Berkshire Hills of western Massachusetts, its extensive library, regular series of symposia and conferences, as well as its guest scholars program foster an environment that was once aptly described as a "greenhouse for ideas." The Clark has close ties to nearby Williams College, recognized for training art historians, curators, and museum directors. The Clark and Williams jointly offer a graduate program in art history which, together with the Clark's visiting Fellows program, brings students and scholars from around the world to this special intellectual community, three hours from the urban centers of Boston and New York. For many of the world's most respected and influential scholars and museum professionals in the visual arts, the Clark has been and remains an important and regular part of their lives.

The Clark is perhaps best known for its Impressionist paintings, especially its more than thirty works by Pierre-Auguste Renoir. The core of the collection—European and American paintings, master prints and drawings, English silver, and porcelain—is the legacy of its founders, Sterling and Francine Clark. A professional explorer, horse-breeder, and art connoisseur, Sterling Clark trained his eye by visiting galleries, attending auctions, and developing relationships with art dealers—most notably the Durand-Ruel family. Clark once wrote, "I like all kinds of art if it is good of its kind." He also relied heavily on the opinion of his wife, Francine, describing her as "an excellent judge, much better than I at times," and referring to her as his "touchstone in judging pictures." The museum they founded together opened to the public in 1955, and in the years since, the collections have been thoughtfully enriched with select new acquisitions and have also expanded into new areas, such as early photography. Visitors to the Clark are amazed by the quality of Impressionist and Old Master paintings that are part of the permanent collection and by the groundbreaking exhibitions the Clark organizes, such as the critically acclaimed *Picasso Looks at Degas*.

Intellectual engagement and scholarly inquiry define the Clark's Research and Academic Program, which has achieved international distinction as a place where both established leaders in the field and young scholars can encounter and directly engage in the changing methods, practices, and theoretical strategies of art history and visual culture. In the past decade, its residential visiting Fellows program has hosted well over two hundred scholars from more than two dozen different countries. With interests ranging from contemporary performance art to Classical studies in perspective to feminist theory, the Fellows themselves testify that some of their most important and groundbreaking work has been a direct result of their experience at the Clark. A wide-ranging program of lectures, colloquia, symposia, and conferences bring additional voices to the campus on a regular basis, fostering countless formal and informal exchanges.

In planning for its future, the Clark is currently engaged in a campus expansion that includes new buildings designed by the Japanese architect Tadao Ando, as well as major renovations by the New York-based Annabelle Selldorf to the existing buildings that house the art museum and the Manton Research Center. These initiatives will reinforce the Clark's ability to realize its program through enhanced gallery spaces, expanded facilities for its research program, and improved visitor amenities. The occasion also affords the Clark the opportunity to engage new audiences by sharing some of its most important works in a series of exhibitions that will travel throughout North America, Europe, and Asia over the next few years.

A recent visiting scholar observed that "the Clark is where ideas happen." Within its galleries, on its walking trails, and within its library, curators, scholars, students, and visitors engage with art in myriad ways. And yet, as much as the sense of place resonates with visitors to the campus, it is the ideas and experiences generated at the Clark that contribute to the greater intellectual advancement of museums and research institutes in the arts throughout the world.

MICHAEL CONFORTI
Director, Sterling and Francine Clark Art Institute

EXHIBITION VENUES

Palazzo Reale, Milan
February–June 2011

Musée des impressionnismes, Giverny
July–October 2011

Fundación "La Caixa," Barcelona
November 2011–February 2012

Kimbell Art Museum, Fort Worth
March–June 2012

Royal Academy of Arts, London
July–September 2012

Montreal Museum of Fine Arts
October 2012–January 2013

Mitsubishi Ichigokan Museum, Tokyo
March–May 2013

Hyogo Prefectural Museum of Art, Kobe
June–August 2013

Shanghai Museum
September–November 2013

National Art Museum of China, Beijing
December 2013–February 2014

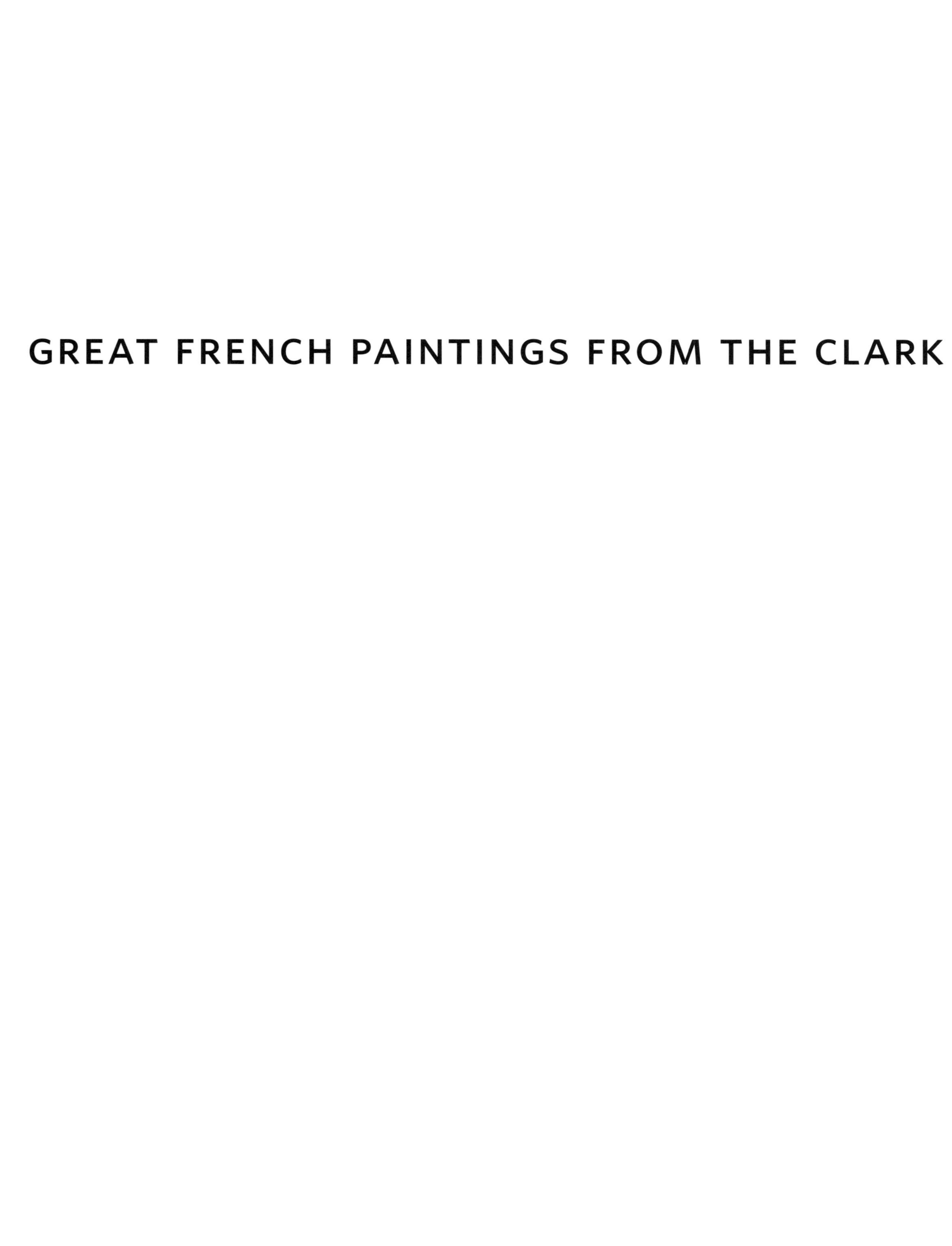

GREAT FRENCH PAINTINGS FROM THE CLARK

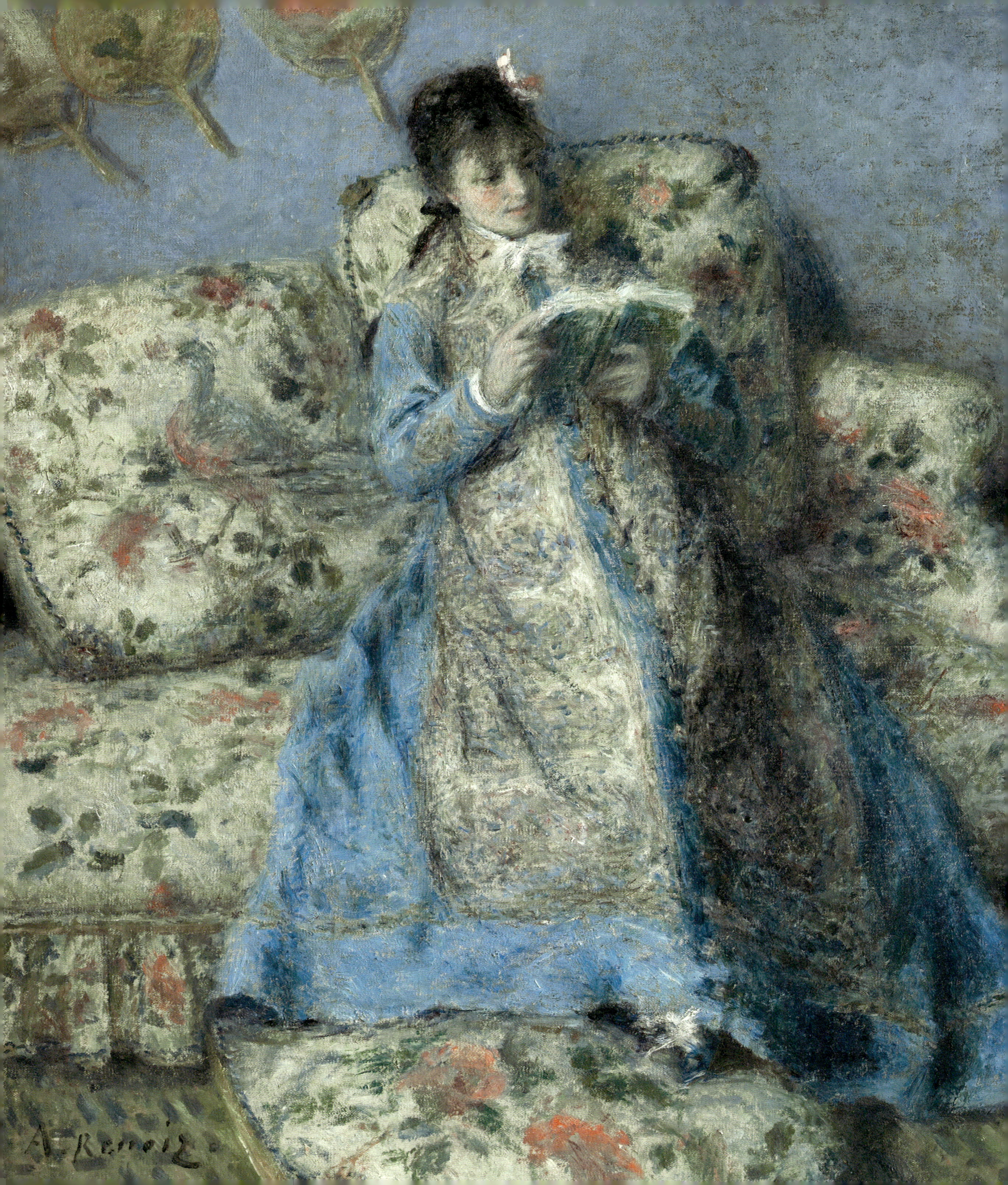
A. Renoir

Sterling Clark as a Collector

JAMES A. GANZ

Robert Sterling Clark was an enigmatic figure. Born into a life of privilege and wealth, he set himself on an independent course from a young age, breaking free of his family's New York ties to live in Europe and travel the world. He was a man of contradictions, a private individual who shunned the spotlight but founded an institution to share his art collection with the public. His death came shortly after the opening of the museum bearing his name, and in the years that followed, the identity of the man became subsumed by the institution. Clark's own diaries and correspondence provide a rich, if fastidious, personal archive that gives insight into how the events of his life shaped the choices he made, and how his art collection and its final disposition in Williamstown reflect his idiosyncratic personality.

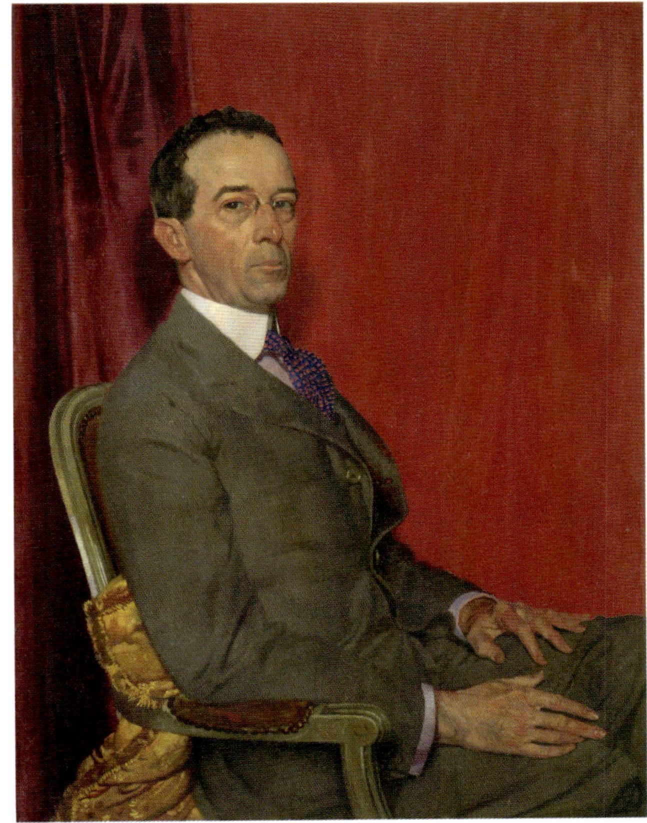

Fig. 1. William Orpen (Irish, 1878–1931), *Robert Sterling Clark*, 1921–22. Oil on canvas, 101.9 x 74.9 cm. Sterling and Francine Clark Art Institute, Williamstown, Massachusetts (1955.824)

FAMILY AND EARLY YEARS

Sterling Clark (fig. 1) was born in 1877, the second of four children of Alfred Corning Clark and Elizabeth Scriven Clark. The family's fortune originated with

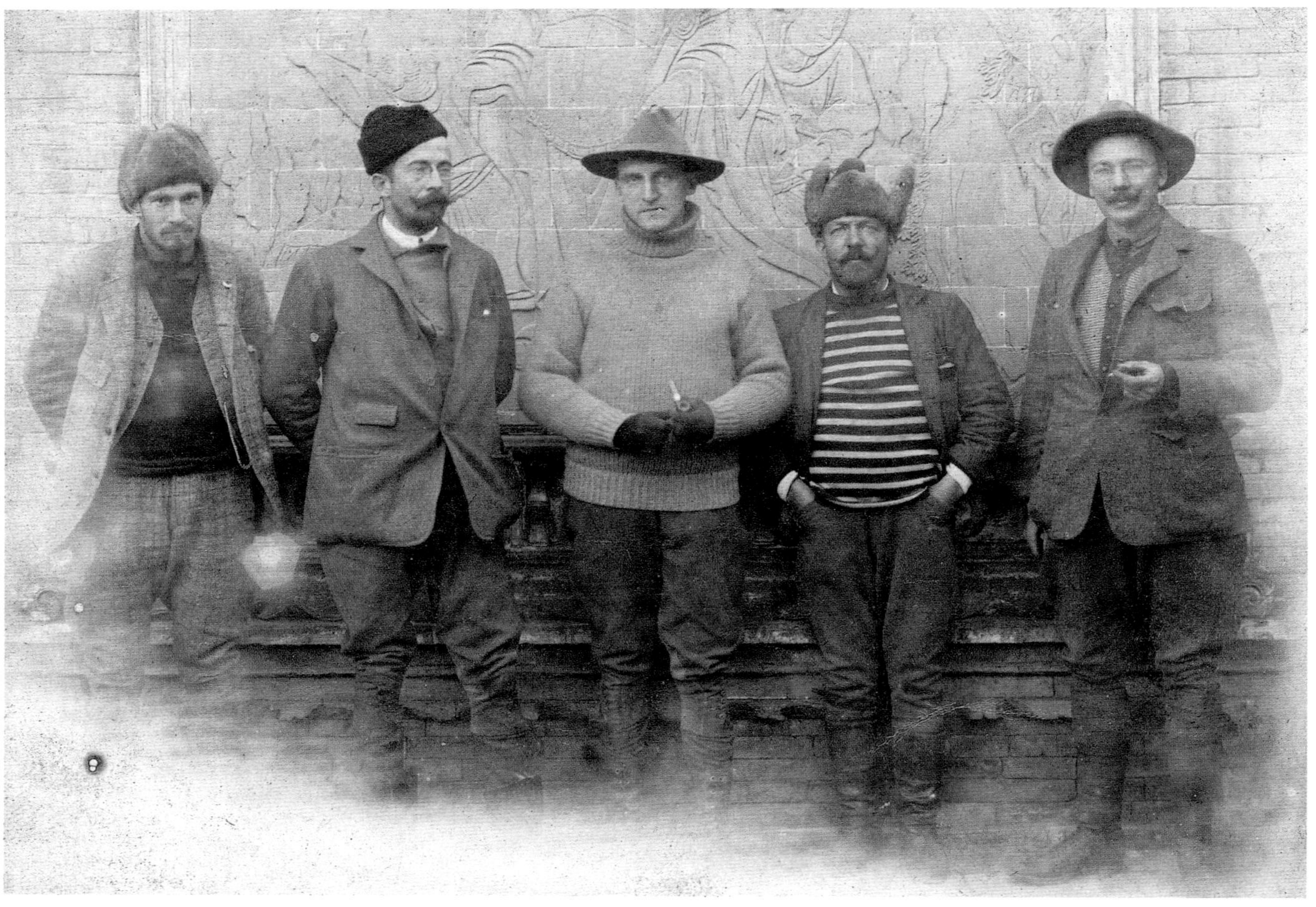

Fig. 2. Sterling Clark (second from left) with the team of explorers who accompanied him during his expeditions into northern China, 1908

Sterling's paternal grandfather, Edward Clark, a young lawyer who was hired by the inventor Isaac Merritt Singer in 1848 to secure the legal status of Singer's improvements to existing sewing machines. Soon the two became business partners, and in the 1850s I. M. Singer & Company became the world's leading sewing machine manufacturer. Much of the company's commercial success is credited to Clark's introduction of an installment plan for payment that made the machine financially viable for the ordinary consumer. By the time Edward died, in 1882, he left his family an estate worth more than $50 million, including an entire city block in Manhattan for each of his four grandsons.

Growing up in a life of luxury, Sterling Clark split his time between New York City and his family's home in rural Cooperstown, New York. He attended Cutler's School in New York and the Sheffield Scientific School at Yale, graduating from its civil engineering program in the class of 1899. He immediately volunteered for the army and was sent to China, seeing action in the Boxer Rebellion. After retiring from the army in 1905, Sterling went back to China in 1908, leading a research expedition on horseback through the mountains of Shaanxi and Gansu provinces, west of current Beijing (fig. 2). He published an account of this trip titled *Through Shên-kan* in 1912.

After his adventures in the Far East, Sterling decided that instead of returning to New York and his family, he would settle in Paris. For a thirty-two-year-old army veteran and adventurer who had traveled extensively during his twenties in such far-flung locales as Manila, Peking, and the West Indies, Paris was hardly exotic. The French capital represented, rather, the height of Western civilization while providing a convenient outpost for a series of projected expeditions funded by his inheritance and fueled by an insatiable wanderlust. For Clark, relocating to Paris was also the means to another end: his escape from the family manse. Although he communicated regularly with his brothers during the 1910s, and continued to frequent Cooperstown through the early 1930s, the move to Europe marked the beginning of a process of distancing himself from his family. In one of his first letters sent from Paris to an agent based in New York working for the Clark Estates, he confessed: "Cooperstown does not interest me in the slightest and were I alone in all of this I would sell out of every stick I had in the place. . . . I consider that the family has done quite enough and too much for Cooperstown already."[1]

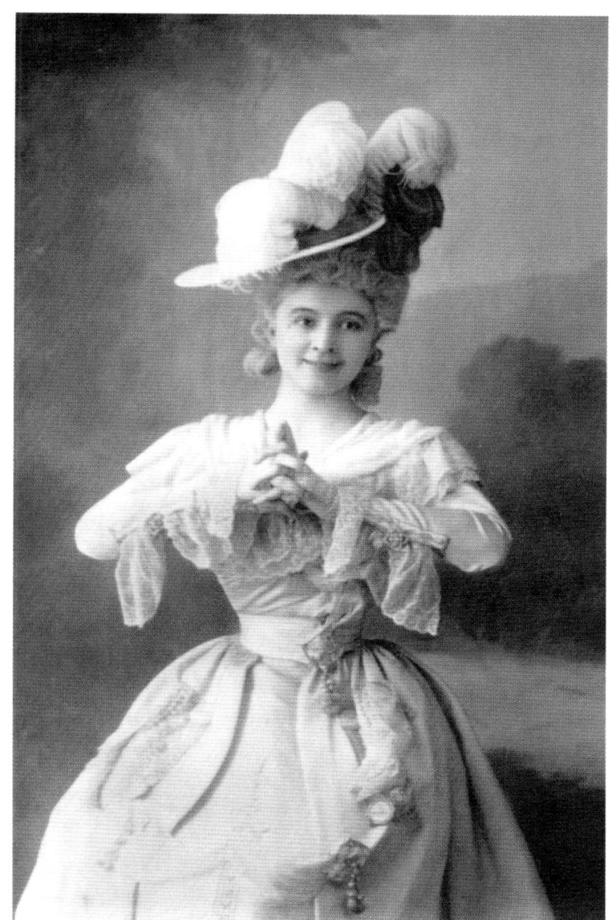
Fig. 3. Francine Clary (later Mrs. Sterling Clark) in costume on the Paris stage, c. 1900

The death of Clark's mother in 1909 added considerably to the fortunes already inherited by Sterling and his three brothers. The windfall enabled Sterling to set himself on a new and entirely independent course. His decision to settle in Paris the following year may have been related to a chance encounter that would further alter the course of his life. For beyond the many attractions of the "City of Light," its relative proximity to the Middle East, and its comfortable distance from the Clarks of Cooperstown, it was Sterling's deepening relationship with an actress of the Comédie-Française that may have clinched his decision to establish his primary residence in Paris.

The cultural and socioeconomic backgrounds of the American bachelor and the French actress could not have been more different. Francine Clary (fig. 3) was born Francine Juliette Modzelewska on 28 April 1876, the daughter of a Parisian dressmaker. A year older than Sterling, Francine had graduated from the Paris Conservatoire in 1897 and assumed the stage name "Clary" in her first appearance at Sarah Bernhardt's Théâtre de la Renaissance in the play *Service Secret* (October 1897). Her career was interrupted by the birth of her only child, Viviane, in 1901. She resumed acting in 1902 and made her debut at the prestigious Comédie-Française in 1904. At the time of Sterling Clark's visit in March 1910 she was appearing in both Tristan Bernard's *L'anglais tel qu'on le parle* and Gaston Armand de Caillavet and Robert de Flers's *L'amour veille*.

While the exact circumstances of the couple's early relationship are shrouded in mystery, it is clear that by 1911 the intense bond the two would share was already forming. Sterling's youngest brother, Stephen, visited Paris in December of that year and noted that although Francine kept her own apartment, she took all of her meals with Sterling and occasionally spent the night in his newly completed residence. "Apparently they lived a good deal by themselves," he observed.[2] This insularity would become one of the couple's enduring traits for the rest of their lives together.

BEGINNINGS OF THE COLLECTION

In the fall of 1910, Clark purchased a modest Second Empire–style *hôtel particulier* at 4, rue Cimarosa in the fashionable sixteenth arrondissement in Paris. He took pleasure in overseeing renovations of the house and spent much time scouring Paris for appropriate furnishings, lighting, fixtures, and wall treatments. The most impressive room in the house was the grand salon on the first floor, which afforded hanging space for a dozen paintings (see fig. 29). Clark called this room his "galleria," and it would become the personal showcase for a selection of his favorite works.

Sterling Clark lost no time in filling his new house with art. This proclivity likely grew out of his childhood exposure to fine art, as both of his parents actively collected and displayed art throughout their homes (figs. 4, 25).[3] In June 1911 he had a shipment of paintings sent from New York, including pictures by Jean-François Millet, Mariano Fortuny y Carbó, Gilbert Stuart (fig. 5), George Inness, and Julian Walbridge Rix.[4] These paintings originated from the estate of Sterling's mother, and their arrival in Paris marked the resolution of an early dispute between Stephen and Sterling. Of these pictures, only the Millet and Fortuny

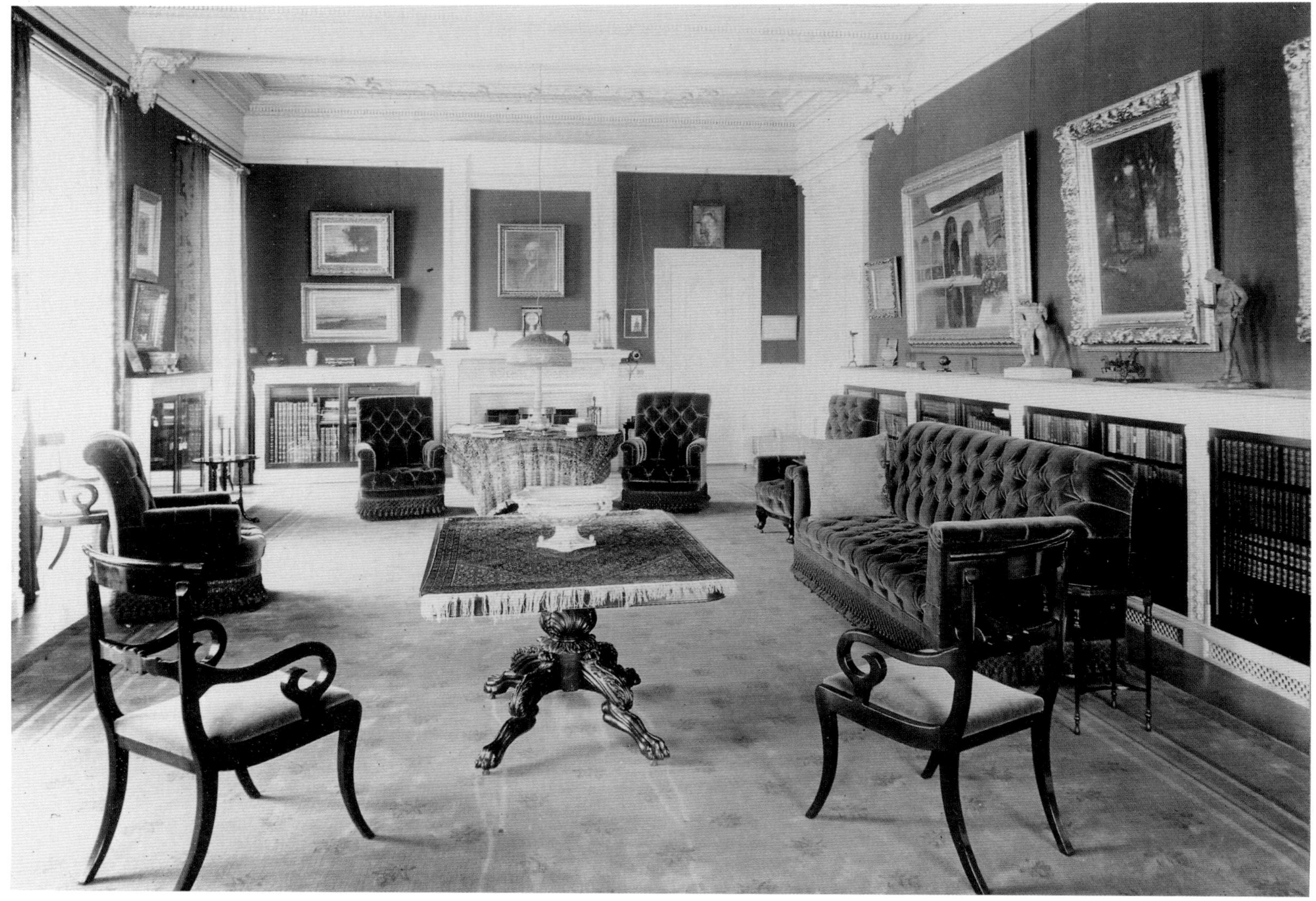

Fig. 4. Sterling Clark's mother filled her New York house with art. Gilbert Stuart's *George Washington* (fig. 5) adorned the mantel of the living room, while Jean-Léon Gérôme's *Snake Charmer* (cat. 40) is visible on the left wall of the drawing room, c. 1898 (see fig. 25).

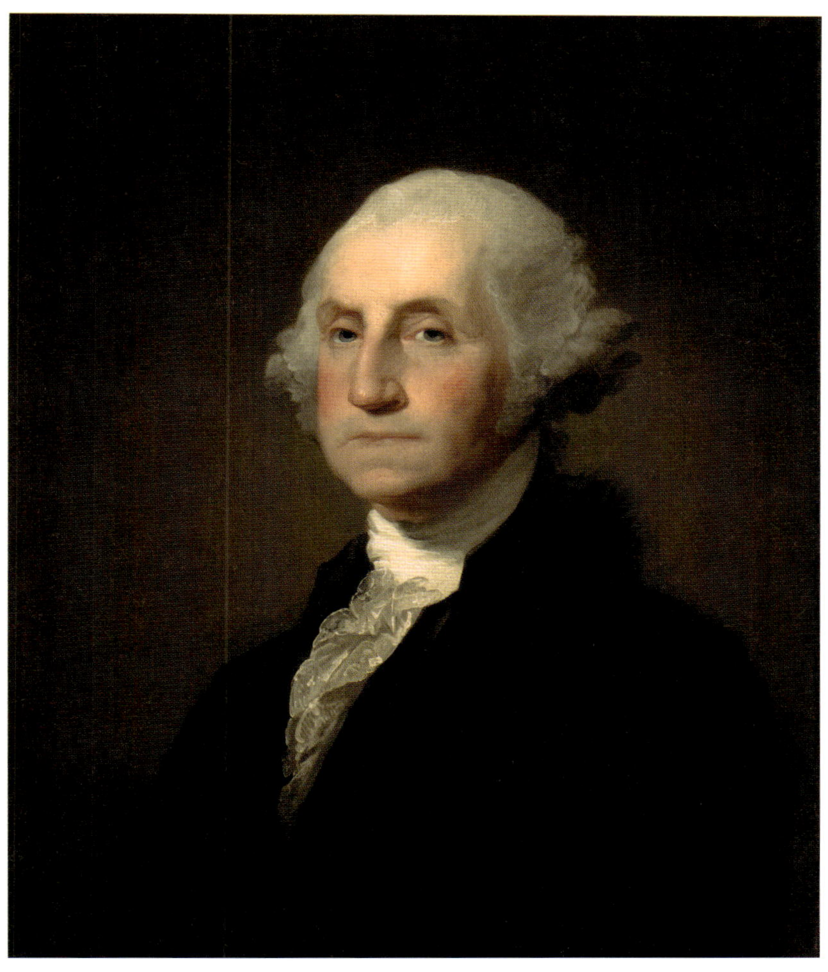

Fig. 5. Gilbert Stuart (American, 1755–1828), *George Washington,* after 1796. Oil on canvas, 73.5 x 61.1 cm. Sterling and Francine Clark Art Institute, Williamstown, Massachusetts (1955.16)

had been assigned to Sterling during the original dispersal of the art collection that Stephen had overseen. At the time, Sterling was traveling in China, and in his absence his siblings were given priority in selecting works of art from their parents' estate. In light of his brother's nomadic lifestyle, Stephen reasoned that he would have little interest in receiving a large group of paintings, but as the second-born son, Sterling felt that his choices should have superseded those of his two younger brothers. Although it was settled amicably, this dispute aroused feelings of resentment on both sides.

At this time Clark also began turning his attention to expanding the small collection he had inherited, and at first he proceeded conservatively. His earliest documented acquisitions, made in February 1912, were a bronze of the *Medici Venus* after the Mannerist sculptor Giambologna, and a pastel portrait by Jean-Baptiste Perronneau.[5] The next month he bought a seascape by Jacob van Ruisdael (now attributed to a follower) and a devotional panel attributed to Matteo di Giovanni from the London firm P. & D. Colnaghi & Obach. During the fall he returned to New York for the first time since his move to Paris, and while there, he made his first purchase from Colnaghi's American partner, M. Knoedler & Co., a dealer with whom he would have a long and lucrative relationship. A panel by the Netherlandish Master of the Legend of Saint Lucy would join the Matteo di Giovanni to form the nucleus of a significant collection of Italian and Northern Renaissance paintings in the Paris residence. He also began purchasing works on paper, and by 1920 had amassed an

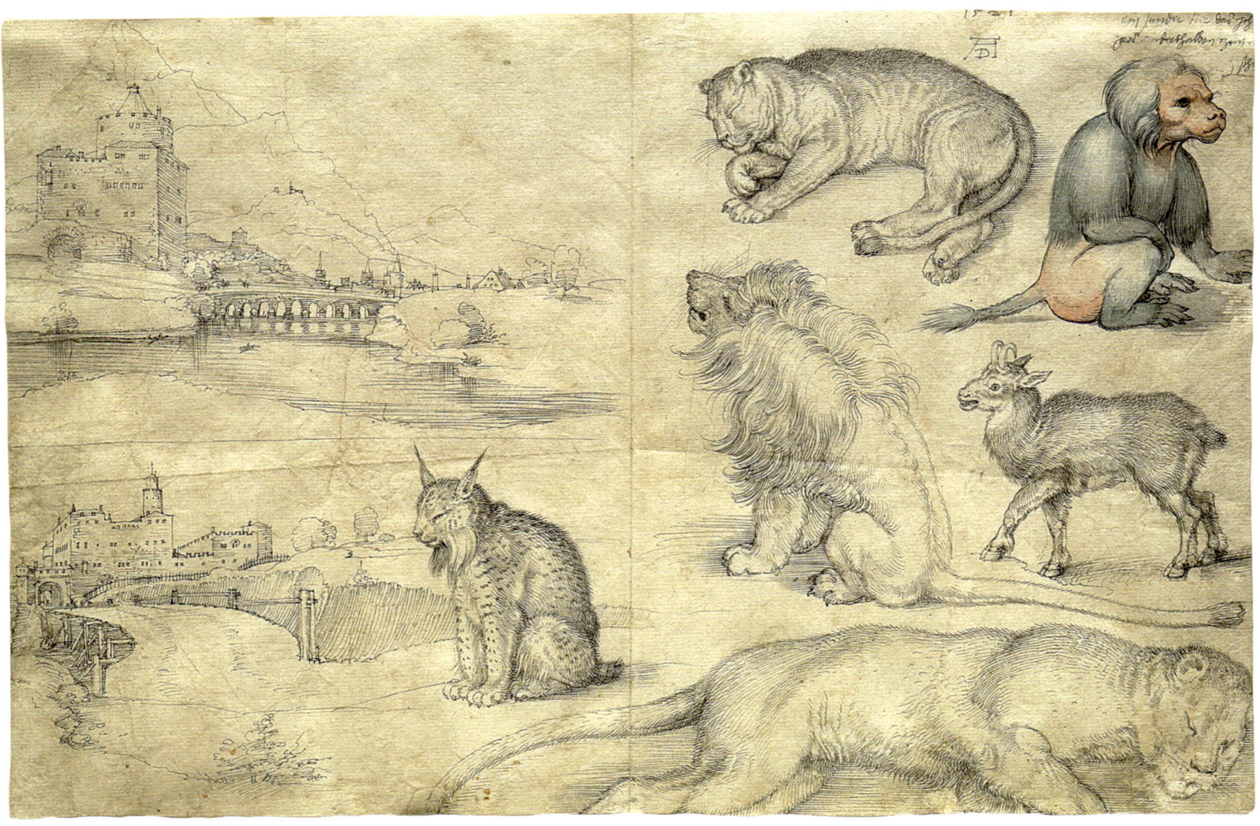

Fig. 6. Albrecht Dürer (German, 1471–1528), *Sketches of Animals and Landscapes*, 1521. Pen, black ink, and gray and rose wash on paper, 26.5 x 39.7 cm. Sterling and Francine Clark Art Institute, Williamstown, Massachusetts (1955.1848)

impressive group of Old Master drawings, including Albrecht Dürer's stunning *Sketches of Animals and Landscapes* (fig. 6).

With this enthusiasm for Old Master paintings and drawings, Clark quietly—and quickly—rose from an inconspicuous American in Paris furnishing his new house to become a player in a field of collecting that previously had been dominated by such figures as J. P. Morgan, Henry Clay Frick, and Joseph Widener. In November 1912 he bought Anthony van Dyck's *Portrait of Ambrogio Spinola* and a *Madonna and Child* by Giovanni Bellini, paying $70,000 for the Bellini alone.[6] In acquiring these two paintings, Clark had taken his place on a competitive playing field of multimillionaire collectors who were setting new standards of luxury consumption and taste, and whose activities were eagerly reported in the newspapers. But unlike these other leading figures, Clark succeeded in maintaining his privacy and anonymity as he slowly built his collection within the domestic environment of his residence, which happened to be in Paris rather than New York.

Among Sterling's and his brother Stephen's transatlantic correspondence of the early teens is a significant exchange, in 1913, on the subject of collecting art toward establishing a private museum. Sterling's letter of 4 February gives insight into the motivations and goals driving this new passion:

> You remember the subject on which we had a conversation last year, namely my idea of founding a gallery in Cooperstown. And also that you thought it would be probably better to have it in N.Y. I have been thinking it over and although I have not arrived at any definite conclusion, I rather think that it would be better to have it as I first planned.[7]

He went on to enumerate the relative advantages of New York ("more people would see it"; "it would be better known") and Cooperstown ("it would help the town"; "it would be better lighted"), concluding "in

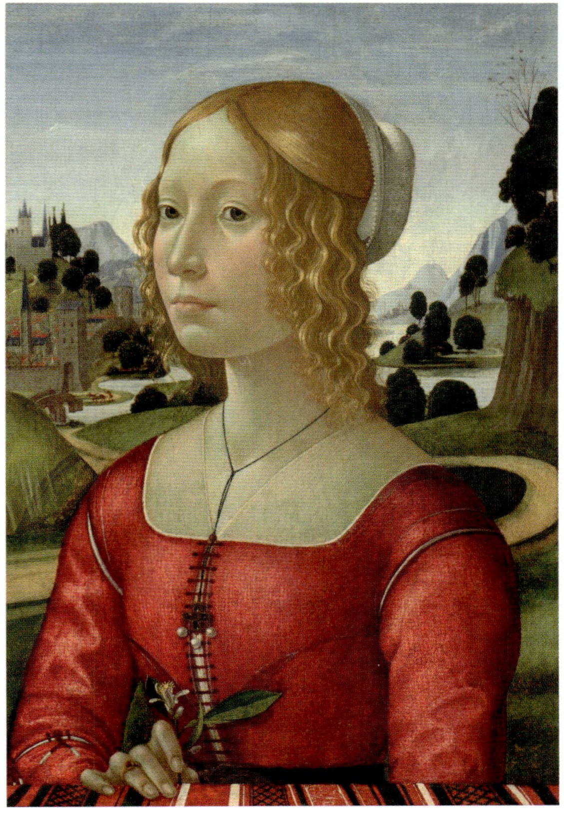

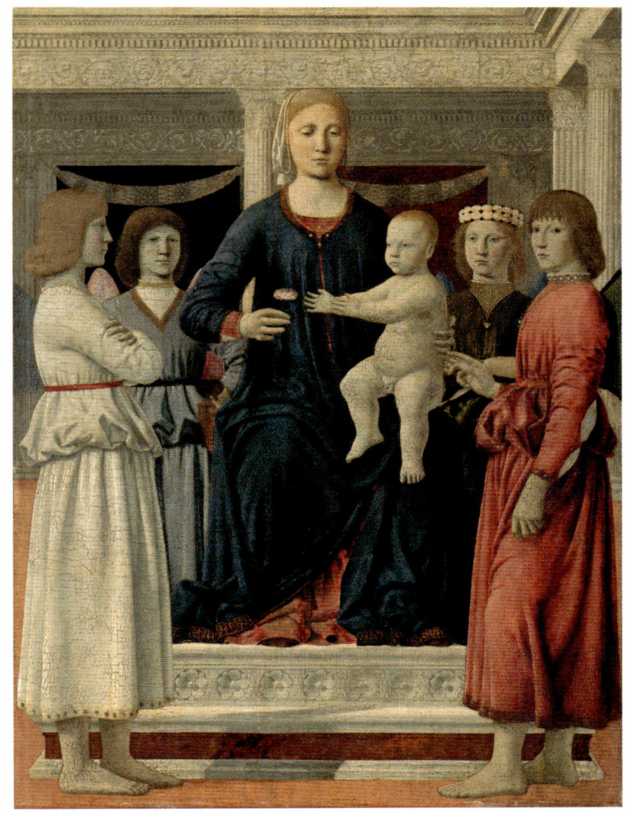

Fig. 7. Domenico Ghirlandaio (Italian, 1449–1494), *Portrait of a Lady,* c. 1490. Tempera and oil on panel, 56.1 x 37.7 cm. Sterling and Francine Clark Art Institute, Williamstown, Massachusetts (1955.938)

Fig. 8. Piero della Francesca (Italian, c. 1420–1492), *Virgin and Child Enthroned with Four Angels*, c. 1460–70. Oil possibly with some tempera on panel, transferred to fabric on panel, 107.8 x 78.4 cm. Sterling and Francine Clark Art Institute, Williamstown, Massachusetts (1955.948)

N.Y. it would be compared with some of the famous collections and some of the best known works of art and would suffer in comparison before the eyes of the common man, even though the art as art might be just as good."[8] Stephen's response was decidedly measured. After pointing out the difficulties of establishing a museum in Cooperstown ("owing to climatic conditions, there would be scarcely a single person who would go to see it during the winter time"), he advised his brother to build his collection first, and his museum later.[9] So ended the discussion for the time being, but this conversation is significant in establishing that the seeds of the Sterling and Francine Clark Art Institute were sewn in Clark's mind as early as 1912.

As Clark continued building his collection, he quickly became disillusioned with the advice of outside advisors and experts. In 1913 he bought *Portrait of a Lady* by Domenico Ghirlandaio (fig. 7) and *Walking Horse*, a bronze by Giambologna. Both purchases were facilitated by the American sculptor George Grey Barnard, who had been a friend of Clark's father. After being assured that the Ghirlandaio had not been retouched and that the *Walking Horse* was a unique cast, Clark subsequently found that both of these claims were false. On a trip to Italy in the summer of 1913 he discovered a postcard of the Ghirlandaio in an altered state, and a copy of the *Walking Horse* in the Bargello in Florence. This experience would color his attitude toward outside experts for the rest of his life, and he quickly learned to rely on his own judgment rather than their advice. Soon after his trip to Italy he wrote to Stephen, warning him that "except for Knoedler and Colnaghi you have got to know the game yourself and that is what I am trying my best to learn."[10]

Clark's taste for works by Old Masters continued to grow, and just weeks after his trip to Italy, he bought Piero della Francesca's sensational *Virgin and Child Enthroned with Four Angels* (fig. 8) from Colnaghi for an astounding 35,000 pounds sterling, which translated at the time to roughly $170,000. The Piero immediately became the focal object in his rapidly expanding collection. Clark's collecting of Italian Renaissance paintings peaked in 1914, with the purchase of panels by such masters as Luca Signorelli, Perugino, and Bartolomeo Montagna. A snapshot of the collection in that year would suggest that he might follow in the footsteps of Isabella Stewart Gardner or James Jackson Jarves. Clark, however, was about to change his course.

At the important sale of the Antony Roux collection held in Paris on 19 and 20 May, Knoedler bid successfully on his behalf for a group of nineteenth-century French paintings and sculptures, including a magnificent plaster cast and bronze by Auguste Rodin of *Man with a Serpent* (fig. 9).[11] Clark's burgeoning interest in the "moderns" was also reflected in his acquisitions of early works by the living American painter John Singer Sargent, beginning in the fall of 1913 with the purchase of *Venetian Interior* from M. Knoedler & Co., Paris. He would eventually acquire twelve paintings and two drawings by Sargent, including his Orientalist masterpiece *Fumée d'ambre gris* (fig. 10).

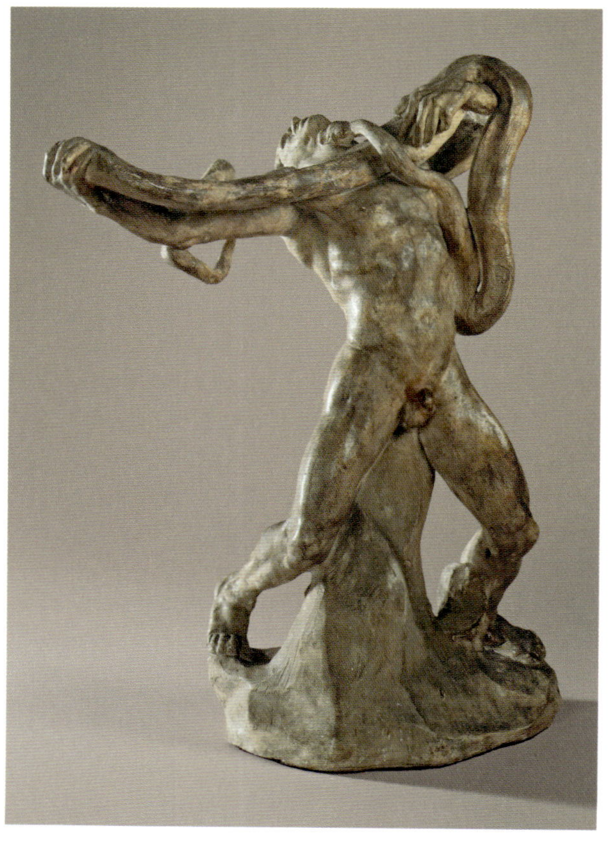

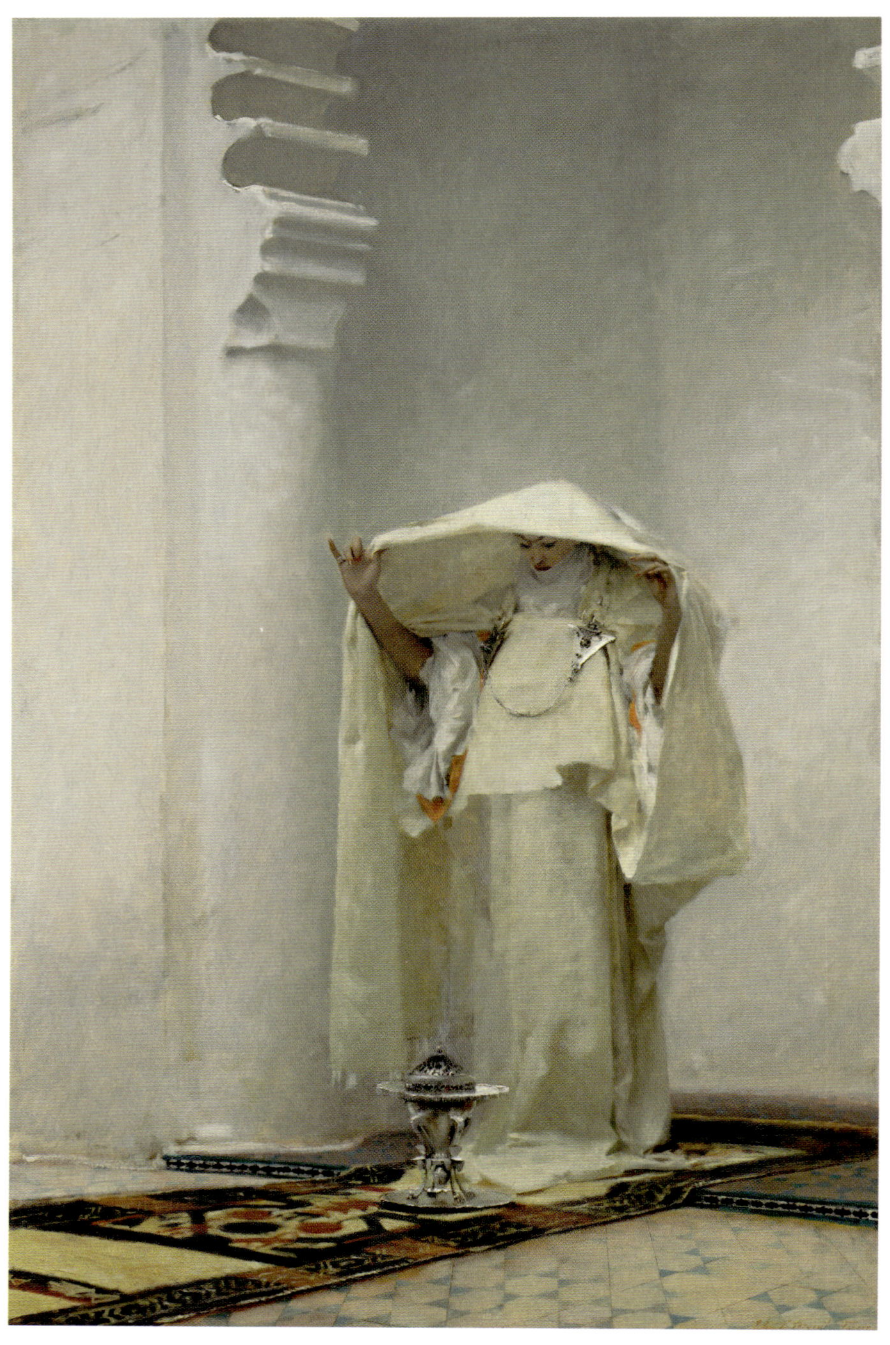

Fig. 9. Auguste Rodin (French, 1840–1917), *Man with a Serpent*, 1885. Plaster, height 69.9 cm. Sterling and Francine Clark Art Institute, Williamstown, Massachusetts (1955.1023)

Fig. 10. John Singer Sargent (American, 1856–1925), *Fumée d'ambre gris (Smoke of Ambergris)*, c. 1880. Oil on canvas, 139.1 x 90.6 cm. Sterling and Francine Clark Art Institute, Williamstown, Massachusetts (1955.15)

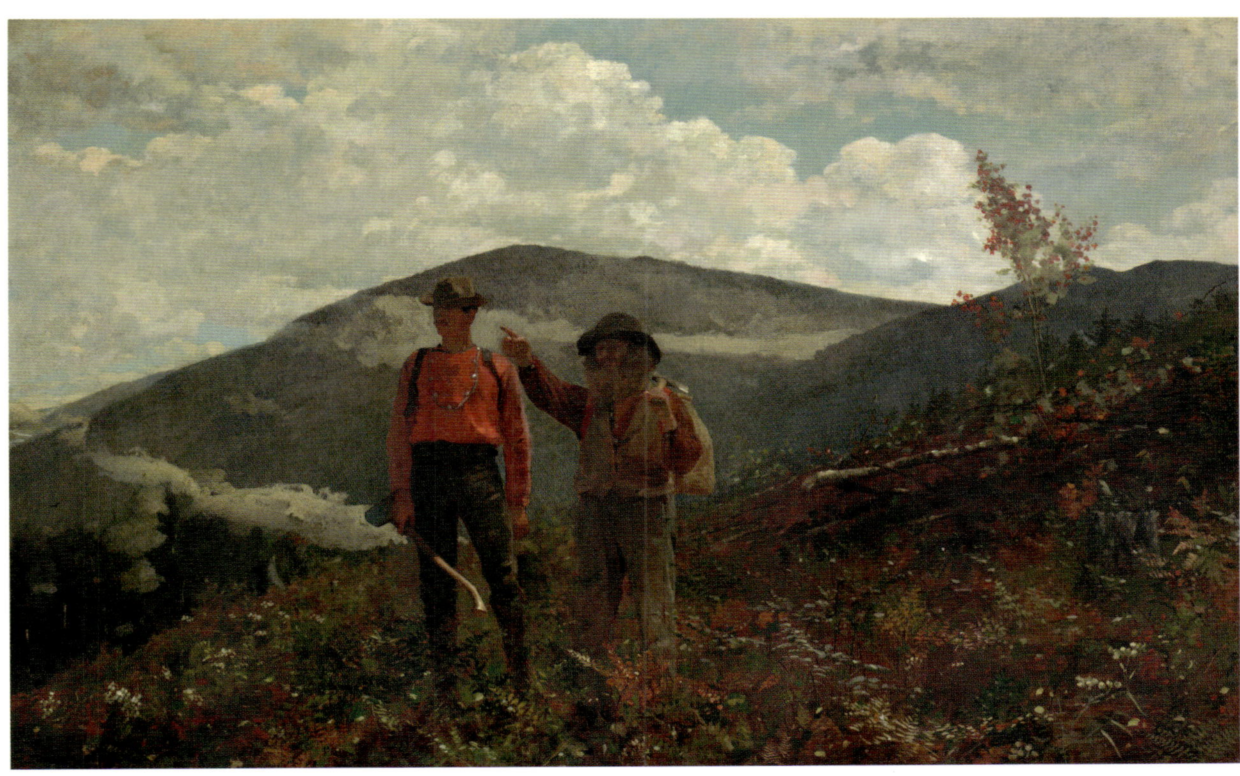

Fig. 11. Winslow Homer (American, 1836–1910), *Two Guides*, c. 1875. Oil on canvas, 61.5 x 97.2 cm. Sterling and Francine Clark Art Institute, Williamstown, Massachusetts (1955.3)

PARIS: WORLD WAR I

Germany's declaration of war on France in August 1914 curtailed Clark's collecting activities and forced him to put his most valuable works into storage. As the war raged on in Europe, Clark maintained his residence in Paris and was able to make several trips to London and New York. He bought only two paintings in 1915. In 1916, however, Clark made two momentous purchases while visiting New York: Winslow Homer's *Two Guides* (fig. 11), and his first Renoir, *Girl Crocheting* (cat. 50). Compared with the prices he was accustomed to paying for important Old Master paintings, the Homer (at $10,000) and Renoir (at $20,000) must have appeared as relative bargains. Even so, he hedged his purchase of the Renoir by requesting a written guarantee from the gallery to buy back the picture at its purchase price within five years if he should decide to return it.[12] Little did Clark realize at the time that instead of returning *Girl Crocheting*, he would go on to become one of the premier collectors of Renoir's work, eventually acquiring more than thirty paintings by the Impressionist master.

Clark's taste for Renoir was relatively advanced for his time, although it would not be long before the field of collectors became crowded. In the first line of his article in *Art News* titled "The Renoirs in America" (1937), Henry McBride stated, "the Renoir cult in America is a story of quiet and steady progress." He went on to single out the silk-weaving magnate Catholina Lambert as "the first American collector to take Renoir seriously," noting that "Mr. Lambert's Renoir was sold [at auction] to the Messrs. Scott & Fowles for $16,200—a price that must have been impressive in 1916."[13] The picture in question was *Girl Crocheting*. Clark took this canvas off the hands of Stevenson Scott (of Scott & Fowles) just ten months later, following the lead of Dr. Albert Barnes, who bought his first Renoir painting in 1912, and Henry Clay Frick, who acquired his first Renoir in 1914.

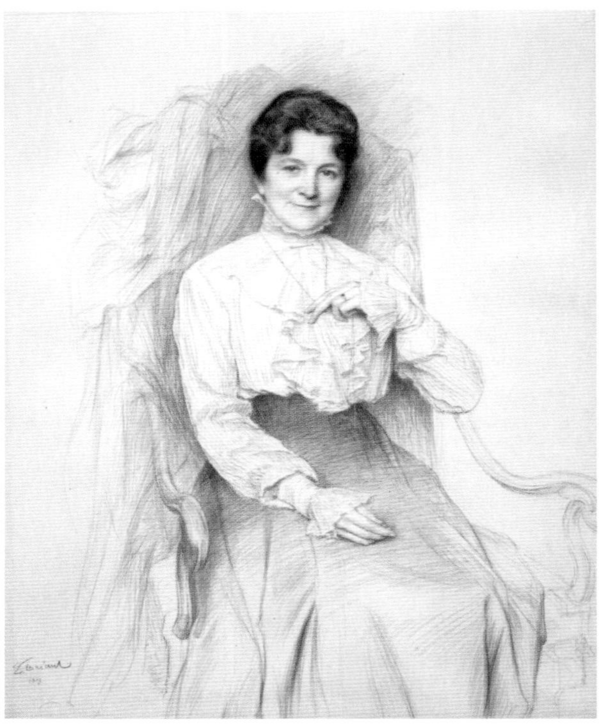

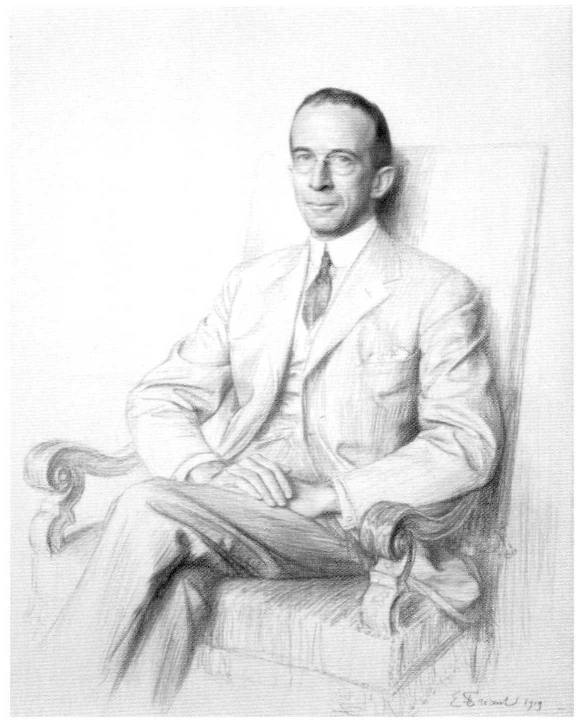

Fig. 12. Émile Friant (French, 1863–1932), *Francine J. M. Clark*, 1919. Pencil on paper, 54.6 x 43.5 cm. Sterling and Francine Clark Art Institute, Williamstown, Massachusetts (1955.743)

Fig. 13. Émile Friant, *Robert Sterling Clark*, 1919. Pencil on paper, 51.2 x 41.9 cm. Sterling and Francine Clark Art Institute, Williamstown, Massachusetts (1955.742)

Upon the entry of the United States into World War I, Clark rejoined the military at the rank of major in the Inspector-General Corps in May 1917 and for the next two years exploited his command of the French language as a liaison officer between the American and French forces. In June 1919 he and Francine married at the local town hall in a civil ceremony, and the next day Francine became an American citizen (figs. 12 and 13). That spring and summer, Clark was among a handful of American collectors to make purchases directly from Edgar Degas's atelier sales, which had surpassed all expectations in attracting enormous crowds and high prices.[14] With Roland Knoedler bidding on his behalf, he acquired three drawings in the third sale, including a pair of late bather studies executed in charcoal on yellow tracing paper. At this early date the taste for this type of drawing was not widespread and Clark's selection of these studies was, for him, so advanced as to be almost out of character. To these works he added eleven more drawings and his first painting by Degas, *Portrait of a Man* (cat. 35), from the fourth sale, held in July 1919.

With the end of the war and the start of a new decade, Clark had reason to look back on his Paris years with feelings of both accomplishment and relief. He had published a book on his China expedition; renovated and furnished a fine house to his own exacting specifications; fallen in love with and married a beautiful French actress; immersed himself in French culture; seen his financial assets grow back home; built a remarkable art collection; served his country for the second time, most recently in the Allied forces' victory over Germany; and escaped a world war without suffering losses to either his family or his property. In a very real sense, Clark was a changed man. While he remained technically an American citizen, he had become a Parisian. The experience of living abroad during the war, and of finding himself in a position of defending not only his country but also his personal effects and his new extended family, had a profound influence on his world outlook, as well as his sense of personal comfort and well-being. Clark had entered the decade a loner, an independent-minded adventurer with unbridled energy and big plans to conquer the world, if only as an explorer.

The war placed him on the defensive, forcing him to adjust his priorities. Never one to fall into a rut, at the age of forty-two Clark decided that it was time to get out of Paris for at least part of the year and establish a presence in New York.

NEW YORK CITY AND THE GROWTH OF THE COLLECTION

As France began the slow process of rebuilding its damaged infrastructure and digging out of debt, New York entered a vibrant new age of prominence and prosperity, and the Clarks made a decision to set up a part-time residence there. In June 1920, Sterling and Francine disembarked together for the first time in New York. Within a year they had settled in a luxurious eighteen-room apartment at 300 Park Avenue and East Forty-ninth Street, the present site of the Waldorf-Astoria Hotel. At the same time, Sterling began buying parcels of farmland in Bowerstown, a small community southeast of Cooperstown, where he would spend much time consumed in his passion for riding, training, and breeding horses. Now that Sterling Clark had a new apartment to furnish in New York City, his collecting activities picked up, although he continued to export certain of his major acquisitions to install among his primary collection in Paris. One of the realities of collecting in the 1920s was the escalation in prices, which applied not only to Old Master paintings but also to the work of modern and even contemporary artists. Faced with this more challenging and expensive marketplace, Clark altered his pattern of collecting. He slowly retreated from the pre-eighteenth-century works that he had favored in the teens and bought increasingly in New York, which had become the center of the global art market.

Although until the outbreak of World War II the Clarks' pictures moved frequently between their New York and Paris homes, rarely did the couple lend to exhibitions, and then only when strongly encouraged to do so by dealers, like Knoedler, with whom they had a significant relationship. In these instances Clark refused to have his name associated with the loans, and he became known in certain circles as "Mr. Anonymous." Sterling Clark's reluctance to lend was based in part on his general disdain for art historians, but even more on a desire to stay out of the public eye. This reticence distinguished him from his American contemporaries like Barnes, Duncan Phillips, and even his brother Stephen, who allowed their names to be publicized along with works in their collections.

Sterling's relationship with his brother Stephen became strained during the early 1920s and broke down completely in 1923. The root cause of the conflict was the distribution of the family trusts related to shares and interests in the Singer Manufacturing Company. Sterling grew increasingly angry at the way the trusts were organized—his wife, Francine, and his stepdaughter, Viviane, were excluded from inheriting Sterling's stock—and at Stephen's refusal to modify the trusts to address this issue. One morning in June 1923 at the New York offices of the Clark Estates, Sterling's dissatisfaction with the state of affairs boiled over, and a verbal confrontation between the brothers over breaking the Singer Trusts escalated into physical violence. So began a feud that would divide the family for the next three decades. The brothers broke off all direct communication, relying on attorneys and other third parties to relay messages. The differences, it would seem, were irreconcilable.

In the aftermath of the break with his brother, Clark reconsidered the scheme to establish an art museum in either Cooperstown or New York City. No firm plans had been drawn up, but the conversations he had had with Stephen on this topic must have echoed in his mind as he began to sift through the terms of his father's will and to contemplate his own mortality. Of great concern to him was the possibility that his assets might fall into the hands of his brothers. On the eve of sailing from New York to Paris in the spring of 1924, he signed a new will specifying that in the event that he and Francine should die together, his Paris house and art collection should be donated

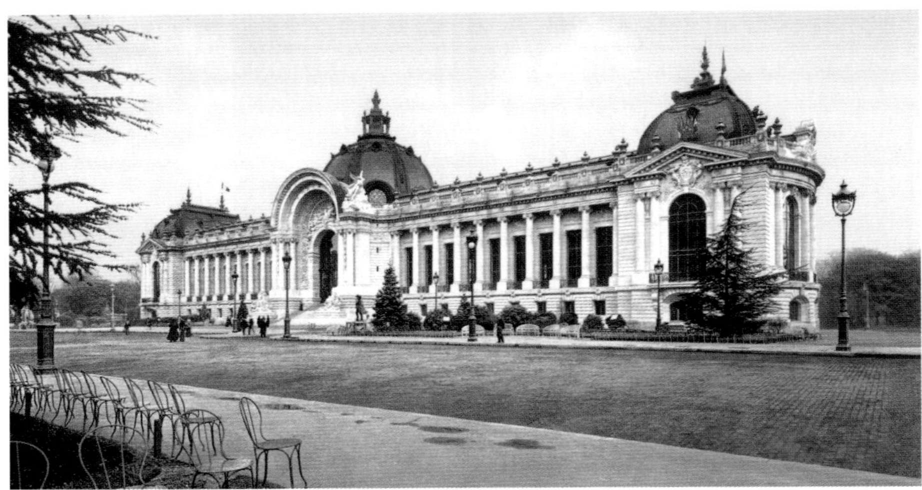

Fig. 14. The Petit Palais, c. 1900

to the Petit Palais (fig. 14) and the rest of his estate should go to Viviane.[15] Clark's choice of the Petit Palais is especially interesting, as it suggests his continuing attachment to the French capital even as he spent less time there. Established in 1902 as the "Palais des Beaux-Arts de la Ville de Paris," the Petit Palais had distinguished itself as a lively art institution with a dynamic exhibition program. Clark must have felt that his collection would maintain its identity and stand out among the eclectic holdings of the Petit Palais, which consisted of some 20,000 works spanning Egyptian and Greek sculpture, medieval ivories, Renaissance jewels, eighteenth-century furniture, seventeenth- and eighteenth-century prints, drawings, and paintings,[16] as well as notable works by Millet, Courbet, Gauguin, Pissarro, Sisley, and Moreau.

At the same time that he was becoming increasingly aware of the importance of maintaining the unity of his collection, Clark began a decided shift in his collecting strategies from serious Old Master purchases toward French Impressionism and academic and genre painting of the late nineteenth century. In October 1924 Clark wrote of his disappointment in the selection of Old Masters at Knoedler's New York gallery, declaring that "they have not been able to buy many good pictures. Stock low. And they could sell if they had them. There is no doubt about it the old master is a thing of the past. The big American collections like Frick, Widener, Taft, Altman, Huntington have absorbed most of the available ones."[17] Illustrating Clark's growing interest in nineteenth-century painting are his purchases in 1924, which included paintings by Giovanni Boldini, Jean-Louis Forain, and Edgar Degas (cat. 36). As in so many aspects of life, Clark bucked the trend of collectors like Frick and Widener, who started out buying Salon pictures and moved on to the Old Masters.

The global depression that began with the American stock market crash in 1929 did little to curtail Clark's leisure pursuits, either in the realm of art collecting or horse breeding. This latter interest led him to open up stud farms in both Normandy and Virginia, and while he would never spend much time in Normandy, his horse farm in Virginia became his primary escape from city life. Although he fretted about the heavy tax burden imposed under the New Deal and railed against the economic policies of President Franklin D. Roosevelt, the Depression turned into the collecting opportunity of a lifetime for Clark.

Taking advantage of the dip in art prices caused by the economic downslide, Clark dramatically increased the pace of his acquisitions. Many collectors were hurt by the crash and began to liquidate their holdings, flooding the market with quality paintings at discount prices. Clark bought J. M. W. Turner's *Rockets and Blue Lights* (fig. 15) in 1932 from Charles M. Schwab, who was forced to sell it at half of what he had been offered during the "boom period."[18] In 1933 alone Clark bought

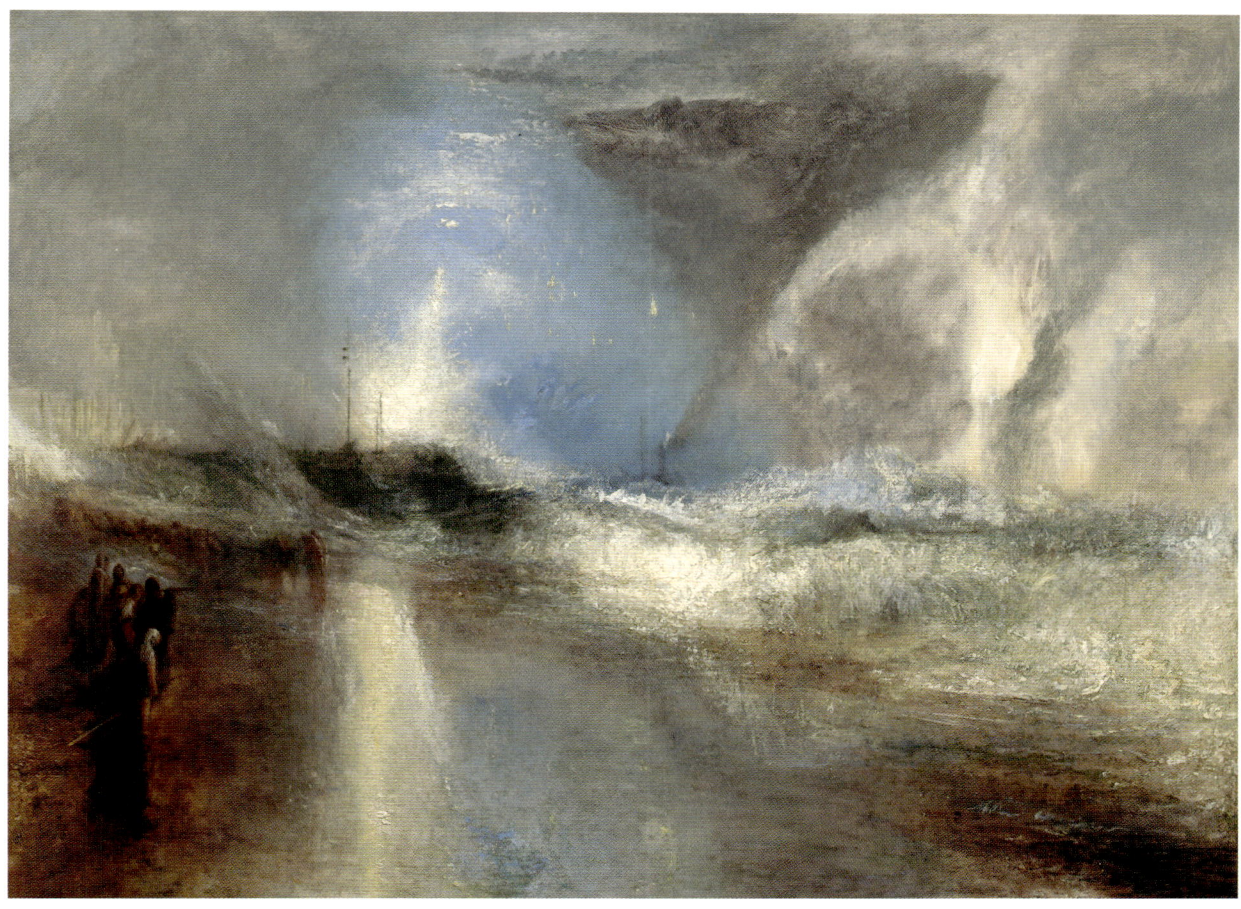

Fig. 15. J. M. W. Turner (English, 1775–1851), *Rockets and Blue Lights (Close at Hand) to Warn Steamboats of Shoal Water,* 1840. Oil on canvas, 92.1 x 122.2 cm. Sterling and Francine Clark Art Institute, Williamstown, Massachusetts (1955.37)

a dozen paintings from Durand-Ruel in New York, and five more from Knoedler in New York and Paris, including major works by Monet and Pissarro.

It was during this period that Clark began seriously cultivating a passion for the paintings of Renoir. While he had been collecting Renoir's work since the teens, and already owned such iconic pictures as *A Box at the Theater (At the Concert)* (cat. 56) and *Sleeping Girl* (cat. 55), between 1930 and 1940 he would acquire no fewer than twenty pictures by the artist. What is perhaps more phenomenal than the number of paintings is their consistently high quality. From the bravura brushwork of *Marie-Thérèse Durand-Ruel Sewing* (cat. 64) (acquired in 1935) to the sheer intensity of the c. 1875 *Self-Portrait* (cat. 47) (acquired in 1939), each work stands out as a superb example of the artist's craft.

Renoir was undoubtedly Clark's favorite painter from the 1930s onward. One can follow this growing passion in Clark's increasingly effusive praise for the artist in his diaries. In an almost lyrical entry from 1939, Clark writes:

> What a great master!!!! Perhaps the greatest that ever lived—certainly among the first 10 or 12—And so varied—Never the same in subject, color, or composition both in figures, portraits and landscape!!!!—As a colorist never equaled by anyone—No one so far as we know ever had an eye as sensitive to harmony of color!!!! . . . And his greys are as fine as Velasquez & his reds as fine as Rubens—His flesh both dark and light as fine as Rubens or the Venetians—the only thing the Venetians, the Primitives, the people like Velasquez

> and Van Dyck were superior in line, the suave line like Leonardo, Ingres, Degas, Bouguereau etc. but Renoir could draw & his best pictures are good in line—But as a painter I do claim he has never been surpassed—As a colorist he has never been equaled.[19]

Passages such as this one make it clear that Clark not only viewed Renoir as a great Impressionist painter, but also saw his work as a continuation of the Old Masters.

Clark's collection of Renoirs also highlights his tenacity in acquiring only the works in which he saw quality. While collectors such as Barnes bought paintings by Renoir almost by the truckload and sometimes seemingly without discretion, Clark was very careful about what he purchased. His overwhelming tendency was toward Renoir's work of the 1870s and early 1880s, particularly the artist's portrayals of young women, although he collected still lifes and landscapes as well. Despite the contemporary fashion for Renoir's later works, Clark did not care for them, once deridingly referring to the "'sausage' bloody Renoirs of the late period,"[20] and subsequently describing the artist's later figures as "limbs filled with air."[21] In the end, while Clark amassed neither the largest number of Renoir's paintings (Barnes owned 181) nor the most important work (Duncan Phillips, who purchased *Luncheon of the Boating Party* in 1923, had that distinction), his highly personal eye for paint and subject matter, and his conviction in his own judgments, turned him into one of the greatest private collectors of the French Impressionist's work.

Although Sterling was the primary force behind the growing collection of art, he highly valued Francine's opinion and often vetted purchases through her. There were times, however, when Francine assumed a more active role in acquisitions. The clearest example of this concerns the purchase of Henri de Toulouse-Lautrec's *Jane Avril* (fig. 16). Sterling first saw the picture in 1939 at Wildenstein, unaccompanied by Francine. He was shown it again in late January 1940, when he noted its "excellent quality" but also remarked that he considered the asking price double its actual worth.[22] Nine days later, while he was visiting Wildenstein with Francine, the painting was brought out again, and Francine reacted immediately. Sterling still felt the price was too high, but upon leaving the shop Francine pressed him to make the purchase. He recalled in his diary that "we got as far as the corner—F. very strong for buying the 'Jeanne Avril'—a Chef d'oeuvre she said—we returned & said we would like it."[23] Evidently such strong advice from Francine was rare, as the episode caused Sterling to comment: "Never saw Francine more enthusiastic about a picture!"[24]

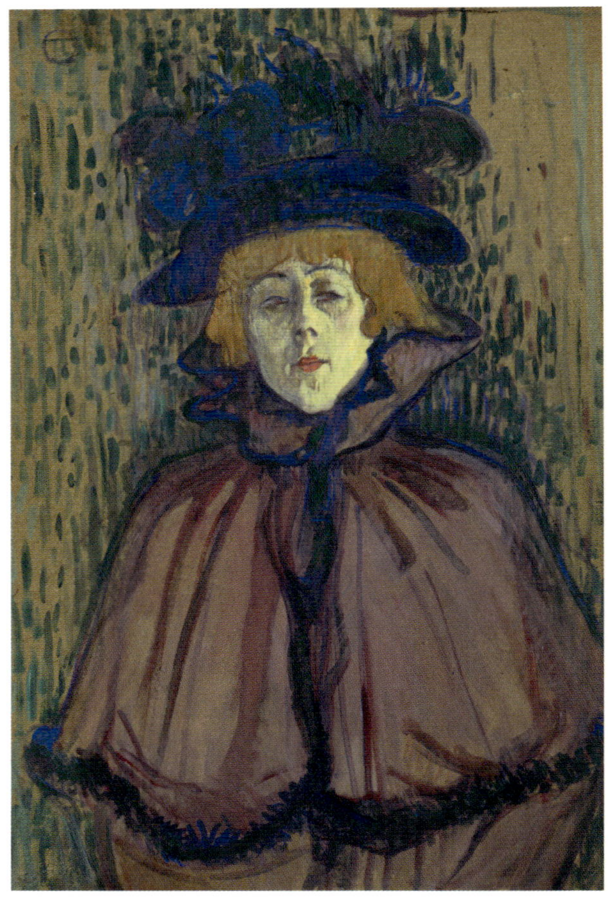

Fig. 16. Henri de Toulouse-Lautrec (French, 1864–1901), *Jane Avril*, c. 1891–92. Oil on cardboard mounted on panel, 63.2 x 42.2 cm. Sterling and Francine Clark Art Institute, Williamstown, Massachusetts (1955.566)

In addition to amassing an excellent collection of "blue chip" artists like Renoir and Sargent, Clark built up a large trove of nineteenth-century cabinet paintings by such lesser-known figures as Jean-Louis-Ernest Meissonier, Alfred Stevens, Giovanni Boldini, and

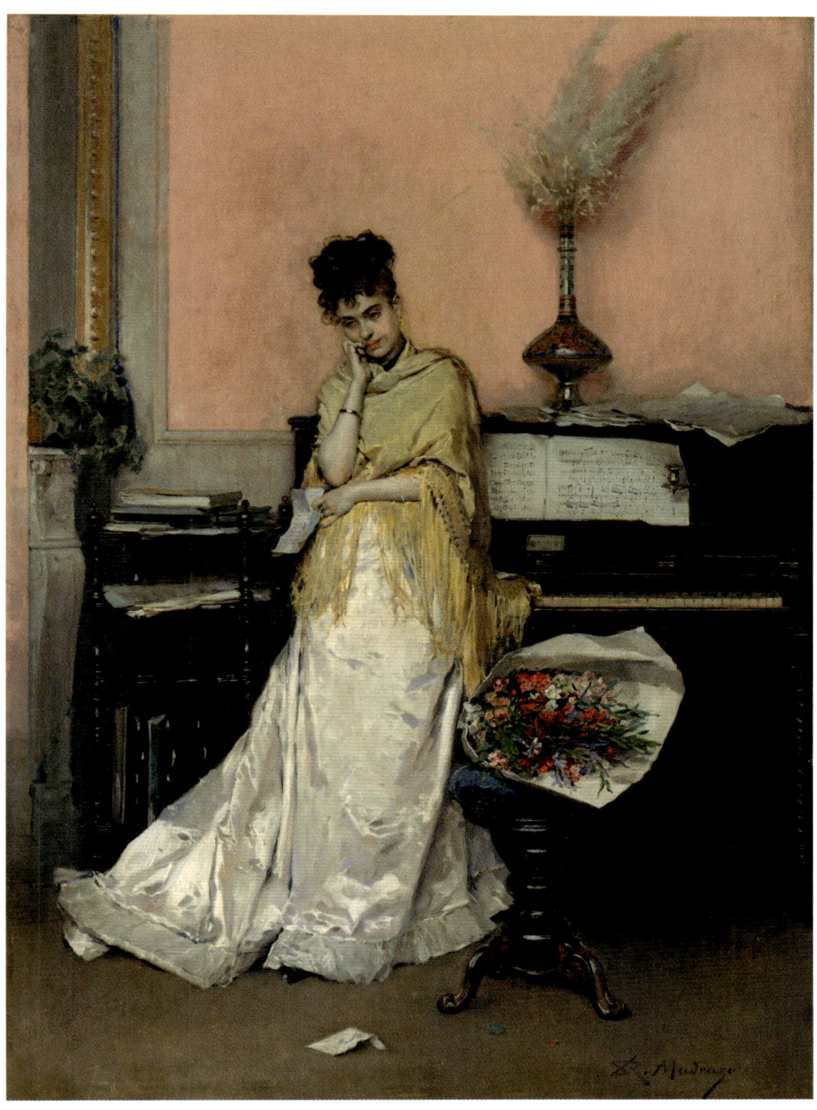

Fig. 17. Raimundo de Madrazo y Garreta (Spanish, 1841–1920), *The Bouquet*, c. 1870. Oil on panel, 67.2 x 48.6 cm. Sterling and Francine Clark Art Institute, Williamstown, Massachusetts (1955.918)

Raimundo de Madrazo y Garreta (fig. 17). In contrast to the Impressionists, who represented the vanguard in their day, this group of artists painted for a broader audience, relying on anecdotal subject matter handled in a slick manner. Clark also admired the highly finished and larger-scale paintings by forgotten academicians like Jean-Léon Gérôme and William-Adolphe Bouguereau, but acquired their works in much smaller quantities. In his taste for these unseen painters, whose works hung in the storerooms of French and American museums alike, Clark may not have been alone but was in very small company.

OUTBREAK OF WORLD WAR II: PLANNING FOR THE FUTURE

Clark's strong bond with dealers grew from years of patronage and in-depth conversations. But it was a very small circle of dealers, like George Davey of Knoedler and Herbert Elfers of Durand-Ruel, whom Clark trusted with intimate knowledge of the scope of his collection and with whom he could share his views on art. These dealer friends rallied to Clark's aid when the anticipation of war forced him to evacuate his collection from Paris. Davey handled most of the arrangements from France starting in the summer of 1938. The first pictures to go were the Renoirs, including the *Blonde Bather* (cat. 62) and *Sleeping Girl*. By the year's end, all of the most important paintings had been packed and shipped by ocean liner to a warehouse in Montreal.[25] The next summer, the paintings in the Clarks' New York apartment and their "reserves" at Durand-Ruel and Manhattan Storage were transferred to a secure facility in the mountains near Denver, Colorado, that Clark shared with the gallery. The bulk of the collection remained in Montreal and Denver for nearly a decade, during which time the Clarks made several trips to see their objects. Even after the war, the Clarks maintained a group of paintings in Montreal.[26]

In the summer of 1939 the Clarks paid their final visit to France prior to the war. As the normally sleepy month of August wore on, the atmosphere in Paris grew increasingly tense, and soon the Clarks found themselves again in a war zone. Sterling filled his days packing his most valuable silver and porcelain objects, which he arranged to store at the Musée de Sèvres, and took inventories of his books and other possessions (fig. 18). Although most of the important pictures had already been shipped to Canada, there were numerous preparations to be made at the farm in Normandy and the house on the rue Cimarosa. On 11 August, Clark wrote in his diary, "What times with the cursed airplanes & the terrible material destruction ahead of us all of so many beautiful things!!!!—

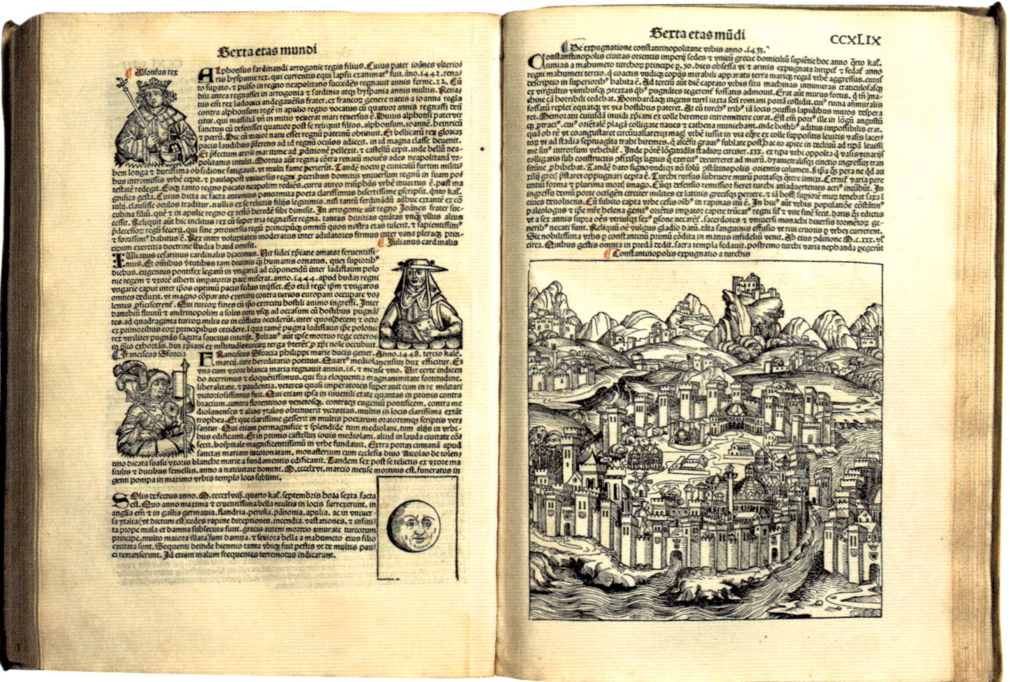
Sexta etas mundi

Sexta etas mũdi CCXLIX

Fig. 18. Hartmann Schedel (German, 1440–1514), *Nuremberg Chronicle*, Nuremberg: Anton Koberger, 1493. Sterling and Francine Clark Art Institute, Williamstown, Massachusetts

It made me sad to think of how much has left the house—Collections of 30 odd years—No rest for the weary."[27]

On 3 September, when England and France declared war on Germany, the Clarks were still in Paris. Walking on the terrace of the Trocadéro, they took in its sweeping panorama of the French capital. They noted how the view had been altered by signs marking bomb shelters dotting the cityscape.[28] The next day they were fitted for gas masks, and when the sirens wailed in the middle of the night, they found themselves huddled in an air-raid shelter in a cellar on the avenue Kléber with a group of their neighbors. With some difficulty, they finally booked a passage back to New York. After their departure on the third of October, seven years would elapse before their return to Paris.

Wary of crossing the Atlantic in wartime, Clark made it his final order of business prior to embarking for New York to update his will. With the situation in Paris looking grim, he made the decision to leave all of his collections to the city of Richmond, Virginia, in the event that he and Francine should die together.[29]

The choice of Richmond at this date is an interesting one. Although Clark did not specify the Virginia Museum of Fine Arts, it was the only art museum in the city, having opened to the public just three years earlier, and was actively seeking collectors like Clark to pledge gifts that would enhance its modest holdings. The museum's core collection consisted of some fifty Old Master paintings donated to the state by John Barton Payne, a prominent judge and secretary of the Interior under President Wilson. No evidence has yet been found that the museum was specifically aware of Clark or made a direct appeal to him, but rather, he may have arrived at this decision through his own knowledge of Richmond's ambitions. From his point of view, the Virginia Museum of Fine Arts would have made an excellent site for his art collection for the same reasons that had led him to select the Petit Palais in 1924; in the context of its relatively small and eclectic permanent collection, Clark's potential donation would have stood out as the museum's main attraction.

The Clarks spent the war years shuttling back and forth between an apartment in the old Ritz-Carlton

Hotel in New York and their Virginia farm, while their art collection remained divided among Paris, Montreal, and Denver. An unusual and historic event, however, occurred at Crichton Brothers in New York during the first week of June 1940. Peter Guille, a dealer in fine silver who had become friendly with the Clarks, convinced the couple to mount an exhibition of their silver collection. Sterling had been acquiring silver at a rapid pace throughout the 1930s, but, like the bulk of their other collections, it was mostly sitting in storage. This would be the first public exhibition of any aspect of the couple's artworks.

The exhibition opened with a dollar admission charge as a benefit for English and French relief organizations. A reviewer in *The Connoisseur* raved:

> A private collection of silver, chiefly English in origin, which an anonymous owner generously permitted to be shown in a benefit exhibition in June at the galleries of Peter Guille, is without doubt one of the finest to be brought together in America, and as its existence has been known to comparatively few, the showing of the collection constituted an event of outstanding importance.[30]

The Clarks seem to have been delighted with the outcome, as it gave them the first opportunity to see their own objects installed all together.

In the beginning of 1944, Clark began seriously considering creating a museum of his own. It is clear from the beginning that The Frick Collection, on the corner of Fifth Avenue and East Seventieth Street, was his primary inspiration (fig. 31). On Clark's first visit, in 1939, he recorded his general enthusiasm for the institution:

> What a collection of very fine things—with some 25 percent subtracted a collection of chefs-d'oeuvre!!!! And even the exceptions not bad—The false Rembrandt bought when Frick would not speak to Carstairs & the Pieter de Hoogh false both labeled "School of"—Some English portraits overcleaned by Duveen—Two out of 4 Whistlers terribly dark and these are about all to find fault with—But what real masterpieces the 2 Rembrandts, the Goya "Forge," the Wonderful Fragonard of Grasse, the Van Dycks etc. etc.!!!! I forgot the Velasquez & the 2 Greco's!!!![31]

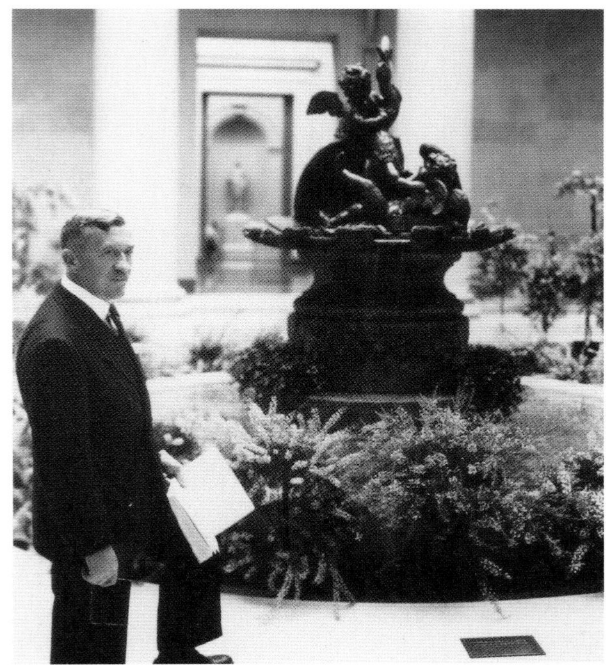

Fig. 19. Chester Dale in the West Garden Court, National Gallery of Art, c. 1943

Clark's attorneys and business associates began to make discreet inquiries on his behalf and arranged tours of several Manhattan town houses. Clark's most important consideration was to find a building with a large façade that received a generous amount of unobstructed sunlight. Eventually he redirected his attention to a plot on the corner of Seventy-second Street and Park Avenue, and instructed his lawyer to make an offer, which was accepted.[32]

In the midst of his search for a place to house his collection, Clark made the fortuitous acquaintance of Chester Dale (fig. 19) and found him to be a sympathetic collector with informed opinions concerning estate planning and bequests to museums.[33] Like Clark, he was an outwardly gruff personality who spoke his mind in no uncertain terms. Unlike Clark, Dale was a benefactor of a number of major museums and had

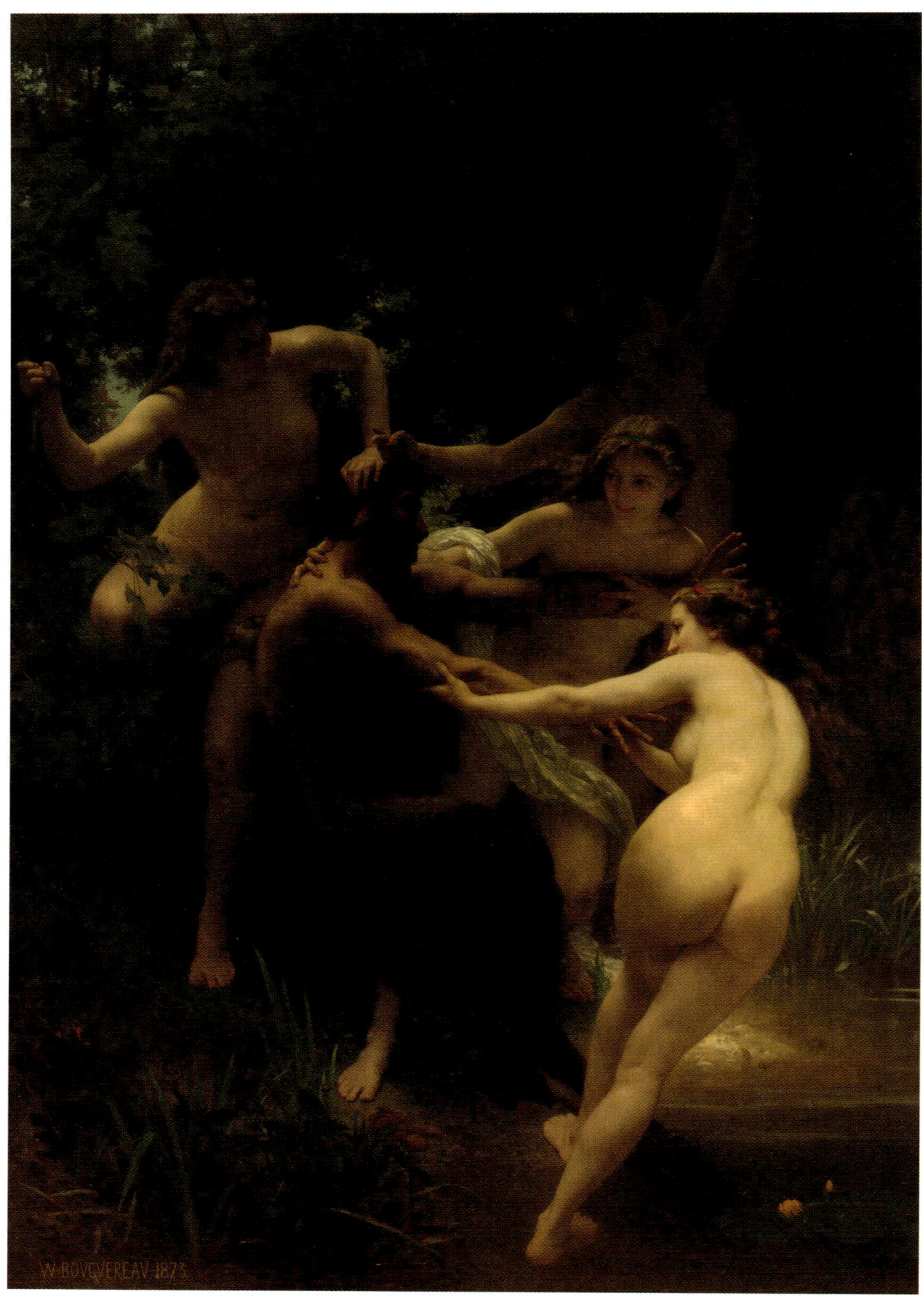

Fig. 20. William-Adolphe Bouguereau (French, 1825–1873), *Nymphs and Satyr*, 1873. Oil on canvas, 260 x 180 cm. Sterling and Francine Clark Art Institute, Williamstown, Massachusetts (1955.658)

placed portions of his collection on long-term loan to the Art Institute of Chicago and Philadelphia Museum of Art, prior to moving them to the newly opened National Gallery of Art in Washington.

When they met at a dinner party at Durand-Ruel's New York gallery, the two collectors bonded immediately. After dinner they left the others and stole down to the third floor, where Clark's great Bouguereau *Nymphs and Satyr* (fig. 20) was installed in a private gallery. He had acquired the painting in 1943 and had exhibited it at Durand-Ruel anonymously to raise money for the Free French Relief Committee. Dale himself owned three large decorative panels by Bouguereau, and the two hard-nosed collectors got lost in a discussion of the artist's supreme craftsmanship until they were discovered by Durand-Ruel and ushered back to the party upstairs.

After bonding over Bouguereau, Clark and Dale extended reciprocal invitations to each other's New York apartments. During the course of their budding friendship, Dale discussed his unhappy experiences attempting to find a permanent home for his collection at the Metropolitan Museum of Art and Columbia University, neither of which could meet his terms. The National Gallery was more receptive and agreed to show his paintings as an inviolable collection in a suite of four galleries. "Chester said his pictures were his children & he had wanted them settled before his death—Urged me to take similar steps,"[34] Clark noted with great interest. After this conversation, he pushed his attorneys to move forward and contact the lawyers of the Frick Foundation to obtain information on establishing his private museum in New York.[35]

Clark's passion for "high Impressionism" was unabated during the war years, but the supply of important masterpieces had been disrupted. Among the few additions were Pissarro's *Road to Versailles at Louveciennes* (cat. 21) and Manet's *Interior at Arcachon* (cat. 30). Clark also continued to add to his collection of Renoir, acquiring eight paintings during the war. Two of his Renoir purchases during the 1940s were particularly gratifying to Clark and reveal the tenacity with which he scoured the art market. In 1939 he had been shown a Renoir still life of white roses at Wildenstein and regretted letting it slip through his fingers. He spent the next three years looking for a still life of comparable quality until one day Charles Henschel of Knoedler showed him *Peonies* (cat. 57). Clark was delighted with the painting and the successful conclusion to his search, describing it as a "really fine picture."[36] Another triumph for Clark came with the acquisition of *Thérèse Berard* (cat. 54), this time for more personal reasons. Sterling knew that the picture had been consigned to Durand-Ruel by his brother Stephen and reveled in taking the "treasure" out of Stephen's collection. How much the picture's provenance contributed to his declaration that the picture was "one of the best portraits I have ever seen by Renoir" is arguable, but it nevertheless stood out in Sterling's mind as a painting of the finest quality.[37]

In preparation for his first trip abroad since 1939, Clark once again met with his attorneys to draw up a new will, which would be the first and only document to spell out his plans to found a museum in New York City. Clark's 1946 will provided for the creation of a nonprofit institution called the R. Sterling Clark Collection "for the purpose of establishing and maintaining a gallery of art and of encouraging and developing the study of the fine arts and advancing the general knowledge of kindred subjects; such gallery of art to be a public gallery to which the entire public shall always have access."[38]

The will goes into some detail concerning the potential uses of the endowment fund. The trustees were empowered to apply it to the construction, upkeep, and expansion of the physical facility, as well as "the acquisition of other suitable works of art to form part of such gallery of art, and the maintenance of a non-profit school or schools for the study of the fine arts and kindred subjects." The stated guidelines for collection care and acquisitions give insight into Clark's own views of conservation and his criteria for adding to his collection:

> It having been my object in making said collection to acquire only works of the best quality of the artists represented, which were not damaged or distorted by the work of the restorers, it is my wish and desire and I request that the said Trustees . . . permanently maintain in said gallery all works of art bequeathed hereunder in the condition in which they shall be at my death without any so-called restoration, cleaning or other work thereon, except in case of damage from unforeseen causes, and that none of them be sold, exchanged or otherwise disposed of; also that in the acquisition of additional property, they be guided by my desire to restrict additional acquisition to works of artists who have died twenty-five years or more prior to such acquisition and to the best works of such artists.[39]

The restriction on buying works by artists dead for more than a quarter of a century was based on the same limitation originally imposed at the National Gallery of Art in Washington, and was clearly meant to keep out the painters of the School of Paris, whom Clark felt were overrated and overpriced.

AFTER THE WAR: PARIS AND NEW YORK

In 1946 the Clarks returned to France for the first time in seven years. The Normandy farm had been bombarded by Allied forces and was a total loss. The Paris house at 4, rue Cimarosa was, however, remarkably intact. The homecoming was marked with relief as well as sadness, for the couple had decided that the time had come to close their beloved Paris house.

Returning to New York, the Clarks moved into a larger apartment in the Carlton House that could accommodate the furnishings from Paris.[40] As the paintings collection began to emerge from storage, the couple had the pleasure of reacquainting themselves with works that they had not lived with for years. They created a new "galleria" to replace their grand painting salon on the rue Cimarosa. The pace of new

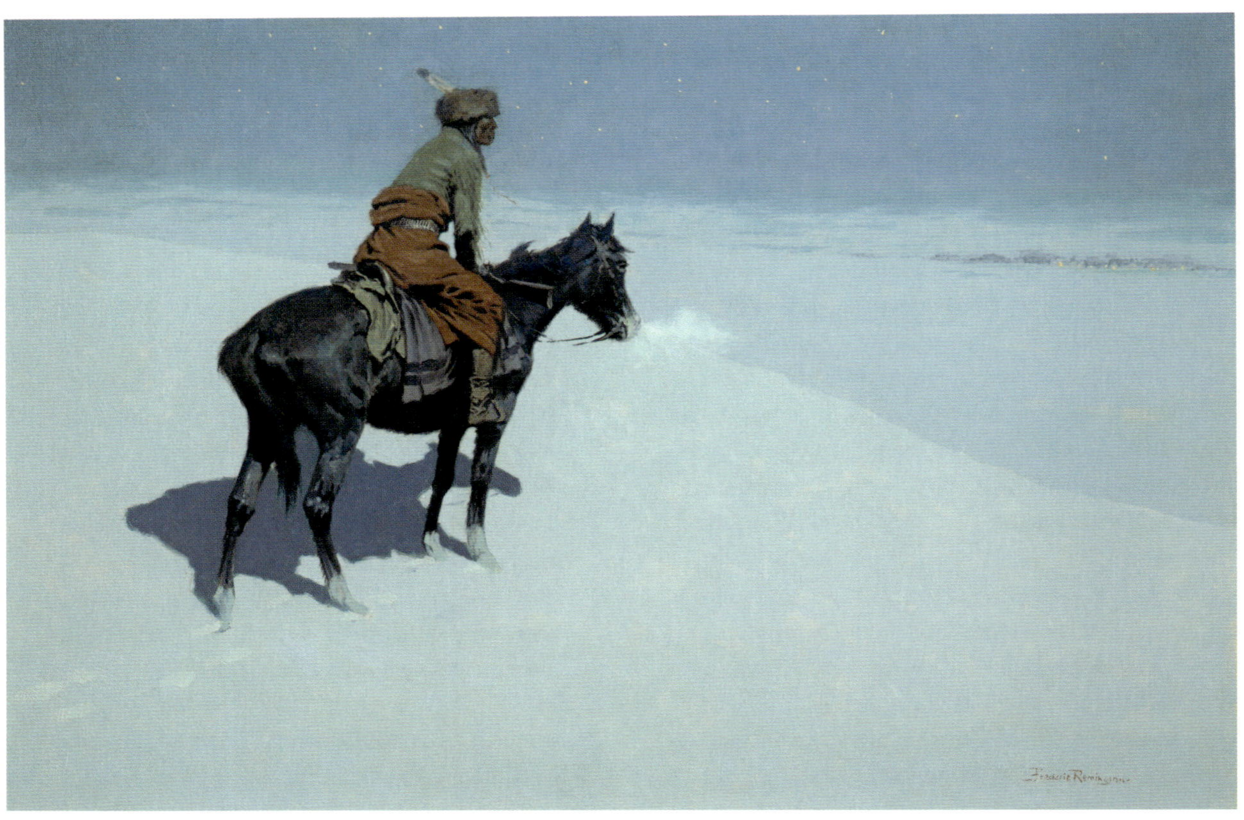

Fig. 21. Frederic Remington (American, 1861–1909), *Friends or Foes? (The Scout)*, c. 1900–1905. Oil on canvas, 68.6 x 101.6 cm. Sterling and Francine Clark Art Institute, Williamstown, Massachusetts (1955.12)

acquisitions slowed considerably, with an average of only three to four new paintings entering the collection each year from 1948 through the mid-1950s. While the quantity dropped, the quality remained higher than ever; among these late acquisitions was a remarkable number of major additions to the paintings collection, including Morisot's *The Bath* (cat. 69), Remington's *Friends or Foes? (The Scout)* (fig. 21), and Toulouse-Lautrec's *Waiting* (cat. 71).

Throughout these last years, the nature of Clark's purchasing habits changed, as he imagined his objects installed in multiple galleries large enough to present his entire collection. He was determined to add works of quality that would both build on the strengths of the existing collection and, if possible, fill gaps. It is important to note that none of these acquisitions represented a compromise in Clark's taste. He still bought only what he liked. In the spring of 1951, he paid a visit to Knoedler and purchased his final Renoir, *Apples in a Dish* (cat. 65). Just a few months earlier he had acquired another Impressionist still life from Knoedler, *Apples and Grapes in a Basket* (cat. 18) by Alfred Sisley, an artist he had only come to admire during the 1940s. The Sisley was still in Clark's storeroom at the gallery when he was shown the Renoir, and it seems likely that he saw the two pictures as complementing each other.

In 1950 the Clarks learned that the Ritz-Carlton, where they had been living since 1934, had been sold to make way for an office building, so they moved their residence to 740 Park Avenue (fig. 22). The Clarks were attracted to the apartment largely because it reminded them of the layout of their Paris home and had ceilings tall enough to hang their enormous Bouguereau.

As they settled into their recently acquired surroundings, Clark, evidently happy in his new abode, wrote:

> The new apartment is a real 'galleria.' . . . Believe it or not 3 Géromes, 2 Claude Monets, a Pissarro, a Mary Cassatt, a Ziem, a Madrazo, a Sisley, 4 Renoirs in the same room go quite well together. And in Francine's bedroom 2 Stevens . . . 2 Corots, a Manet, a Sargent, and 2 Renoirs look extremely well together.[41]

While this somewhat eclectic arrangement pleased Clark, it represented only a portion of the more than two hundred paintings that eventually hung in the apartment.

WILLIAMSTOWN: STERLING CLARK'S LEGACY

As he entered his seventies, Clark decided that the time had come to move forward with his museum so that he could actively participate in creating the institution, rather than handing it down to his executors. Although he owned a plot of land in Manhattan that had been earmarked for this purpose, he had grown increasingly concerned about modern methods of warfare, which had radically changed the threat to civilians since his early days fighting the Boxers in China. Clark had spent World War I in France, assisting the Allies and protecting his own property. Less than twenty years later, he found himself caught in France during the outbreak of World War II and was forced to secure his irreplaceable collection in advance of the Nazi invasion. He considered himself a lucky man that the Allied bombing of his French farm caused his only real losses. But these experiences had instilled in Clark a sense of anxiety. More than any other American collector of his generation, he had known the ravages of war firsthand.

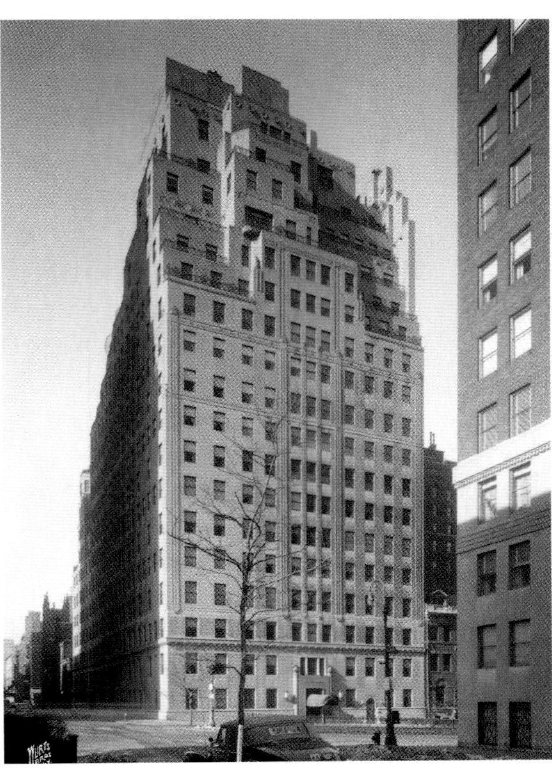
Fig. 22. 740 Park Avenue (also known as 71 East Seventy-first Street), 1937

Having miraculously safeguarded his collections through two world wars, Clark had reason to be concerned. If and when World War III broke out, he felt that New York City would be a primary target. What he needed was a small New England village a safe distance, but reachable, from New York. Cooperstown was now out of the question as a potential site for his museum. The Clark family had earlier ties to Williams College, Sterling's grandfather's alma mater. Both his grandfather Edward Clark and his father, Alfred Corning Clark, had been trustees, and the family had erected a building on campus called Clark Hall. These ties, however, may not have been Sterling Clark's primary attraction to Williamstown, Massachusetts. After some forty years of imagining a home for his works of art in such far-flung locales as Cooperstown, Paris, Richmond, and New York City, Clark decided that the final resting place for the collection, and the collector, would be a site not on the radar, and that is precisely what he found so appealing.

Clark's plan was nothing more than an idea until late 1948, when his attorney contacted William Sidley, a Chicago lawyer and alumnus of Williams College, and mentioned that he had a client who was searching for a home for his art collection.[42] The college administration and its savvy art professors lost no time in pursuing this lead, and in January 1949, retired professor Karl Weston and his successor as head of the art department (and a former student), S. Lane Faison Jr., traveled to New York to meet the Clarks and view their collection. What they found astonished them, and the duo returned to the Berkshires with the thrilling prospect that an extraordinary and virtually unknown collection might be destined for their community.

After this meeting, the pace accelerated toward the founding of the museum. The warm personal relationships that developed between Sterling Clark and both Karl Weston and J. Phinney Baxter, president of Williams College, were crucial to the plan moving forward. The Clarks paid their first visit to Williamstown in the fall of 1949, and by February 1950 a suitable site was identified. In April the "Robert Sterling Clark Art Institute" was officially incorporated as a charitable and educational organization. The original charter clearly stated the Clarks' intentions that the museum would be much more than a treasure house to showcase their art collection, but would serve as an educational institution promoting the study of the fine arts. Williamstown offered a bucolic setting not unlike Cooperstown, where Clark had first imagined building an art museum, but with the added advantage of a prestigious college at its doorstep. After developing a rapport with members of its administration, Clark recognized that his museum could only benefit from its proximity to Williams College.

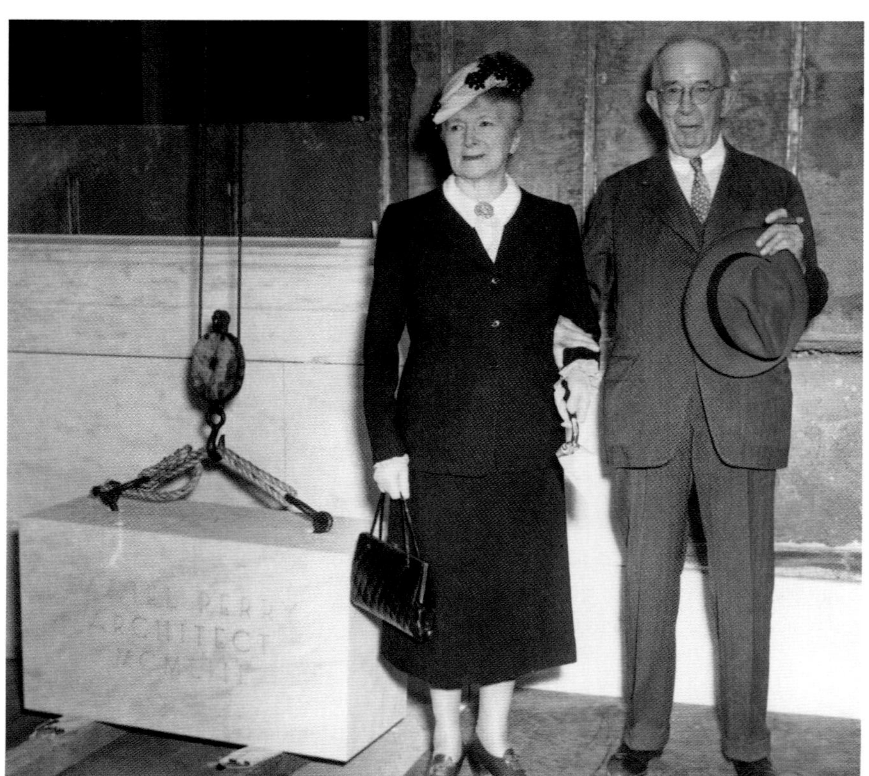

Fig. 23. Sterling and Francine Clark at the cornerstone-laying ceremony of the Institute, August 1953

During the course of 1950–51, Clark rejected two different architectural firms, and the project was at a standstill. Clark's demands for a modestly scaled, classically organized building with natural light were finally met when Daniel Perry, an architect introduced to Clark by Peter Guille, submitted his preliminary plans in December 1951. Clark took Perry to see The Frick Collection, which he admired for the domestic scale of the gallery spaces, something he wanted to emulate; however, he found the building's ornamentation excessive. Perry worked diligently to understand and meet the approval of his demanding client.

Site work commenced in late 1952, and in August 1953 a simple ceremony was held marking the laying of the cornerstone (fig. 23). A month later, the name of the institution was changed to include Francine's name as well. Clark himself wrote: "It is a particular gratification to me that the Institute . . . bears not only my name but also that of Mrs. Clark. Her constant enthusiasm for the Institute's objectives, her participation in the accumulation of the collections which the Institute will house and her contributions to the planning of the project, make the new name wholly appropriate."[43] Sterling had always called Francine his "touchstone" in judging pictures, and now the world would know her role in forming the collection.

Construction of the museum took nearly two years at a cost of just under $3 million.[44] The Clarks monitored the progress, and as the building neared completion in the spring of 1955, they began the complex process of moving their collection from their New York apartment, their storeroom at Knoedler, and the storage facility in Montreal that they had retained since the war. Peter Guille was the founders' choice to be the first director, although in the selection and arrangement of the inaugural installations, Clark maintained control. In correspondence with Herbert Elfers of Durand-Ruel dating from March 1955, just

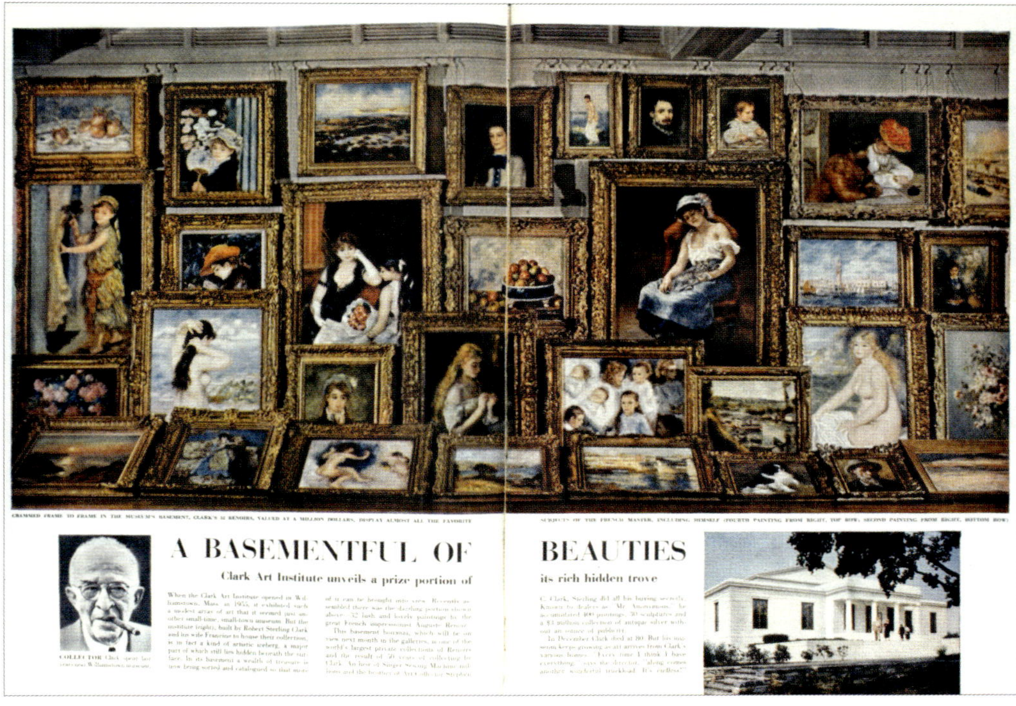

A BASEMENTFUL OF BEAUTIES

Clark Art Institute unveils a prize portion of its rich hidden trove

Fig. 24. In 1956, *Life* magazine featured an extraordinary photographic spread of works by Renoir at the Clark.

two months prior to the opening, he described his participation:

> We have just returned from 6 days in Williamstown. We hung 19 pictures & expect to have in all about 30—6 or 7 Winslow Homers; 2 Sargents; 2 Remingtons; 2 Inness; 1 Mary Cassatt; 1 Puvis de Chavannes; 3 Gérômes; 1 Dagnan-Bouveret; 1 Chartran (Calvé); 1 Ruysdael; 1 Troyon; 1 Géricault; 1 Van Dyck; 1 Goya; 1 Gilbert Stuart; 1 Gainsborough; 1 Carolus-Durand; 1 Claude Lorrain; Perhaps Renoir "Fournaise"—The Degas portrait; these last simply to show a representative lot of men's portraits by good artists.[45]

The eclecticism of this selection echoes the installations that Clark had made in his own residences. Most surprising was the emphasis on American art and French academic painting and the relative scarcity of Impressionism in the opening display; while only a single Renoir was included, seven Homers and three Gérômes were placed on view. The decision to hold back what would certainly be the most crowd-pleasing portion of the collection was a calculated one on the part of the founder. Writing to Charles Durand-Ruel of the first installation, "I think you would be surprised to see how well the Gérômes look among much more expensive pictures—I am keeping the Renoirs & Impressionist pictures for later on—I expect the critics will give me the works! But I also expect I shall be amused."[46]

Francine Clark cut the ribbon on opening day, 17 May 1955, before an invited crowd of sixty. Just two galleries were unveiled, containing thirty-three paintings, seven sculptures, and an assortment of silver. At the time of the opening, the museum building included a suite of rooms that the Clarks intended to use as a private apartment when they were visiting Williamstown, and this ended up becoming Sterling Clark's final permanent home. The couple stayed in the Berkshires to greet the many friends who came through to see the new museum; in September, Clark suffered a stroke and remained hospitalized for four months. He spent the last year of his life in his museum, tended by Francine and a professional nurse. He was present for the second summer season and the opening of the large Impressionist gallery in the fall of 1956, which at last revealed his extraordinary collection of Renoirs, an event that garnered national coverage in the press (fig. 24).

It was in his temple of art, surrounded by his treasures, that Sterling Clark died on 29 December 1956. A private funeral service was held in the museum's central gallery, with his remarkable collection of paintings by Renoir providing an idyllic backdrop. In his final years he had seen his prize thoroughbred, Never Say Die, win the prestigious Epsom Derby, and had created a fine museum to house his cherished collections. If he had any regrets, he kept them to himself. Clark's cremated remains were interred in a marble vault beneath the front steps of the museum.

Francine Clark continued to sit on the museum's board until her own death in April 1960. Correspondence reveals that she asserted her opinions on the arrangement of paintings in the galleries, looking to maintain her husband's wishes.[47] She also supported the appointment in 1958 of the museum's first curator, William Collins, formerly of Knoedler in London and New York, who was put in charge of prints and drawings. Under Collins's guidance, the Clarks' large collection of works on paper, still stored in the portfolios that had been kept at Knoedler for many years, was inventoried and organized, and a gallery for changing exhibitions of prints and drawings was inaugurated.

In creating the Sterling and Francine Clark Art Institute, the founders established an institution with a unique personality, one that reflected a true labor of love. Acquiring remarkable works in a variety of media—paintings, sculptures, drawings, prints, silver, porcelain, and books—was more than a hobby for the Clarks: it was a joint project through which they bonded over the course of nearly fifty years. With both of their names carved in the lintel, and their tombs beneath the front steps, the museum in Williamstown marked the end of their long adventure together, many miles from their families, but with their "children."

In the half century that followed, the Clark has evolved into an institute with an expansive mission that reaches well beyond the limits of the small New England town in which it is situated. Sterling Clark did not intend his museum to function as a glorified mausoleum; indeed, he left a large endowment combined with a liberal charter that has enabled the institution to grow into a world-renowned research center in the field of art history, a place where objects, ideas, and people come together. The unique personality of the Clark is defined not merely by its art collection but by an atmosphere of intellectual vitality that builds upon its founders' vision.

NOTES

An expanded version of this essay was published as "From Paris to Williamstown: Robert Sterling Clark's Life as a Collector," in Michael Conforti et al., *The Clark Brothers Collect: Impressionist and Early Modern Paintings*, exh. cat. (Williamstown: Sterling and Francine Clark Art Institute, 2006), pp. 35–121. Unless otherwise indicated, original correspondence and diaries are in the archives of the Sterling and Francine Clark Art Institute, Williamstown, Massachusetts.

1. Sterling Clark to W. Beach Day, 13 Jan. 1911.
2. Stephen Carlton Clark, unpublished memoir (private collection, c. 1935), p. 2.
3. For an in-depth discussion of the collecting activities of Alfred Corning Clark and Elizabeth Scriven Clark, see Michael Conforti, "The Clark Brothers: An Introduction," in Michael Conforti et al., *The Clark Brothers Collect*, pp. 7–23.
4. Douglas Johnston to Sterling Clark, 21 June 1911. The paintings are as follows: Jean-François Millet's *The Water Carrier* (Sterling and Francine Clark Art Institute, 1955.551); an unidentified work by Mariano Fortuny y Carbó; Gilbert Stuart's *Portrait of George Washington* (fig. 5) (Sterling and Francine Clark Art Institute, 1955.16); an unidentified work by George Inness; and Julian Walbridge Rix's *Road Through the Woods* (location unknown).
5. The bronze is in the collection of the Clark (1955.1015). The Perronneau pastel was sold by Clark at an unknown date.
6. Soon after buying the Bellini, however, Clark became dissatisfied with the painting's seriously compromised state and traded it back to the dealer, who eventually sold it to the Boston collector Isabella Stewart Gardner.

7. Sterling Clark to Stephen Carlton Clark, 4 Feb. 1913.
8. Ibid.
9. Stephen Carlton Clark to Sterling Clark, 26 Feb. 1913.
10. Sterling Clark to Stephen Carlton Clark, 12 Aug. 1913.
11. Sterling kept the plaster cast of the Rodin and gave the bronze to his brother Stephen.
12. Scott & Fowles dealer's file, Sterling and Francine Clark Art Institute Archives.
13. Henry McBride, "The Renoirs in America: In Appreciation of the Metropolitan Museum's Exhibition," *Art News* 35, no. 31 (1937): p. 60.
14. Ann Dumas and David Brenneman, *Degas and America: The Early Collectors,* exh. cat. (Atlanta: The High Museum of Art, 2000), pp. 27, 30. Gardner bought eight drawings in four lots from the fourth sale through her agent Fernand Robert. Paul Sachs was in attendance for at least one of the sales, but did not make any purchases; see Agnes Mongan, *Memorial Exhibition: Works of Art from the Collection of Paul J. Sachs, 1878–1965: Given and Bequeathed to the Fogg Art Museum, Harvard University,* exh. cat. (Cambridge, Mass.: Fogg Art Museum, 1965), p. 10.
15. Sterling Clark Diary (hereafter, RSC Diary), 4 and 10 Mar. 1924. No copy of the will of 1924 has been found.
16. Henry Lapauze, *Le Palais des Beaux-Arts de la Ville de Paris (Petit Palais)* (Paris: Lucien Laveur, 1910); Juliette Laffon, "Avant-propos," in *Catalogue sommaire illustré des peintures,* vol. 1 (Paris: Palais des Beaux-Arts de la Ville de Paris, 1981), pp. 7–10.
17. RSC Diary, 2 Oct. 1924.
18. Sterling Clark to George H. Davey, 13 Jan. 1933.
19. RSC Diary, 21 Jan. 1939.
20. RSC Diary, 21 May 1937.
21. RSC Diary, 22 Jan. 1942.
22. RSC Diary, 25 Jan. 1940.
23. RSC Diary, 3 Feb. 1940.
24. Ibid.
25. Clark's TFR-500 form, a census of his property in foreign countries filed with the U.S. Treasury Department in November 1943, itemizes the works in his collection that remained in Paris, as well as the objects stored in Montreal. A copy is in the archives of the Sterling and Francine Clark Art Institute.
26. An inventory dated 15 July 1955, shortly after the opening of the museum in Williamstown, lists forty-three paintings still in Montreal, including Ghirlandaio's *Portrait of a Lady* (fig. 7), Monet's *Tulip Fields at Sassenheim, near Leiden* (cat. 14), and Renoir's *Portrait of Madame Monet (Madame Claude Monet Reading)* (cat. 49).
27. RSC Diary, 11 Aug. 1939.
28. RSC Diary, 3 Sept. 1939.
29. RSC Diary, 19 Sept. 1939.
30. Helen Comstock, "Silver in a Benefit Exhibition," *The Connoisseur* 106, no. 468 (Sept. 1940): p. 72.
31. RSC Diary, 23 Apr. 1939.
32. The plot was located at 754–56 Park Avenue on the southwest corner of East Seventy-second Street, and contained three-, four-, and five-story dwellings. Clark kept the site until 1950, when he turned it over to a developer. The sale was reported in "Buyer Takes Title in Park Ave. Deal," *New York Times,* 14 June 1950.
33. RSC Diary, 28 Sept. 1945.
34. Ibid.
35. RSC Diary, 7 Nov. 1945.
36. RSC Diary, 31 Jan. 1942.
37. RSC Diary, 27 Nov. 1945. Why Stephen decided to sell the picture is not clear, although according to Sterling, "Francine I think gave the true explanation—young girl reminded him too much of Betsy, his daughter, who died a few months ago! But Mlle. Berard does not look like Betsy."
38. Sterling Clark's will, dated 12 July 1946, Sterling and Francine Clark Art Institute Archives.
39. Ibid.
40. Sterling Clark to Paul L. Clemens, 20 and 23 Apr. 1947.
41. Sterling Clark to Clemens, 28 Apr. 1950.
42. See Michael Conforti, "The Mind and the Eye: Williams College and the Establishment of the Clark Art Institute and Its Research and Academic Mission," *CAI: Journal of the Clark Art Institute* 2 (2001): p. 16.
43. Sterling and Francine Clark Art Institute, Report of President for Fiscal Year Ending February 28, 1954, p. 2, Sterling and Francine Clark Art Institute Archives.
44. Predictably, Clark did not want the construction costs released to the media. The George A. Fuller Company of New York was hired as the general contractor for the project and submitted an estimate of $2,450,000 on 8 October 1952 based on Daniel Perry's designs; Robert Sterling Clark Art Institute Minutes, vol. 1, Sterling and Francine Clark Art Institute Archives. Land, building, and construction costs indicated in the corporation's balance sheets between 1952 and 1956 amount to approximately $2,917,000.
45. Sterling Clark to Herbert Elfers, 19 Mar. 1955.
46. Sterling Clark to Charles Durand-Ruel, 20 Mar. 1955.
47. See correspondence between Peter Guille and Hugo Kohlmann from Jan. 1957, concerning Francine Clark's objections to moving the Rubens painting *Holy Family Under an Apple Tree* from the "Primitives Gallery" to the "Dutch and Flemish Gallery," Sterling and Francine Clark Art Institute Archives.

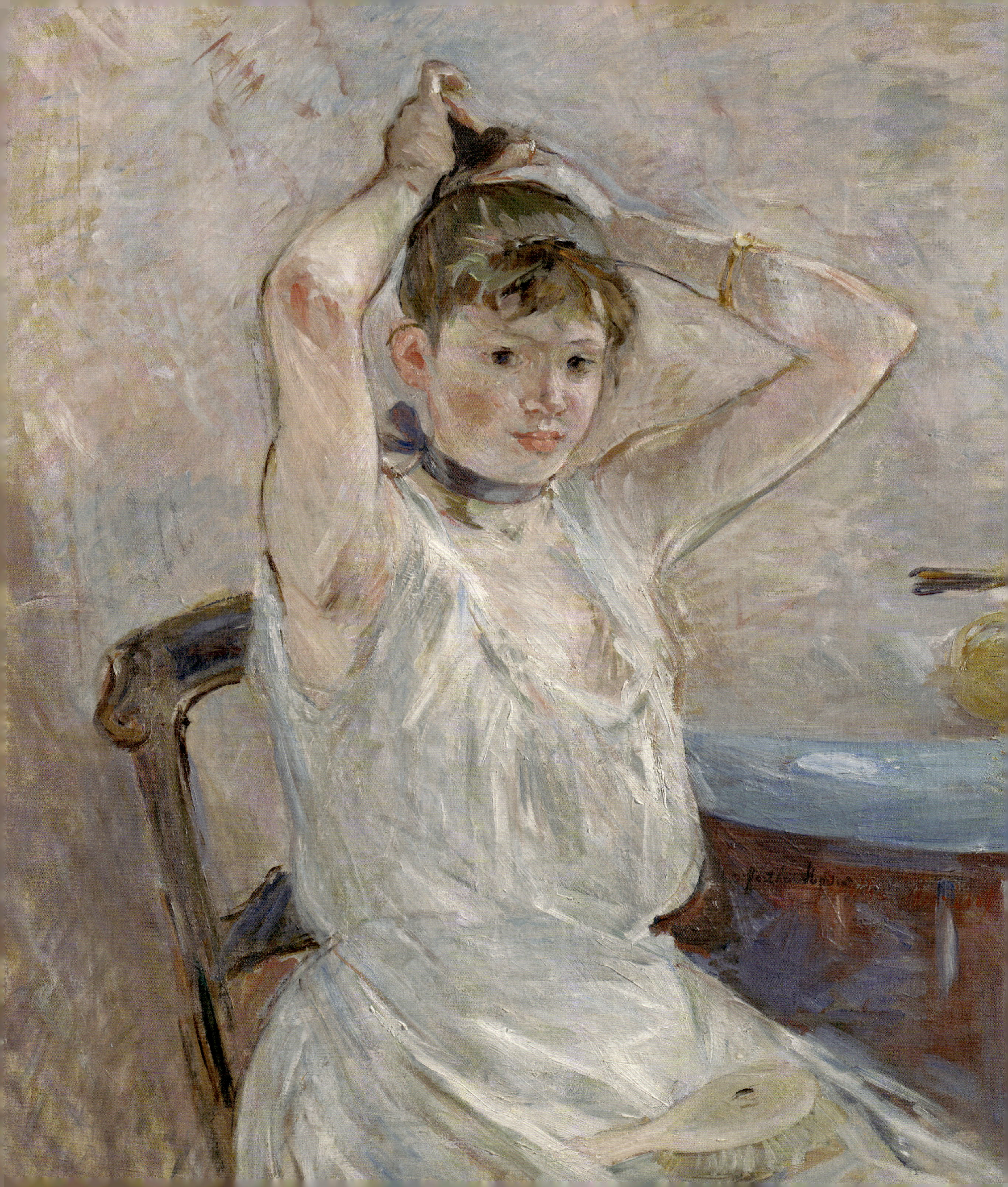

Refined Domesticity: Sterling Clark's Aesthetic Legacy

RICHARD R. BRETTELL

When Sterling Clark began to buy art seriously in 1912, he was in his mid-thirties, independently wealthy, handsome, and had traveled the world as both a soldier and explorer. Some two years earlier he had settled in Paris, becoming the only member of his fabulously wealthy American family to buy a permanent home in Europe.[1] He had also fallen in love—in a way familiar from nineteenth-century plays, novels, and opera libretti—with a beautiful young comedic actress, who stepped aside from a successful career to devote herself to her slightly younger American lover, whom she married in a French civil ceremony in 1919. Thus, Sterling Clark almost could have been a character in a novel by Henry James or Edith Wharton: a wealthy American expatriate gentleman who engages in dangerous liaisons and lives to enjoy—and to suffer—the consequences. Indeed, a bitter falling-out with his brothers in 1923 resulted directly from that marriage, making Sterling and his wife, Francine, into a Franco-American couple with roots nowhere and allegiances only to each other.

It was not difficult for Sterling Clark to find important works in the years before the onset of World War I. Both London and Paris had well-organized networks of art galleries, paid advisors, and decorators, the last of whom made connections among the various parties when an important residence was being prepared for a wealthy American. Yet, unlike many of the heroes and heroines of stories and novels by James and Wharton, Sterling Clark was largely self-educated as an art collector. Although he had been exposed to major works of European and American academic art in his mother's New York home (fig. 25), he chose to study the sciences at Yale and traveled as a young man not in search of museums but as a military adventurer. He earned a Silver Star for his service as a U.S. soldier in suppressing the Boxer Rebellion in 1900 (fig. 26), and in 1908 he led an exploratory expedition into northern China, mapping the topography of 24,000 square miles and fixing the position of twelve cities little known to Westerners at the time. His early history reminds us more of T. E. Lawrence than a young American aesthete of the Jamesian sort.

All of this explains the reticent and, in a sense, conventional beginnings of his collection. In the first ten years of his collecting, he preferred Old Master

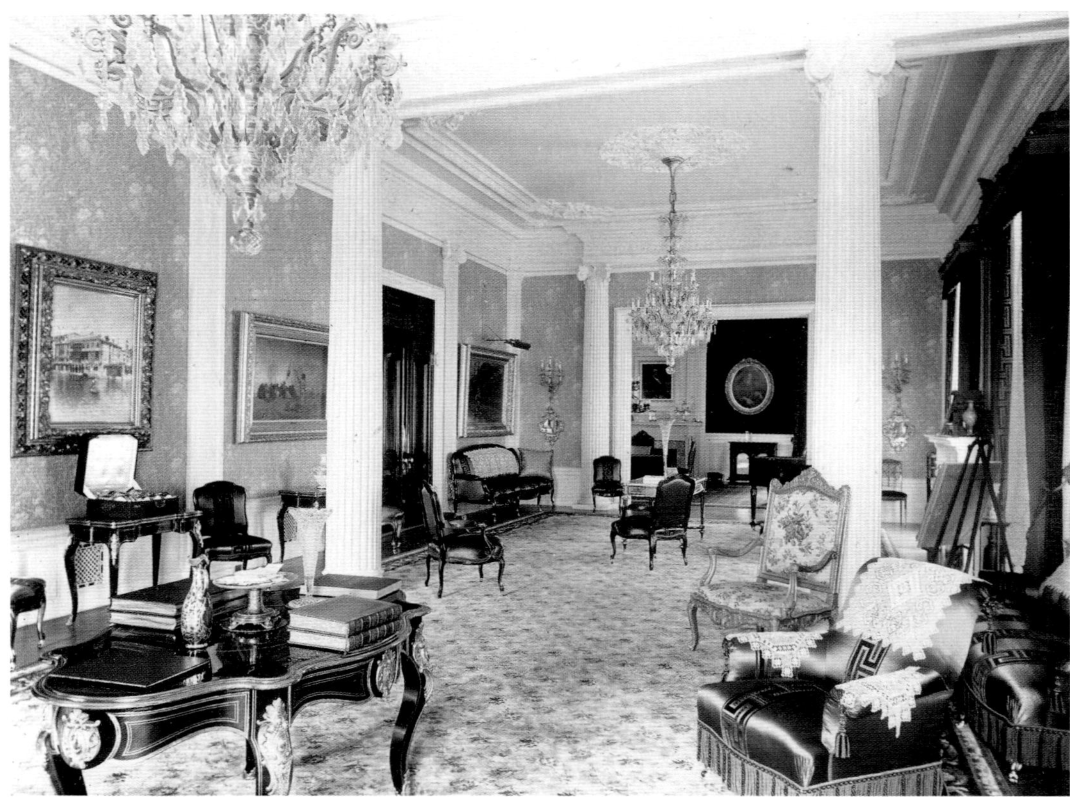

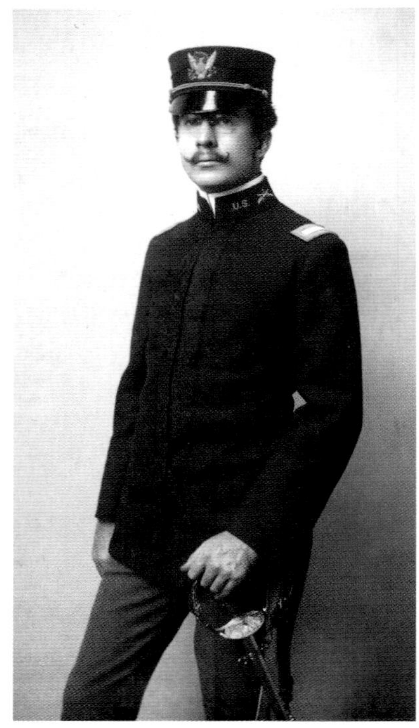

Fig. 25. Drawing room of Elizabeth Scriven Clark's residence at Riverside Drive, c. 1898

Fig. 26. Sterling Clark, c. 1900

paintings and sought out older works in both London and Paris, often with the advice of others. His first truly expensive purchase, a portrait of a woman by Domenico Ghirlandaio (fig. 7), was made in April 1913 and was negotiated by the American sculptor/art advisor George Grey Barnard, who helped Clark with a number of early acquisitions made in Italy. But on Clark's own trip to Italy that summer, the neophyte collector discovered that many of Barnard's assertions about the painting (significantly, Barnard's claim that it had not been restored) were incorrect. This early experience colored the rest of Clark's life as a collector, giving him an abiding suspicion of dealers, art advisors, and art historians. Clark's stubborn independence, even insularity, in both life and collecting culminated in his eventual decision to create his own private museum. Unlike most American collectors of the late nineteenth and early twentieth centuries, he established no close relationship with a museum or university until he founded the institute in Williamstown, Massachusetts, in 1955. Indeed, for much of his life, Clark was best known in social circles as a horse breeder and an aficionado of horse racing rather than as an art collector and cultural philanthropist. He maintained stables in both Virginia and Normandy, and in 1954 his prize thoroughbred Never Say Die became just the second American-bred horse to win the prestigious Epsom Derby.[2]

Although Clark remained primarily interested in Old Masters throughout the 1910s, he was also sowing the seeds of his future interest with a handful of early purchases of works by the American painters John Singer Sargent (fig. 10) and Winslow Homer (fig. 11). He also acquired his first Renoir in 1916 (cat. 50), and while it is the French nineteenth-century masterpieces that would eventually constitute the core of Sterling and Francine Clark's collection, this was by no means the only area in which the couple maintained a lasting interest. Indeed, if one were to make generalizations about "the Clark taste" from these works alone, the conclusions would be false. In addition to the French masterpieces, the Clarks collected not only Old Masters and American painting, but amassed as well truly extraordinary holdings of European and American prints and drawings from the Renaissance to the early twentieth century (fig. 6). They also put together a superior collection of English and American silver and an impressive library of rare books. The works in this exhibition—wonderful as they are—are but part of a larger, more complex, and evolving pattern of collecting practiced by Sterling and Francine Clark throughout the period from 1912 to 1950, when they were most active in assembling the works that hang in their eponymous institute.

This essay is an attempt to put their collecting of modern art into two contexts—that of the Clarks' own larger collections and that of the Euro-American collecting of art in the years 1880 to 1950. The first is easier to do because Sterling and Francine Clark parted with very few works of art and left both their collections and the records associated with them to the institution that bears their names. Because they supervised the construction of the museum, the building itself reflected their own particular sense of the relationship between the parts of the collections—Old Master paintings shown in domestically scaled rooms (fig. 27); eighteenth- and nineteenth-century works of smaller scale in a corridor gallery; and two bigger galleries for the large-scale French, British, and American academic paintings and for the Clarks' fabled collection of paintings by Pierre-Auguste Renoir (fig. 28). Interestingly, however, the Clarks made no stipulations whatsoever about the future installation of their collections, or about the nature of future acquisitions made possible by the generous endowment they established.

In the main, the works in Sterling and Francine Clark's collection are domestically scaled and were shown during their lifetime in rooms of ample but noninstitutional proportions with furniture and decorative arts. The very idea of domesticity, of works appreciated privately in rooms sized for that purpose,

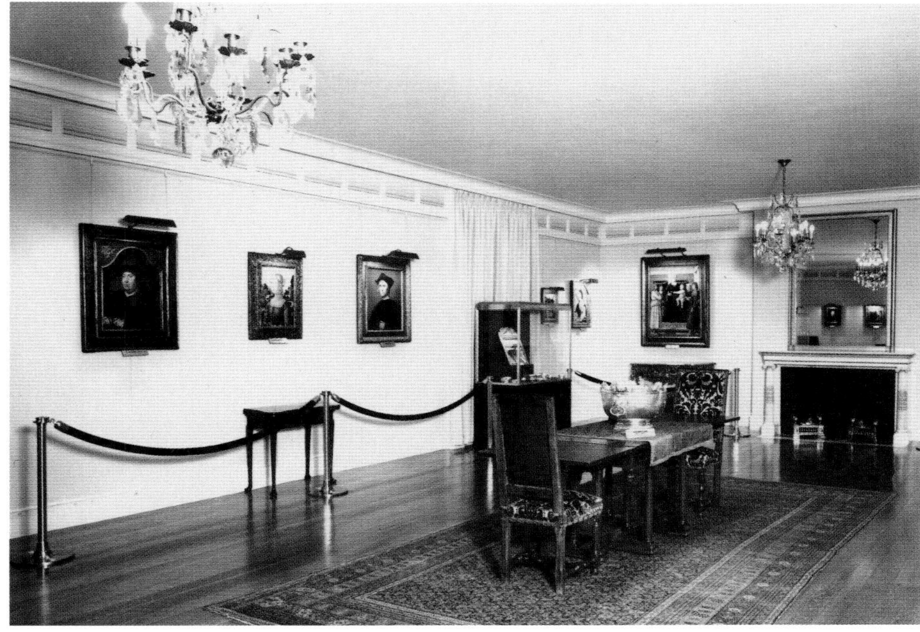

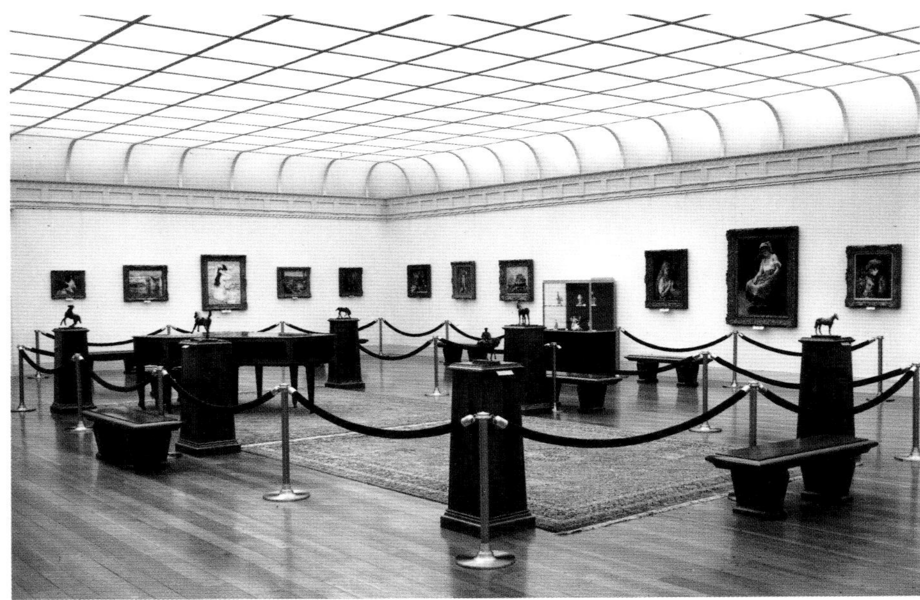

Fig. 27. Old Master gallery at the Sterling and Francine Clark Art Institute, 1957

Fig. 28. Renoir gallery at the Sterling and Francine Clark Art Institute, 1957

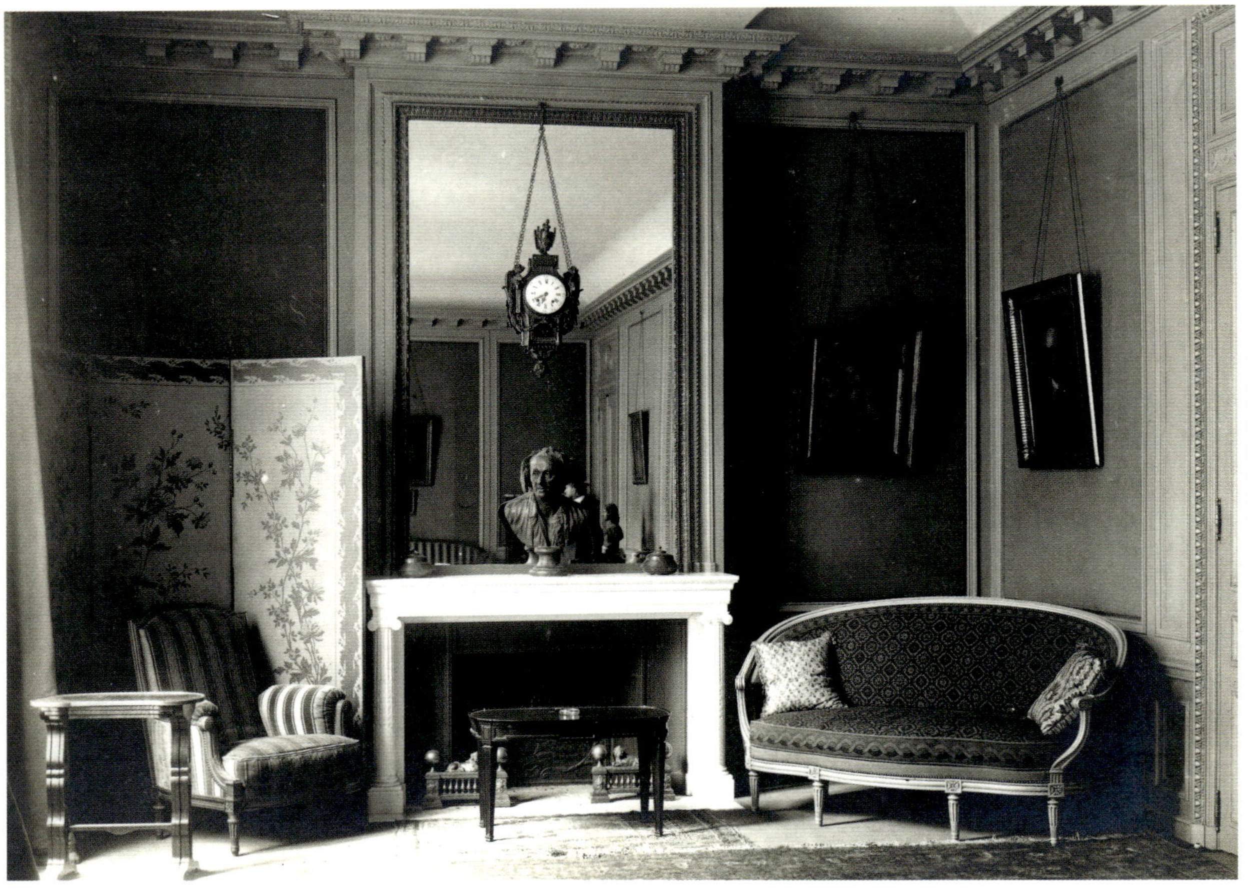

Fig. 29. Grand salon of Sterling Clark's house at 4, rue Cimarosa, Paris, c. 1913

is essential to an understanding of the Clarks' taste. Unlike many other aesthetically doctrinaire collectors of his generation, Sterling Clark saw remarkable links between Old Master and modern art and between academic and Impressionist art, and his collection celebrated what were for him the shared formal and aesthetic qualities of these often segregated subfields in capitalist collecting. Though there is little evidence that they ever placed Italian Renaissance paintings in the same room with works by Renoir and Pissarro, a letter written in 1950 does indicate that pictures by Gérôme, Madrazo, Pissarro, and Renoir were all in the same room, proving that the affinities were more important to them than the differences.[3] Both the artists and Clark's brother Stephen, an accomplished art collector and museum trustee, would have been horrified by this display of aesthetically opposite works.[4]

What other conclusions can one make about the Clarks' tastes? Most important is that they were centered in the pictorial arts. Sculpture, though not entirely absent from the collection, was never acquired with comparable depth and sweep. Perhaps because Sterling Clark had had a negative experience in an early purchase of a work of Renaissance sculpture in 1913, he remained cautious with bronzes, terra cottas, and plasters, all of which could be made in multiple versions and even produced posthumously.[5] He preferred drawings and paintings because they are, most often, the direct product of the artist's hand, and when they are copies or versions, this fact is evident when examined in the original.

A second generalization has to do with the Clarks' taste in the decorative arts, which was confined to the late eighteenth and early nineteenth centuries—and mostly to silver and porcelain. Unlike many wealthy

American collectors of European art, the Clarks did not buy furniture, ceramics, tapestries, and textiles contemporary with their paintings—Florentine chests and chairs to go with Italian Renaissance paintings, linen-fold paneling and period chairs for late Gothic painting, Dutch cabinets and chairs for Ruisdael and Hobbema, Louis XV chairs and commodes for Boucher. Instead, they preferred to live in rooms with expensive modern re-creations of Louis XVI furniture and paneling and with decorative objects from the period evoked by the rooms themselves. Hence, the atmosphere of their homes was of a consistent, refined simplicity without specific historical character. What it was not was modern. Although most of the Clarks' interiors were produced by skilled workers during their own lifetimes, they were not stylishly contemporary in character. Nothing Art Nouveau, Arts and Crafts, Art Deco, or Art Moderne would ever have been found in a Clark interior. No Guimard or Ruhlmann for the Clarks, no matter how refined they might have been. In this they were more like many contemporary European collectors, less anxious about historical accuracy than Americans and less interested in being fashionably modern.

Not surprisingly, given Sterling Clark's reticence, indeed suspicion, of publicity, only one known photograph of the interior of any of his residences exists (fig. 29). Taken around 1913, just as Clark was starting his collection and had been in the house for only two years, it shows a room that is nonetheless startlingly spare by the standards of other American millionaires of the time, who tended to stuff their homes with furniture, books, bibelots, *objets de luxe*, and many works of art. A simple comparison with Mrs. Potter Palmer's gallery in Chicago (fig. 30) or any of the Havemeyer rooms in New York makes this clear. This lack of documentation of Sterling Clark's homes is unusual, since many other American collectors of European art, including his brother Stephen, commissioned detailed photographic "surveys" of their various residences, generally focusing on the rooms with art. For that reason, the account books and Sterling's persistent use of the Parisian decorating firm of Schültz and Leclerc are the sole clues to the interiors of their Paris town house and their various apartments in New York. The rooms in the Sterling and Francine Clark Art Institute provide the most compelling evidence of the Clarks' refinement, simplicity, obsession with good proportions, and *fin de l'ancien régime* nostalgia. Clark's wealth—with its origin in the Singer Manufacturing Company—was, like most American money of the early twentieth century, relatively new. But with enough of it, one could seek refuge in a supremely private and determinedly "timeless" aristocratic past.

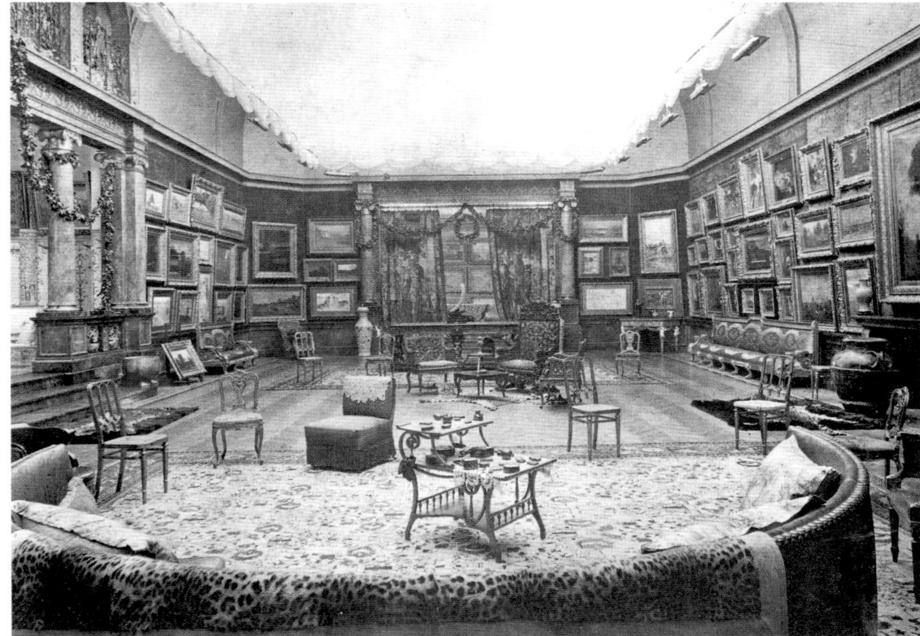

Fig. 30. Main gallery in the home of Mr. and Mrs. Potter Palmer, Chicago, c. 1900. Chicago History Museum (ICHi-01266)

How original and important was Sterling Clark as a collector and philanthropist, and what roles does he play in the larger narrative of capitalist art collecting in what we wistfully call the Gilded Age? To begin with, his generation was the last of that period (he was, after all, living in Paris during World War I, when the Gilded Age is thought to have ended), and his experiences of war and its horrors were such that he looked hesitantly into the future. As a collector of European and American art, Clark was far from alone. Indeed, the number of comparably large art collections formed in Europe and the United States in the period of 1880 to 1950 is in the thousands, even though fewer than thirty of them are well known today. Of these, there were basically two types of private collectors.

The first were the aesthetes, for whom the private experience of acquisition and appreciation was paramount. The second were the civic or, in the case of national galleries, patriotic philanthropists, who joined forces with other like-minded people in their communities or nations to share their wealth with the public at large.

Of the aesthetes, there were more in Europe than in the United States. Like Clark, these men and women had sufficient disposable income and enough leisure time that they could shop more or less continuously for works of art. And many of them lived in one of the three international cities in which that was easily possible—Paris, London, and New York. Aesthetically minded collectors determined their tastes in two ways—one by reading and looking at museum collections to arrive at a collecting idea (Northern Renaissance painting, Old Master drawings, eighteenth-century French art, etc.), the other (and more commonly), simply by selecting the best available works on the market at any given time for their living spaces. With his discerning taste and highly personal vision, Sterling Clark can easily be compared to these predominantly European collectors, which is understandable, considering that he lived for much of his life in Paris.

The most famous of the civic collectors are, conversely, American—the Havemeyers, Morgans, Marquands, Altmans, and others in New York; the Scrippses, Dodges, Tannahills, and others in Detroit; the Palmers, Ryersons, Hutchinsons, Bartletts, and Eddys in Chicago; the Holdens, Wades, and Severances in Cleveland; the list could go on and on for Boston, Hartford, Toledo, and other American cities. These were what today we would call "joiners," people who believed that their own efforts in collecting should best play a much larger role in the future "civilizing" of modern society when combined with those of others in an institution that reflected not personal but regional wealth and aspiration.

Clark does not fit neatly into either the aesthete or civic collector category, although he certainly shared the aesthetic motivation and discrete inward focus of the former. At various points in his life, however, Sterling Clark considered donating his collection to museums in Paris, Richmond, and New York,[6] but in the end he parted company with his younger brother Stephen, whose collection found its way not to a museum bearing his name but to the Metropolitan Museum of Art, the Yale University Art Gallery, the Museum of Modern Art, and twelve other museums and institutions. Sterling rarely loaned works to public exhibitions and was, on the whole, not interested in joining his legacy to a specific institution or even a region. In fact, even though Williams College president J. Phinney Baxter worked diligently to help Clark find a site for the museum in Williamstown near the college, Clark nevertheless insisted that the museum remain a separate entity from the school.[7]

In creating the Sterling and Francine Clark Art Institute, he joined another breed of hybrid collectors who considered their collections to be of such importance (and who wanted to control the destiny of those collections) that they formed their own museums in facilities they commissioned. Sterling Clark had begun to talk and write about his idea of a private museum with his brother Stephen as early as 1913—well before his collection was worthy of such aspirations (and even before his marriage), and this idea surfaced at many later points in his life, particularly after World War II, when he purchased three buildings on the corner of Park Avenue and Seventy-second Street as a potential site for his museum.[8] The museum Clark loved the most and wanted, in part, to emulate was the Frick, which opened to the public in 1935 and was assiduously visited by Sterling Clark four years later (fig. 31). Yet if Clark's collection were to be installed temporarily in the opulent rooms of the Frick, it would look out of place, because Clark's aim was never majesty but the articulation of an intimate and personal vision. His pictures were also decidedly smaller, and the "slant" of his collecting toward the mid- and later nineteenth century was very different from that of Frick, who stuck to Old Master painting with real determination. Instead of Sterling Clark's thirty-nine

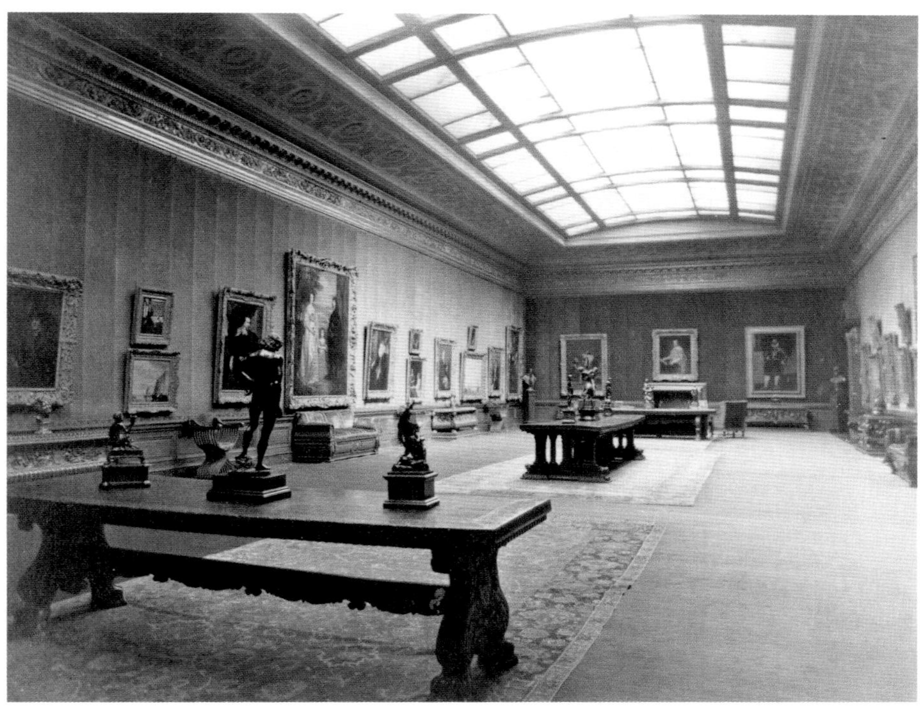

Fig. 31. The Frick mansion, c. 1927, before the museum opened to the public

paintings by Renoir, the Fricks (actually Mrs. Frick, rather than her husband) bought one—a large-scale portrait-like work (larger than any in the Clark collection) that could easily hang with The Frick Collection's Van Dycks, Gainsboroughs, Reynoldses, or Whistlers. Any viewer would be shocked to see Clark's *Onions* (cat. 61) in the Frick mansion, and, equally, the large-scale paintings by artists as diverse as Velázquez, Rembrandt, Fragonard, Van Dyck, Goya, Constable, and even Corot would have looked completely out of place in any of Clark's homes or in his museum in Williamstown.[9] Illustrative of this difference is the fact that Clark's only painting by Vermeer, which he sold before founding the museum, could be held easily in one's hand, while the Frick's *Mistress and Maid* is one of the artist's largest and most ambitious canvases.[10]

The comparison between these two great American founders of private museums actually makes clear Clark's difference as a collector—and his truly hybrid vision. The museum he created was emphatically unlike the Frick, not only because it is in Williamstown and not New York, but also because his collection was conceived in an evolving and altogether unpretentious manner. This becomes evident when one compares the ways in which the two institutions have evolved—the Clark into an ever-expanding collection, whose founder, though crucial to it, is not as omnipresent as are the Fricks in theirs; indeed, a former director of the Frick once remarked that his job was "to re-weave the rugs," so perfect and so apparently permanent is the collection and environment of the founder.[11]

What private museums had Clark seen in 1913 when he first wrote to his brother Stephen about his idea to create his very own museum? There were very few, but the one he surely knew was the venerable Wallace Collection in London, which opened its doors on 22 June 1900.[12] This institution included the collections of four generations of the Marquesses of Hertford, which had been inherited by Richard Wallace, the illegitimate son of the fourth marquess. The collection was so large and important that it would have been difficult to subsume into the National Gallery, which, in any case, could never have accepted its huge holdings of arms and armor, decorative arts, and books; fortunately, the family house itself was more than suitable to become a museum, both for its location and for the scale and arrangement of its rooms. The Wallace Collection would undoubtedly have impressed the young American, who was commencing a lifelong obsession with art collecting. Yet little about the Hertford-Wallace collections comes to mind when entering the Clark, reflecting less Sterling's smaller fortune than his decision to do something very different with art. It is only the privacy and role of the donor at the Clark that is reminiscent of the Wallace Collection. So again, what Clark actually did swerves from any apparent model.

The year 1913, when Sterling first wrote about founding his museum, also saw the opening of the incredibly grand Musée Jacquemart-André in Paris (fig. 32). This vast Second Empire home and museum was completed in 1875 for the Protestant banker Édouard André and his talented artist-wife, Nélie Jacquemart, after whose death in 1912 it was opened to the public. Yet the house had been accessible to the knowledgeable public for more than two decades before it formally opened on 14 December 1913, and its inhabitants acted like earlier aristocratic collectors, who separated their private rooms from those opened on a limited basis to socially or intellectually qualified visitors. This was a model the Clarks followed when they planned their museum, which included small-scale private domestic spaces where they could live while "in residence" in Williamstown. Yet again, the grand scale and formal aesthetic character of the Wallace or Jacquemart-André could not have been more different from what Sterling Clark envisaged. In its initial catalogue, the Musée Jacquemart-André included entries for 1,239 objects of diverse origin, material, and age. Had the Wallace Collection created such a catalogue when it opened, it would have contained even more works. And neither of these listed the prints, drawings, and books not visually accessible to the casual viewer. By contrast, the Sterling and Francine Clark Art Institute displayed thirty-three paintings and a small assortment of sculptures and silver when it opened on 17 May 1955, forty-two years after Sterling tentatively proposed his museum plan to his brother.

In effect, there was no obvious model in 1913 for Sterling Clark's idea of a museum, and few of the hundreds built throughout Europe and America between that year and the opening of his museum in 1955 provide a precise archetype. Perhaps the closest is that of Duncan Phillips, whose collection opened to the public in 1921 in the home of the patron's parents in Washington, D.C., and grew gradually on the site. Like Clark, Phillips collected Old Master and modern painting, and both men were preeminent collectors of Renoir. Yet at the Phillips Collection, Old Master paintings were numerically limited and tended to include works by artists considered by early historians of modern art to be precursors to modernism, or even protomodern—Rembrandt, El Greco, Chardin, and the like. In this way, Old Master painting was conceived as a kind of orchestral prelude to the fully modern symphony of the collection.

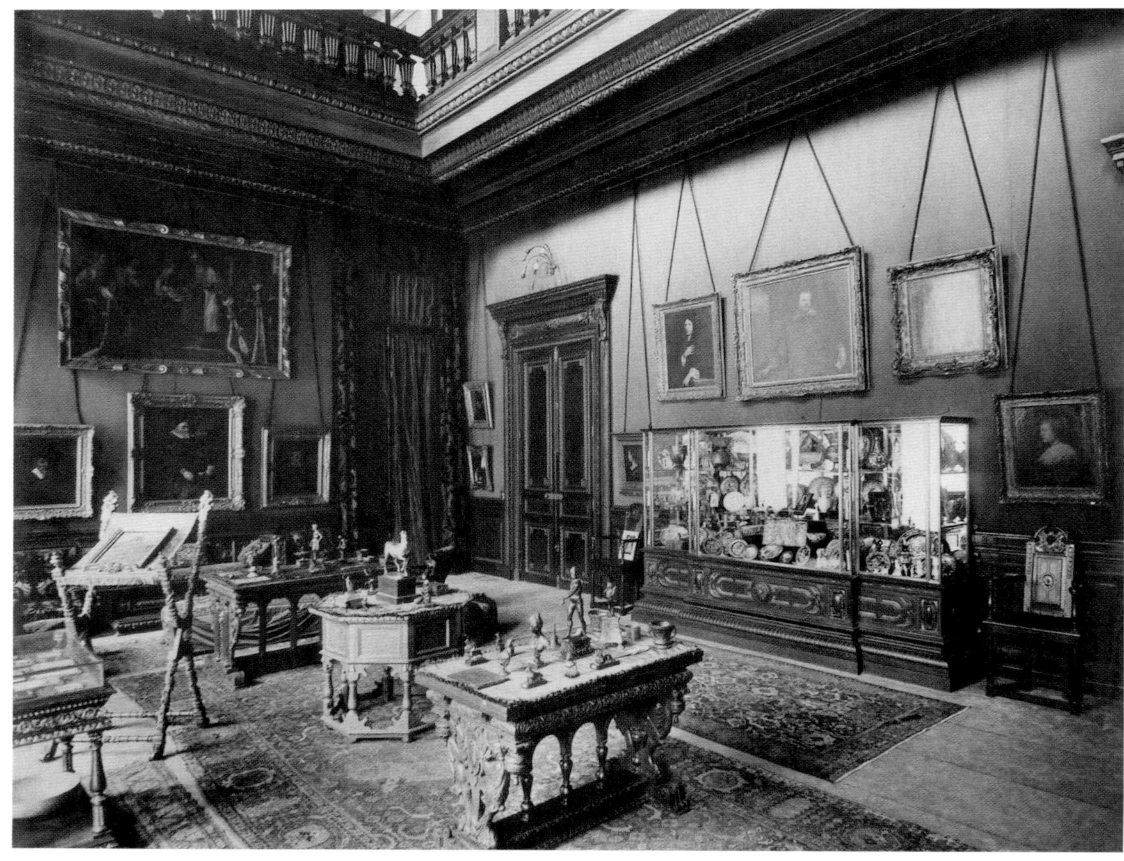

Fig. 32. Music room at the Musée Jacquemart-André, 1913 (photo © Bulloz)

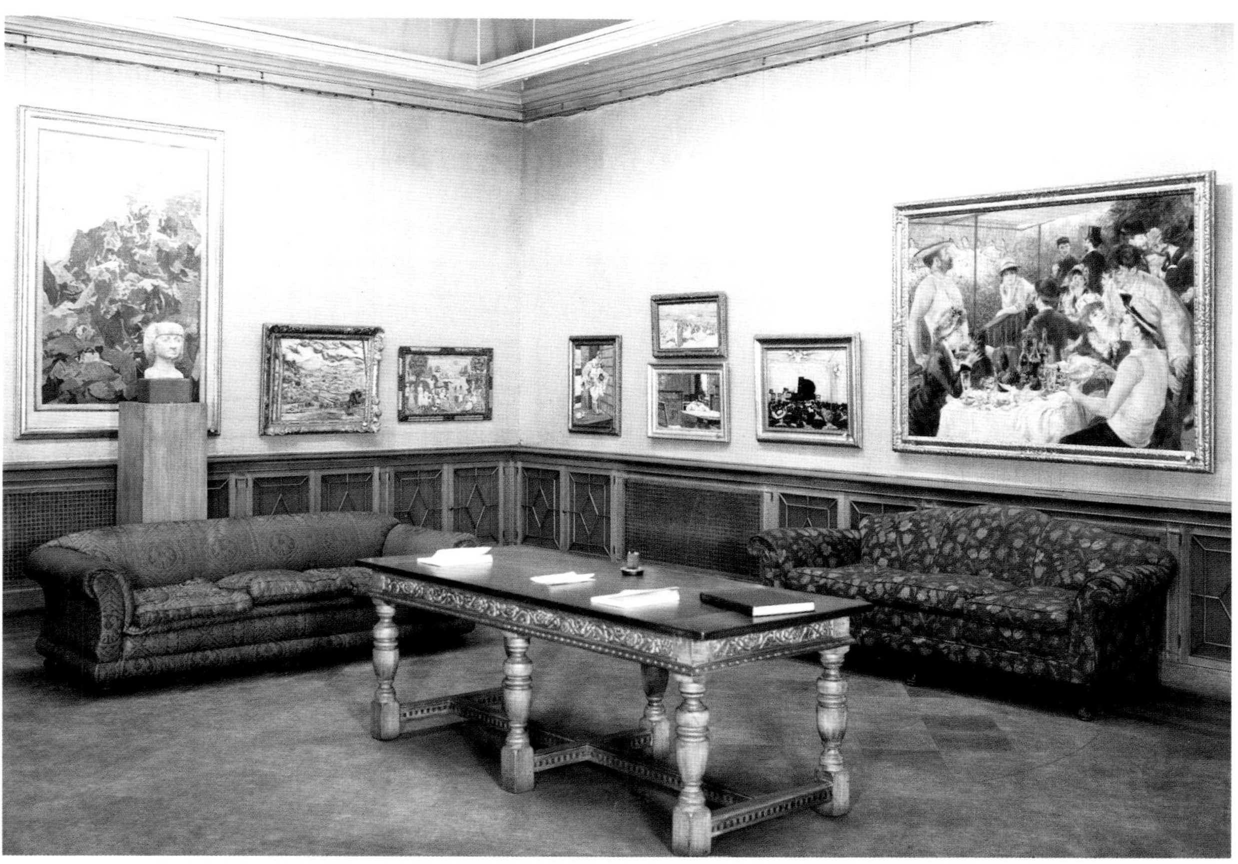

Fig. 33. Main gallery of the Phillips Collection, c. 1930–35

The same can be said when one compares the functional balance of Old Master with modern painting in other private museums that concentrated on modern art, such as the Barnes Collection outside Philadelphia or the Kröller-Müller Museum in Otterlo, the Netherlands. Both Albert Barnes and Helene Kröller-Müller included works by the Old Masters in their museum displays—indeed, the Kröller-Müller Museum, when it opened in 1938, commenced with a white modernist room of Old Master paintings, which visitors dutifully looked at before moving on to the major part of the collection, devoted to modern art. Similarly, Dr. Barnes, who collected Old Master paintings mostly for educational purposes—to teach the public the differences between the practice of painting before 1850 and the best avant-garde practice since then—installed his galleries of Old Master works on the upper floor of his house-museum, far from the entrance and from the glories of the avant-garde.

Yet all these collectors also valued domesticity and either adapted houses or created museum buildings that are essentially house-like. Even the skylit white galleries of Mrs. Kröller-Müller's museum are scaled domestically, and she was insistent on rugs and gallery furniture. So too Barnes, who envisioned for his collection a completely new building based on the designs of Paul Cret, as if he were erecting a "house for art." This domesticity was even a principle of the most forward-thinking of American collectors, such as the Steins in Paris and Katherine Dreier in New York and Connecticut, who installed avant-garde art in settings that are insistently domestic and, in important senses, unmodern. In this Clark was perhaps most like Phillips, who placed important Old Master and modern works in rooms that were easily identifiable as parlors, dining rooms, music rooms, bedrooms, etc., none of which had important furniture but retained their aura of refined domesticity (fig. 33).

For most collectors of modern as well as Old Master paintings, this imbalance persists. The two great Swiss collectors Oskar Reinhart and Emil Bührle included works by artists from the fifteenth through the eighteenth century as a kind of prelude to their predominantly modern collections. Reinhart, like Clark before him, concentrated on avant-garde art of the second half of the nineteenth century; however, the majority of passionate collectors of modern art were more interested in finding the best of the most advanced art around them than in making profound links between the qualities of modern artists and those of various Old Masters. There is not a single collector of modern art who opened an important private museum—not Karl Ernst Osthaus, Sergei Shchukin, Ivan Morozov, Phillips, Barnes, or Kröller-Müller—who excluded twentieth-century art to such a degree as Clark or who, again like Clark, chose not to collect such major figures before that as Cézanne, Seurat, and Gauguin.[13] One should, however, be careful not to fault the Clarks for their taste, because they never attempted to be adventurous in their purchases. They did not think that the art of Renoir was an improvement on that of the Old Masters. Instead, they found continuities everywhere and disdained difference.

It was the ongoing rather than the summarizing qualities of modernism that interested the majority of its collectors. By contrast, Clark looked to past art to set standards of quality and felt strongly that even his beloved Renoir had lost his way by 1890. Clark rejected the art of his own time just as he rejected modern furniture. When Clark did purchase work by contemporary artists, they tended to be *retardataire* in style, like Paul Lewis Clemens, who was disparaged in *Art News* as a Renoir imitator and whom Clark not only patronized but welcomed to his intimate circle of friends.[14] The Clark collection celebrates pictorial subtlety and high standards of craft rather than some overarching developmental narrative of art history. And two of Clark's heroes—Degas and Renoir—were alike less in their artistic style than in their fascination with the great art of the past. Degas's role in Clark's collection is actually rooted in the graphic arts, and one finds the greatest rhymes with the works by Degas in Clark's extensive collection of drawings by earlier artists, many of whom were admired by the brilliant yet irascible Impressionist. Renoir was a consummate painter, and Clark had a supreme sense of this quality. Oddly, however, he didn't collect major works by Renoir's most obvious painterly precursors. For instance, he purchased no significant work by either Boucher or Fragonard.[15] Again, he wasn't forming a consciously historical collection, but one with particular aesthetic values. This is clear with his early and enduring commitment to certain artists like the Americans Homer and Sargent and his lifelong devotion to Old Master drawings and prints, few of which he kept around him, preferring to store them in boxes safeguarded by one or another dealer, visiting these prized works with Francine to study privately.

Clark was also unique among important collectors of Impressionism in his complete acceptance of academic painting. He admired painters such as Bouguereau (cat. 41) with the same eye for quality that defined his Impressionist holdings. He knew that these paintings were held in low regard by some of his contemporaries, and when the esteemed art historian Lionello Venturi told him flatly that his *Fellah Women Drawing Water* by Gérôme (cat. 39) was a "bad picture," Clark replied that he liked "all kinds of art if it is good."[16] Clark was much more concerned with painterly craftsmanship than with the art historical narrative of modernism, and in this as so many other aspects of his life, he followed his passion regardless of popular opinion. To him paintings by Boldini, Fortuny, Madrazo, and Stevens could hang in the same collection with those by Manet, Monet, Degas, Renoir, Sisley, and Pissarro. In creating a collection with important holdings of both academic and Impressionist painters, Clark actually achieved a kind of pre-Postmodernism, eschewing the political and aesthetic values of the avant-garde for its pictorial achievements measured in the terms set by the predominant museum culture of the late nineteenth and early twentieth centuries.

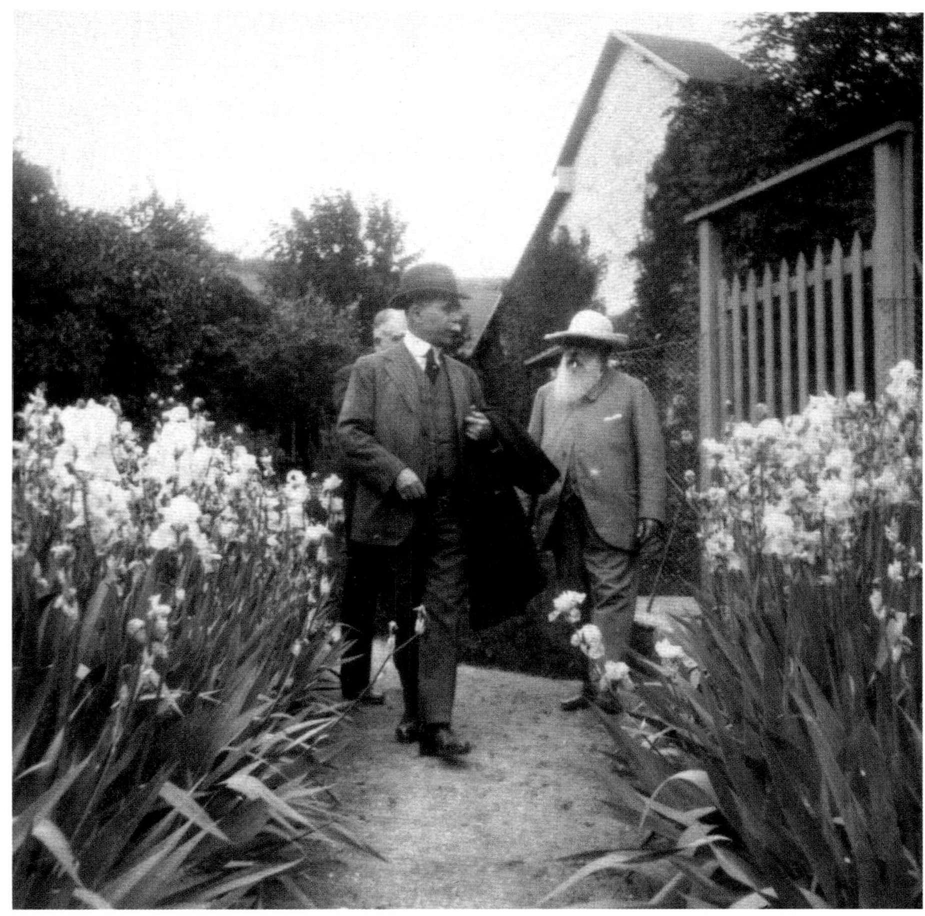

Fig. 34. Martin A. Ryerson (center) with Claude Monet (right) and possibly Joseph Durand-Ruel (back) in Giverny, France, June 1920

In thinking about collectors with similar values, only one comes to mind: the great Chicago collector Martin A. Ryerson. Born in 1856 to considerable wealth from timber and real estate, Ryerson was supremely well educated and had an abiding interest in collecting. Like Clark after him, Ryerson created a collection rooted in Old Master paintings, and he owned a major group of masterpieces from the fourteenth and fifteenth centuries. He was also, like Clark, an important collector of drawings and kept abreast of current trends in modern art. He amassed major works by most of the canonical figures of Impressionism, including an important group of paintings by Renoir.

Yet pride of place in Ryerson's collection went not to Renoir and Degas but to Monet, whom the Chicago businessman knew personally and whose career he followed both assiduously and knowledgeably (fig. 34). Although he never owned as many paintings by Monet as his Chicago contemporary Mrs. Potter Palmer (who purchased more than ninety paintings by Monet during her lifetime), the thirteen in Ryerson's collection were more carefully chosen and represent all the key aspects of that painter's oeuvre. Ryerson even made the incredibly bold decision to offer Monet a million dollars in 1920 for the as yet unfinished water-lily paintings now in the Musée de l'Orangerie in Paris.[17] Ryerson also owned major paintings by Cézanne, Gauguin, and Redon, although he never ventured into truly avant-garde twentieth-century movements.

The real difference, however, between these two fascinatingly comparable collectors of different generations is that Ryerson was an institutional man, while Clark avoided any connection with existing museums. Not only did Ryerson keep many of his greatest works on permanent loan at the Art Institute of Chicago after it opened at its present site in 1893 (his house was not large enough for his entire collection), but also he acquired art with the institution in mind. It is likely that he avoided entire phases in the history of art because other Chicago collectors focused on these areas, and Ryerson was as much a curator of private collections in Chicago as he was of his own. His best friend, Charles L. Hutchinson, seriously collected northern Baroque painting, and Ryerson left that significant field to him. Many other Chicagoans, including Marshall Field and Bertha Palmer, had extensive holdings of Barbizon School painting—again an area Ryerson avoided.

Sterling Clark had no such civic aspirations, and there were few other collectors he sought either to compete with or to complement. Clark did form a short-lived friendship with the great collector Chester Dale in the 1940s (fig. 19), but only after each man had essentially completed his respective collecting project. Indeed, it was Dale's notion of his collection as his "children" and his desire to keep it intact that appealed so strongly to Clark. Dale did not have the resources to build his own museum, and he eventually donated his paintings, which he stipulated be shown as an inviolable collection, to the National Gallery of Art in Washington. Another collector who created a similar, yet larger-scale, donation strategy was Robert Lehman, who required the Metropolitan Museum of Art in New York to build a separate wing exclusively for the display of his collection. Lehman is known to have been disappointed that the extraordinary impact of collectors like J. P. Morgan or Horace and Louisine Havemeyer was diluted because the enormous collections they donated to the museum were scattered throughout the vast building and were, hence, virtually invisible to the public. It is interesting to note that Clark himself had pondered a strategy similar to those of Dale and Lehman as early as 1943, when he executed a will stating his intention to leave his art collection to the Met, with the stipulation that it be maintained and exhibited as a separate entity, designated as the "R. Sterling Clark Collection."[18] All three of these great twentieth-century collectors had strong desires to control the display of their collections. Of the three it is ironically Clark, who in the end chose to build his own museum rather than work with an existing institution, who gave his successors the most freedom. Whereas Dale and Lehman left strict covenants as to the future use and display of their collections, in his museum's liberal charter, Clark included only general recommendations, leaving the institute the freedom to grow and adapt over time.

Before concluding this essay, one must consider Sterling Clark's superb collection of Renoir's work. Although one of the greatest collections of paintings by Renoir in history, it was certainly not the largest, nor did it attain the same extraordinary dimensions as other equally obsessive collections of particular artists. One thinks immediately of the ninety-plus paintings by Cézanne bought by Auguste Pellerin after meeting Ambroise Vollard in 1897, or the truly spectacular group of works by Van Gogh purchased by Mrs. Kröller-Müller. Then there are the mind-bogglingly numerous paintings by Cézanne (69), Matisse (59), Picasso (46), and Renoir (181) in the collection formed by Dr. Albert Barnes.

Yet Clark was unlike Barnes, who balanced Renoir with Cézanne. Indeed, Barnes followed this canonical pairing of the "Rubens and Poussin" from Julius Meier-Graefe's great history of modern painting published in 1904. There was no such "idea" for Sterling Clark. Rather, it becomes clear that he simply enjoyed living with and looking at Renoir and that, in the act of admiring most of the finest paintings by the artist that came onto the market in his long life, he selected one and then another and then another, all the while delving into Renoir's aesthetics and technique as well as forming an idea of his variable greatness. Also, unlike Barnes, but like many other collectors of Renoir (including Ryerson), Clark had no patience for the painter's late works, and his collection is steeped in the 1870s and early 1880s, reaching a kind of climax in 1882, when Durand-Ruel sent so many important figure paintings by Renoir to the seventh Impressionist exhibition (Clark owned three of the most significant figure paintings as well as one landscape and still life from that show).[19] Yet unlike Chester Dale, Clark was equally uninterested in the early Renoir and would never have bought his 1867 Salon painting *Diana* or his immense 1870 *Odalisque*, both now in the National Gallery in Washington.

In interpreting the Renoir paintings Clark purchased for his collection, it is important to remember that he could easily have bought more works, and that certain of the greatest Renoirs now in museums throughout the world were on the market, often for lengthy periods, during the years when Clark was most actively collecting. The two dealers Clark favored, Durand-Ruel and Knoedler, had scores of major paintings by Renoir during those years, sometimes because they were purchased by one or the other at auction and kept for variable periods in the gallery, and other times—particularly for Durand-Ruel—because they were part of an old stock of works. Knoedler sold *Mother and Children (La Promenade)* to Mrs. Henry Clay Frick in 1914 (fig. 35), just at the beginning of Clark's collecting, but held on to other major paintings considerably longer.[20] What is instructive here is that the Clarks had the opportunity to buy even more major works by Renoir than they did; it was their own particular tastes, very well known to the dealers, that steered these men to show the couple works by the artist that fit with others they already owned. Unlike other major collectors who chose certain artists to dominate their holdings, the Clarks never had an "idea" that Renoir would be represented by a certain number of pictures of a certain type. History and coverage were not important to them; their own enjoyment and private assessment were.

When we study Sterling Clark's purchase history, we find a collector who was anything but impulsive or obsessive. He rarely bought more than a handful of pictures in a single year, and few years can be called banner years in his collecting. Even his Renoirs were bought over virtually the entire history of his collecting, the first in 1916 and the last in 1951. The most Renoirs he purchased in one year was six, proving that he did not like to part with large sums of money or take advantage of market trends by buying at auction when major collections came onto the market. As he started to conceive of the collection installed in a museum, however, it is clear that he began to temper his monographic focus on Renoir with acquisitions of significant works by that artist's friends and colleagues. Indeed, Clark's two early works by Monet—the subtle view of Sainte-Adresse (cat. 11) and the powerful small seascape (cat. 10)—were purchased in 1952 and 1950, respectively. So too for Pissarro, who had been represented by only two works until World War II, during which Clark bought four superb landscapes by the artist from the 1870s (cats. 21-24);[21] it was in 1950 that he purchased the wonderful late painting of the Louvre (cat. 27). And Morisot's masterpiece *The Bath* (cat. 69) was purchased in 1949, in part no doubt as Clark recognized her importance to Renoir and vice versa.[22] It is clear that Sterling Clark did his reading, and there is no doubt that he devoured John Rewald's 1946 *History of Impressionism*, in spite of the fact that it was published by the museum that he loved to hate—the Museum of Modern Art in New York.

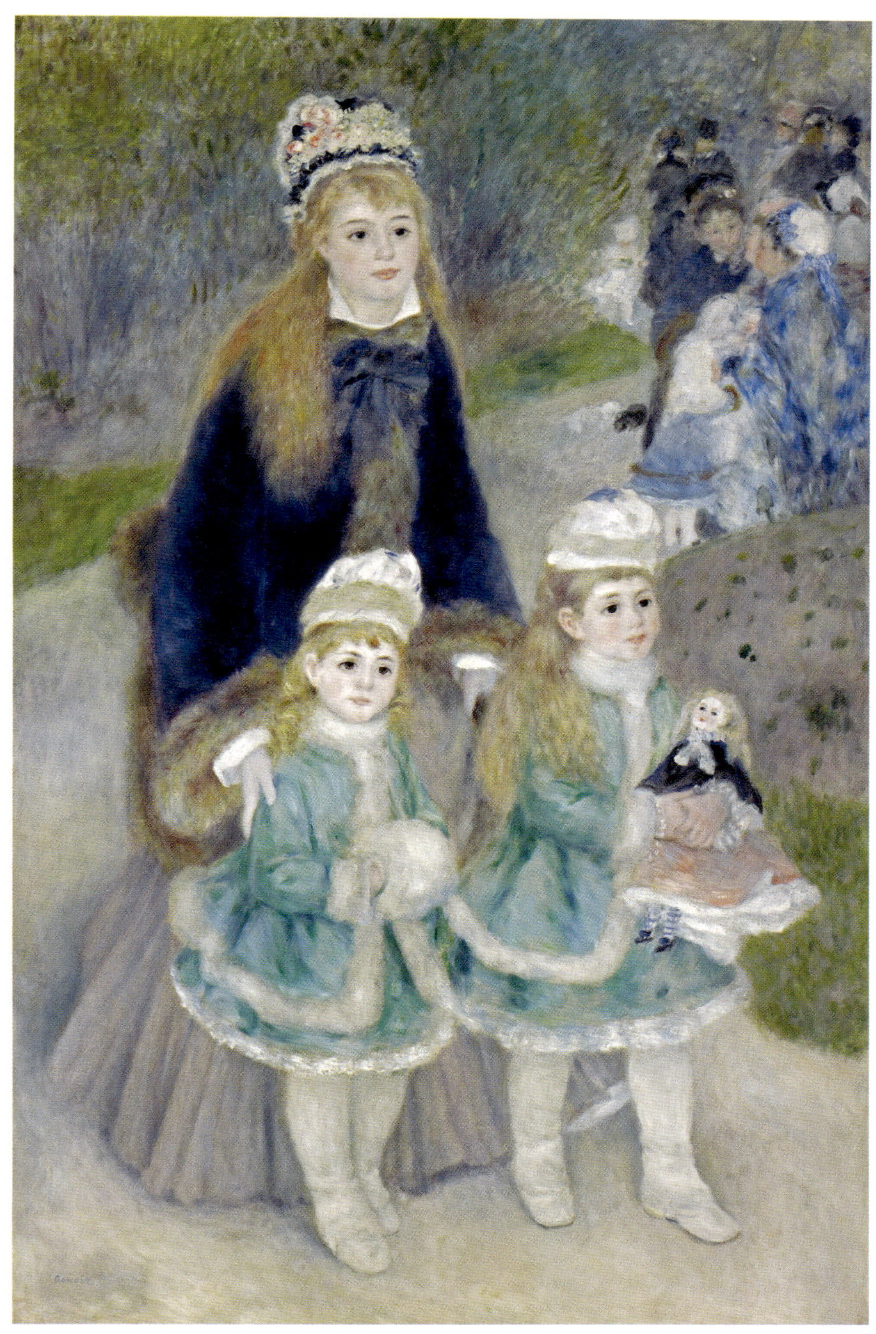

Fig. 35. Pierre-Auguste Renoir (French, 1841–1919), *Mother and Children (La Promenade)*, 1875–76. Oil on canvas, 170.18 x 108.27 cm. The Frick Collection, New York

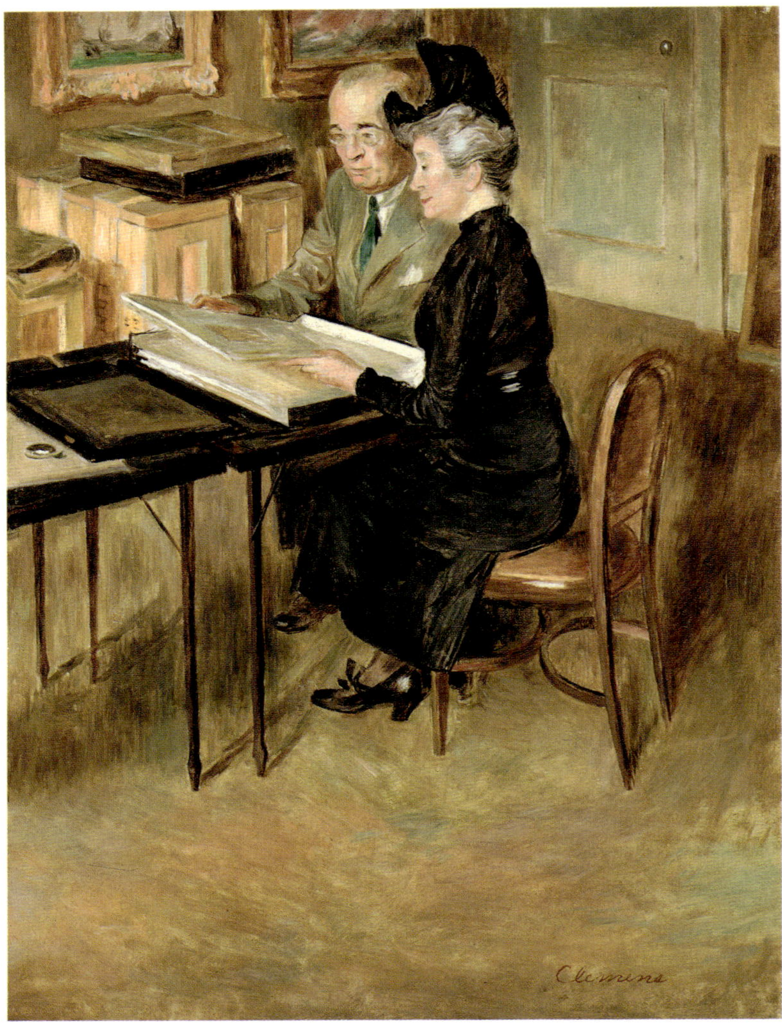

Fig. 36. Paul Lewis Clemens (American, 1911–1992), *Mr. and Mrs. Clark*, 1967, after 1942 original. Oil on canvas, 48.7 x 36.2 cm. Sterling and Francine Clark Art Institute, Williamstown, Massachusetts (1967.84)

Had Sterling Clark been a "joiner" like his younger brother Stephen, he would most likely be less well known as a collector today. One can imagine a comparable split of his collection among the Metropolitan Museum, the Yale University Art Gallery, and perhaps even the National Gallery of Art. If the collection had been divided in this manner, the greatest works in it would today have pride of place in galleries with equally great works by the same or similar artists given by other collectors. And many of his greatest treasures would be found in boxes in the departments of prints and drawings. What Clark achieved by applying the "Wallace/Frick" model to what was a supremely intimate collection formed slowly over a lifetime for various homes was to give us the feeling of communing with a fully private sensibility in a fully public setting. Unlike the "Wallace/Frick" model, however, Clark left his museum a generous endowment with no binding restrictions, which has enabled the institution to increase its global impact through a scholarly exhibition program as well as an ambitious research and academic curriculum supported by a major art library.

Before assessing the growth and transformation of the Clark since its founding in 1955, it is important to stress that Sterling and Francine were never able to get a complete sense of their collection until their museum was built. They lived in various homes in France and

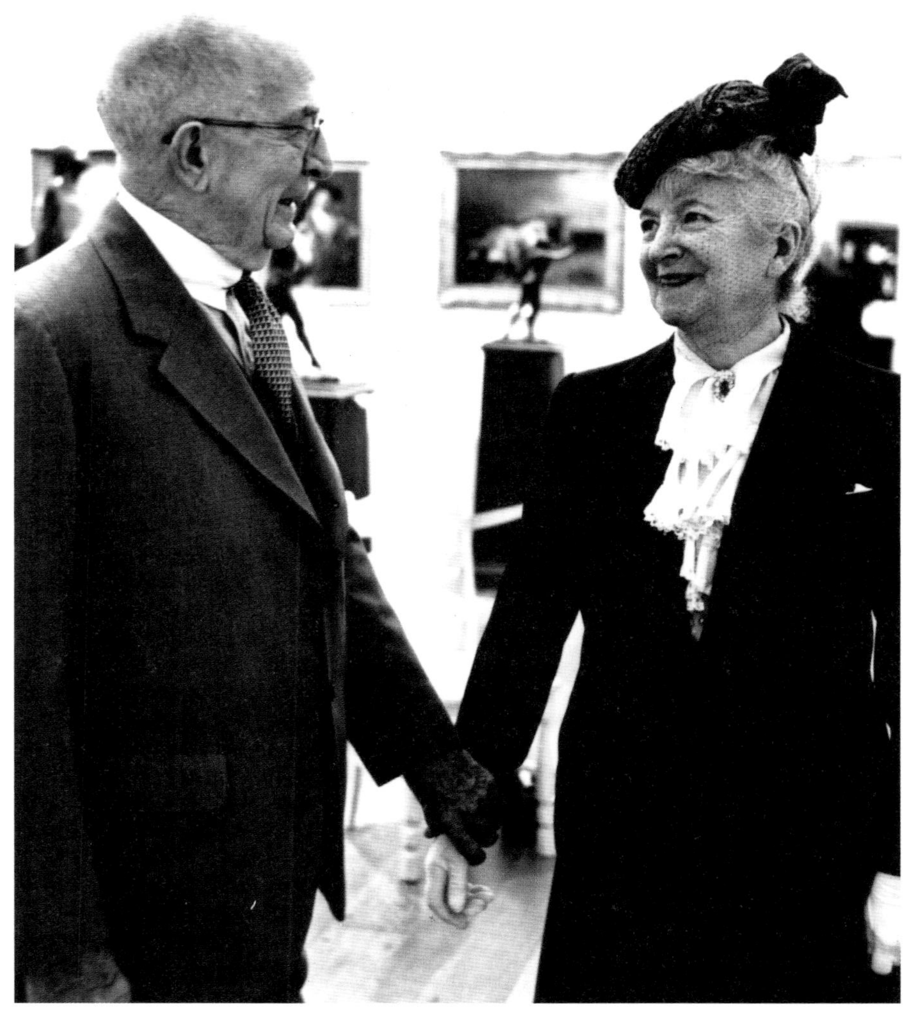

Fig. 37. Sterling and Francine Clark at the opening of the Sterling and Francine Clark Art Institute, 17 May 1955

the United States, each of which had collections of paintings and decorative arts, none of them "definitive." They kept a good deal of their art, particularly their few large paintings, almost all of their works on paper, and most of their books in various forms of accessible storage. A wonderfully wistful painting of Sterling and Francine done by their friend Paul Clemens shows them looking at a group of their works on paper then stored at Durand-Ruel's New York gallery (fig. 36). This very image makes it clear that their holdings were larger and more varied than even they knew.

When the Clark opened in 1955, both Sterling and Francine were there to greet their guests (fig. 37). After dinner, they retired to their bedrooms in the museum. Their private rooms were off-limits to the public until Francine's death in 1960, but early visitors keenly felt the presence of the Clarks. As the museum grew to include the private rooms, and as it began to define itself as a major research institution, it has kept true to the Clarks' vision of refined domesticity and quiet study. It has also, in an important way, become an institution that is probably not so far from the one first envisioned by Sterling and Stephen Clark in 1913. At that point neither young man owned a single work for which they are now famous as collectors, but they foresaw a museum in a beautiful rural place, away from the distractions of the city, where one could quietly contemplate works

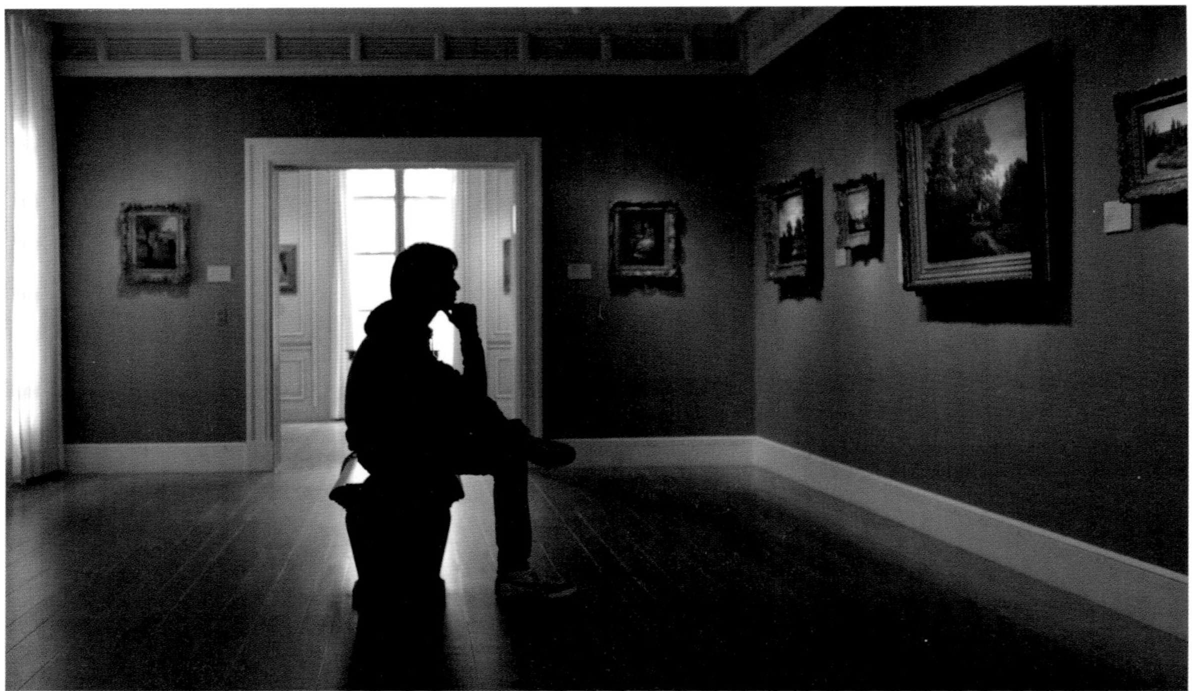

Fig. 38. European painting galleries at the Sterling and Francine Clark Art Institute

of art in an environment conducive to little else but that (fig. 38).

Because Sterling and Francine Clark left the museum few instructions and a good deal of money, the directors and curators of the Clark have been free to interpret and to extend the Clarks' legacy. Indeed, of the works in the present exhibition, nine have entered the collection of the Clark since its founding. Would Sterling Clark have bought any of them himself? Sadly, we will never know; yet he left us enough evidence in what he did buy that we can surely guess. My own sense is that he would have approved utterly of the purchase of the paintings by Rousseau, Tissot, Jongkind, and Morisot (cats. 7, 46, 8, and 68, respectively), and would have happily accepted the Boudin seascape (cat. 9) and Caillebotte landscape (cat. 16) as gifts. While it is unclear whether he would have bought Pissarro's *Port of Rouen: Unloading Wood* (cat. 26), as its gritty industrial subject is one that Clark largely avoided, it rhymes well with the superb *The River Oise near Pontoise* (cat. 23), which Sterling bought in 1945. What would Clark have thought of the Bonnard or the Gauguin (cats. 72, 73)? Each artist was too modern to fit tidily into the aesthetic defined by Sterling Clark's collection. Indeed, one thinks more readily of his brother Stephen's taste when looking at these two works.

What we know, though, is that Sterling and Francine Clark grew as collectors throughout their lives and that the real ambition and variety of their late purchasing shows us both a greater range and a better-focused art historical idea than their earliest acquisitions. And, whatever they might think of the institute's Bonnard and Gauguin, both of them would have been very pleased to see the fine group of French paintings by Boucher, Fragonard, David, and Boilly that have entered the collection since their deaths. What one can know is that they would have loved the extensive art library and the idea that scholars and students from throughout the world can now study their works of art in an atmosphere of serious scholarship. They too read and studied art almost daily—both from the original and from their own extensive library. They created the best kind of institution: one at once defined by—and liberated from—its founders.

NOTES

Unless otherwise indicated, original correspondence and diaries are in the archives of the Sterling and Francine Clark Art Institute, Williamstown, Massachusetts.

1. For further information on the Clark family and its history, see Michael Conforti, "The Clark Brothers: An Introduction," in Michael Conforti et al., *The Clark Brothers Collect: Impressionist and Early Modern Paintings,* exh. cat. (Williamstown, Mass.: Sterling and Francine Clark Art Institute, 2006), pp. 7–23.
2. Never Say Die's Epsom Derby success was also the first of an incredible nine Derby victories for the jockey Lester Piggott. Piggott, who would go on to become one of the greatest British jockeys of all time, was just eighteen years old when he rode Never Say Die.
3. Sterling Clark to Paul L. Clemens, 28 Apr. 1950.
4. For more information about Stephen Carlton Clark and his collection, see Gilbert T. Vincent and Sarah Lees, "A Life with Art: Stephen Carlton Clark as Collector and Philanthropist," in Conforti et al., *The Clark Brothers Collect*, pp. 122–99.
5. The bronze is *Walking Horse (Hogged Mare and Saddle Cloth)*, now attributed to Circle of Giambologna. It is in the Sterling and Francine Clark Art Institute's collection (1955.1004). When Sterling bought the piece, he was assured by the dealer that it was a unique cast, but he subsequently found another version of the statue in the Bargello Museum in Florence.
6. While Sterling executed a number of wills throughout his life bequeathing his collection to the Petit Palais in Paris, the Virginia Museum of Fine Arts in Richmond, and the Metropolitan Museum of Art in New York, these plans should be seen as secondary, rather than Clark's primary wish. For a more in-depth discussion of Clark's various wills, see the essay by James A. Ganz in this volume, pp. 3–27.
7. For more on the role of Baxter and other Williams College faculty and alumni in courting Clark and ultimately convincing him to build his museum in Williamstown, see Michael Conforti, "The Mind and the Eye: Williams College and the Establishment of the Clark Art Institute and Its Research and Academic Mission," *CAI: Journal of the Clark Art Institute* 2 (2001): pp. 13–26.
8. On Clark's 1913 plans, see Sterling Clark to Stephen Carlton Clark, 4 Feb. 1913.
9. There are a few exceptions to Clark's proclivity for smaller-scale paintings, notably William-Adolphe Bouguereau's enormous (260 x 180 cm) *Nymphs and Satyr* (fig. 20).
10. The painting Clark bought and returned is *Girl with a Flute.* It was subsequently bought by Joseph Widener and eventually donated to the National Gallery of Art, Washington, D.C. The attribution of the painting to Vermeer has since come to be disputed by specialists on the artist.
11. Everett Fahy, conversation with the author, c. 1985.
12. While it is not known when Clark first saw the Wallace Collection (he did frequent London often throughout the 1910s and 1920s), he strongly recommended the Wallace's Fragonards to Paul Clemens in 1944.
13. The Clark's four prints by Cézanne were acquired between 1962 and 1977, and Gauguin's *Young Christian Girl* (cat. 73) was acquired in 1986.
14. *Art News* 43, no. 5 (15–30 Apr. 1944): p. 25.
15. Clark did acquire one drawing by Boucher and revered his painting *Pygmalion and Galatea*, which he believed was by Fragonard (it has since been attributed to Circle of Fragonard). The Clark Art Institute's beloved paintings by these artists were acquired after Sterling Clark's death—Fragonard's *The Warrior* in 1964, Boucher's *Vulcan Presenting Arms to Venus for Aeneas* in 1983, and Boucher's *Laundresses in a Landscape* in 2002.
16. Sterling Clark Diary, 26 Mar. 1942.
17. Gloria Groom et al., *The Impressionists: Master Paintings from the Art Institute of Chicago*, exh. cat. (Chicago: Art Institute of Chicago, in association with the Kimbell Art Museum, Fort Worth, 2008), p. 13.
18. Sterling Clark's will dated 23 Nov. 1943.
19. The paintings that were shown at the exhibition and subsequently bought by Sterling Clark were *A Box at the Theater (At the Concert)* (cat. 56), *Sleeping Girl* (cat. 55), *A Girl Gathering Flowers* (deaccessioned), *Venice, the Doge's Palace* (cat. 59), and *Peonies* (cat. 57).
20. A short list of the greatest such pictures available at either Durand-Ruel or Knoedler (or both, as they often collaborated in business deals) is instructive: the fabled *La Loge* from the first Impressionist exhibition was not sold to Samuel Courtauld until 1925; the Philadelphia Museum of Art's sublime *Portrait of Mademoiselle Legrand* was not sold to Henry McIlhenny until 1934; *At the Theater (La Première Sortie)*, now in the National Gallery, London, was sold in 1923; the enormous and poetic *Mussel Fishers at Berneval* was not sold to Albert Barnes until 1942; the fabled *Luncheon of the Boating Party*, the pride and joy of Duncan Phillips, was in Durand-Ruel's stock until 1923; and the list could could go on and on with canonical figure paintings, landscapes, and still lifes, many of greater importance and scale than their counterparts—or than anything—in the Clark collection of paintings by Renoir.
21. It is interesting that the first Pissarro bought by Clark (in 1933) was the daring and pointillist-inspired *Saint-Charles, Éragny* (cat. 25), which is one of the most avant-garde paintings in his collection.
22. Aside from the many stylistic and iconographic links between the two artists, Renoir was the executor of Morisot's estate and the appointed guardian of her only child, Julie Manet.

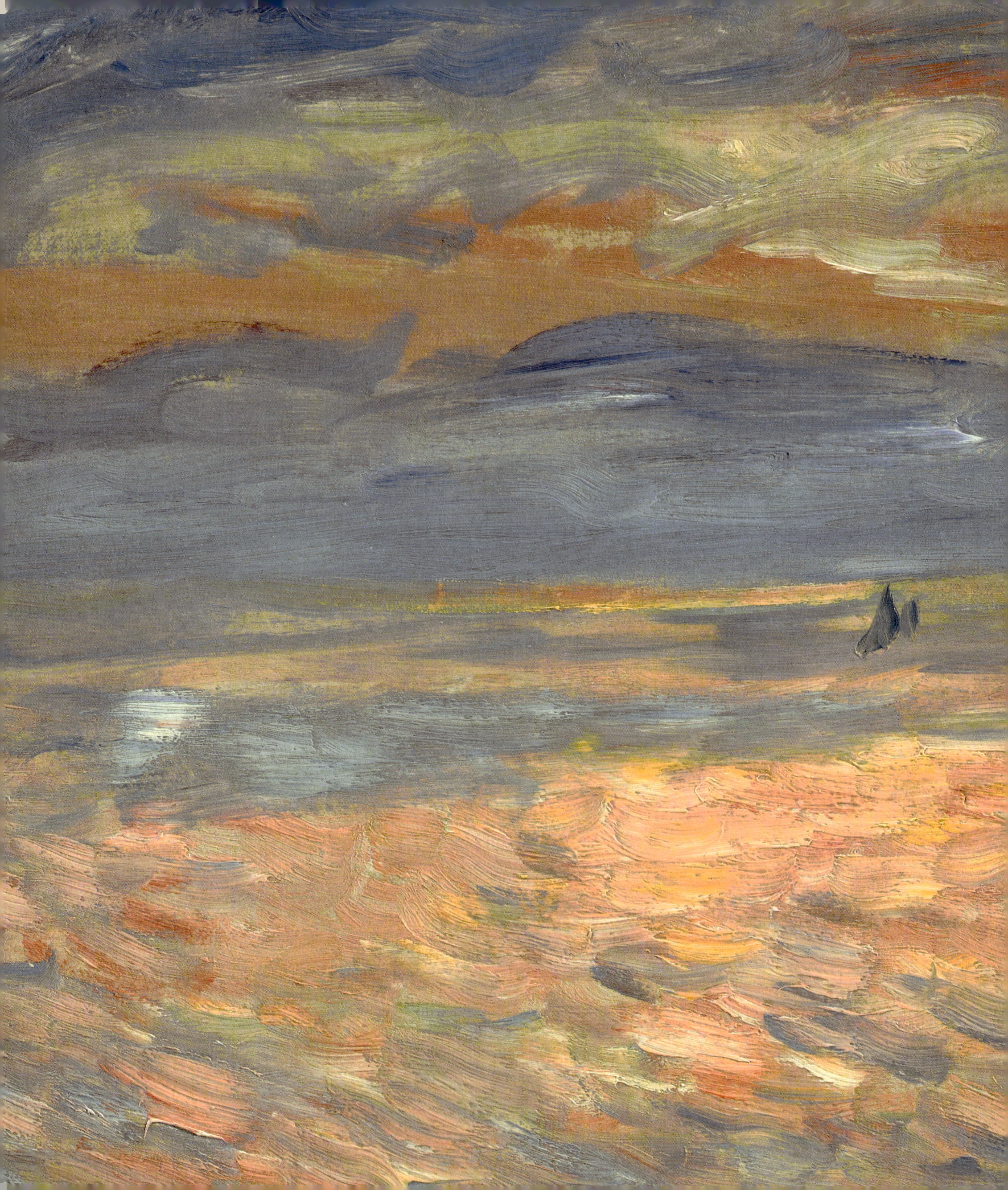

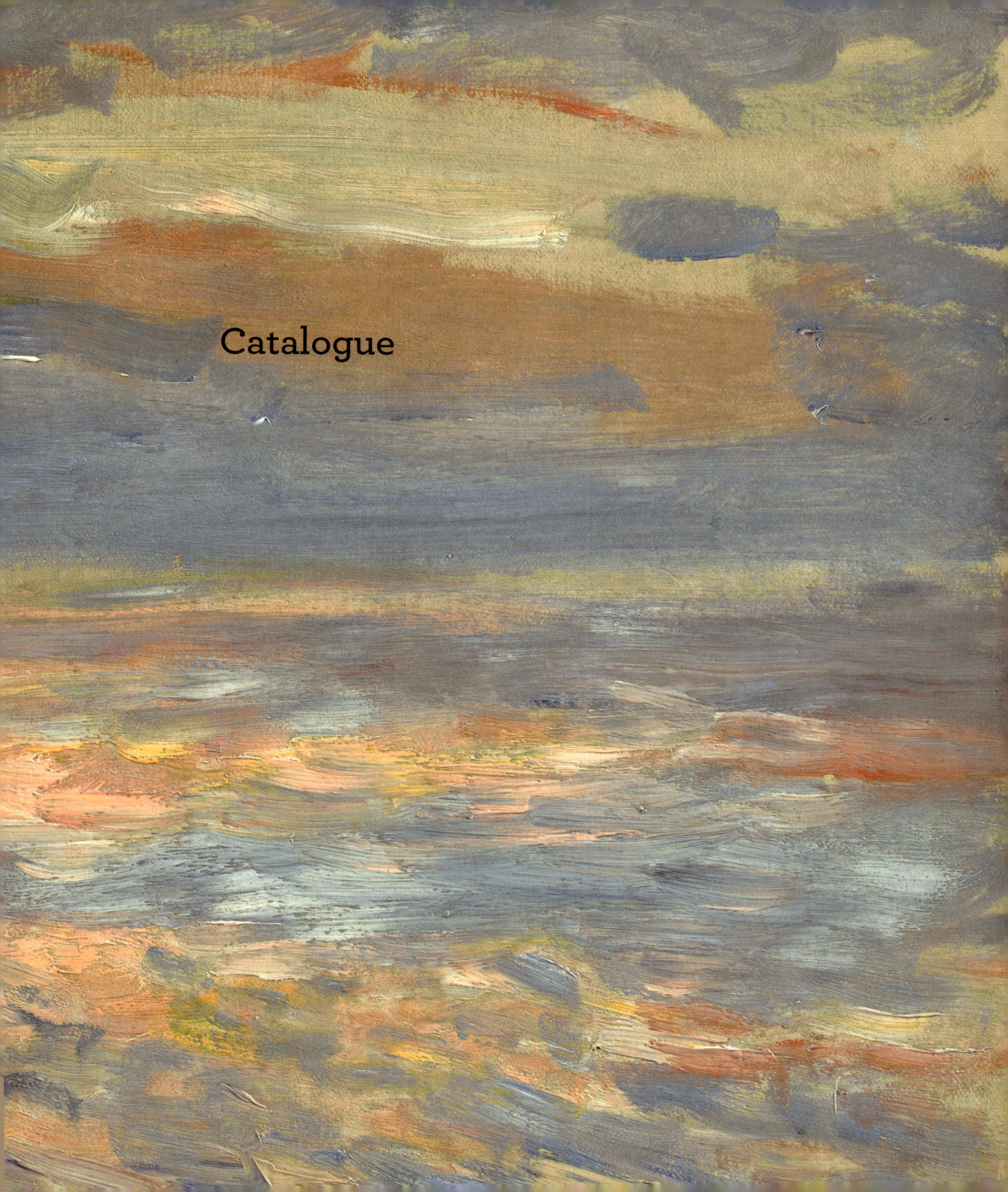

Catalogue

1 CAMILLE COROT French, 1796–1875

Castel Sant'Angelo, Rome

1835–40
Oil on canvas
34.3 x 46.7 cm
Signed lower left: COROT/COROT/Corot
Acquired by Sterling and Francine Clark, 1946
1955.555

CASTEL SANT'ANGELO IS A FINISHED VERSION of a plein-air oil sketch Corot made in Rome about 1827 (now in the Fine Arts Museums of San Francisco). Corot's view of the Castel Sant'Angelo (Hadrian's tomb) from the southwest in the afternoon sunshine is a tour de force of mass and light. The arches of the bridge mimic the dome of Saint Peter's Basilica in the center of the canvas, and the row of houses on the left is a subtle counterpoint to the gleaming monument on the right. Not only does Corot capture the sense of a city steeped in history; he also conveys the palpable quality of a humid, sun-drenched day in Rome. The painting offers a subtle balance between a carefully organized compositional structure and a fresh, seemingly spontaneous touch of open-air painting. Careful examination of the paint layers reveals that the canvas was executed in stages over a number of years. Corot possibly began the painting while in Rome, finishing it at a later date in his Paris studio at the request of a patron.

Castel Sant'Angelo also holds a unique place in the Clark family. Sterling Clark originally bought the painting in 1914 but subsequently sold it to his older brother, Edward. When Edward died in 1933, the painting was left to Sterling's youngest brother, Stephen, with whom Sterling was not on good terms. With the help of a dealer, however, Sterling successfully bought *Castel Sant'Angelo* from Stephen without the latter's knowledge. Sterling was very proud of his purchase, and he derided Stephen, who had traded the work to a dealer as credit toward the purchase of a painting by Paul Cézanne. In typical bombastic fashion, Sterling commented that he would not sell the *Castel Sant'Angelo* "for all the Cézannes in existence."

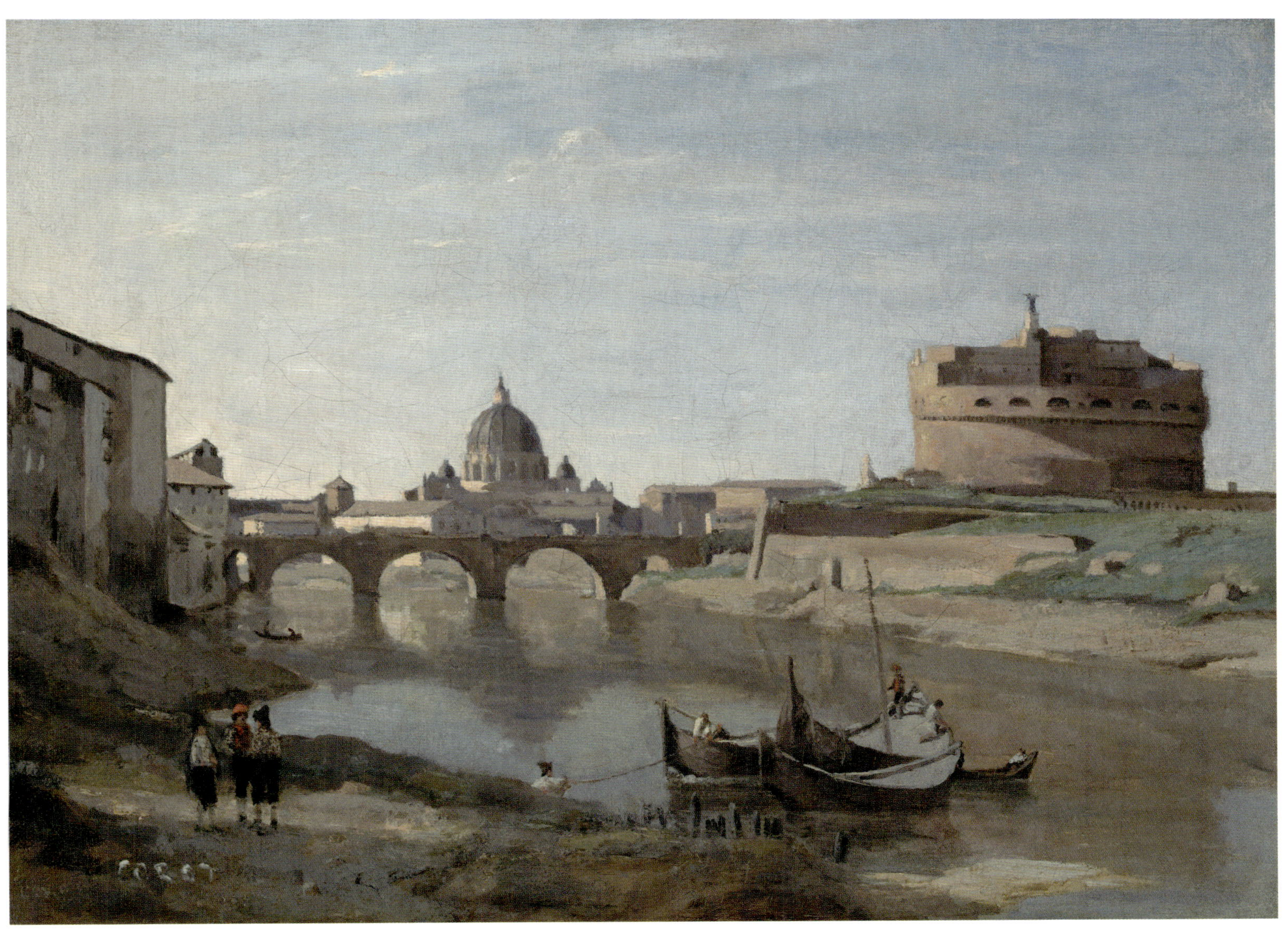
COROT

2 CAMILLE COROT French, 1796–1875

Louise Harduin

1831
Oil on canvas
55.1 x 46 cm
Signed and dated lower right: C. Corot. / 1831
Acquired by Sterling and Francine Clark, 1955
1955.539

DURING COROT'S LIFETIME, HIS PORTRAITS were less well known than his landscapes, and many went straight into private hands soon after completion. *Louise Harduin* remained in the sitter's family for many years and was first exhibited in public only after it was acquired by Sterling Clark in 1955. Corot's mastery of portraiture greatly impressed his contemporaries; Edgar Degas thought that the older artist's painting of figures surpassed even his much-lauded landscapes. The present picture was one of a number of portraits executed during the late 1820s and early 1830s, after Corot's return from a trip to Italy.

The young girl in this portrait, identified as Louise Harduin at age fifteen, sits on a small embankment alongside a dirt road, as if resting from a walk. A panoramic landscape stretches out behind her, creating a dramatic leap in scale. At the time the picture was painted Louise was in the care of her uncle Théodore Scribe, a close friend of the artist. Corot depicted her as somewhat tentative in demeanor yet staring directly at the viewer. She is dressed in a charcoal gray redingote and cape, white neck ruff, and fashionably slender shoes; she clutches a parasol and has placed her wide-brimmed straw hat on the ground. Corot's exacting recording of her clothing reflects the time he spent in his mother's millinery shop. Some scholars have interpreted Louise's dark dress as a sign of mourning—she had recently lost both her parents—but this explanation is unlikely, since details such as the white trim on her hat and white stockings do not suggest bereavement. Furthermore, Corot executed other contemporary portraits of women in dark attire that are not associated with mourning.

Louise Harduin is one of the few portraits in which Corot included a landscape in the background. The expansive view bathed in light depicts the area near Nogent-le-Phaye, outside Chartres, home to the Scribe family. The broad, planar construction of the scene was undoubtedly inspired by the artist's recent trip through the Roman Campagna. By 1831 Corot was clearly already experimenting with some of the techniques that would become staples throughout his mature oeuvre, such as the dabs of red flowers in the foreground and the adjacent flecks of grayish-green foliage.

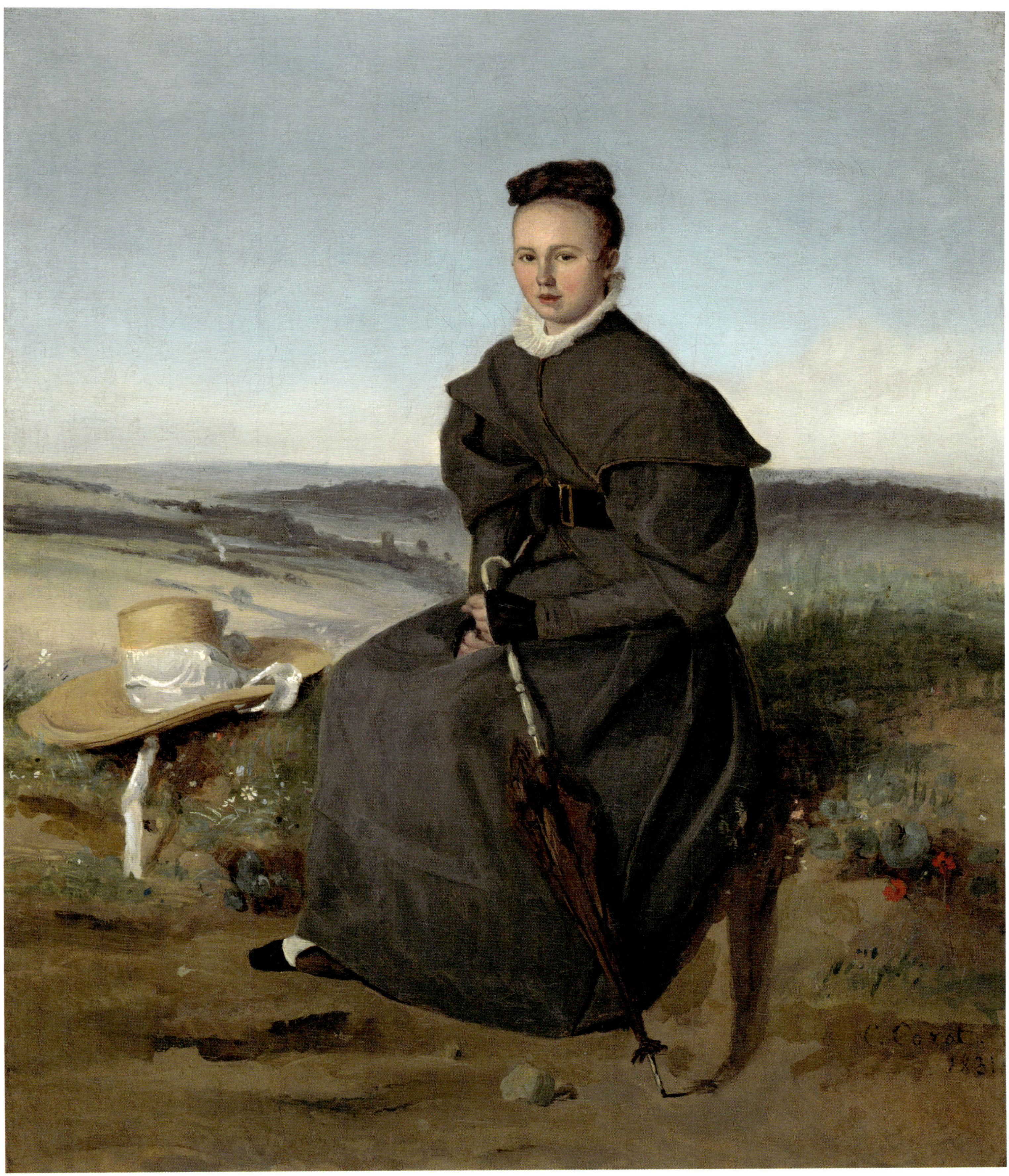
C. Corot
1831

3 **CAMILLE COROT** French, 1796–1875

Road by the Water

c. 1865–70
Oil on canvas
40.3 x 60.6 cm
Signed lower right: COROT
Acquired by Sterling and Francine Clark, 1945
1955.553

WITH ITS SOFT LIGHT, MUTED PALETTE OF HARMONIZED COLORS, and peaceful mood, *Road by the Water* has many of the qualities of Corot's later work that were highly valued by collectors. The locale is one that Corot knew well: the environs around his family's country house in Ville-d'Avray, just west of Paris, between Sèvres and Versailles. The artist's intimate knowledge of the area is evident in the manner in which he endows the natural beauty of the landscape with a subtle and timeless quality. The peaceful idyll of the scene is accentuated by the figures that inhabit the winding country road. In the foreground, two women stop to chat in the shade of a cloud; farther down the road a rider on a horse or donkey seems to be leisurely making his way, and in the background two more figures walk side by side. The women's bundles and the panniers on the animal ahead suggest work and toil, but Corot understates this aspect. Rather, there is a feeling of harmony and quietude.

The balance between naturalism and idealism in paintings such as *Road by the Water* was central to Corot's vision of the French landscape. His interest in conveying a persuasive sense of textures and light effects through scumbles and glazes of paint coexisted with a desire to create harmonious compositions. Corot described his formal process as one of discernment, whereby he would not hesitate to change elements of a given scene as long as the adjustments enhanced the character of the landscape he saw before him. Certain trees and foliage in *Road by the Water*, for instance, are decidedly different from those in other views of the same area. His pictures are not a didactic search for pictorial truth but rather observed meditations on a given view. In the late nineteenth century, one critic singled out *Road by the Water* as a work in which Corot embodied "all that man thinks and feels about nature."

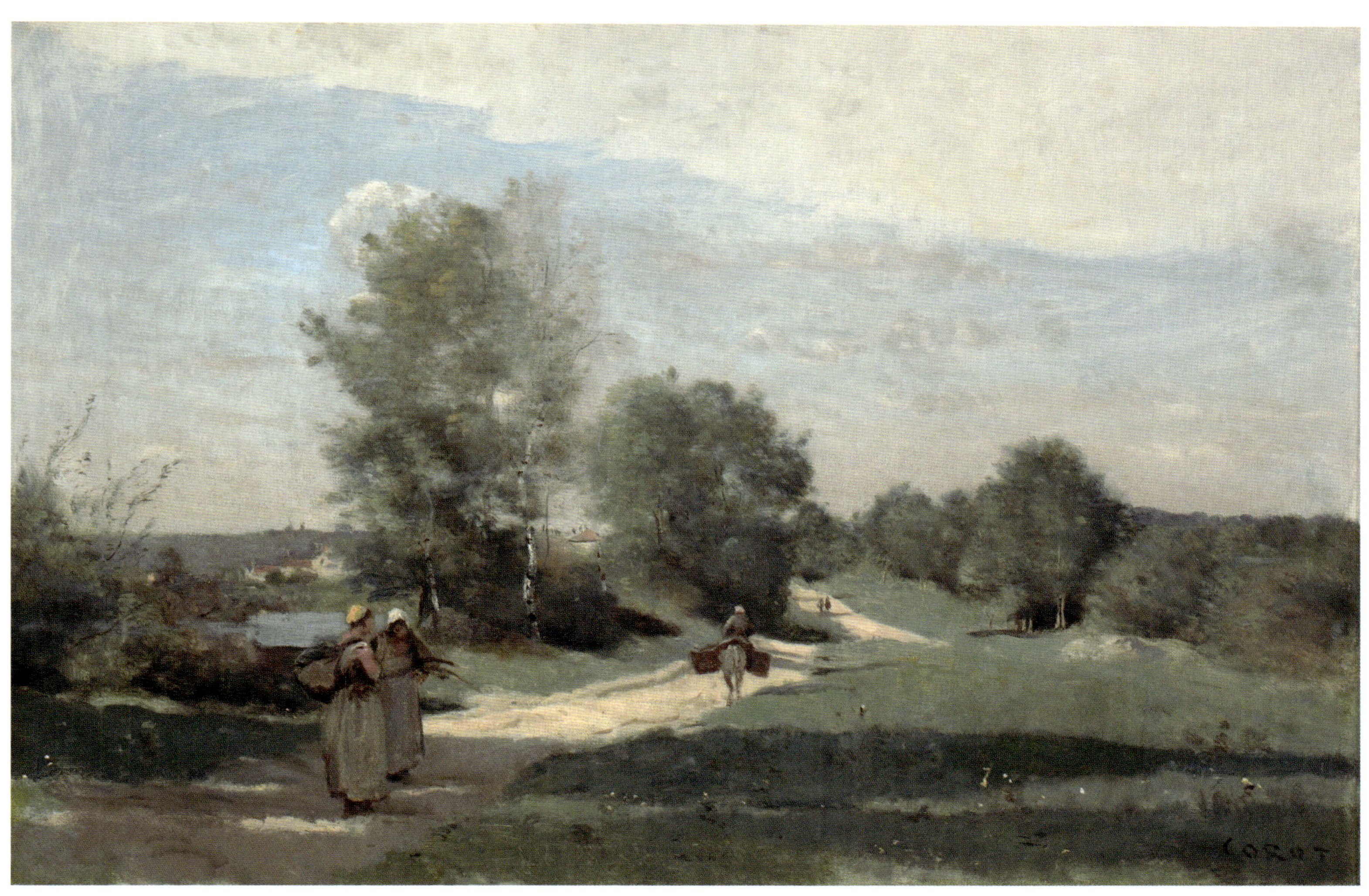
COROT

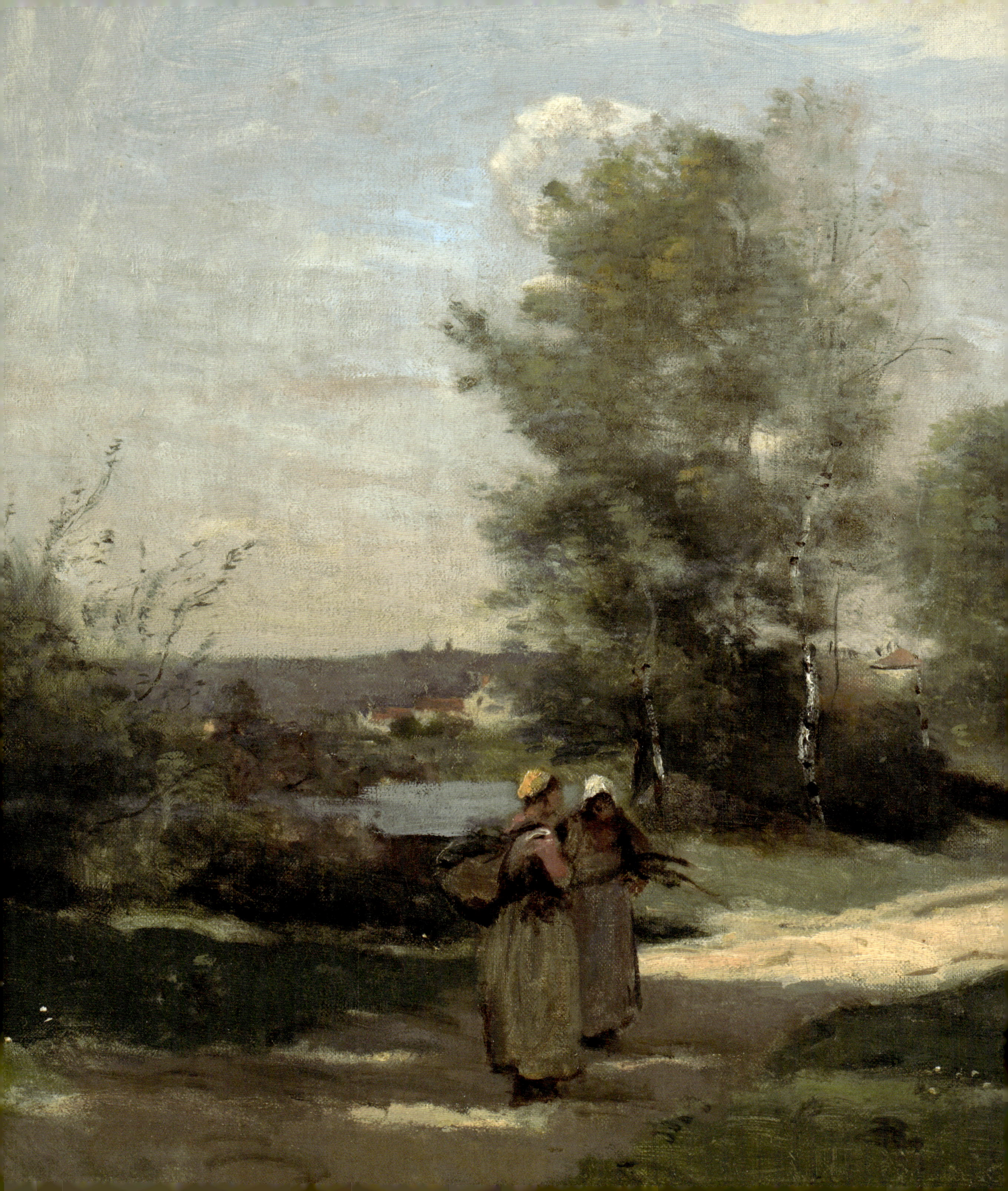

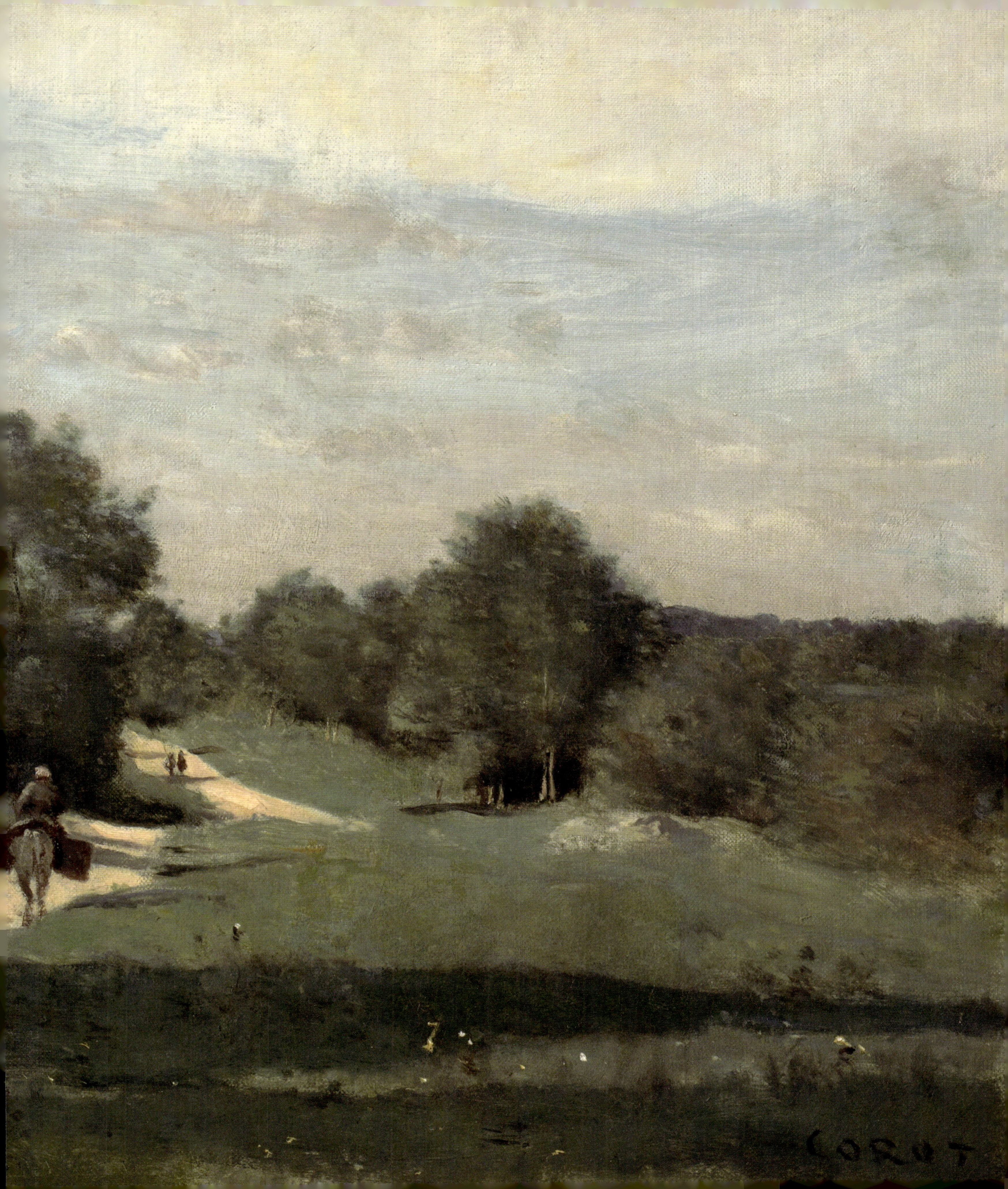
COROT

4 CAMILLE COROT French, 1796–1875

Bathers of the Borromean Isles

1865–70
Oil on canvas
79.1 x 56.7 cm
Signed lower left: COROT
Acquired by Sterling and Francine Clark, 1930
1955.537

PAINTED WHEN COROT WAS ABOUT SEVENTY YEARS OLD, *Bathers of the Borromean Isles* exemplifies the artist's ethereal late style. Corot had last been to Italy twenty years before and had likely not seen Lake Maggiore (in which the Borromean Islands are located) since 1834; not surprisingly, the scene in the painting has an idealized, dream-like quality. Lake Maggiore is the largest of the northern Italian lakes, but Corot chose to portray an intimate view of a small cove populated by two bathers. A large backlit tree growing out of the water dominates the canvas, giving the scene a feeling of enclosure and privacy, which is further accentuated by the rock on the right and the brush-filled bank on the left. Using delicate layers of glazes, Corot beautifully captured the sense of soft sunlight filtering through the foliage and reflecting off the rippling water. The suggestion of buildings in the distance heightens the feeling that the scene takes place not in the everyday world but rather in some utopian fairyland.

Bathers of the Borromean Isles is Corot's earliest known attempt to paint a view of Lake Maggiore, although he had depicted scenes of bathers as early as the 1830s. The lack of distinguishing details in the bathers in the Clark picture has at times been criticized, and indeed these figures are not as meticulously rendered as in certain of Corot's other scenes of bathing. Yet in their very lack of specificity the bathers harmonize well with their surroundings and add to the otherworldly aspect of the scene. In fact, *Bathers of the Borromean Isles* was evidently admired by collectors, as Corot repeated the composition several times, though never with the freshness of the Clark picture, the first one completed.

Sterling Clark was a great admirer of Corot, eventually acquiring eight of his paintings. The two Italian scenes in his collection, *Bathers of the Borromean Isles* and *Castel Sant'Angelo, Rome* (cat. 1), display markedly different aspects of Corot's oeuvre. *Castel Sant'Angelo* was painted early in the artist's career and is a very direct portrayal of a famous monument, while *Bathers of the Borromean Isles* is indicative of the artist's late, and often meditative, "*souvenirs.*" While certain *souvenirs,* such as the present one, are associated with a specific location, others came more out of meditations on a landscape's atmospheric effect than from a direct portrayal of the scene. Indeed, around the time *Bathers of the Borromean Isles* was painted, the French writer and photographer Maxime Du Camp wrote that Corot "never copies nature, he dreams it and reproduces it as he sees it in his reveries: gracious reveries that belong to the land of fairies."

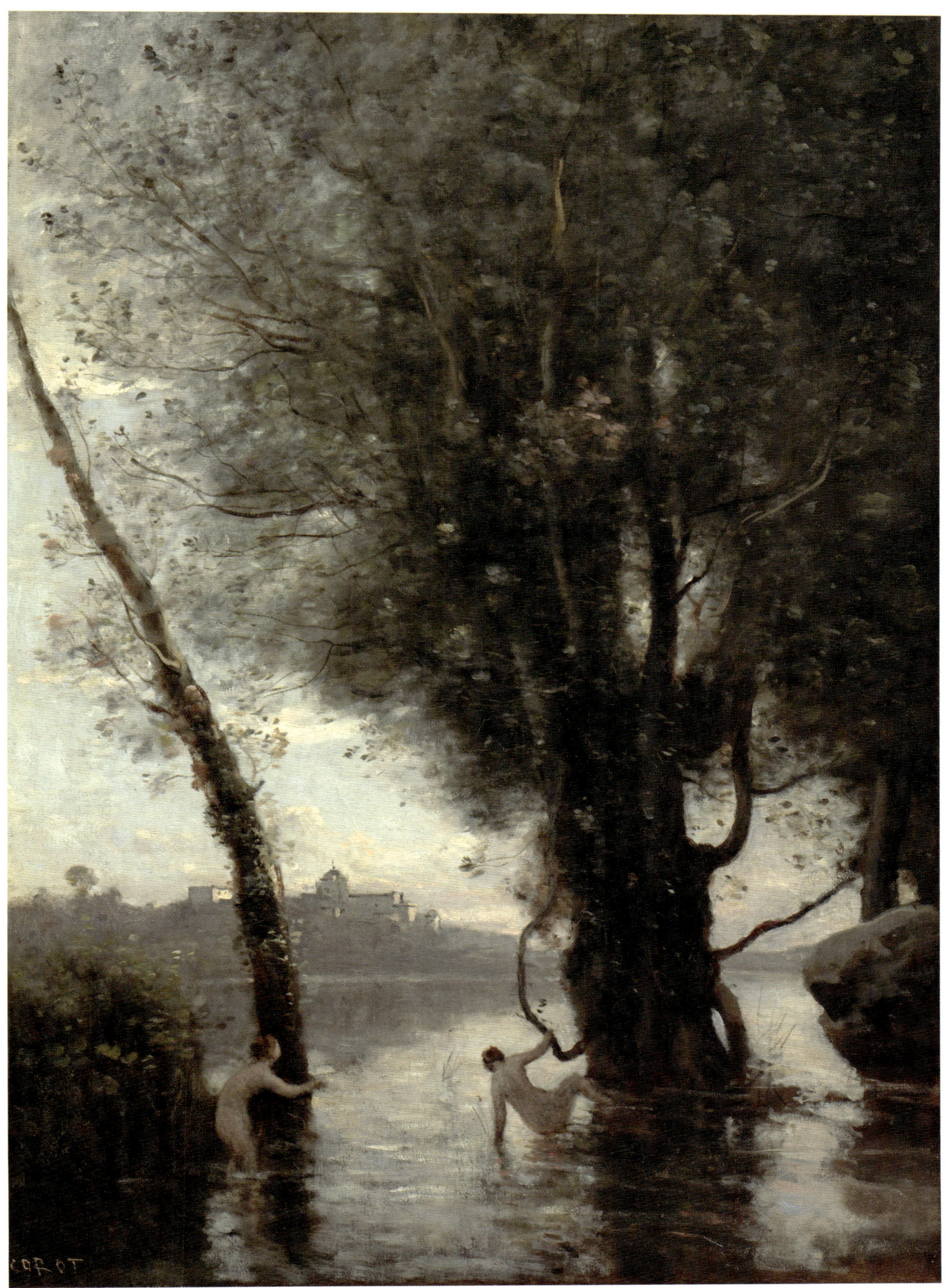
COROT

5 JEAN-FRANÇOIS MILLET French, 1814–1875

Shepherdess: Plains of Barbizon

Before 1862
Oil on panel
38.1 x 27.5 cm
Signed lower right: J. F. Millet.
Acquired by Sterling and Francine Clark, 1945
1955.532

MILLET WAS A CENTRAL FIGURE IN THE BARBIZON SCHOOL, whose members painted the life and countryside of rural France in the mid-nineteenth century. One of Millet's favorite motifs was that of a single shepherdess. He first began exploring its possibilities in the late 1840s, and through the years he was able to use the theme as a foil to express differing moods of melancholy, lassitude, or, as in the present picture, quiet industry.

In *Shepherdess: Plains of Barbizon*, a young girl stands at the edge of a grazing flock of sheep. Ostensibly minding this flock, she leaves her job to a small black dog and instead focuses on knitting a brown sock. This type of agrarian idyll is typical of many of Millet's pictures, which often portray an empathetic view of the stability and continuity of daily life in Barbizon. Women mending or making clothes is another recurring theme in Millet's oeuvre; here the subject has a certain poignancy in that the wool the girl is knitting likely came from the sheep behind her. In this way, the painting seems to touch on the self-sufficiency of the rural culture in which Millet lived. The small scale of the painting adds to the intimate and humble nature of the image.

While it is highly probable that Millet saw such a scene, it is not a painting that was made outdoors or even from sketches made directly from the subject. His brother Pierre, who often walked with Millet, recalled that "all of his [Millet's] pictures or drawings were made at the studio . . . François always went home full of these impressions, and during the evening the memory of what we had seen would suggest to him some composition for a picture." Millet himself corroborated this information, and he did not hesitate to comment on the deliberation that went into his carefully considered compositions. The combination of Millet's skill as a painter, choice of subjects, and methodical approach to composition is at the heart of what gives pictures such as *Shepherdess: Plains of Barbizon* a timelessness and depth of feeling.

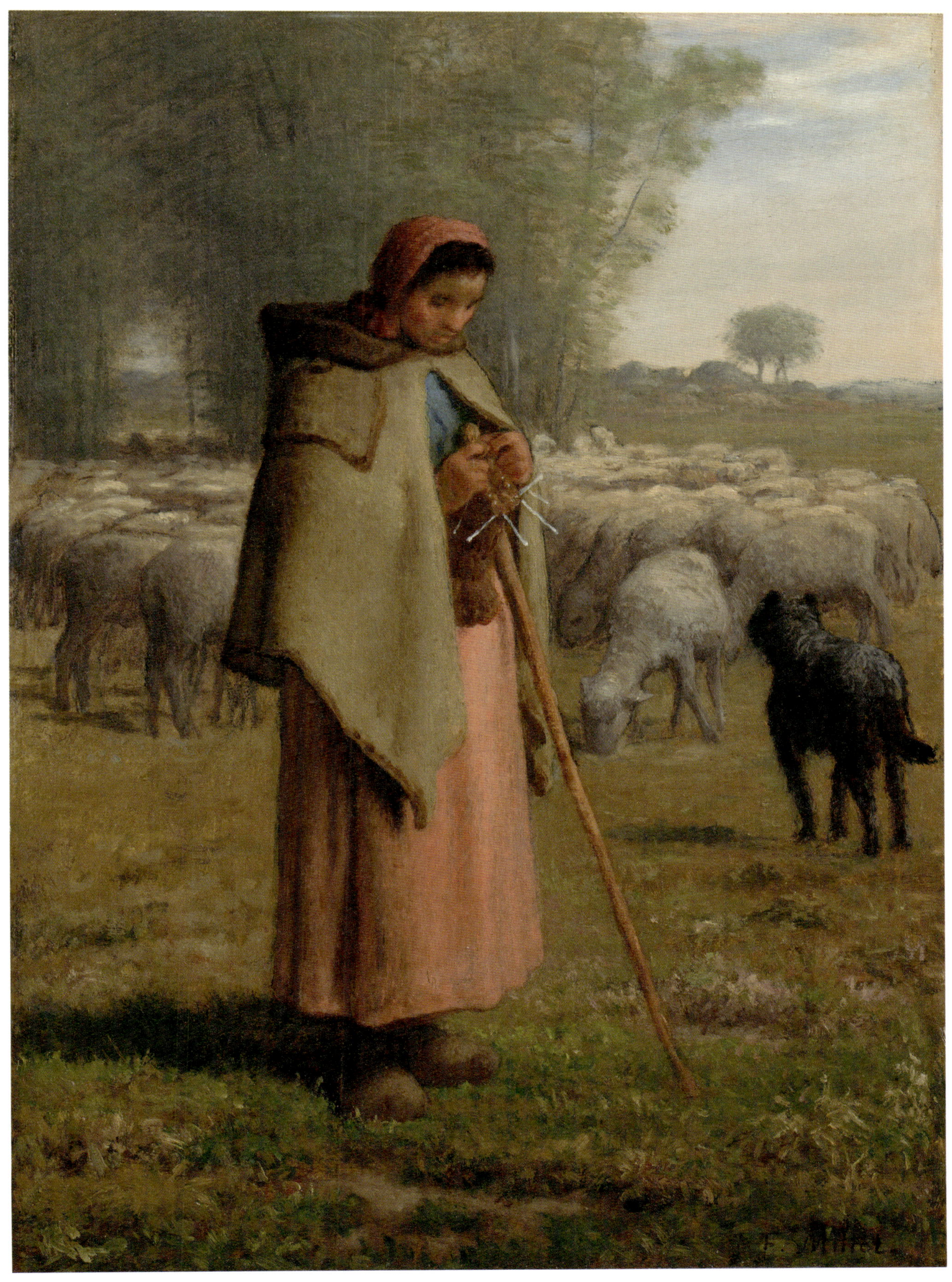

6 CONSTANT TROYON French, 1810–1865

Gooseherd

c. 1850–55
Oil on panel
46 x 37.1 cm
Signed lower left: C. TROYON.
Acquired by Sterling and Francine Clark, 1919
1955.550

TROYON WAS BORN IN SÈVRES, and he first trained as a decorator at the famous porcelain factories there. His first public success was as a landscapist, but his reputation now rests on his animal paintings. In the 1830s he was introduced to the Barbizon School painters Théodore Rousseau and Jules Dupré, whose rural imagery and fluid, seemingly spontaneous brushwork greatly influenced his art. A fellow artist recounted that "year after year I went with Troyon to Barbizon. On rainy days, when we were unable to sketch in the forest, we visited the farms where the watchers of cows and the tenders of geese posed as our models." *Gooseherd* is a fine example of Troyon's mature style, in which the figure and the gaggle of geese are harmoniously integrated within the landscape setting. The small picture, delicately painted on a wooden panel, was likely intended for the private delectation of a collector. The lively brushwork imparts a sense of activity and movement, which is accentuated by the geese looking in many different directions. Troyon often gave his pictures a sense of drama through the introduction of a stormy sky, but in this case the scene is placid and pleasing.

Although Troyon had exhibited animal paintings as early as 1838, his interest in this genre was heightened by a trip in 1847 to Belgium and Holland, where he was exposed to the animal paintings of earlier Dutch masters, in particular those of Aelbert Cuyp and Paulus Potter. From the late 1840s until his death in 1865 Troyon concentrated almost exclusively on animal paintings, often to great acclaim, supposedly creating a finished picture almost every day. It was said that his studio was "a veritable factory for pictures . . . [producing] paintings as a chicken does eggs." *Gooseherd*, in fact, is closely related to at least one other painting (and perhaps other lost ones) that depicts a similar boy tending geese. It is likely that the Clark picture is an early product of a practice that Troyon called *retourner son veau* (returning to his calf), by which he created a number of finished paintings based on a single sketch. This reuse of sketches and motifs helps explain the large volume of works the artist produced during a relatively short mature career.

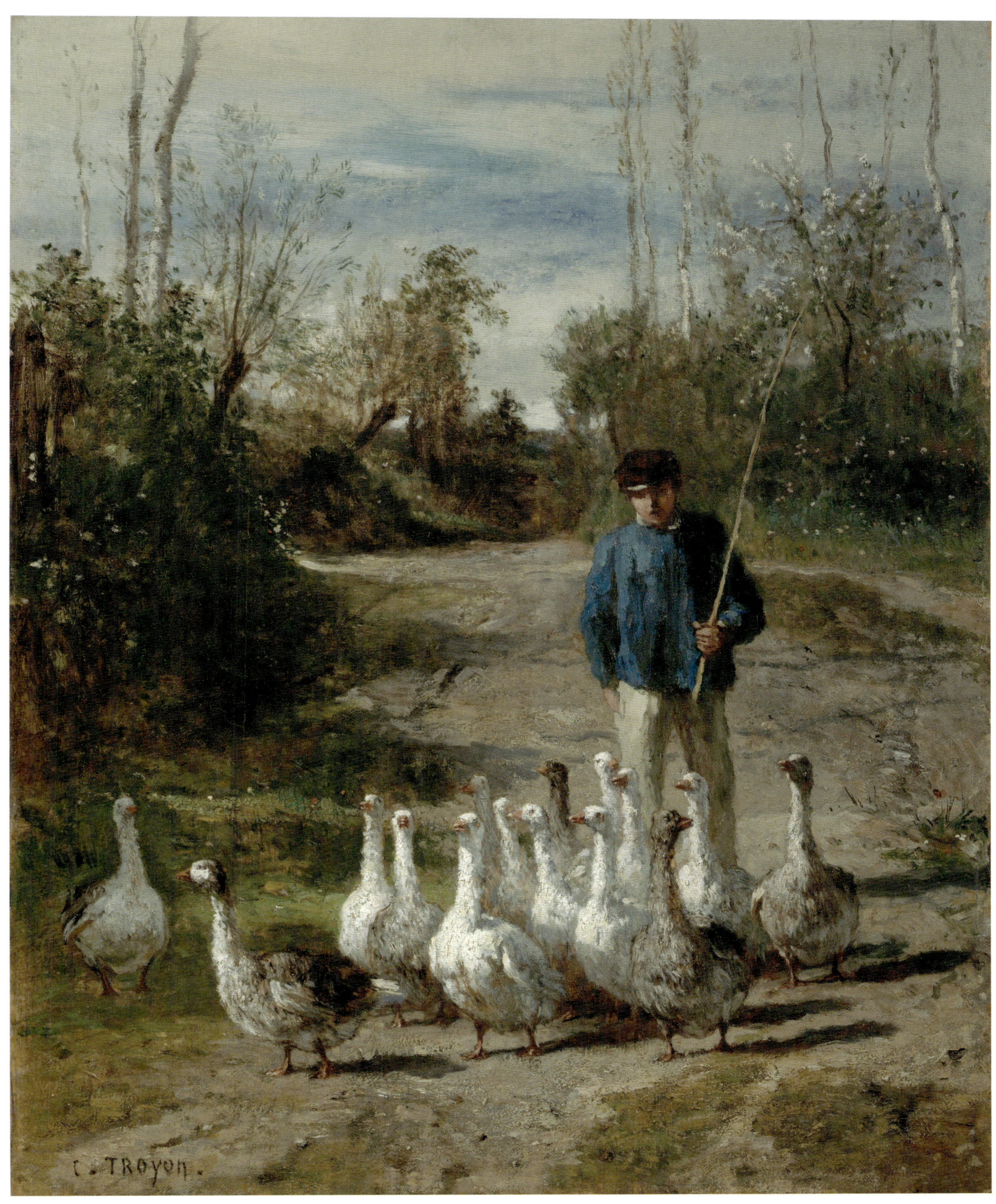
C. TROYON.

7 THÉODORE ROUSSEAU French, 1812–1867

Farm in the Landes

1844–67
Oil on canvas
64.8 x 99.1 cm
Signed lower right: TH · Rousseau
Acquired by the Clark, 2009
2009.8

FARM IN THE LANDES IS A PRIME EXAMPLE of a great Barbizon School landscape. Painted by the most celebrated landscapist of the mid-nineteenth century, it depicts a region of southwestern France that the artist likened to Eden. Monumental oaks, silhouetted against an intense blue sky, dominate a scene of a humble farm warmed by late afternoon sunlight. A dusty path leads through a rustic gate into a busy farmyard where a dog sits patiently, a man repairs a wagon wheel while a child looks on, a woman feeds cows, and at the right a second woman hangs washing before a barn with a great thatched roof. The painting is a moving testament to Rousseau's abiding love for rural life and unadorned nature.

Rousseau worked on *Farm in the Landes* for nearly twenty-five years. The painting had its origins in a trip to the region, just south of Bordeaux, in 1844. At that time he made a composition drawing (private collection), followed by a grisaille oil painting nearly as large as the final work (Ny Carlsberg Glyptotek, Copenhagen). Upon returning to his Barbizon studio, Rousseau worked on the canvas over the ensuing decades, refining the evocation of the play of southern light on the leaves of the trees. The painting was initially purchased in 1852 by Frédéric Hartmann, an Alsatian industrialist and one of the artist's most important patrons. Hartmann also agreed to purchase two other paintings of similar size, *The Village of Becquigny* (The Frick Collection, New York) and *Communal Oven in the Landes* (Museum der Bildenden Künste, Leipzig). Owing to Rousseau's obsessive work, Hartmann was unable to collect the pictures until well after the artist's death in 1867.

In a series of remarkable letters, artist and patron debated the progress of the three pictures, particularly the question of the high degree of finish that characterizes Rousseau's late style. Rousseau explained that *Farm in the Landes* "is for me the object of serious thought and a study at once sweet and bitter," sweet in that his long work on the composition finally brought pictorial form to his experience of the place itself, and bitter because the meticulous technique he had developed was at odds with the current fashion for quickly painted landscapes. Rousseau exhibited *Farm in the Landes* at the Salon in 1859, where it was criticized by conservative writers but admired by younger ones who saw it as a significant experimental work. After Rousseau's death, the three paintings were taken by his good friend Jean-François Millet, who is said to have put the final touches to *The Village* and *Communal Oven* (and possibly *Farm in the Landes*). Hartmann finally took possession of the works, recognized as the artist's greatest late paintings, in 1873, some twenty years after he had purchased them.

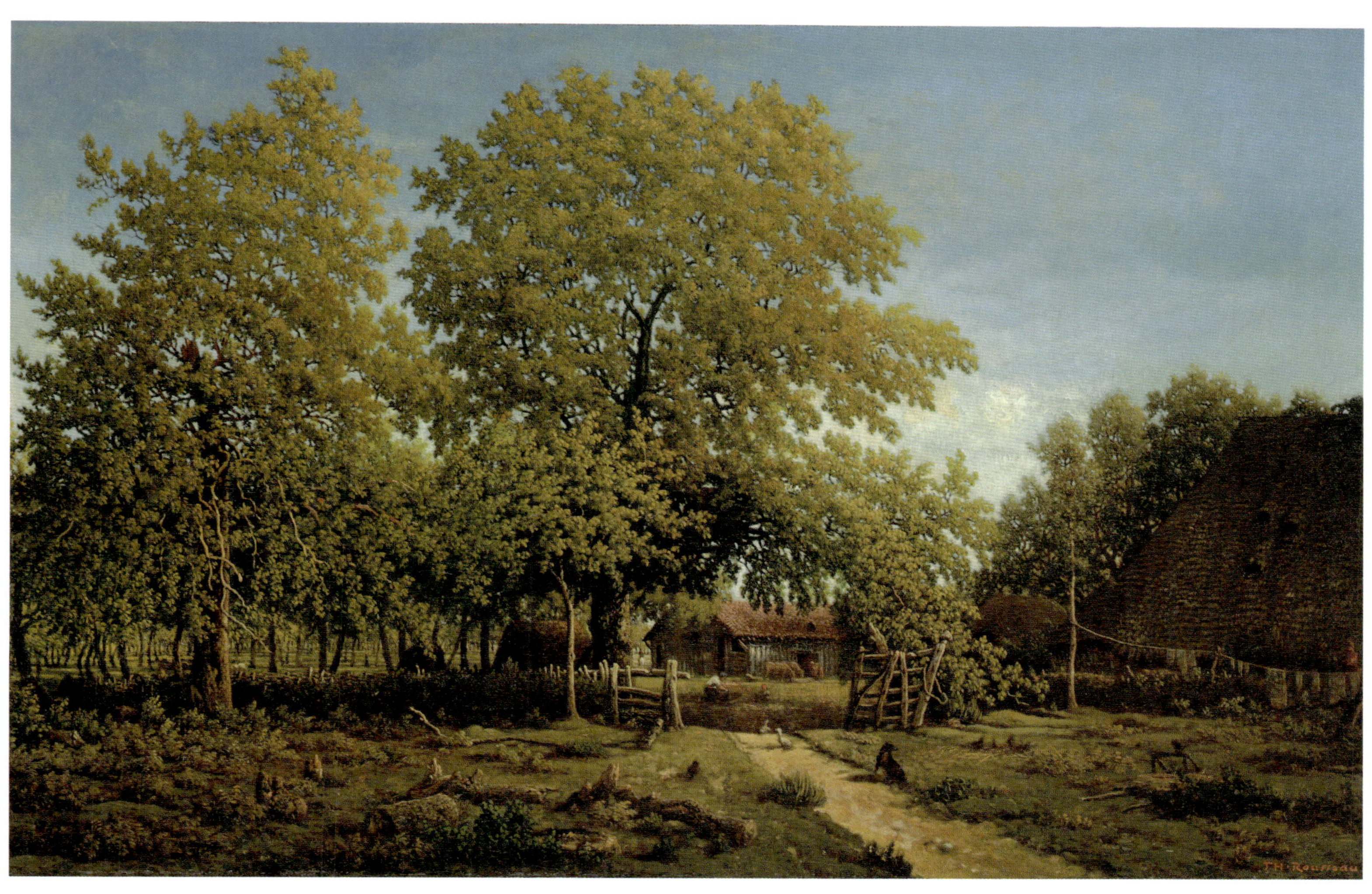
TH·Rousseau

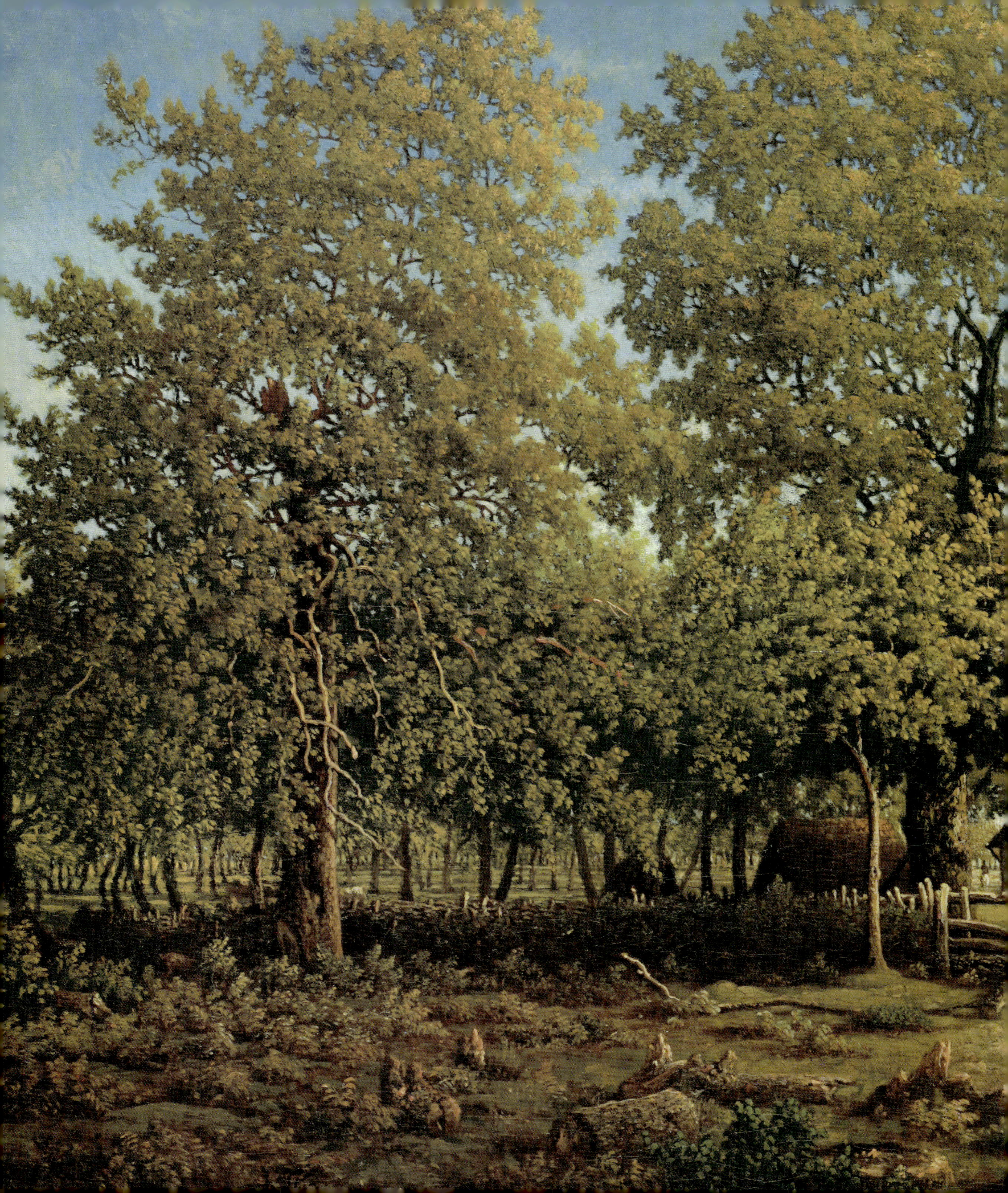

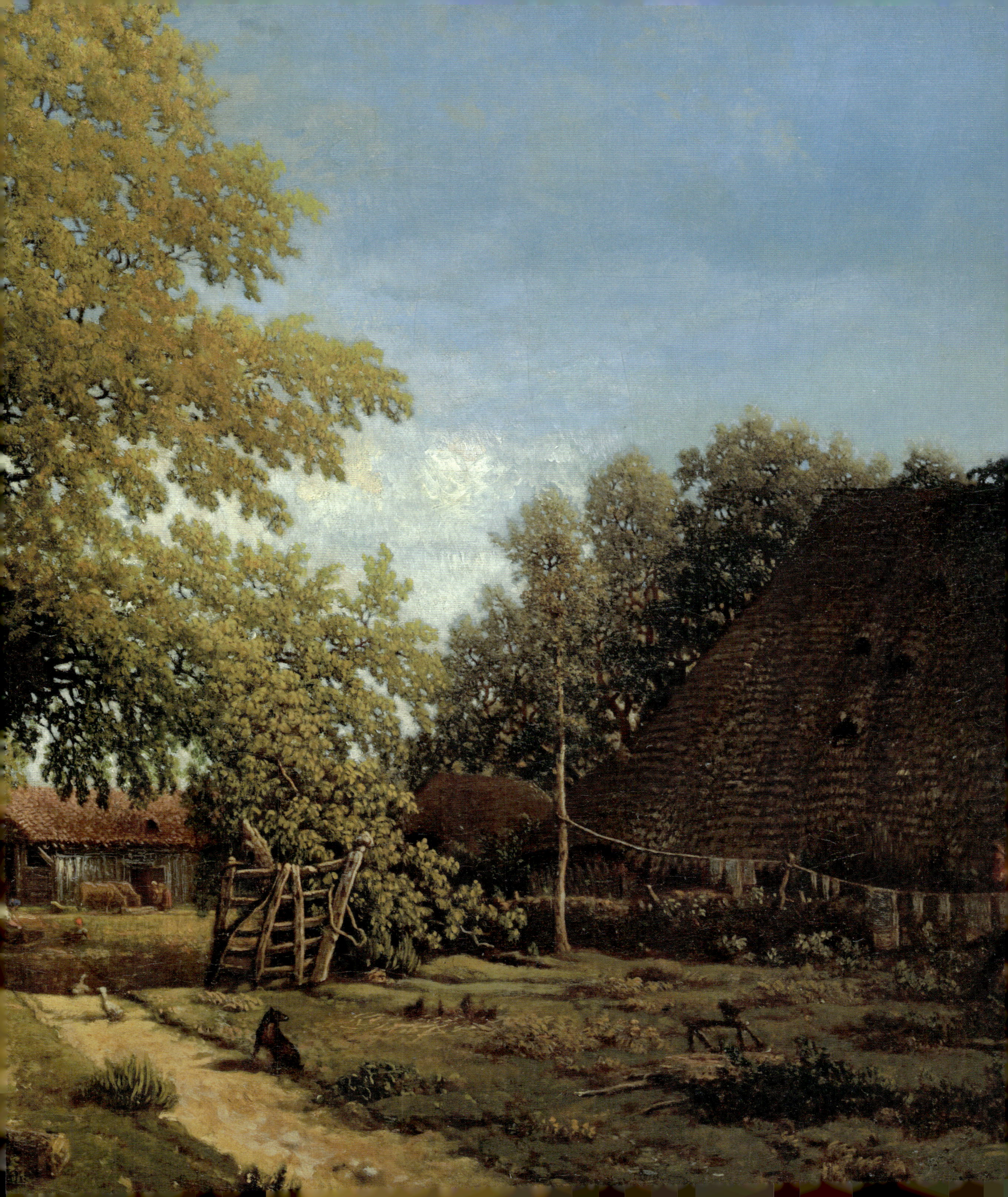

8 JOHAN BARTHOLD JONGKIND Dutch (active in France), 1819–1891

Frigates

c. 1852–53
Oil on canvas
54.6 x 80.6 cm
Signed lower right: Jongkind
Acquired by the Clark in memory of Eugene W. Goodwillie (Institute Trustee, 1959–74), 1974
1974.4

AFTER RECEIVING PRELIMINARY TRAINING IN THE NETHERLANDS, Jongkind moved to Paris in 1846 to study with Eugène Isabey, a prominent painter of seascapes. While still under the tutelage of Isabey, Jongkind quickly became associated with artists such as Eugène Boudin and Théodore Rousseau, and he eventually came to be an early inspiration for Claude Monet. *Frigates*, painted soon after Jongkind moved to France, documents an important stage in both his own development and that of nineteenth-century French landscape painting.

Jongkind often made trips to the Normandy coast to paint the seaside there and its shipping industry. His art is often topographically precise enough to locate the exact geographical areas he portrayed. The subject of the present painting has traditionally been identified as Harfleur, one of Normandy's principal seaports, but the image was more likely produced in the artist's studio from an amalgam of watercolor sketches. While it is possible that some of the elements derive from Harfleur, the city's signature landmark, the spire of the church of Saint-Martin, is missing. In addition, the amount of shipping activity depicted seems impossible, since by the mid-nineteenth century the river Lézarde had silted up considerably and the larger city of Le Havre had become the primary port.

Frigates represents the pinnacle of Jongkind's early mature style, when he was still adhering to conventions of mid-century naturalism in art. The relatively tight handling of paint, the emphasis on shipping's role as a commercial enterprise, and the precise delineation of such details as rigging are typical of much marine painting of the period. Yet the picture also hints at the changes that Jongkind would bring to his art and that would be so important to the younger generation of Impressionist painters. This is most evident in the convincing depiction of atmosphere and light effects and reflections of the ships in the rippling water, rendered with broader and more fluid brushstrokes than was his earlier practice. It was these aspects of his later painting style that strongly influenced artists like Claude Monet, who first met Jongkind in the mid-1860s and, forty years later, could still declare that he owed to him "the final education" of his eye.

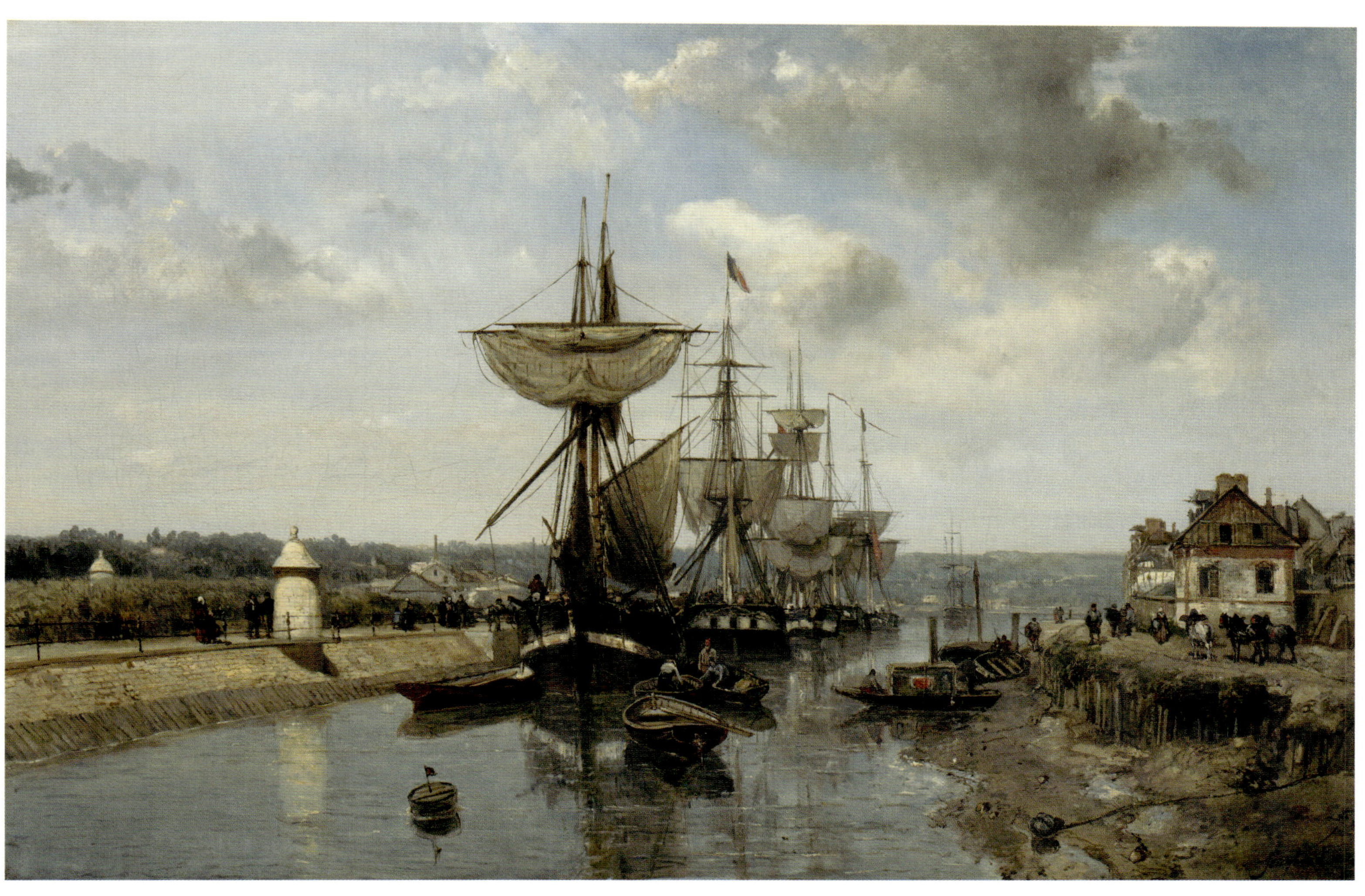

9 EUGÈNE BOUDIN French, 1824–1898

Boats Returning to Port, Trouville

1894
Oil on canvas
65.7 x 92.2 cm
Signed, dated, and inscribed lower left: E. Boudin-94 / Trouville
Bequest of Mildred Cox Howes, 1973
1973.7

BOUDIN PLAYED A CRUCIAL ROLE in the history of nineteenth-century French landscape painting. He was one of the first artists to work predominantly out of doors, portraying the characteristic light and ever-changing atmospheric effects of the Normandy coast where he lived. Boudin had a particularly strong influence on Claude Monet, whom he first met and began mentoring when the latter artist was only eighteen years old. Monet remained a lifelong friend, and as late as 1892, after he had become an established and successful artist, he wrote to Boudin, "I haven't forgotten that you were the first to teach me to see and to understand."

Over the course of his career, Boudin traveled throughout Europe, but he regularly returned to Normandy in the summers to paint the beaches and waters of the coast he knew so well. *Boats Returning to Port, Trouville*, executed when the artist was seventy years old, explores a motif that Boudin painted numerous times in the last thirty years of his life. While many of these paintings focused on the fashionably wealthy beachgoers and their leisurely activities, here Boudin turned his gaze to the sea and the boats upon it.

The composition centers on a sailboat plowing through the waves with several other sailboats behind it and a steamship on the right, creating a triangular composition. The billowing sails and blowing black smoke accentuate the tempestuous weather conditions and give the scene a sense of urgency. Boudin used quick diagonal brushstrokes to render the choppy waves that blow from left to right, and the looming gray clouds in the expansive sky and the relatively low horizon line further add an ominous tone to the canvas. *Boats Returning to Port, Trouville* is notable in that it is one of the rare instances in which Boudin depicted ships out at sea, although it seems that he was becoming more interested in this subject late in his life.

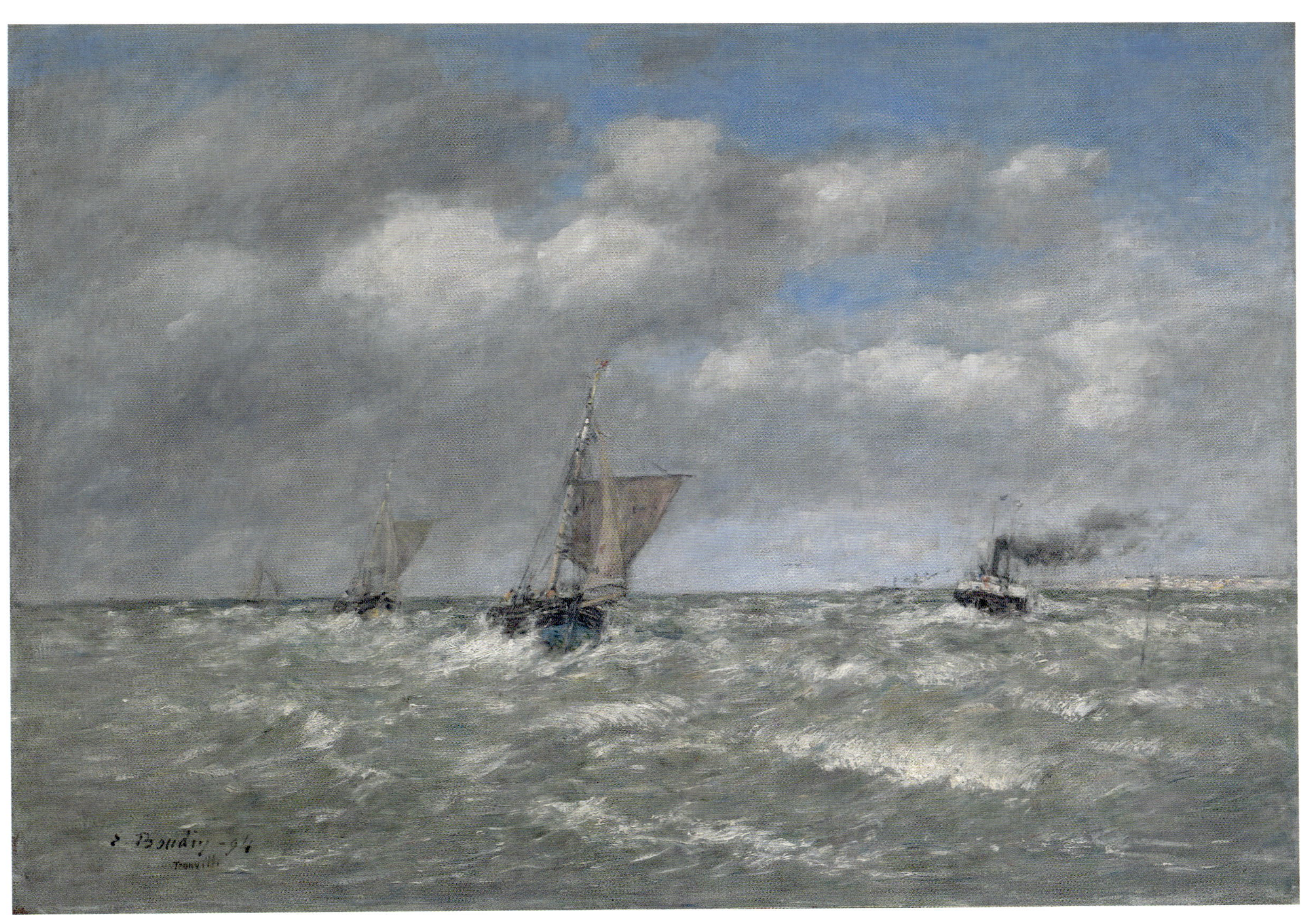

10 **CLAUDE MONET** French, 1840–1926

Seascape: Storm

c. 1866–67
Oil on canvas
48.7 x 64.6 cm
Signed lower right: Claude Monet
Acquired by Sterling and Francine Clark, 1950
1955.561

EXECUTED WHEN MONET WAS IN HIS MID-TWENTIES, *Seascape: Storm* was painted as the artist struggled to find a distinctive style. The canvas has the feel of an audacious youthful experiment, with its stark color scheme and broad strokes of paint, some of which were applied with a palette knife. Throughout the 1860s Monet was beginning to form the ideas and practices that would later bring him fame and success, an arduous process of discovery that sometimes led the artist to despair. The somber tone of *Seascape: Storm* was perhaps informed by the young man's moodiness, which becomes explicit in letters from the period that describe painting as "a terrible business" and even recount an occasion when he was so distraught that he "was stupid enough to hurl myself into the water" in an attempt at suicide.

The composition of the painting is remarkable for its simplicity and boldness. The canvas is divided horizontally into a zone of sky and a zone of sea, which is interrupted only by the boat's sail and mast. Unlike most of Monet's sea paintings, which are drenched in sunlight that plays off the water, this one places a dark sky and deep shadows at center stage. The fishing boat, apparently in danger on the choppy waters, is set off from the sea by its brightly painted foamy wake, creating the sense that it is barreling directly toward the viewer.

Although often compared to a group of sea subjects that Monet's contemporary Édouard Manet first exhibited in 1865, *Seascape: Storm* is not without other precedents in Monet's development. Having spent most of his childhood on the Normandy coast, Monet was keenly aware of the myriad appearances of the sea and the feelings it could evoke. While the intense application of paint, often in passages of wet-on-wet, is distinct from the style of his mentors Eugène Boudin and Johan Barthold Jongkind, certain elements of the composition's spareness and low horizon line can be seen as part of Monet's debt to these artists. It has been suggested that Monet's broad use of the palette knife in *Seascape: Storm* was inspired by the Realist painter Gustave Courbet, who also used a palette knife to portray the textures of the Normandy coast. Indeed, in 1865 Monet was close enough to Courbet to invite him to his studio in Paris, and they would subsequently exhibit together.

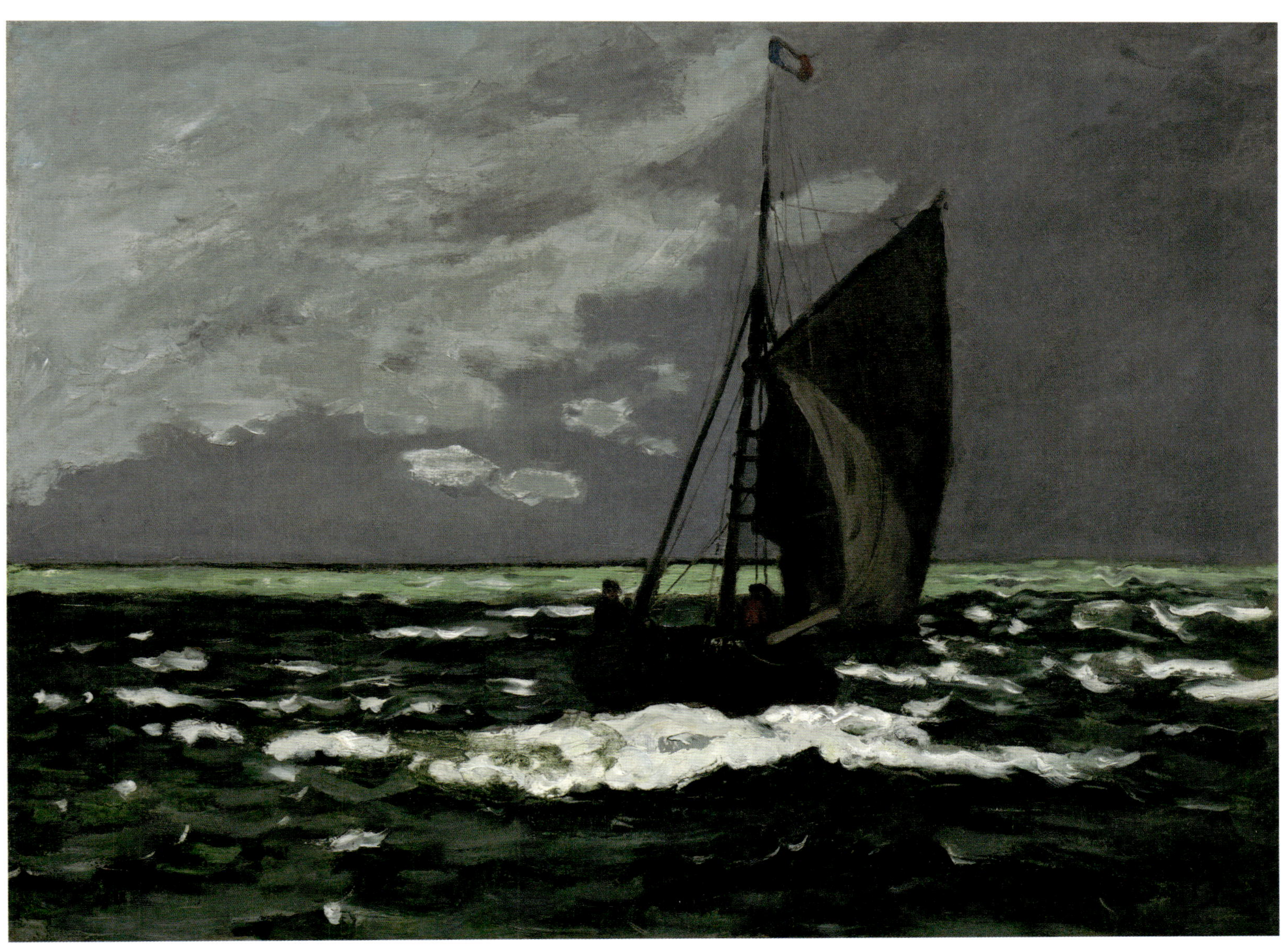

11 CLAUDE MONET French, 1840–1926

Street in Sainte-Adresse

1867
Oil on canvas
80 x 59.2 cm
Signed lower left: Claude Monet
Acquired by Sterling and Francine Clark, 1952
1955.523

JUST NORTH OF LE HAVRE, the large port city where Monet spent his childhood, lies the small fishing village of Sainte-Adresse. Early in his career, Monet would often visit his aunt's summer home in Sainte-Adresse and paint the beach and the view from her house. Many of these scenes include wealthy vacationers who are enjoying time away from the city. In *Street in Sainte-Adresse*, by contrast, Monet turned his attention away from the coastline with its tourists and boats to focus instead on the streets and the people of the village itself. The downward-sloping perspective leads the viewer into the scene, sparking a curiosity about what lies below, which is accentuated by the woman and child walking down the road with their backs to us.

Monet's mastery of light effects, so often focused on water, is here brought to bear on the cobblestone street and the town's vernacular architecture. The stone walls and roofs appear to glimmer in the coastal light, an effect heightened by the patch of green and yellow foliage in the center of the painting. The dominant architectural feature is the town church and its steeple, which is emphasized by a plume of blue-gray smoke that obscures one of its windows. The spire rising above it, however, is itself overwhelmed by the large and imposing tree across the street. Due to the high vantage point, this tree becomes even more monumental. The large expanse of sky, with its dark gray clouds, adds a slightly ominous note to this otherwise warm and comforting scene.

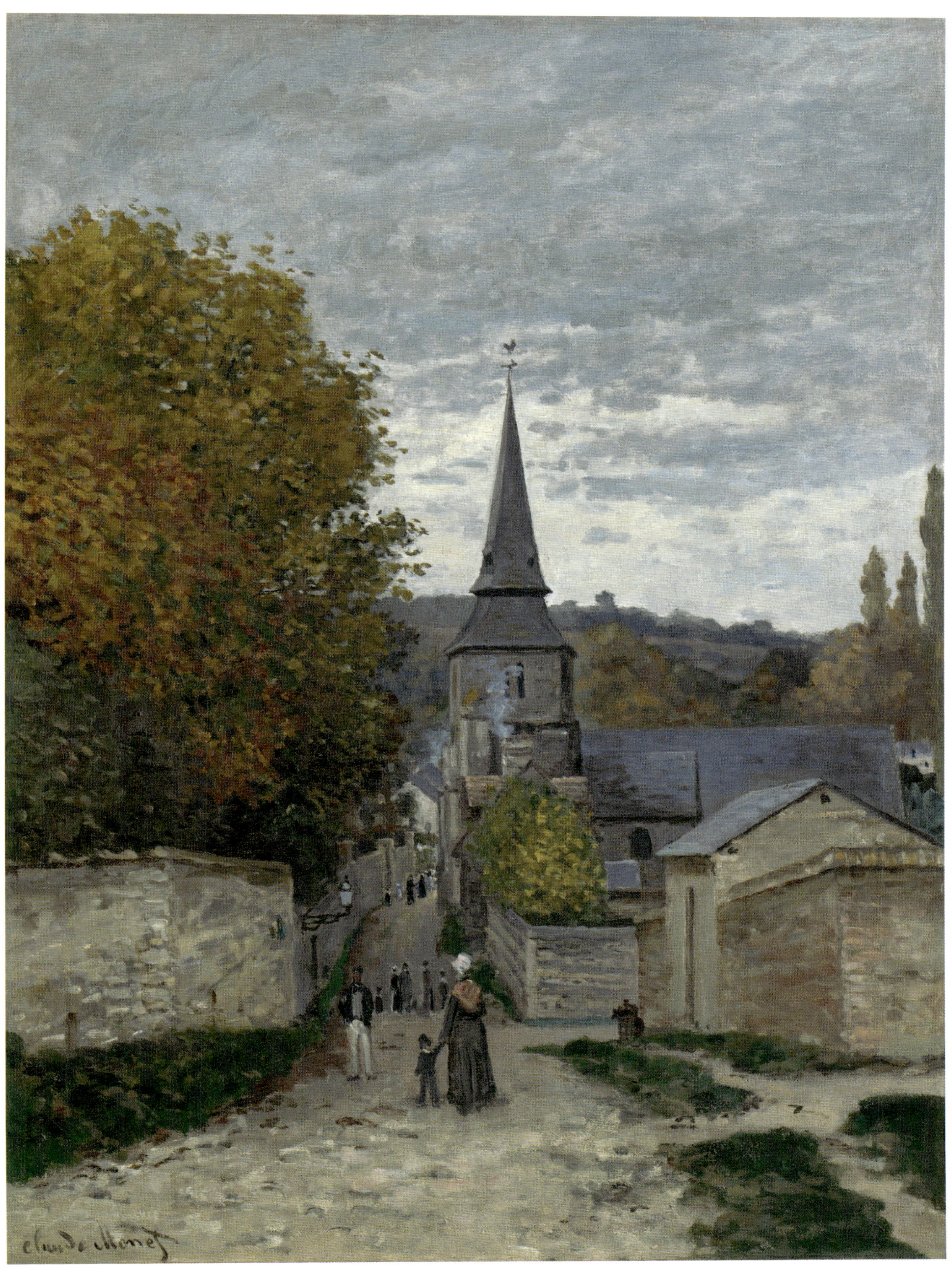
Claude Monet

12 CLAUDE MONET French, 1840–1926

Geese in the Brook

1874
Oil on canvas
73.7 x 60 cm
Signed and dated lower left: Claude Monet 74
Acquired by Sterling and Francine Clark, 1949
1955.529

PAINTED WITHIN MONTHS OF THE FIRST IMPRESSIONIST group exhibition in 1874, *Geese in the Brook* has the bright, multicolored palette and thick impasto that is characteristic of Monet's work during this seminal period. The glittering autumnal scene is dominated by the soft oranges and yellows of foliage, which sparkle in the sunlight and are reflected in rippling water. A picturesque tree-lined path leads to a sunlit, whitewashed farmhouse, while geese gather in the foreground and a mother and child approach an open door in this idyllic country setting.

While the bright palette and the manner of painting are typical of Monet's work of the mid-1870s, in certain ways *Geese in the Brook* is highly idiosyncratic and departs from the artist's oeuvre up to that time. The vertical orientation was a format that Monet rarely used for rustic subjects, which he usually depicted in grand horizontal views that give the viewer a sense of open space. Here, however, the tall trees on both the left and right emphasize the narrow path and give the painting an enclosed and intimate feeling. This sense is further accentuated by the lack of a defined horizon line, which is similarly atypical of Monet's paintings of the period.

It is unknown exactly what motivated the artist's spatial experimentation in *Geese in the Brook*, but scholars have suggested that he was in some ways paying homage to the country scenes of the Barbizon painters. The subject of an informal path of trees slightly obscuring a distant farmhouse bathed in sunlight is indeed reminiscent of certain paintings by Camille Corot and his contemporaries. The conservatism in subject and point of view, however, is countered by Monet's bright palette and radical handling of paint. In this light, *Geese in the Brook* can perhaps be viewed as Monet's attempt to adapt his avant-garde painting style to traditional subjects.

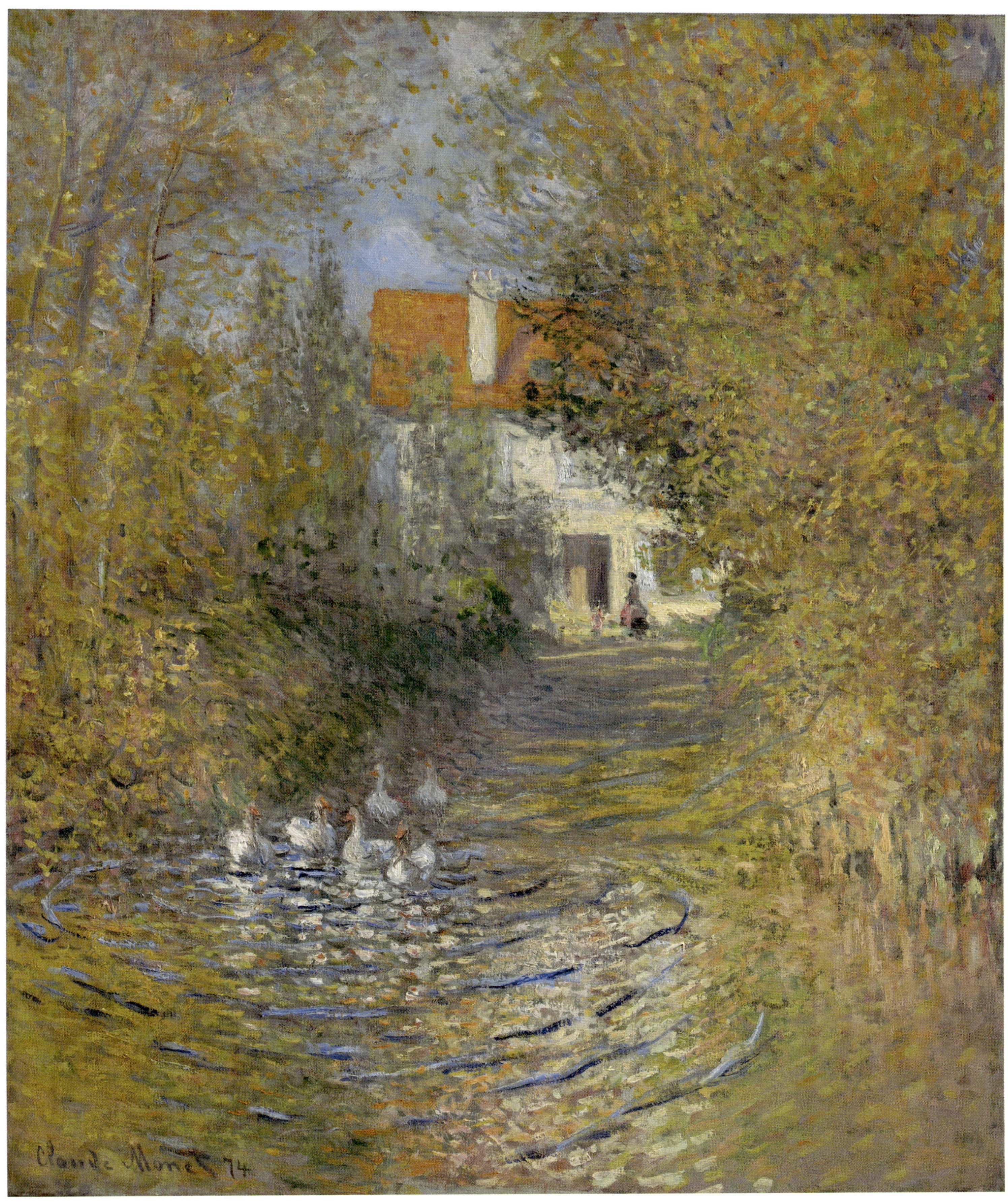
Claude Monet 74

13 CLAUDE MONET French, 1840–1926

The Cliffs at Étretat

1885
Oil on canvas
65.1 x 81.3 cm
Signed and dated lower right: Claude Monet 85
Acquired by Sterling and Francine Clark, 1933
1955.528

THE CLIFFS AT ÉTRETAT IS ONE OF ABOUT FIFTY PAINTINGS of the Normandy coast that Monet worked on between October and December of 1885. The particular motif of the present painting—the needle-like rock and the prominent arch that forms the Porte d'Aval—are signature landmarks that had previously been painted by Monet's mentors Eugène Boudin, Johan Barthold Jongkind, and Gustave Courbet. One has the sense of the mature and successful Monet coming back to the Normandy coast to measure up against his predecessors and secure his place in the tradition of French landscape art.

As was his custom, Monet laboriously worked to capture the ephemeral effects of light and movement in *The Cliffs at Étretat*. Early morning light sets off the glowing tip of the rock pillar, and the undulations in the eroding rocks are reflected and transformed in the rippling sea. The writer Guy de Maupassant, who watched Monet paint in Étretat, described the artist at work: "standing in front of his subject, he waited, watched the sun and the shadows, capturing in a few brushstrokes a falling ray of light or a passing cloud. . . . I saw him catch a sparkling stream of light on a white cliff." The prominent shadows in *The Cliffs at Étretat* underline the fact that the view will change within minutes.

What sets this picture apart from depictions of the Porte d'Aval by other artists is not only Monet's impressive command of light and color but also his choice of viewpoint. The celebrated landmark is seen from a small beach southwest of the rocks, accessible on foot only by means of a precipitous cliff path. It is likely, in fact, that Monet transported himself and his materials by water while working on the painting. Unlike many other views of the area, which exist in a number of different variations, *The Cliffs at Étretat* is the lone example of this particular prospect.

For all the splendorous light in *The Cliffs at Étretat*, Monet's letters from his 1885 trip to the coast are filled with gloomy reports of rain and cold weather. Variations in the weather were both an inspiration and a bane for Monet, who, to observe the effects he was painting, needed to visit the same places under the same conditions a number of times to fully capture the moment. His correspondence makes this clear when he wrote, "the weather is so variable I cannot finish anything." Similarly, one can sense the artist's excitement when conditions were favorable in his comments about "delicious days" of sunshine, when everything was "exactly right for several motifs."

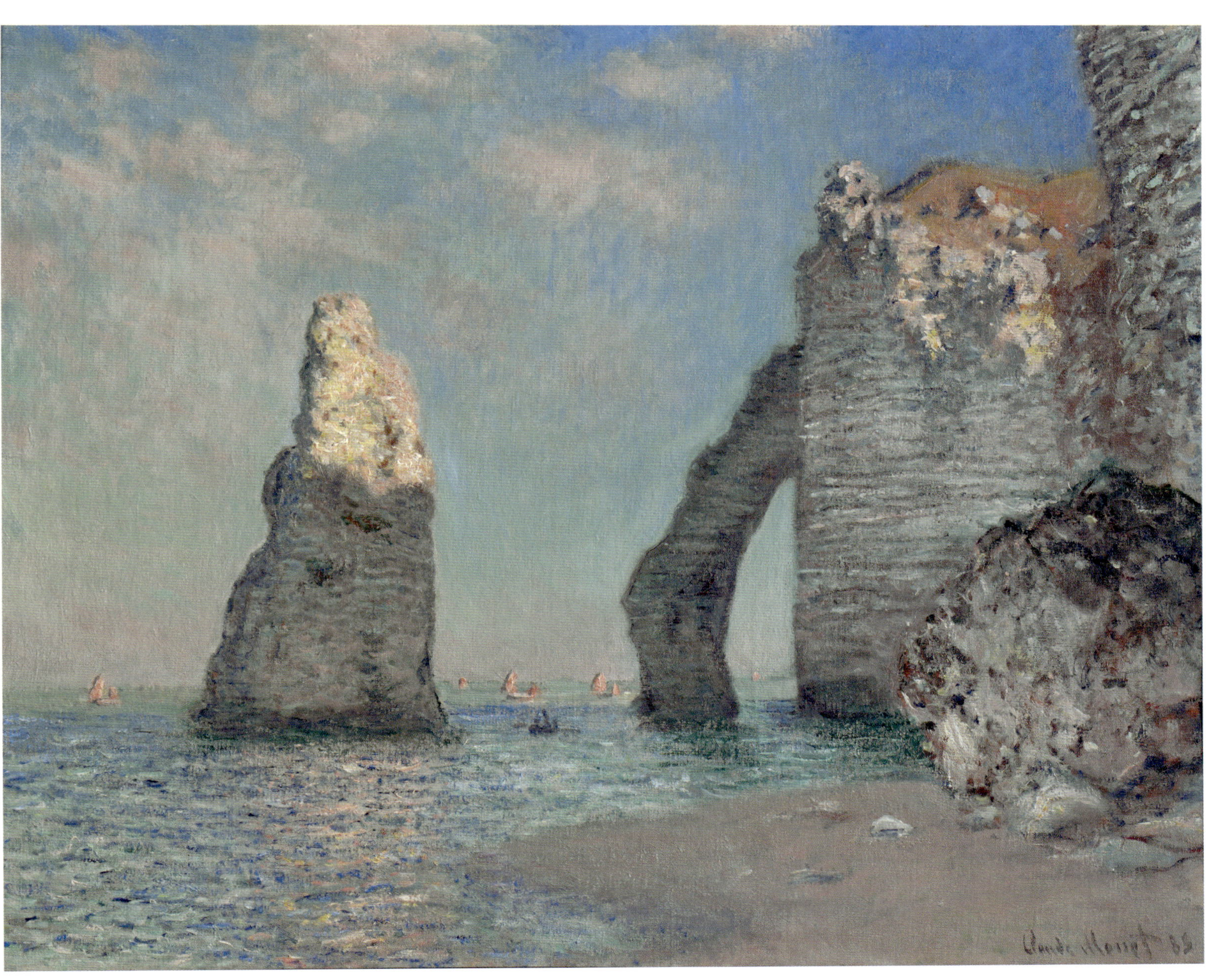

14 CLAUDE MONET French, 1840–1926

Tulip Fields at Sassenheim, near Leiden

1886
Oil on canvas
59.7 x 73 cm
Signed and dated lower left: Claude Monet 86
Acquired by Sterling and Francine Clark, 1933
1955.615

PAINTED DURING HIS THIRD TRIP TO THE NETHERLANDS, *Tulip Fields at Sassenheim* is one of five related works that Monet made of Holland's tulip fields. In fact, the impetus behind the trip in 1886 was an invitation by a French diplomat based in The Hague to study these fields. According to a letter Monet sent to the writer Théodore Duret, the diplomat was "an admirer of [his] painting who wanted to show [him] bulb cultivation, [and] the enormous fields in full flower."

The intense color of the tulip fields clearly appealed to Monet, although he felt that he had insufficient means to translate their glory onto a canvas. He commented that the mix of colors one sees in a tulip field "is certainly admirable but drives the poor painter crazy; it cannot be conveyed with our poor colors." Even so, Monet pressed on in his quest to capture the brilliant hues he was encountering. In *Tulip Fields at Sassenheim* he re-creates this color by painting the blooms of the tulips in broad patches of bright reds, yellows, and creams. The leaves of the flowers are rendered in green and purple, and the whole scene is placed under a brilliant blue sky. Monet's use of thick impasto strokes adds not only richness to the color but depth to the surface of the painting as well, echoing the visual texture of the field, where the tulips sway in the breeze.

Monet was sufficiently pleased with the end result of *Tulip Fields at Sassenheim* to include it in an important exhibition in Paris just weeks after its completion. The critics seized on the painting's bright colors, some praising their "extraordinary intensity," with others disparaging the "exaggeration of reds and blues." *Tulip Fields at Sassenheim* eventually ended up in the private collection of Monet's dealer, Paul Durand-Ruel, from whom Sterling Clark bought the work in 1933.

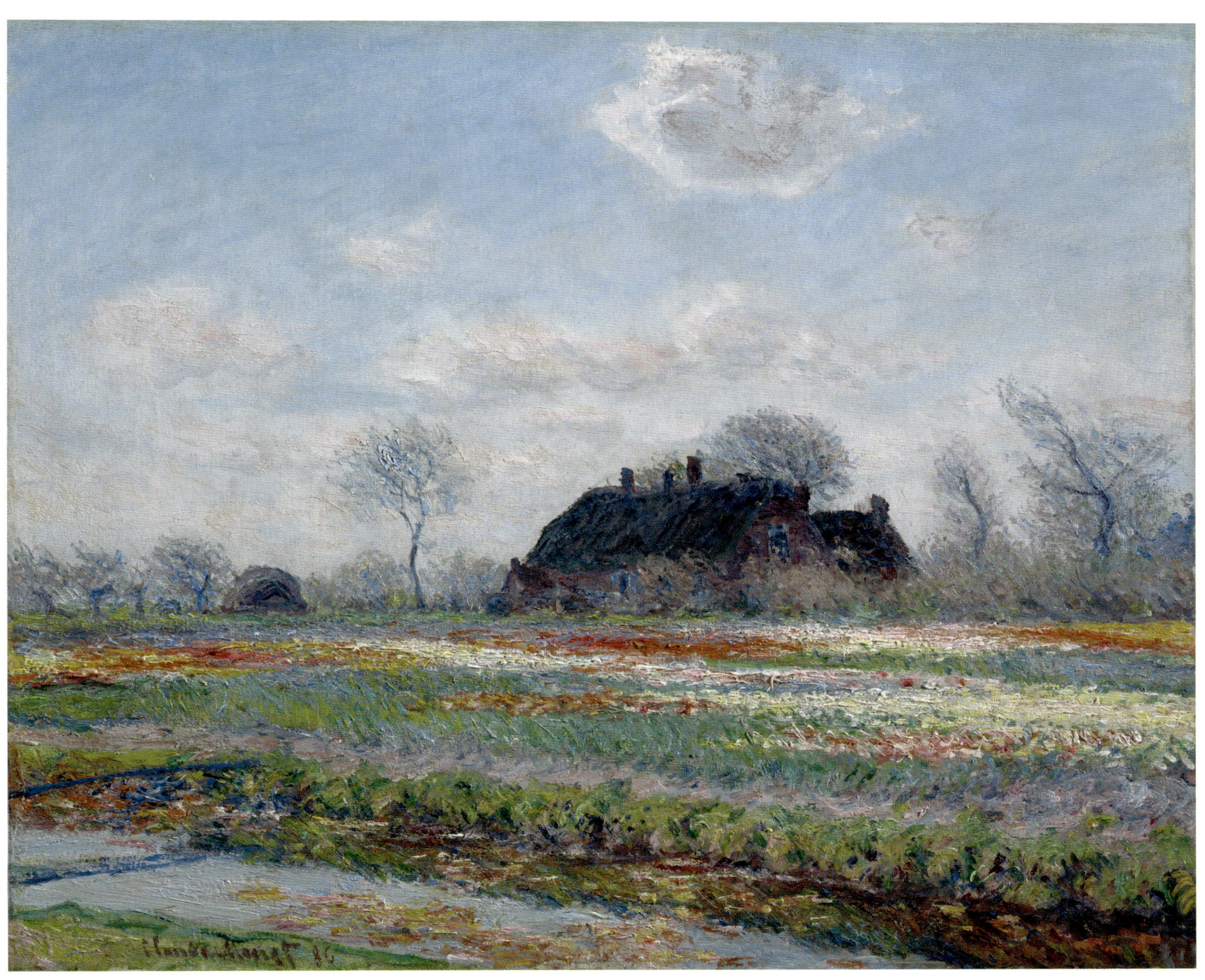

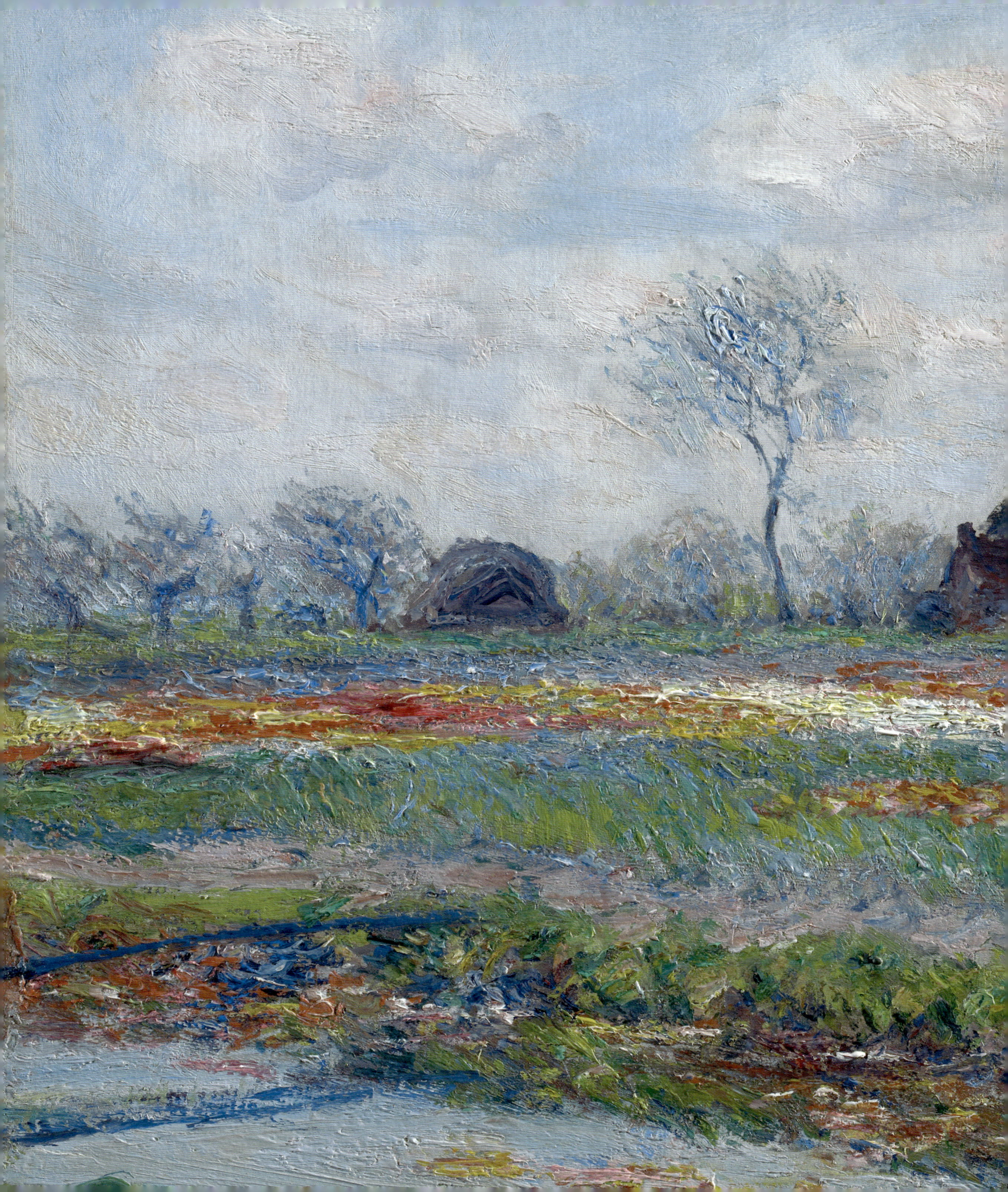

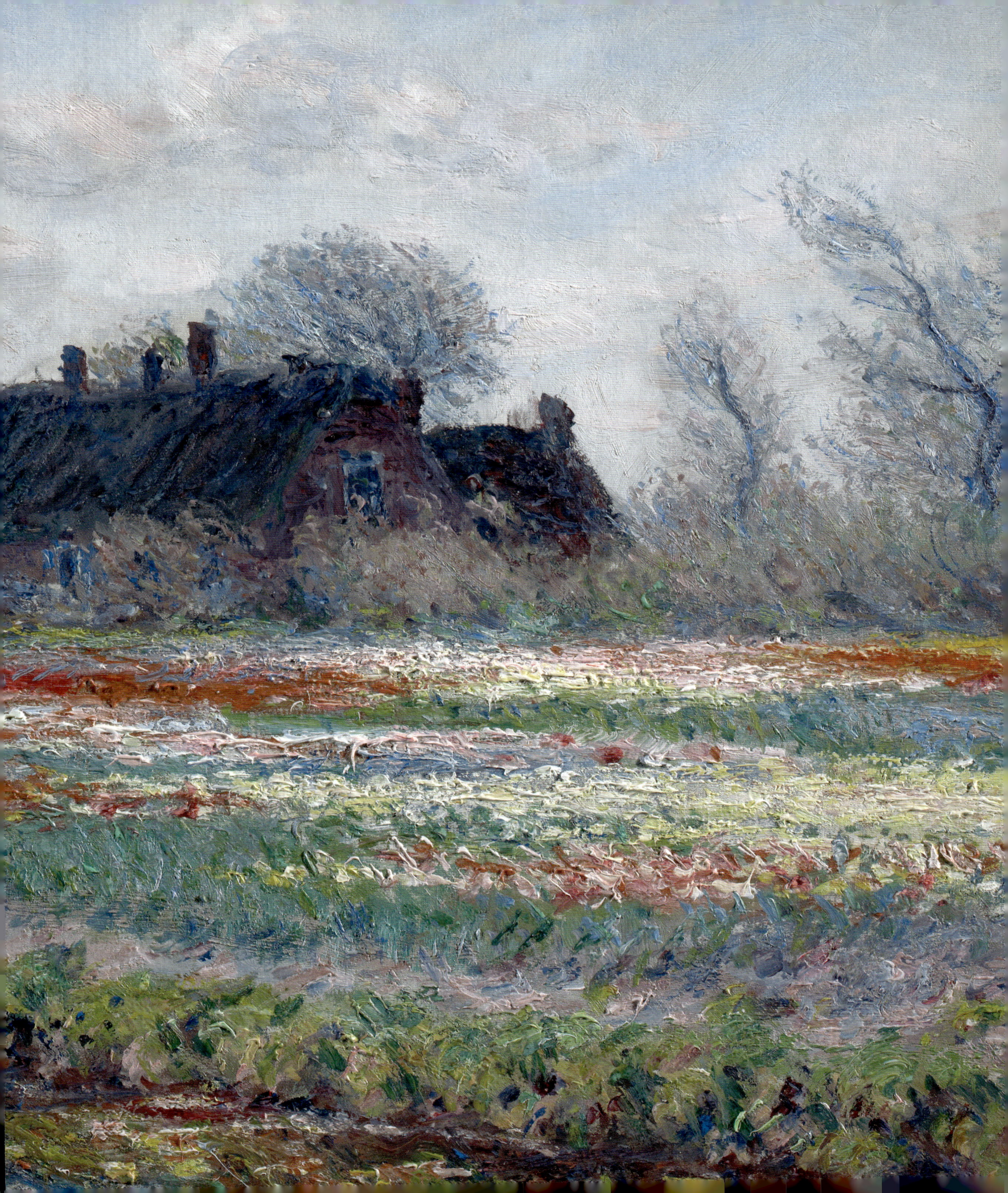

15 CLAUDE MONET French, 1840–1926

Spring in Giverny

1890
Oil on canvas
64.8 x 81 cm
Signed and dated lower left: Claude Monet 90
Acquired by Sterling and Francine Clark, 1933
1955.616

MONET MOVED TO GIVERNY IN 1883, renting a house for his family that could also serve as a base for painting trips to Holland and the coasts of France and Italy. He responded to the commonplace open farmland of the region by experimenting with new styles of painting that would profoundly affect his subsequent work. *Spring in Giverny* is one of a number of pictures in which Monet deemphasizes a central point of view and minimizes the notion of receding space. This is in stark contrast to the majority of his earlier works, which often lead the eye from foreground into deep space along a road or line of trees, and marks a break from the classical tradition of European landscape painting.

In *Spring in Giverny* Monet placed the viewpoint perpendicular to a line of trees and filled the bottom third of the canvas with a field rendered as a continuous speckled band of color. Details such as the suggestion of a house in the far distance are obscured by the trees and the artist's uniform brushwork. Unable to find a fixed point of interest, the viewer lingers on the play of color and the visceral texture of the picture. The effect of the whole is more a sensation of color and texture than a depiction of particular landscape features.

Spring in Giverny belongs to a series of works in which Monet was experimenting with different compositional structures while exploring the ways the landscape changed through the seasons. As early as 1884 he made three sketches that show a budding interest in the parallel interplay between farmland and trees. From 1885 through 1887 he began incorporating more strip-like arrangements of riverbank views as well as focusing on the screening effect of trees. At the same time, he was busy recording the seasonal variations of his surroundings, concentrating on orchards in full bloom, summer wheat, and snowy woodlands. His interest in seasonal scenes is manifest in the present painting's sun-drenched palette.

Although Monet's dealer Paul Durand-Ruel bought the painting shortly after its completion, *Spring in Giverny* was not shown in an exhibition until 1899. It stayed in the possession of the Durand-Ruel family until Sterling Clark bought it in 1933, one of three Monet paintings he purchased that year.

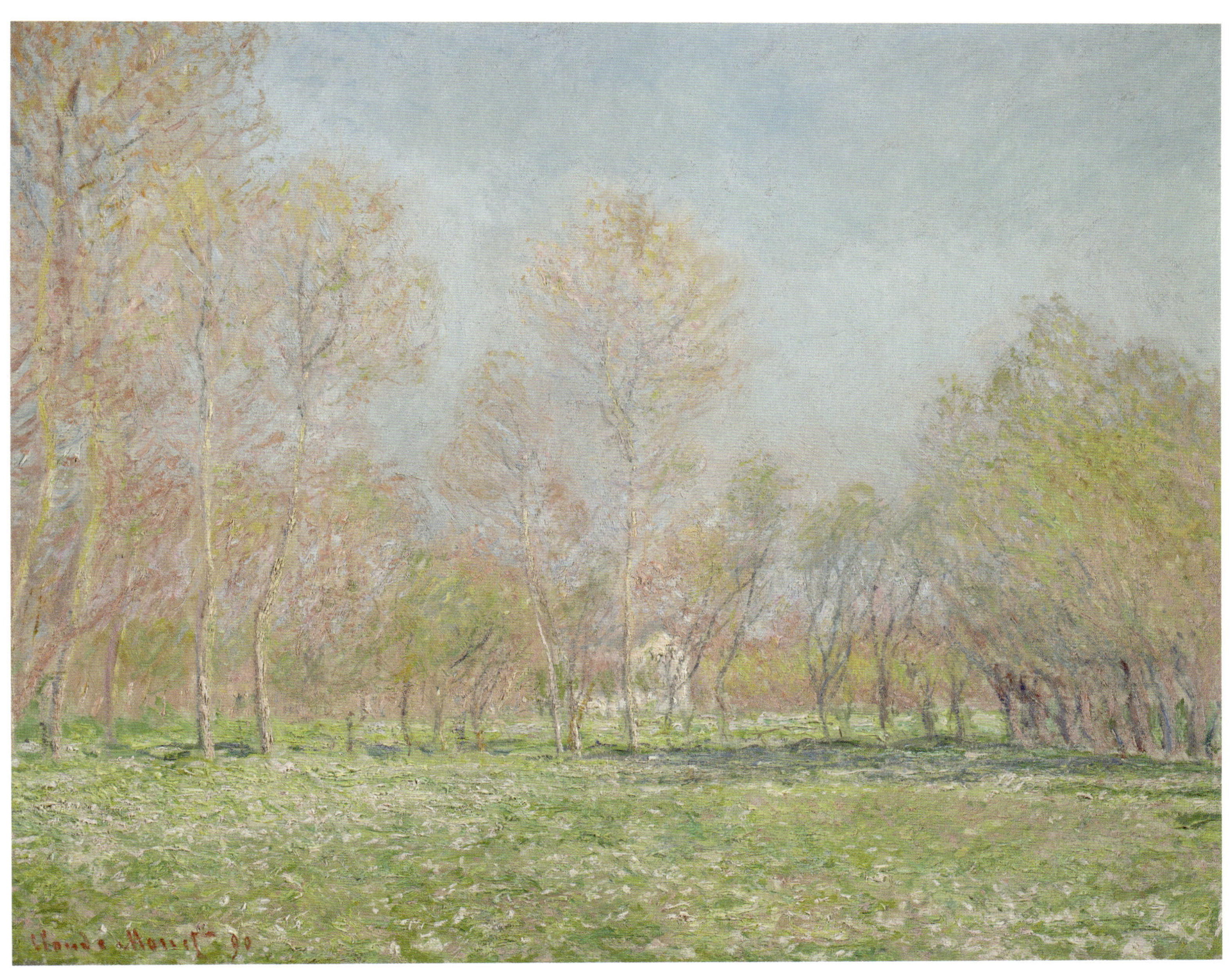
Claude Monet 90

16 GUSTAVE CAILLEBOTTE French, 1848–1894

The Seine at Argenteuil

c. 1892
Oil on canvas
54.3 x 65.1 cm
Signed lower left: G. Caillebotte
Gift of George Heard Hamilton and Polly W. Hamilton, 1973
1973.35

CAILLEBOTTE, WHO OBTAINED A LAW DEGREE before settling on a career as an artist, was the quintessential urban Impressionist. His repertoire included the full range of genre scenes, portraits, and still lifes, but he is best known for his paintings of modern Paris, with its open squares, stately rows of apartments, and lively boulevard life. His most innovative pictures focus on the city dweller, whether the bourgeois promenader or the workman plying his trade. Yet Caillebotte was also interested in portraying rural subjects, particularly in the 1880s and 1890s, after his move from the capital to Petit Gennevilliers, a town about seven miles northwest of Paris on the banks of the Seine, near Argenteuil. The area had been since the 1870s one of the favored stomping grounds of the Impressionists, particularly Claude Monet and Édouard Manet, both of whom maintained houses close by.

For *The Seine at Argenteuil*, Caillebotte set up his easel just upstream from his home, looking across the river toward Argenteuil. One of the motivations for Caillebotte's move to the area was his enthusiasm for boating, both rowing and sailing, activities that were well accommodated by the wide expanse of the Seine at this locale. Caillebotte's view emphasizes this geographical fact, yet in this case, as in several other pictures, he did not include any boaters or day sailors. His attention was instead drawn to the town of Argenteuil on the distant bank, in particular its factories, whose smokestacks pierce the skyline. Caillebotte was on occasion drawn to these signs of industry in the countryside, sometimes painting the factories up close or the iron railway bridge crossing the river. This integration of modernity with a rural or suburban idyll was typical of his Impressionist friends like Monet or Pissarro. In the Clark's picture, Caillebotte relegated this aspect to the far horizon, giving over much of the composition to the organic forms of the riverbank in the foreground and the densely wooded bank in the left middle ground. Indeed, the chimneys of the factories, most likely at a shipyard, barely intrude on the large expanse of summer sky, the smoke emanating from them melding seamlessly with the clouds.

As was typical for Caillebotte, his handling of paint in *The Seine at Argenteuil* is vigorous and varied. The foreground is thickly painted, and the impasto gives the grassy bank a visceral texture. More impressive—and indicative of the quickness with which he was capable of painting—is Caillebotte's rendering of the river, which is made up of varying hues of cobalt blue and white, often unblended and swiftly applied. Although some clouds are heavily painted, the sky is for the most part very thinly brushed, with some of the off-white ground of the canvas left visible and adding texture to the blues and whites.

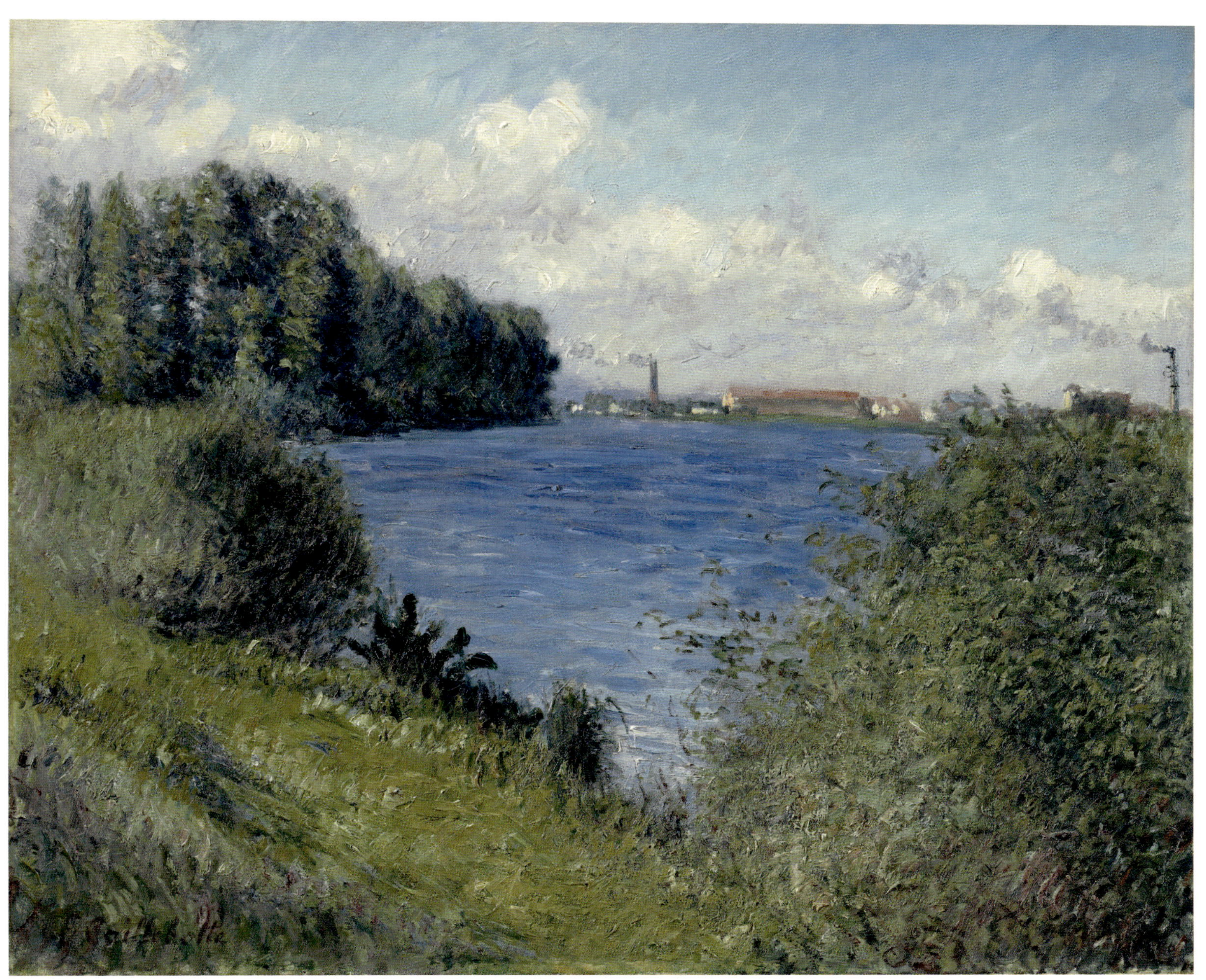

17 ALFRED SISLEY English (active in France), 1839–1899

The Thames at Hampton Court

1874
Oil on canvas
38.1 x 55.2 cm
Signed and dated lower left: Sisley. 74
Acquired by Sterling and Francine Clark, 1937
1955.560

SOON AFTER EXHIBITING FIVE PAINTINGS in the first Impressionist group show in 1874, Alfred Sisley traveled to England for six months, settling at Hampton Court on the Thames, southwest of London. Unlike his contemporaries Monet and Pissarro, who chose to focus on urban subjects during their trips to England in the 1870s, Sisley concentrated on painting the broad expanse of the river, producing a dozen canvases of the area around Hampton Court Palace, visible in the middle distance in the Clark's striking picture. In a letter written late in his life Sisley singled out the work he did in Hampton as particularly important for his development.

In *The Thames at Hampton Court*, Sisley focused on a stretch of the river bathed in sunlight. Geese and sailboats punctuate the foreground, while billowing clouds fill the sky. On the left a large tree rises from the bank, adding texture and color to the expanse of bright summer sky. As a balance to this natural element, Sisley painted an ornate brick building on the right bank. What seemed to interest him most, however, was the interplay of light and water and their various reflections and atmospheric effects, which he portrayed with fluid strokes of paint. Sisley's mastery of the tonal variations of summer sunlight was a direct result of his penchant for painting out of doors directly in front of his landscape subjects. This practice, however, did not inhibit him from altering certain topographical elements in order to create more harmonious compositions. X-ray photography has revealed that the right bank of the river initially included clumps of trees that were eventually painted out. Moreover, the brick building prominent on the riverbank at right is not easily identifiable. While a number of structures near Hampton Court have been proposed as the model, it is possible Sisley introduced a building from another area because it unified the picture better than the actual scene.

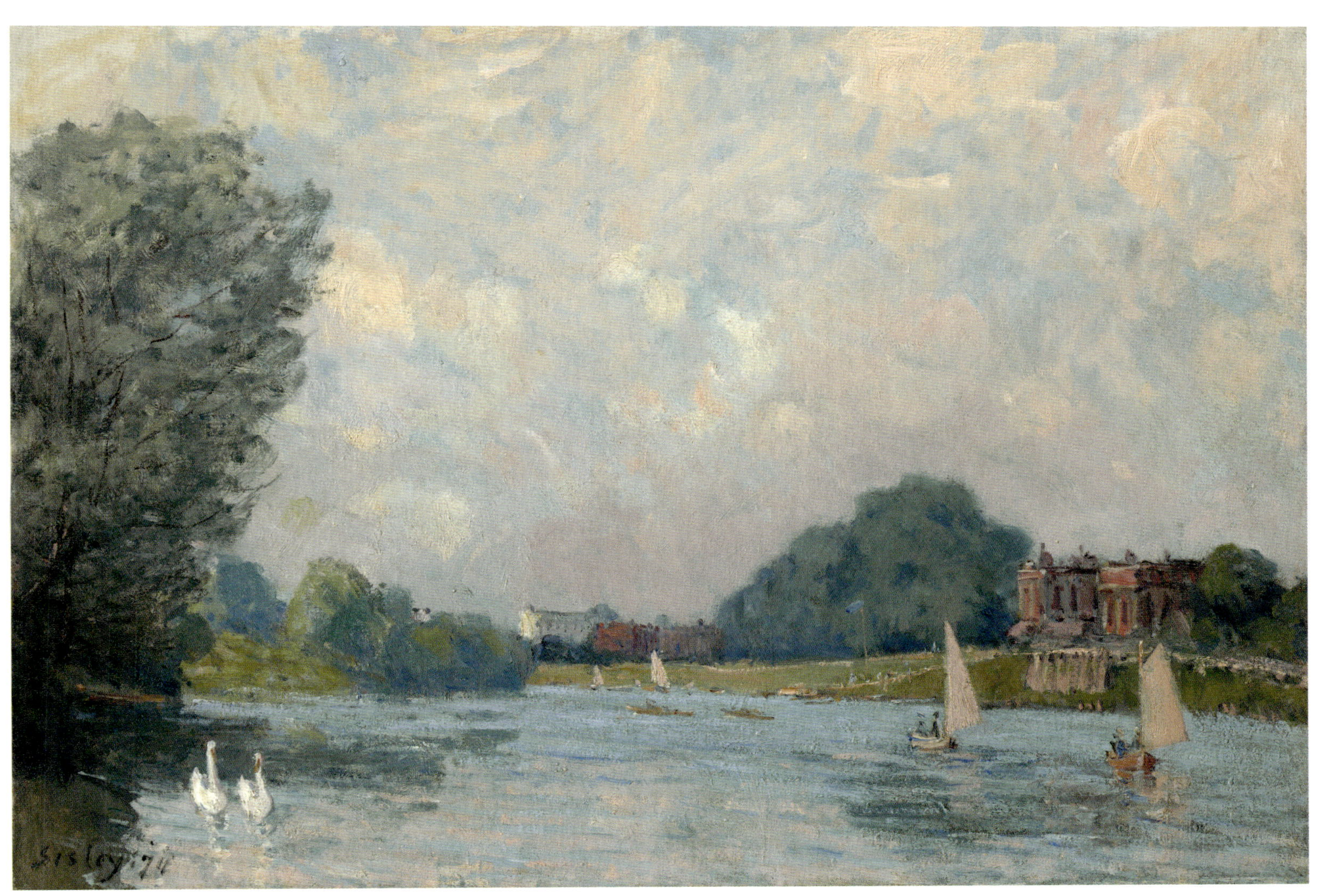
Sisley.74

18 ALFRED SISLEY English (active in France), 1839–1899

Apples and Grapes in a Basket

c. 1880–81
Oil on canvas
46 x 61 cm
Signed lower right: Sisley.
Acquired by Sterling and Francine Clark, 1951
1955.543

APPLES AND GRAPES IN A BASKET is one of only nine still lifes by Sisley, who throughout his career much preferred to paint landscapes. Sisley's impetus for making the picture is unknown. It is possible it was begun as an exercise in form and space, or perhaps as an attempt by the perpetually impoverished artist to attract new patrons. It is equally plausible that it represents a response to some of the still-life paintings of Sisley's contemporaries, such as Claude Monet. Whatever the reason, *Apples and Grapes in a Basket* shows the artist's aptitude for creating bold compositions, no matter what the motif. He chose a high viewpoint, looking down on a round table adorned with a patterned cloth on which sits a wicker basket piled high with grapes and apples near the far edge, a sprig of grapes, four more apples, and a paring knife. Centrally placed in a bold, pyramidal composition, the basket of fruit establishes a note of density that pervades the work; its rounded forms and palpable textures seem to defy the flatness of the canvas. The rich reds of the apples and the cool, metallic grays of the tablecloth intensify these oppositions, while the midtones and delicate handling of the grapes create a vibrant counterpoint. Particularly notable is the play of light throughout, with the deep shadows prominently punctuating the tablecloth pattern.

Despite his lack of practice in the genre, Sisley clearly was familiar with both the traditional motifs of still-life painting and the modern innovations in the field. Echoes of the sumptuous spreads of seventeenth-century Dutch still-life masterpieces are juxtaposed with the angled knives and solitary fruits of the eighteenth-century painter Jean-Baptiste-Siméon Chardin. At the same time, there is an affinity in the tonal variation and compositional structure with some of Paul Cézanne's still-life paintings of the time. Sisley was certainly familiar with Cézanne's work, as both were included in the 1874 and 1877 Impressionist exhibitions.

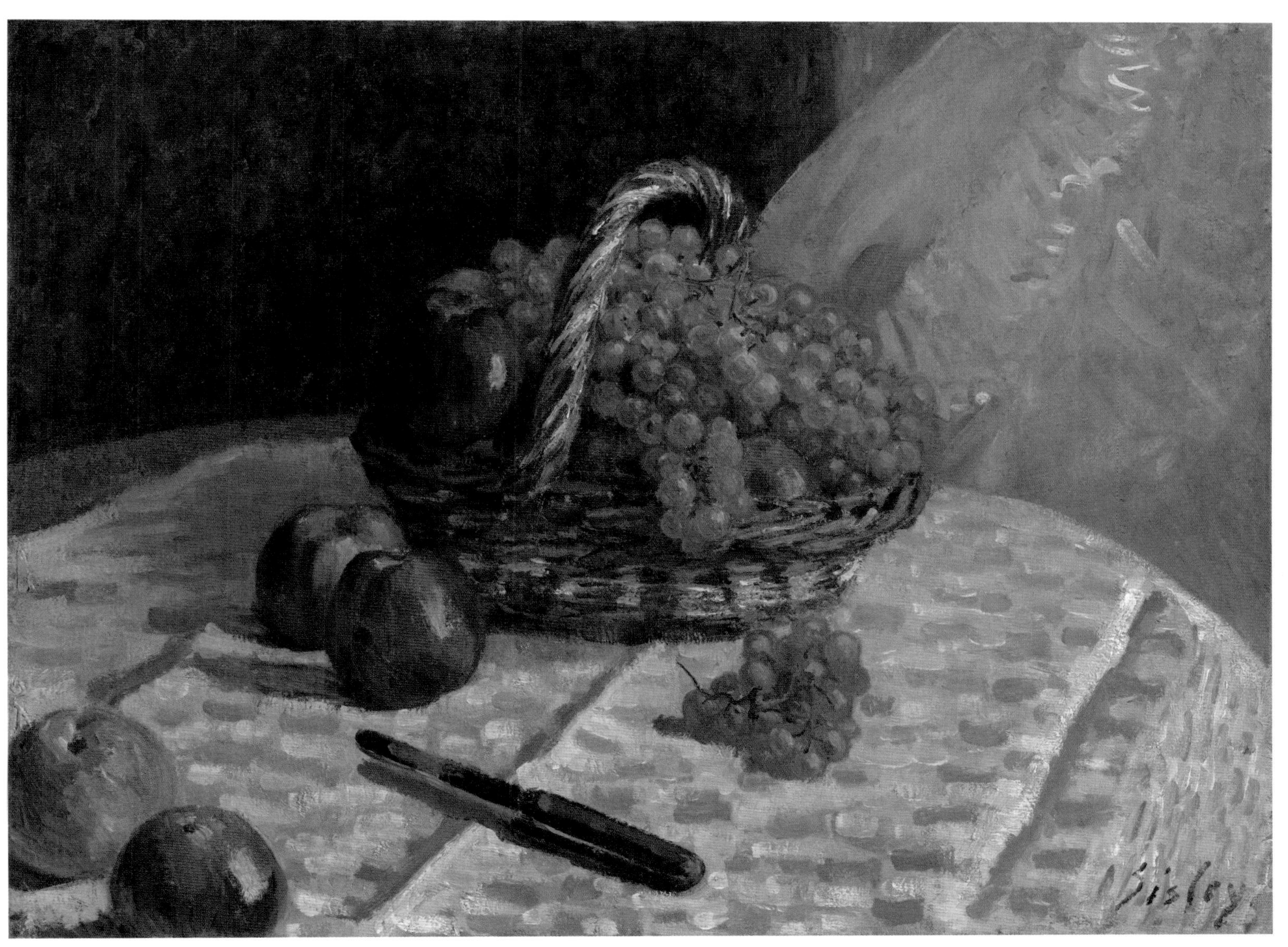
Sisley

19 ALFRED SISLEY English (active in France), 1839–1899

Banks of the Seine at By

c. 1880–81
Oil on canvas
54.3 x 73.3 cm
Signed lower left: Sisley.
Acquired by Sterling and Francine Clark, 1948
1955.534

BANKS OF THE SEINE AT BY was painted soon after Sisley moved to the area around Moret-sur-Loing, in north-central France, in 1880. This relocation would profoundly shape Sisley's output throughout the rest of his career, as depictions of Moret-sur-Loing and its environs provided inspiration for a large part of the artist's later oeuvre. The view in *Banks of the Seine at By* is of a stretch of the riverbank just west of the village now known as By-Thomery. Sisley turned his back on the town, with its buildings and modern railway line, and instead focused his composition on the riverside and its tree-lined path. A woman dressed in blue with a straw hat adds a human dimension to this portrayal of dappled sunlight by the river.

Many of Sisley's early landscapes featured an angled road, street, or bridge, which often helps draw the viewer's eye into the scene. The path in *Banks of the Seine at By* serves a similar function, although here the recession is less emphatic than usual, and one's visual progress is diverted at several points. We first notice the woman in blue, while farther down the road a screen of trees blocks the view. Due to these recessional obstructions, our eye begins to linger more casually on the surface of the painting, with its intricate pattern of brushwork and vibrant colors. *Banks of the Seine at By* is one of the first paintings in which Sisley employed techniques that bring his quick handling of paint and staccato coloristic effects to the forefront.

The glowing light and fluid, creamy brushstrokes evoke a wet luminescence, as though we are witnessing the immediate aftermath of rain. There is an exuberance of color throughout the canvas, from the gradations of blue and gray in the sky to the vibrant greens and yellows of the land. Touches of crimson and pink add warmth to the painting's overall tonality. The dense layering of paint suggests that *Banks of the Seine at By* was executed over a number of sittings. Sisley slowly worked from the more general to the specific, first building up the forms of the trees and establishing a blue sky, later adding twigs, leaves, and more intricate details. Throughout this process, however, he never lost his fluent, seemingly spontaneous style. In fact, *Banks of the Seine at By* has been aptly described as an example of controlled improvisation. Sisley's handling of the subtle nuances of light, color, and atmosphere is a tour de force of mature Impressionism.

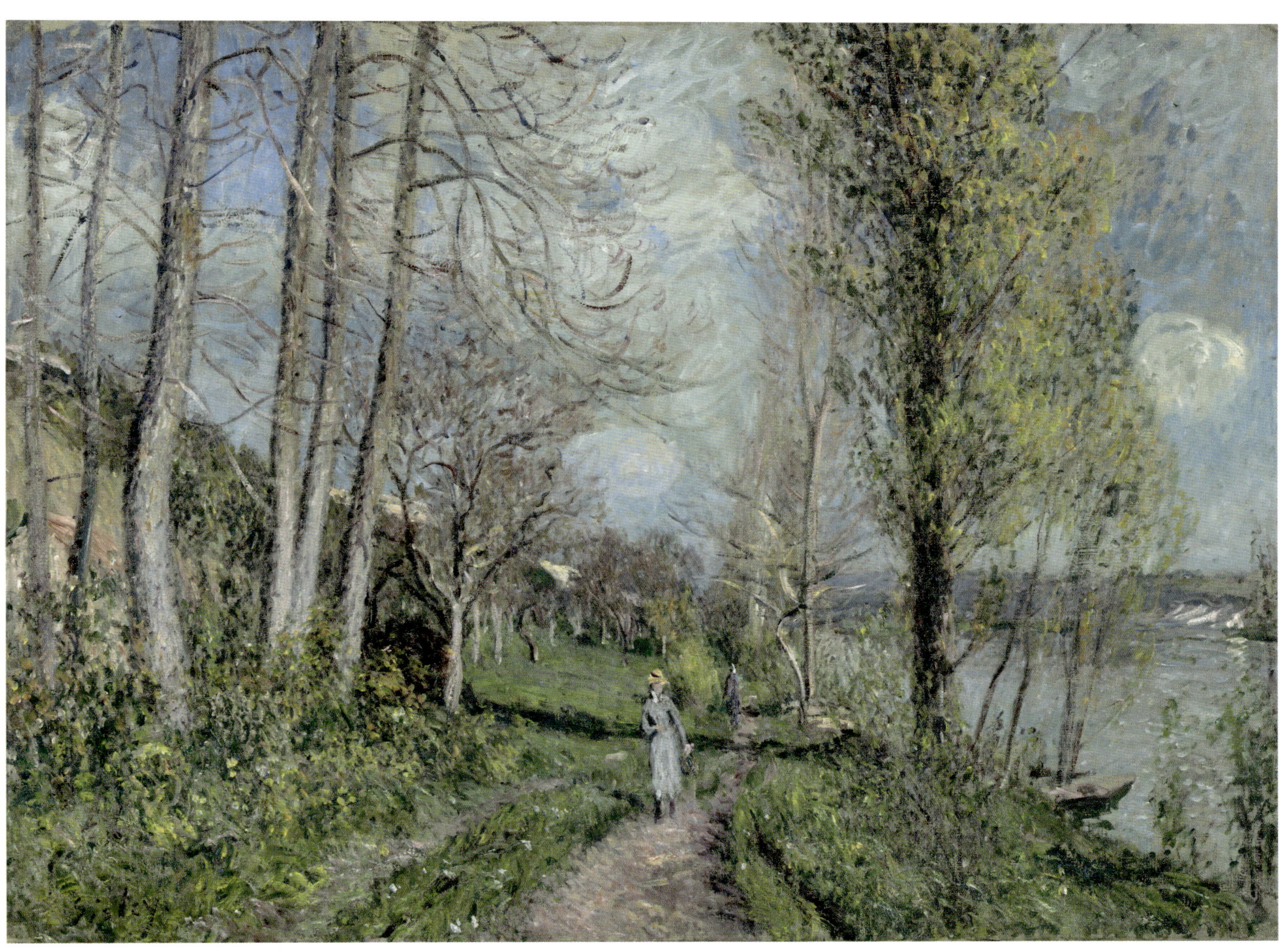

20 ALFRED SISLEY English (active in France), 1839–1899

The Loing and the Mills of Moret—Snow Effect

1891
Oil on canvas
58.7 x 81.6 cm
Signed and dated lower left: Sisley. 91
Acquired by Sterling and Francine Clark, 1946
1955.545

THE LOING AND THE MILLS OF MORET—SNOW EFFECT exemplifies Sisley's continuing devotion to the challenges of Impressionism into the 1890s. River views had been a staple Impressionist subject for almost twenty years at this point, and they continued to inspire artists such as Sisley to find equivalents in paint for the vibrant atmospheric effects of water, land, and sky. The Clark's picture captures a section of the river Loing near the town of Moret, close to Fontainebleau. Sisley had settled in Moret in 1880 and painted the area extensively over the following two decades. The signature structures of Moret's mills, which prominently anchor the right side of the composition, appear in more than thirty of Sisley's paintings between 1888 and 1892. Similar to the contemporary serial campaigns of Monet and Pissarro, Sisley's Moret pictures reveal the artist's attempts to capture different atmospheric effects of a single subject or location.

In *The Loing and the Mills of Moret—Snow Effect*, Sisley turned away from the mills, focusing his gaze on the far bank of the river mediated through the watery reflections and the pale blue sky. Examination of the painting's surface shows that Sisley completed the canvas in one sitting, which is not surprising, given how difficult it is to paint in the open air during winter. Working mostly wet-on-wet, he employed varied brushstrokes to suggest the rippling water and wispy golden poplar trees in the distance. *The Loing and the Mills of Moret—Snow Effect* is a compelling account of cold and solitude, painted with extraordinary technical assurance, and is a prime example of the refined sensibility of late Impressionism.

Although he did not acquire Sisley's work in great numbers, Sterling Clark praised the artist often in his diaries. Clark bought three of his four paintings by Sisley in the late 1940s and early 1950s as his plans for a museum were becoming more concrete. It seems that these works, therefore, appealed to Clark not only for their visual impact but also because they helped fill some gaps in his collection, giving the museum a more comprehensive scope.

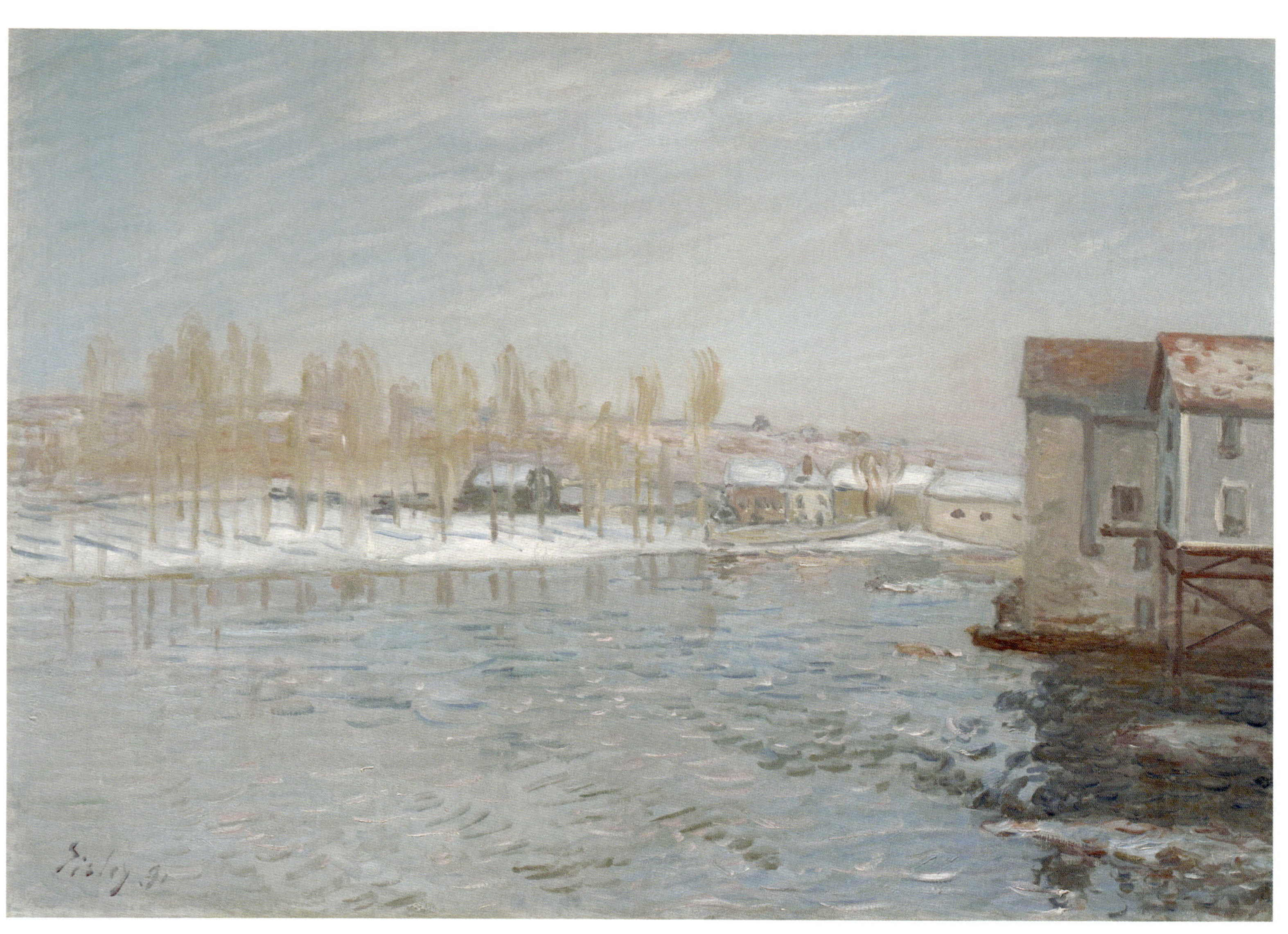

21 CAMILLE PISSARRO French, 1830–1903

Road to Versailles at Louveciennes

1870
Oil on canvas
33 x 41.3 cm
Signed and dated lower right: C. Pissarro. 1870
Acquired by Sterling and Francine Clark, 1942
1955.828

IN 1869 PISSARRO MOVED FROM PONTOISE TO LOUVECIENNES, a village about fifteen miles west of Paris that overlooks the Seine. The move was likely inspired by the fact that his friends Claude Monet, Pierre-Auguste Renoir, and Alfred Sisley all worked in the region. There, Pissarro explored portraying fleeting light effects and became increasingly devoted to plein-air painting. In his numerous images of Louveciennes and its environs, he seems to have been particularly drawn toward depicting the streets near where he lived, as in this composition.

The wide diagonal view of the tree-lined road gives a sense of depth and brings the viewer into the painting. The horse-drawn cart and farmer walking up the road add a figural element, while the raking sunlight plays off the cobblestones and allows shadows to punctuate the modulated earth tones of the walls and buildings. Numerous touches of wet-on-wet painting hint at the immediacy and responsiveness of the artist's technique—traits that would become more pronounced later in his career. While undoubtedly the result of direct observation, the picture shows Pissarro's willingness to adjust the realities of landscape to create a more harmonious painting. He arranged the trees in regular symmetrical rows on either side of the composition and altered the rooflines and the placement of chimneys for artistic effect.

Painted four years before the first Impressionist exhibition, *Road to Versailles at Louveciennes* shows an artist experimenting with new ideas and techniques. Although the canvas has traces of another painting underneath (Pissarro's financial exigencies probably led him to recycle materials), there is no indication of any preparatory drawing for the present picture. It is also an early example of Pissarro's interest, which would later become more pronounced, in recording similar scenes in different seasons. The winter before *Road to Versailles at Louveciennes* was painted, he had depicted the same road from a similar vantage point covered in snow.

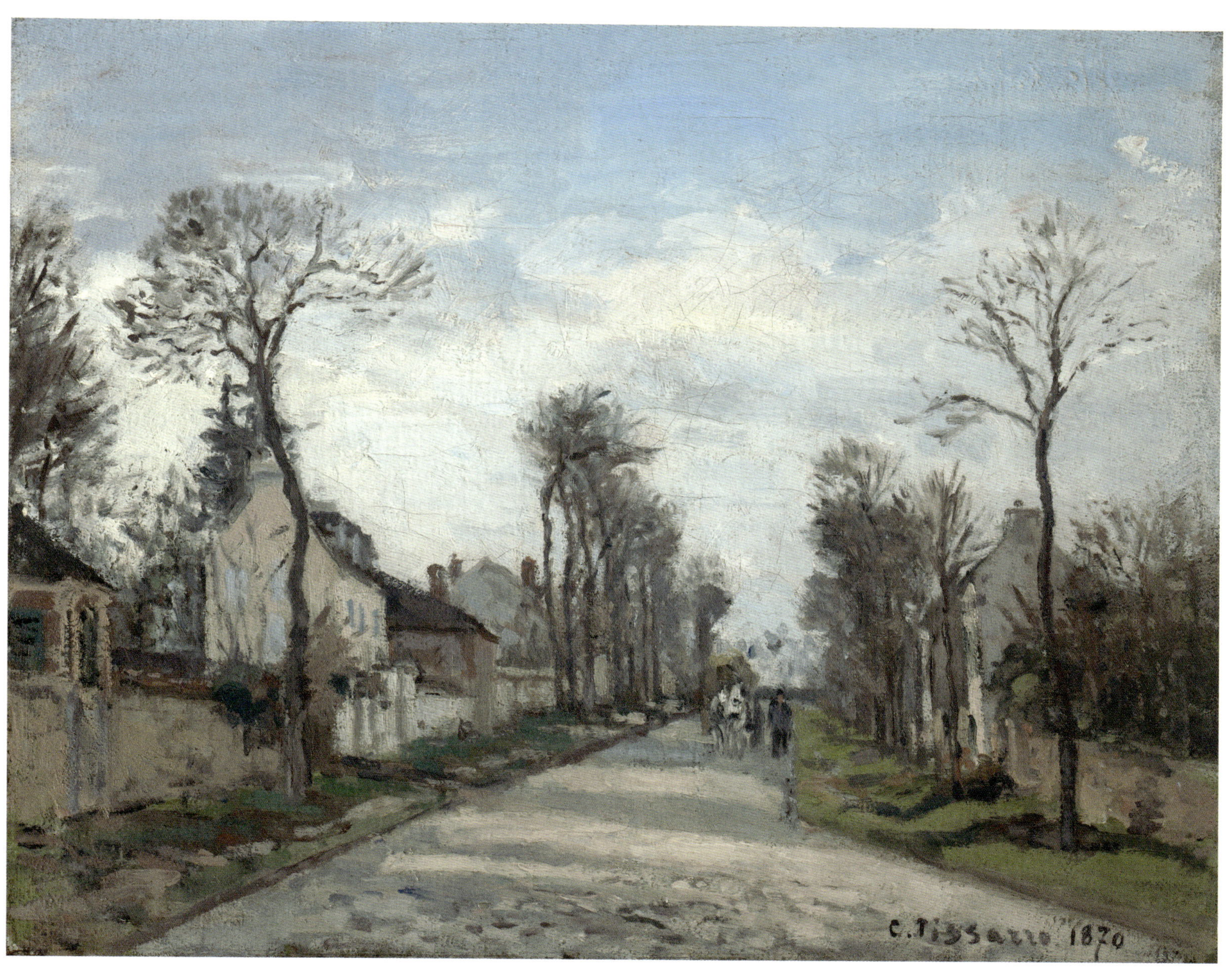
C. Pissarro 1870

22 CAMILLE PISSARRO French, 1830–1903

Road: Rain Effect

1870
Oil on canvas
40 x 56.2 cm
Signed and dated lower left: C. Pissarro 1870
Acquired by Sterling and Francine Clark, 1941
1955.825

ROAD: RAIN EFFECT IS ONE OF A NUMBER OF PAINTINGS Pissarro made soon after his move to Louveciennes, near Versailles. Pissarro's work during this period is marked by a sense of exploration and experimentation, closely attuned to that of his colleagues Renoir and Monet. It was in the years preceding the first Impressionist exhibition of 1874 that these artists began their collective project to capture ephemeral atmospheric effects in their paintings.

Like many works from this era, *Road: Rain Effect* focuses on the particulars of time and place. Pissarro knew this road well, as he not only lived on it (his house is visible at left in the present composition) but also painted it on numerous occasions. A familiar motif offered the opportunity to explore the variations of light, atmosphere, and weather. Indeed, the fact that the receding road was a traditional staple of the landscapist's art might have helped Pissarro see past the motif itself and more fully home in on his quest to portray particular light effects.

Road: Rain Effect is a superb example of the possibilities inherent in the new manner of painting. The wet road, worked up in small, splotchy brushstrokes, shimmers in the pale light and captures colorful reflections. The grass on either side of the road is visibly moist and varied in color and texture. The open, seemingly improvised brushwork is a result of the new stress on painting outdoors and directly in front of the subject. Yet for all this emphasis on capturing a particular moment, close study reveals that the picture was worked on in a number of sessions, suggesting that its casual and at times rough look was studied and deliberate.

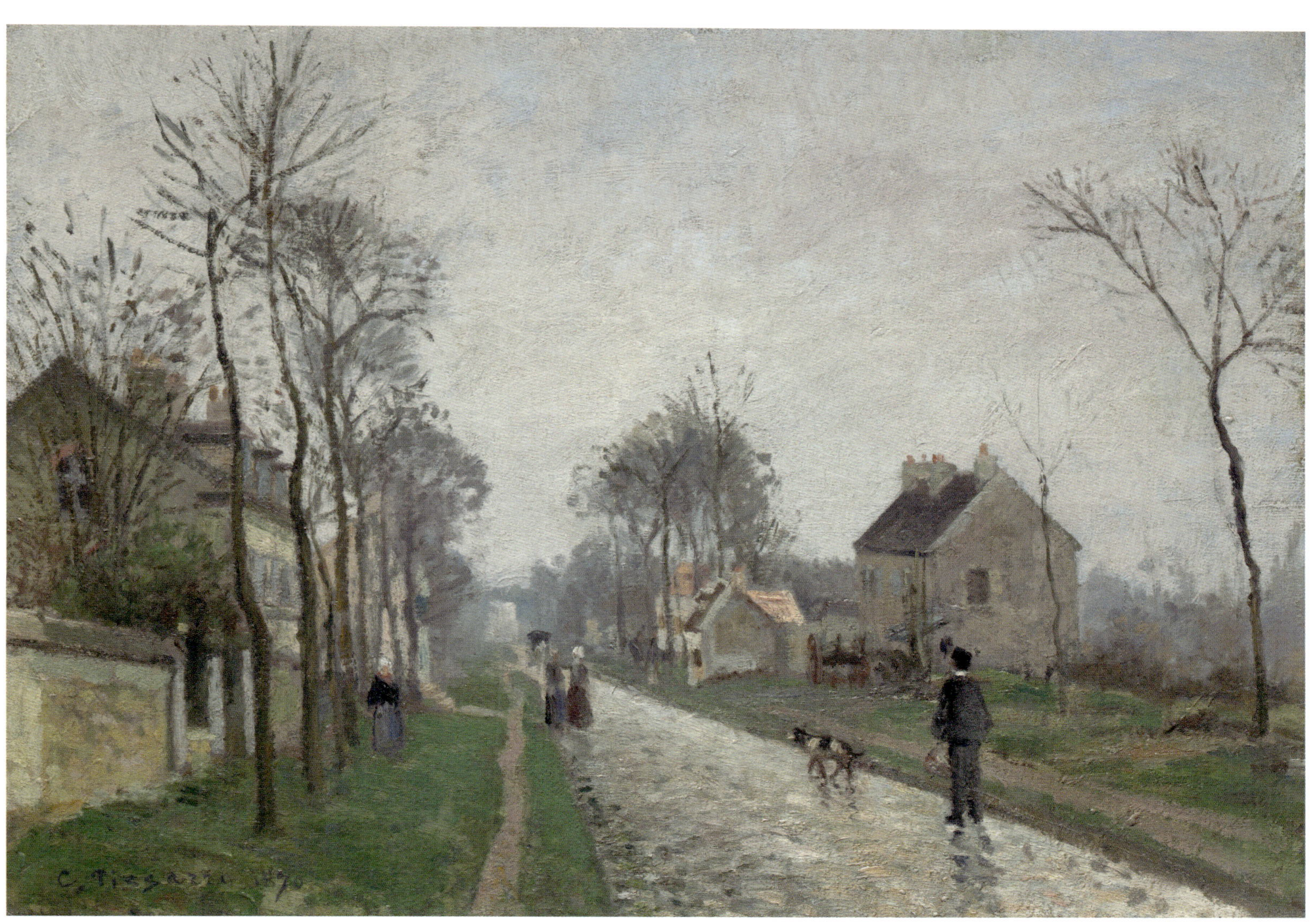

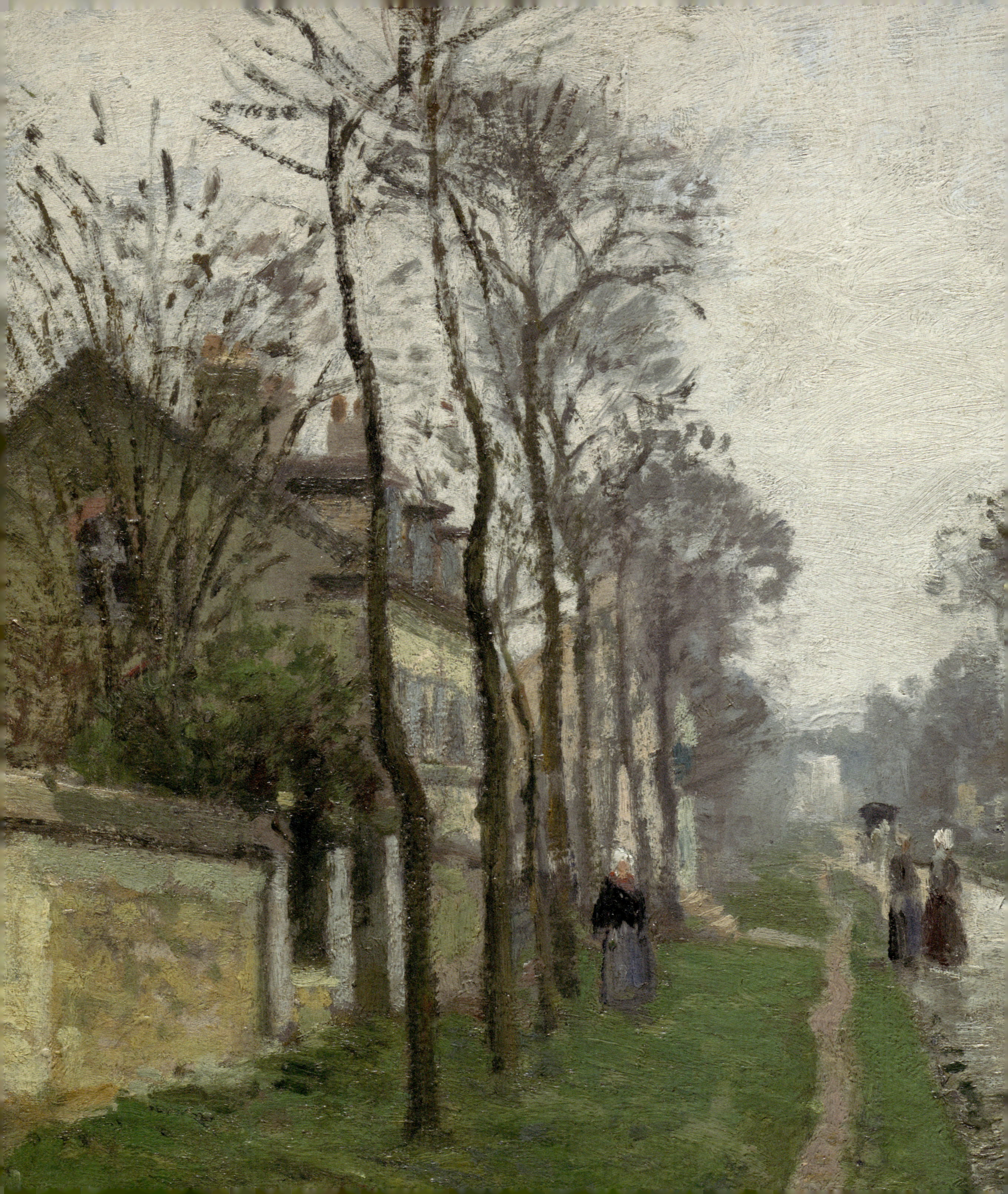

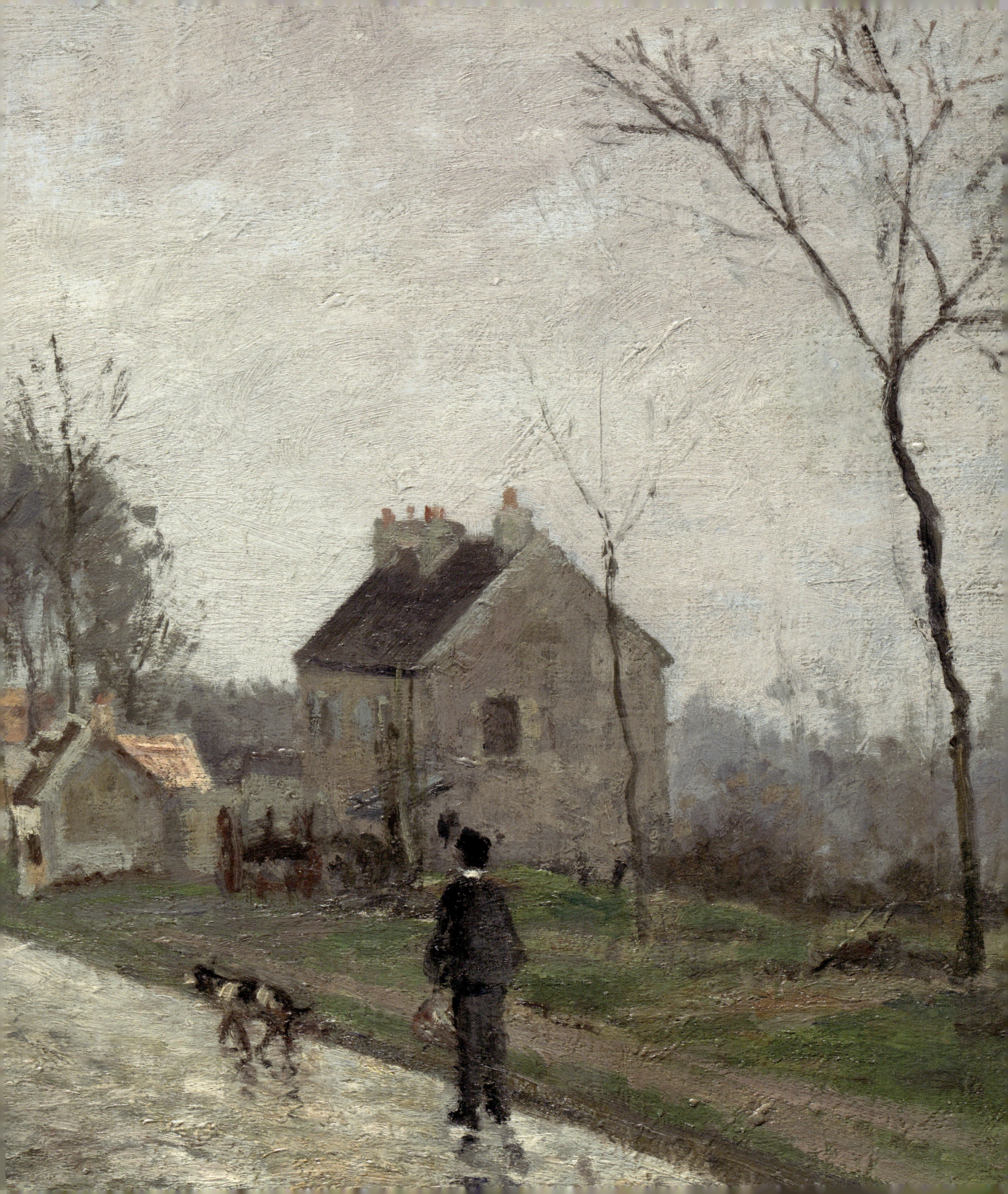

23 CAMILLE PISSARRO French, 1830–1903

The River Oise near Pontoise

1873
Oil on canvas
46 x 55.7 cm
Signed and dated lower right: C. Pissarro. 1873
Acquired by Sterling and Francine Clark, 1945
1955.554

THE RIVER OISE NEAR PONTOISE is one of four pictures Pissarro painted in 1873 that feature the Chalon et Brenot alcohol distillery, located on the outskirts of Pontoise, northwest of Paris. During this time Pissarro lived across from the factory and would have seen it every day. Intensely evocative of a summer scene, the picture is also exceptionally compact and finely resolved. Painted just a year before the first Impressionist exhibition, *The River Oise near Pontoise* is a bravura achievement of nascent Impressionism that shows the artist's delight in the transient effects of light. Especially effective is Pissarro's shifting focus from the scudding clouds to the warm foreground haze, from the sharply geometric rooftops to their blurred echo in the water. Described by Paul Cézanne as "a man to consult and something like the good lord," Pissarro was often seen as the father of Impressionism and is the only artist who exhibited at all eight Impressionist shows.

Pissarro's paintings of the Chalon et Brenot factory show a commitment (in line with other Impressionist painters) to include nontraditional modern features in his landscapes. In some of Pissarro's paintings of the factory in Pontoise, the buildings and their black smoke dominate and overwhelm the scene, while in others they become harmonious parts of a congruent whole. In *The River Oise near Pontoise*, for instance, the factory nestles comfortably into its bucolic surroundings. Even the smoke that comes out of the chimneys seems to mesh with the clouds in the sky. In fact, it is possibly the factory's subdued presence in the landscape that attracted Sterling Clark to the painting. While Clark was a great admirer of Pissarro, he tended to prefer the artist's brighter landscape pictures, particularly praising Pissarro's mastery of the color green, and to avoid his depictions of urban subjects.

Like many of Pissarro's other works, *The River Oise near Pontoise* is painted with crisp brushwork, and there is no sign of any preparatory drawing on the canvas, suggesting a rapid execution directly in front of the subject. For all this, it is a finely resolved composition in a compact space. There is no doubt that the painting was born from a sustained period of studying the motif before brush was laid to canvas.

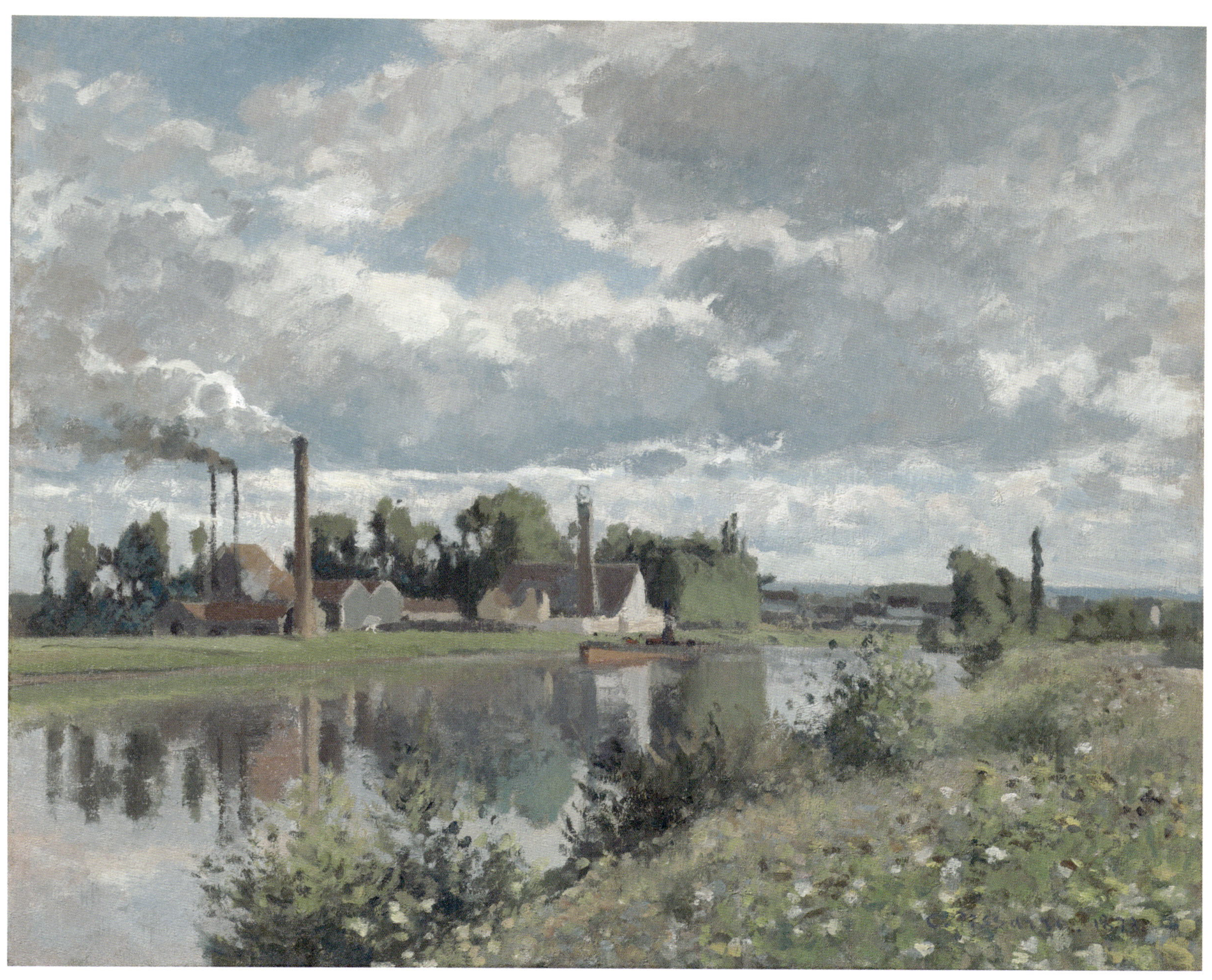

24 CAMILLE PISSARRO French, 1830–1903

Piette's House at Montfoucault

1874
Oil on canvas
46.4 x 68.6 cm
Signed and dated lower left: C. Pissarro. 1874
Acquired by Sterling and Francine Clark, 1941
1955.826

PIETTE'S HOUSE AT MONTFOUCAULT was painted in the winter after the first Impressionist exhibition of 1874, when Pissarro was struggling to support himself and his family. He had moved from Pontoise to stay with his friend and colleague Ludovic Piette-Montfoucault at Piette's farm in Melleray, a remote village between Chartres and Le Mans. Pissarro took the opportunity to paint scenes of rural life and to study figures and animals of the countryside. During his time there he produced fifteen pictures, a handful of them portraying the area covered by snow.

While the challenge of painting snow was taken up by several Impressionist artists, it was rarely depicted so forcefully as in *Piette's House at Montfoucault*. Pissarro rendered thick impastos of white on tree branches that seem to bend under the weight of the paint. The canvas is covered throughout with whites and gray blues indicative of the winter landscape. Pissarro was encouraged by Piette to paint winter scenes, and the year before, he had described how exciting winter could be to the critic Théodore Duret. In *Piette's House at Montfoucault* the white snow is stunningly luminous, the palpably frigid atmosphere wholly enveloping the trees, buildings, and two figures in the center of the composition.

Although some of Pissarro's snow scenes were painted from indoors looking out, it is likely that *Piette's House at Montfoucault* was painted outdoors. This is suggested not only by the vantage point of the composition, which is clearly away from the house, but also from investigation of the picture's surface. The rapid brushstrokes with few revisions attest to the fact that the artist was painting quickly in cold, wet surroundings. Pissarro brushed on pure color in places, letting the whites and blues mix on the canvas as he added subsequent layers. There also seems to be a slight clumsiness to the forms of some of the trees, which is likely due to the adverse working conditions. The forthright engagement with the extremes of nature adds to the painting's allure.

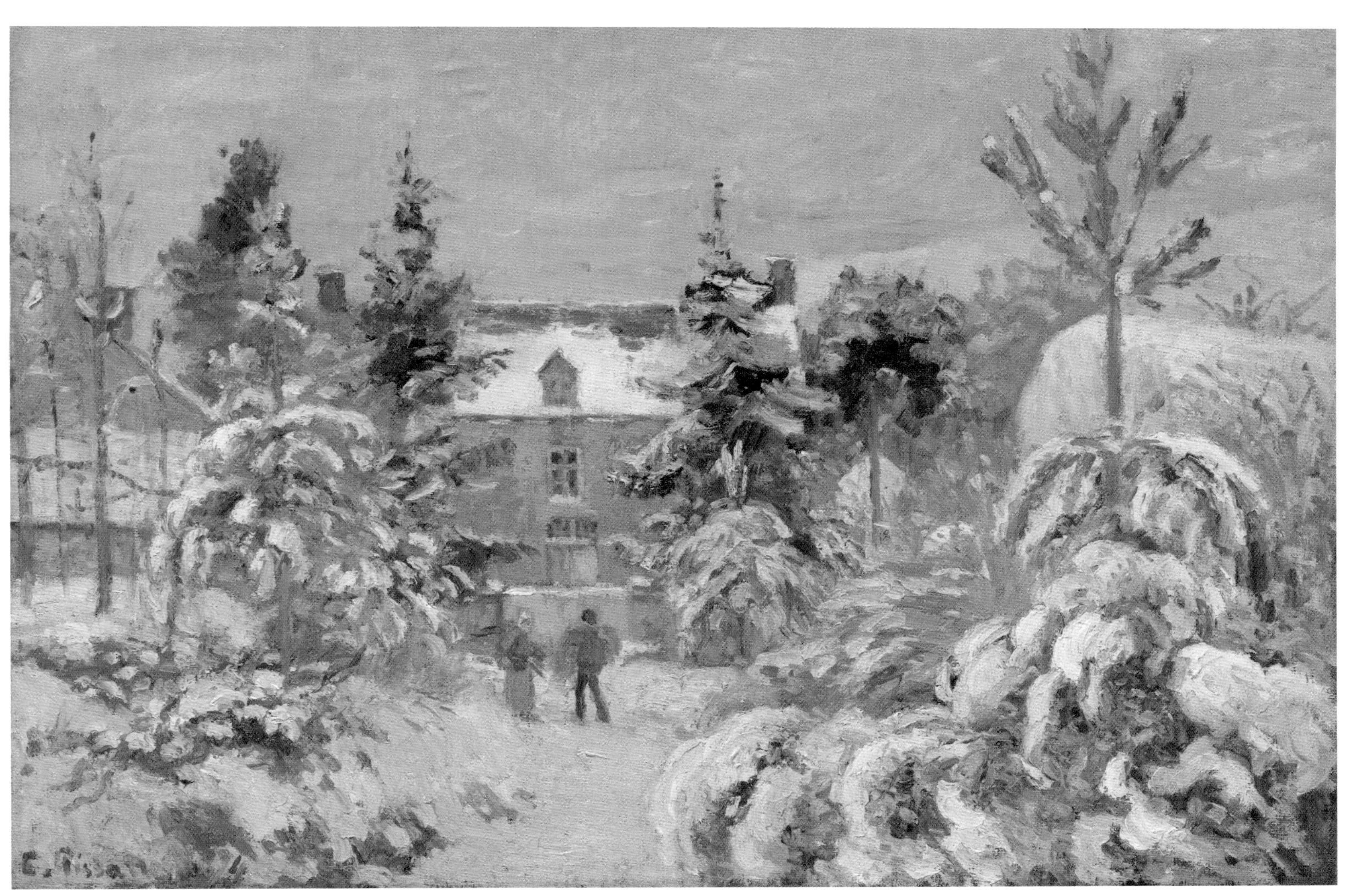

25 CAMILLE PISSARRO French, 1830–1903

Saint-Charles, Éragny

1891
Oil on canvas
81 x 65 cm
Signed and dated lower left: C. Pissarro. 1891.
Acquired by Sterling and Francine Clark, 1933
1955.524

PISSARRO PAINTED *SAINT-CHARLES, ÉRAGNY* IN 1891, just as he was moving away from the Neo-Impressionist style that he had been using since 1885. In this period he had become friendly with Georges Seurat and Paul Signac, who both inspired Pissarro to begin painting in a more "scientific" pointillist manner. Pissarro grew excited about this new technique that embraced the color theories of Michel Chevreul, which involved breaking color tones into their constituent parts. Both his Impressionist colleagues and the critics were skeptical of the stylistic change, and they pressured him to return to his old manner of painting. The artist maintained a strict ideological faith in the pointillist approach for a few years, but as early as 1888 he began to question whether it was possible to "combine the purity and simplicity of the dot with the fullness, suppleness, liberty, spontaneity, and freshness of sensation postulated by our impressionist art."

In *Saint-Charles, Éragny*, executed a few years after this soul-searching question was posed, the fruits of Pissarro's laborious project of combining the merits of two different styles of painting are in evidence. In place of pointillist dots, he used a range of flicks, dabs, and angled strokes that create a weave-like continuity across the surface of the painting. Furthermore, Pissarro's dense application of paint (often in three or four layers) results in a highly textured surface that enhances the tonal vibrations throughout the picture. Although he eschewed the dot painting of Neo-Impressionism, Pissarro maintained the practice of creating shocking tonal effects through juxtaposing wildly vivid colors, such as the brilliant pinks placed next to blues and greens in the lower left corner of the canvas. Pissarro's deft painterly touch in controlling and manipulating these patches of bright colors creates optical illusions that cause parts of the canvas to advance while others recede.

The sheer visual intensity of *Saint-Charles, Éragny* is unmatched in any of Pissarro's subsequent paintings. On a trip to Paris soon after the work was finished, Pissarro found that several of his pictures had recently sold. Adding to this good fortune, he managed to sell the present picture to Paul Durand-Ruel, who had initially discouraged Pissarro's foray into Neo-Impressionism. Even with this taste of success, Pissarro could not help but continue his artistic development. Just a few years later he would once again reinvent himself as a painter of modern urban life.

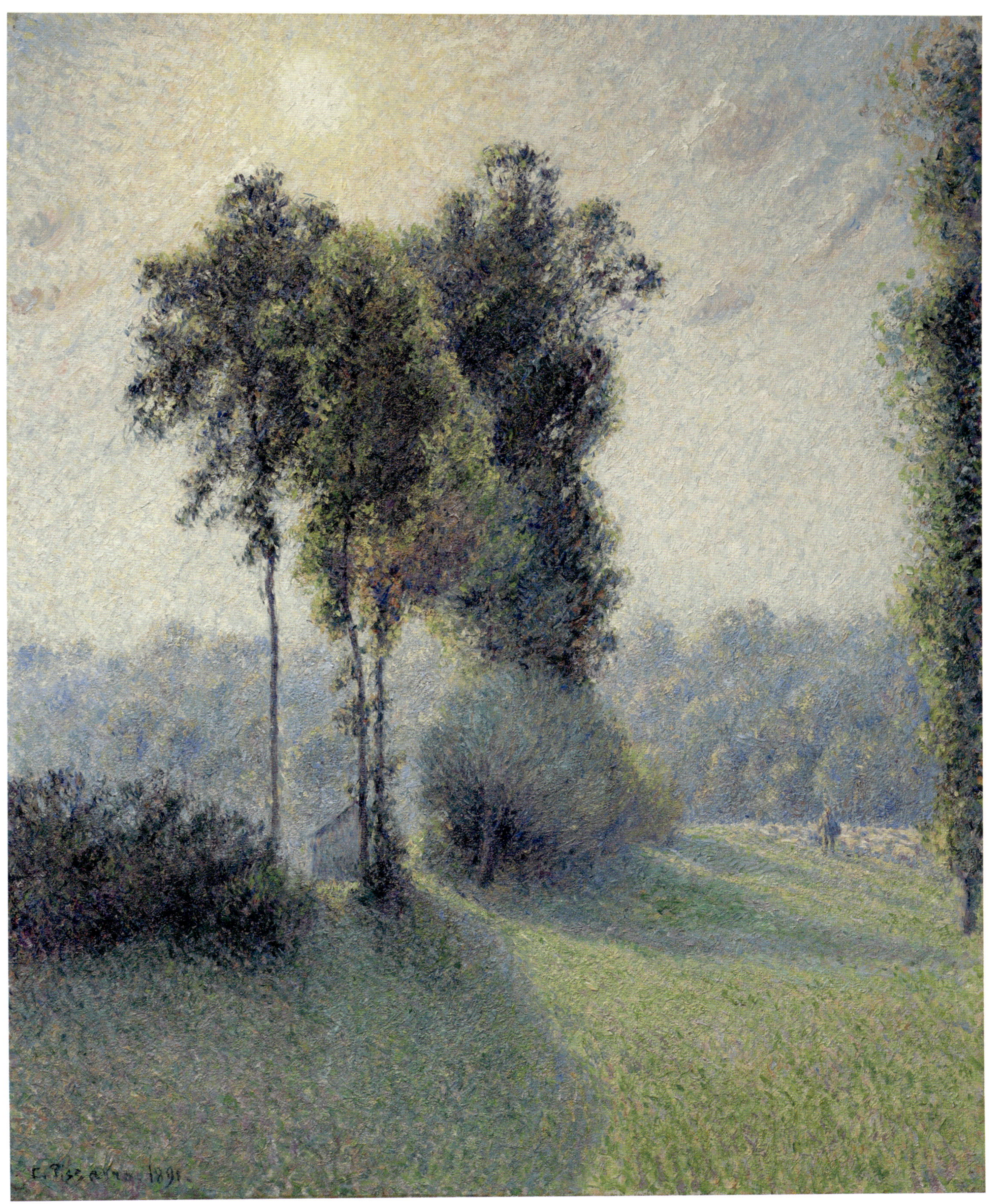
C. Pissarro. 1891.

26 **CAMILLE PISSARRO** French, 1830–1903

Port of Rouen: Unloading Wood

1898
Oil on canvas
74 x 92 cm
Signed and dated lower left: C. Pissarro. 98
Acquired by the Clark in honor of John E. Sawyer (Institute Trustee, 1962–89), 1989
1989.3

DURING THE FIRST THIRTY YEARS OF HIS CAREER, Pissarro focused almost exclusively on painting landscapes of rural France. In the last decade of his life he dramatically shifted toward depicting urban scenes. He took up his new specialty with a marked intensity, creating more than three hundred pictures of the cities of Dieppe, Le Havre, Paris, and Rouen from 1896 to 1903. As with his previous landscapes, Pissarro often produced these urban scenes in series in which he explored the same subject from different angles or in varied light conditions. These city pictures sold well, allowing the aging artist to attain financial stability for the first time in his life.

Port of Rouen: Unloading Wood typifies Pissarro's urban scenes in its stress on the modern landscape. While Rouen was a beautiful city boasting a picturesque market square and massive medieval cathedral, Pissarro turned away from its center and concentrated on its industrialized port. Painted from a hotel room that overlooked the scene, the composition is dominated by a large ship that has brought wood down the river to the city. On the far bank, factory buildings are clouded in the smoke from no less than five large steamships. Many of Pissarro's urban scenes focus on the hustle and bustle of crowds, but this painting is almost bereft of people and is more austere in its emphasis on large industrial structures. The few workers portrayed near the central ship seem dwarfed by the scale of enterprise around them.

Pissarro has managed to infuse the gritty scene with a certain elegance. The painting is divided into four horizontal planes (the quay, river, warehouses, and sky) that are punctuated by the verticality of the ships' masts and plumes of smoke. Thick passages of richly colored paint and the articulated shimmer on the river's surface add a pronounced sensuousness to this otherwise bleak landscape. Indeed, when first viewing the budding industrial complex around Rouen's riverbanks, Pissarro is known to have commented that what he saw was "ugly and banal," but he nevertheless insisted that it could be "as beautiful as Venice."

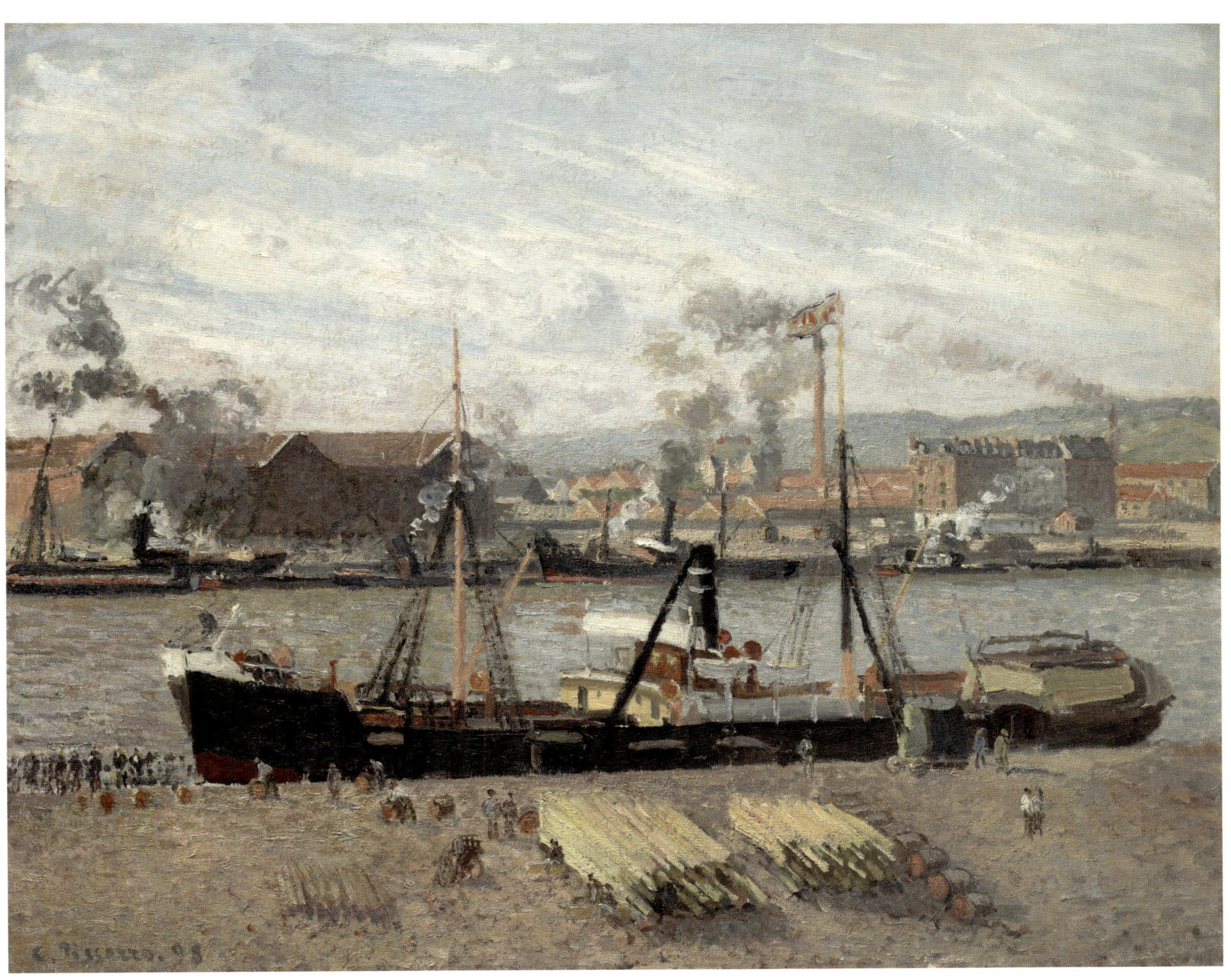
C. Pissarro. 98

27 **CAMILLE PISSARRO** French, 1830–1903

The Louvre from the Pont Neuf

1902
Oil on canvas
60.8 x 92.5 cm
Signed and dated lower left: C. Pissarro. 1902.
Acquired by Sterling and Francine Clark, 1950
1955.558

THE LOUVRE FROM THE PONT NEUF IS ONE OF MORE THAN FORTY variants on this motif, which Pissarro painted near the end of his life, depicting the view across the Seine toward the extraordinary palace and museum that has dominated central Paris since the late twelfth century. Pissarro captured the scene from the window of an apartment he had rented just off the place Dauphine on the Île de la Cité. The base of the pedestal for the equestrian sculpture of Henri IV on the Pont Neuf is visible in the lower left corner, though the picture focuses on the play of light across the water and the buildings of the great palace. In December 1902 Pissarro wrote of the beauty of the Parisian landscape, with its "winter effects that charmed me in their finesse," remarking that "the view of the Louvre on the Seine is an absolutely exquisite and captivating subject." Though he was in ill health and would die the following year, Pissarro had not lost his drive to paint.

Since the mid-1890s, Pissarro had turned his focus toward urban scenes, exploring different atmospheric conditions of a singular subject as well as the hustle and bustle of modern life. It was during this period in Paris that he remarked to his son that it sometimes took "six or seven sessions" to complete even a modest canvas. This technique, similar to that of Monet, was in stark contrast to Pissarro's rapid practice of his youth; the resulting canvases from this late period have an air of intense deliberation and concentration. The Clark's picture is exemplary in this regard, with its intricate weave of small brushstrokes built up out of innumerable individual moments of perception.

Like many of Pissarro's late cityscapes, *The Louvre from the Pont Neuf* filters out most signs of the modern city. Despite including the tourist boats that dot the river and the occasional sightseers that obliquely allude to contemporary Parisian life at the time, he framed the view to focus on the venerable former royal palace. As a young artist Pissarro had railed against the established painting practices of the day, once suggesting that the Louvre be burned down so as to free art from the shackles of tradition. In so lovingly rendering the buildings he had once longed to destroy, one senses a tempered older man coming to terms with his youth.

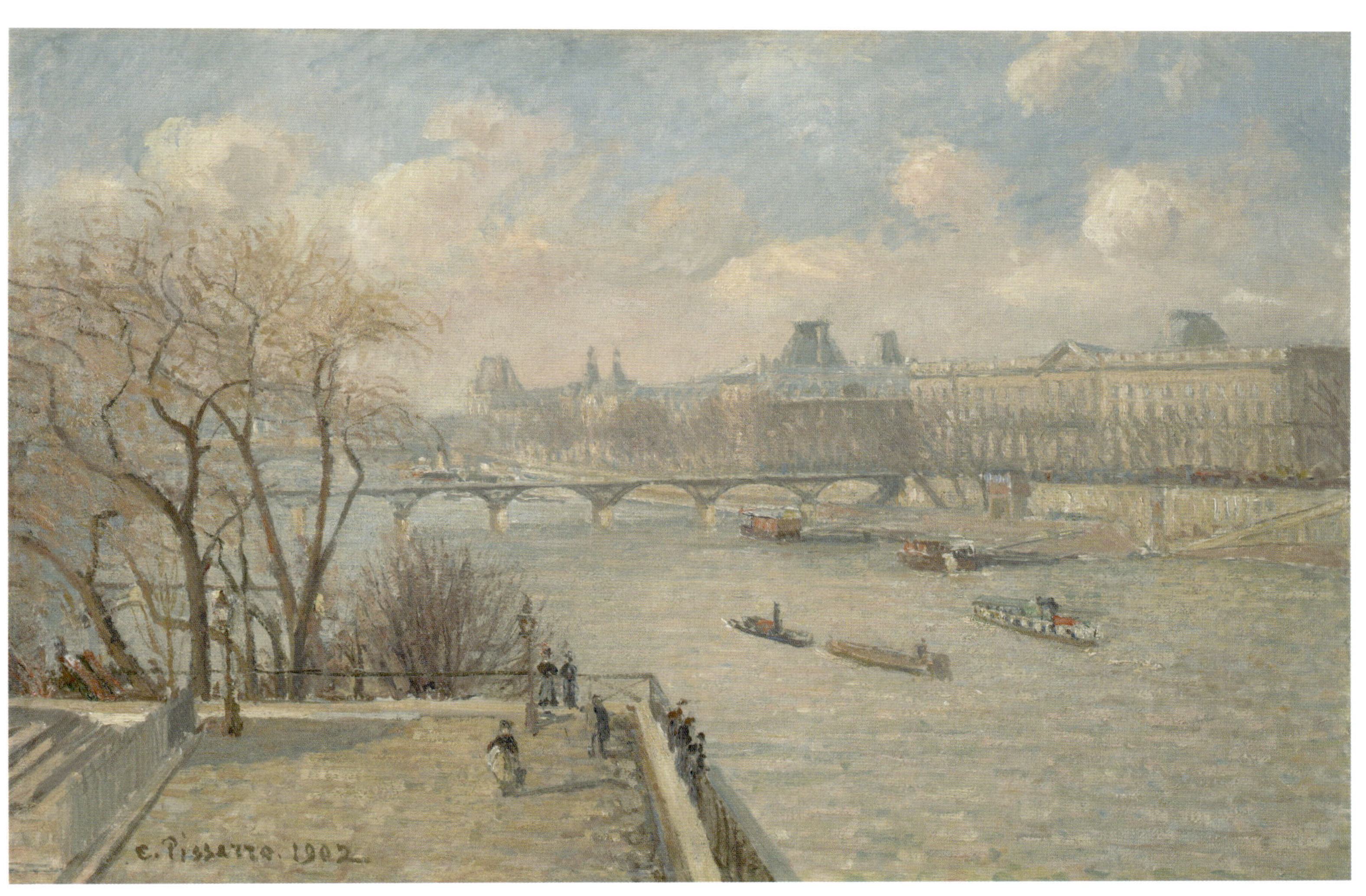
C. Pissarro. 1902.

28 HONORÉ DAUMIER French, 1808–1879

The Print Collectors

c. 1860–63
Oil on panel
30.8 x 40.6 cm
Signed lower right: h. Daumier
Acquired by Sterling and Francine Clark, 1925
1955.696

FAMOUS FOR HIS CARICATURES OF MODERN FRENCH LIFE, which appeared in publications such as *Le Charivari,* Daumier was also an innovative painter, draftsman, and sculptor. *The Print Collectors* is one of about forty paintings that explore the life of artists and collectors—one of his favorite subjects. In general, Daumier's paintings avoid the overt satire of his popular prints. *The Print Collectors* is no exception: it portrays four connoisseurs huddled together and focused on a single sheet held by the central figure. Prints and albums cover the table, and the background walls are lined with paintings. The setting is likely not a gallery but the private study of the central figure, who is attired in a dressing gown, leaning back as if bringing the print into focus. There is little trace of Daumier's often biting mockery in *The Print Collectors*; for the most part, the figures are respectfully depicted engaged in a serious endeavor. The one possible exception lies in the man at the upper right, who juts forward and stares with an intensity somewhat out of proportion to the nature of the proceedings. The painting's small size, dark palette, and tightly gathered figures all contribute to create a feeling of intimacy and close friendship. Daumier's expressive brushwork further accentuates the quiet pleasure of the scene.

Daumier's fascination with connoisseurs and collectors of art was most likely fueled by the artist's direct interaction with the art-loving public, as well as his awareness of and engagement with the artistic traditions of the past and present. In fact, it has been suggested that Daumier was reacting in certain ways to the aristocratic scenes of Jean-Louis-Ernest Meissonier that celebrated the French heritage of connoisseurship and collecting. Reaching back to older traditions, Daumier used dramatic lighting and chiaroscuro in a way that has drawn comparisons to the seventeenth-century master Rembrandt van Rijn. Sterling Clark himself explicitly made this connection, commenting that *The Print Collectors* was "as good as any Rembrandt." Clark was a great admirer of Daumier's oeuvre, acquiring more than twenty of the artist's works on paper and two of his paintings.

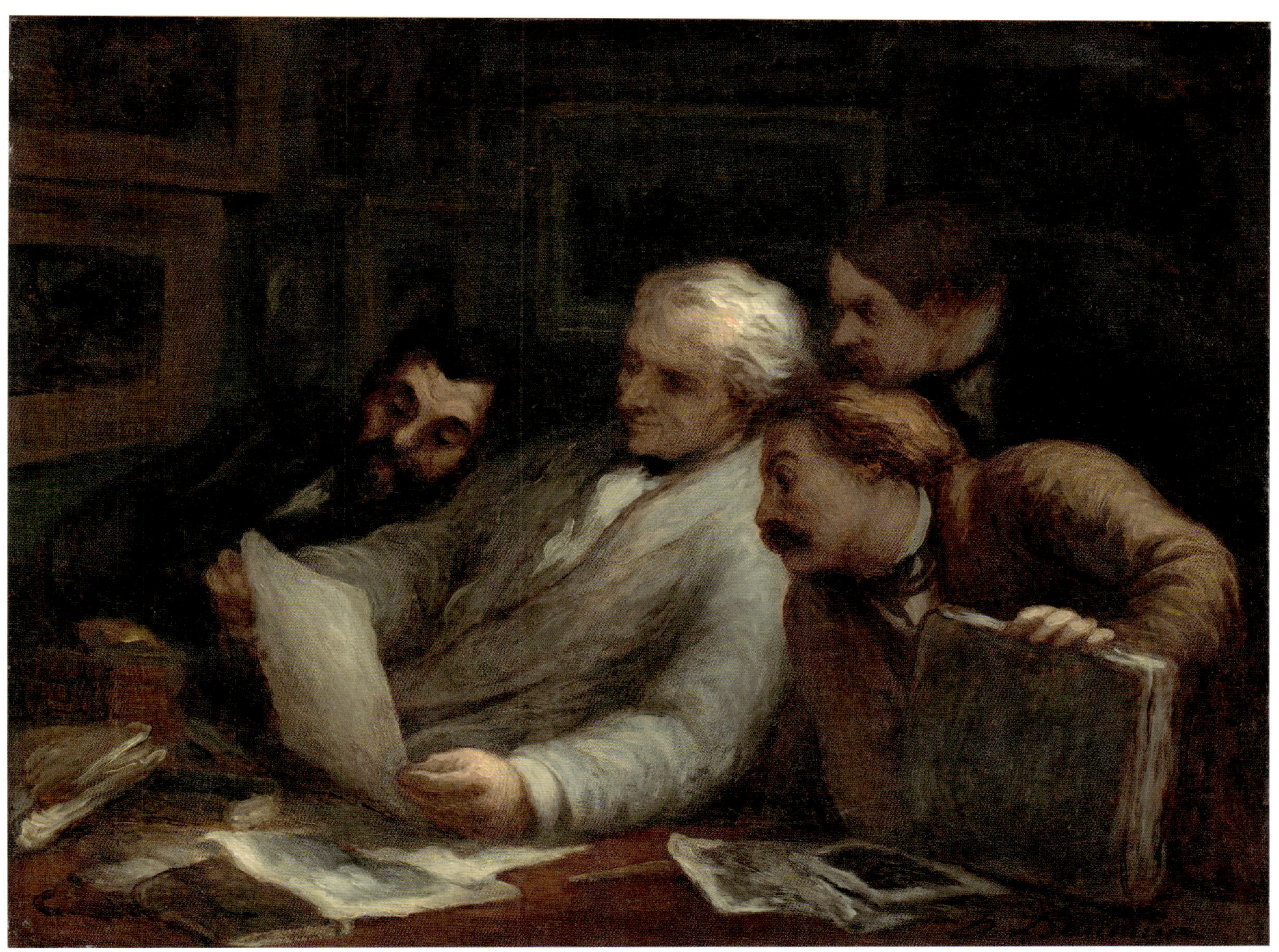

29 MARY CASSATT American (active in France), 1844–1926

Offering the Panal to the Bullfighter

1873
Oil on canvas
100.6 x 85.1 cm
Signed, dated, and inscribed lower right: Mary S. Cassatt. / Seville. / 1873.
Acquired by Sterling and Francine Clark, 1947
1955.1

FIRST EXHIBITED AT THE PARIS SALON OF 1873, *Offering the Panal to the Bullfighter* is one of four large paintings Cassatt produced during a seven-month stay in Seville. Typical of her work from that sojourn, the canvas depicts a scene focusing on local customs. A young woman and a handsome bullfighter are engaged in a flirtatious discussion. The woman offers a glass of water to the bullfighter, who dips a piece of *panal*—honeycomb or sponge sugar—into the water to make a refreshing drink. He is evidently quenching his thirst after a turn in the bullring. He has draped his red cloak over one shoulder and across his body, although his elaborately decorated *traje de luces* (suit of lights) is prominently visible.

Completed when Cassatt was still struggling to find success as an artist, *Offering the Panal to the Bullfighter* shows a painter in command of her craft. Cassatt had received a traditional academic training at the Pennsylvania Academy of the Fine Arts in Philadelphia and in Paris under Jean-Léon Gérôme (see cats. 38–40). With its thick and fluid brushwork, however, *Offering the Panal to the Bullfighter* is clearly indebted more to the painterly style of the seventeenth-century Spanish artist Diego Velázquez. She acknowledged as much when she first encountered Velázquez's work in Madrid, praising the artist's "fine and simple manner" and commenting that "one learns how to paint" in Spain.

Cassatt did not exhibit with the Impressionists until four years after painting *Offering the Panal*, but the contemporary subject matter, freely applied paint, and careful observation of light suggest a kindred purpose to that of the young avant-garde artists. Edgar Degas, who would grow close to Cassatt, commented early on that in her work he found "someone who feels as I do." *Offering the Panal to the Bullfighter* was painted during a key phase in Cassatt's development, when she was seeking new influences and beginning to create a personal style. In less than two years after the picture was completed, she moved to Paris and, in conjunction with a group of contemporaries, began painting images of modern life in a unique and inimitable manner.

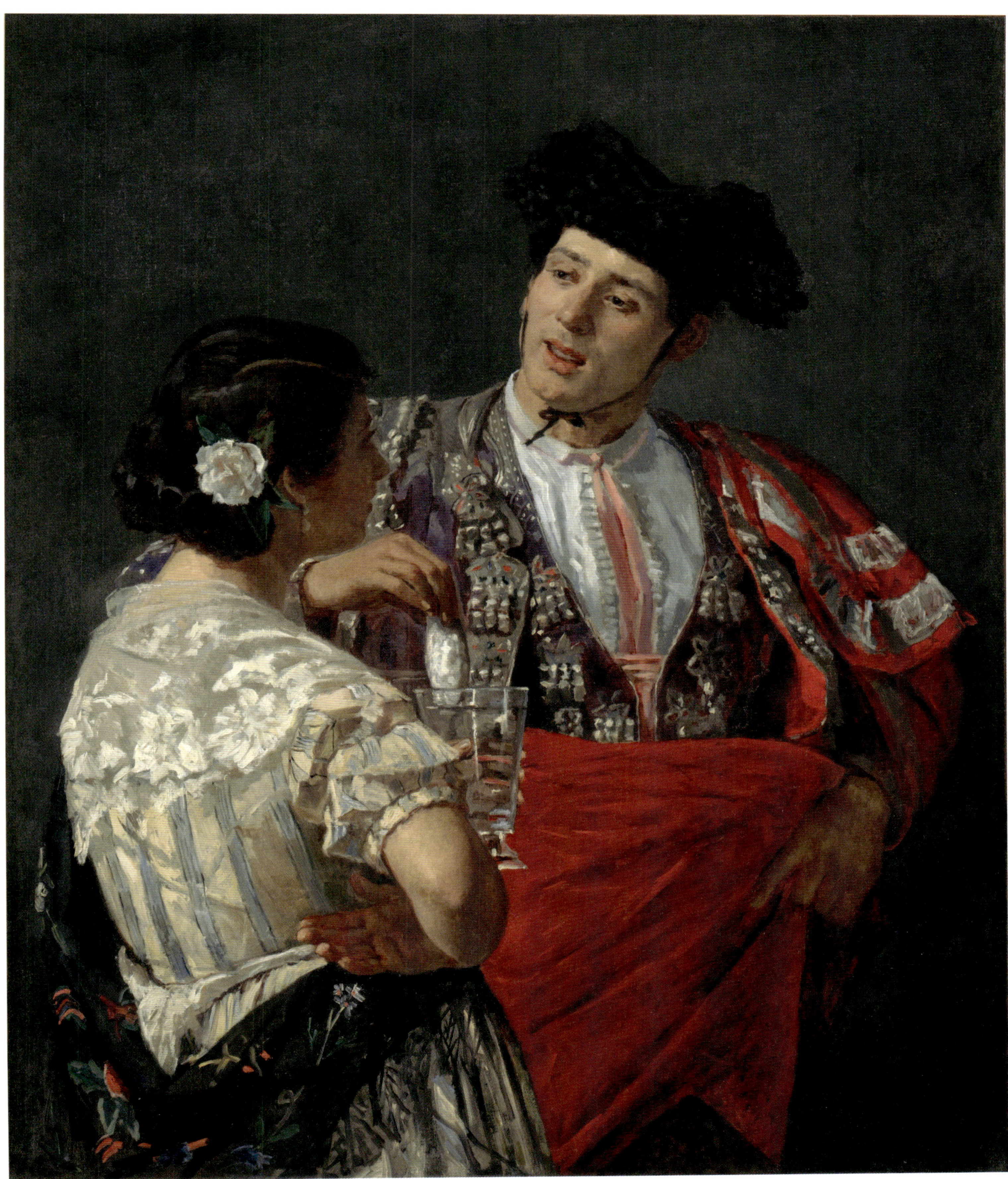

30 ÉDOUARD MANET French, 1832–1883

Interior at Arcachon

1871
Oil on canvas
39.2 x 54 cm
Signed lower right: Manet
Acquired by Sterling and Francine Clark, 1943
1955.552

INTERIOR AT ARCACHON WAS PAINTED in the immediate aftermath of the 1870 siege of Paris during the Franco-Prussian War. After enduring an especially harsh winter while serving in the national guard, Manet left Paris to join his family in the south of France in February of 1871. They first spent time in Bordeaux, and then in March moved to the small coastal town of Arcachon, where they rented a newly built chalet overlooking the bay. A traditional fishing village, Arcachon was developing into a seaside resort following the introduction of a railroad line from Bordeaux in 1857. The view out the window of the Clark's painting gives a sense of the locale, with the corner of a beachside villa on the left and the dunes of Cap Ferret visible across the blue-green water. The beauty and calm of the village must have been a welcome respite from the continuing chaos in Paris, which was engulfed in the turmoil of the Commune.

Interior at Arcachon offers a view of a relaxed family on holiday. Manet's wife, Suzanne, sits comfortably in an armchair, gazing at the ocean while taking a break from writing a letter. Her son Léon, an open book on his lap, stares thoughtfully into space, a cigarette or, more likely, a pen held to his lips. A preliminary drawing probably done on the spot depicts Léon standing by the window reading a letter, although Manet redrew him seated sideways on the chair, as he appears in the final canvas. The Clark's picture may have been painted using the drawing as a guide rather than from life. Throughout it, there is a sense of carefree intimacy and warmth, and in places the work is no more than a sketch. Manet seems to have executed *Interior at Arcachon* quickly and without restraint, the rough finish and patches of bare canvas adding a visceral immediacy to the painting, which is probably unfinished.

Sterling Clark was undoubtedly drawn to the work for its clear manifestation of Manet's masterful brushwork as well as its domestic subject matter. It is possible, however, that he also felt sympathy for the circumstances of the painting's creation. Clark bought *Interior at Arcachon* in 1943, as World War II raged throughout Europe after he and Francine had fled from Paris.

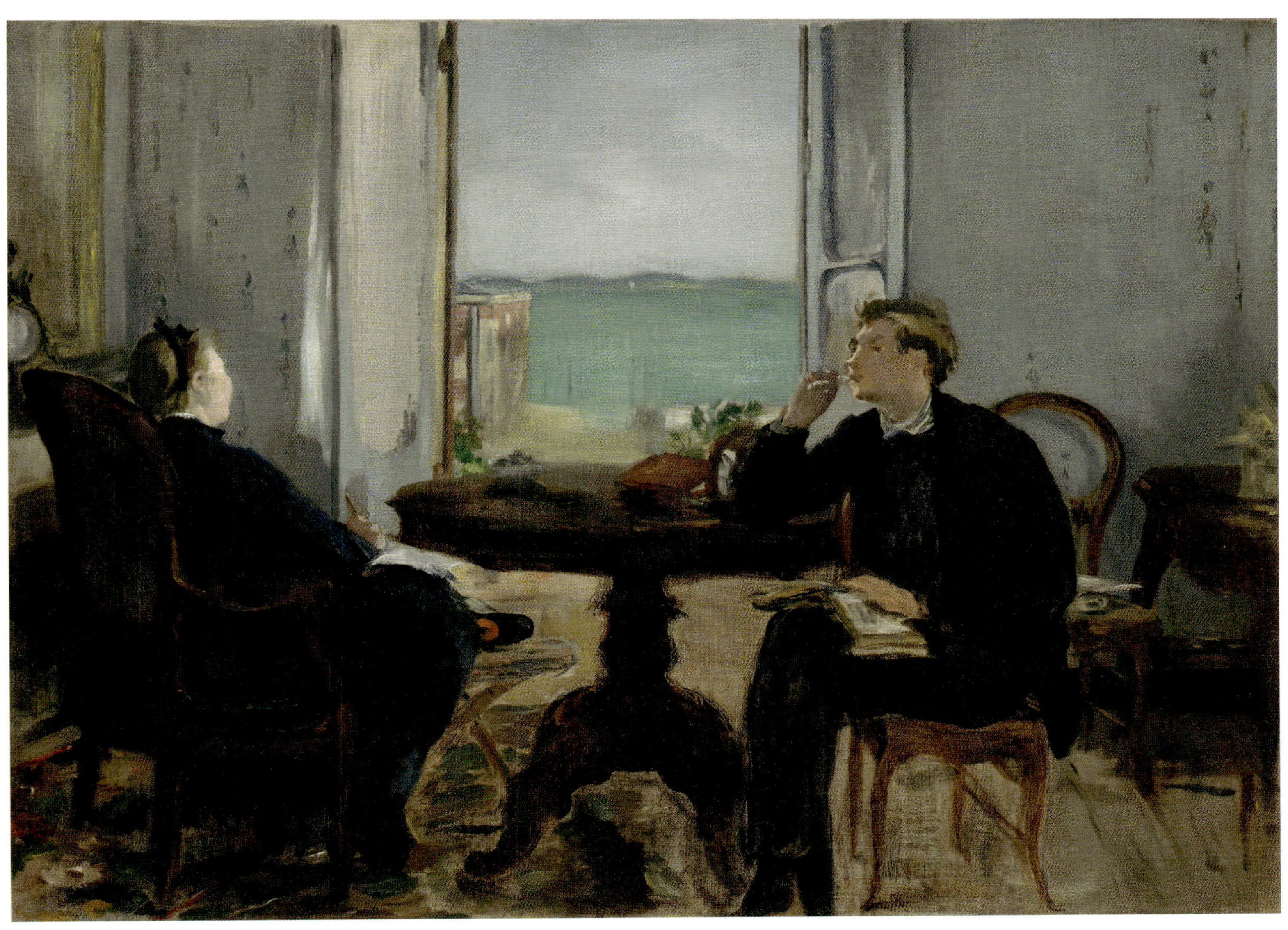

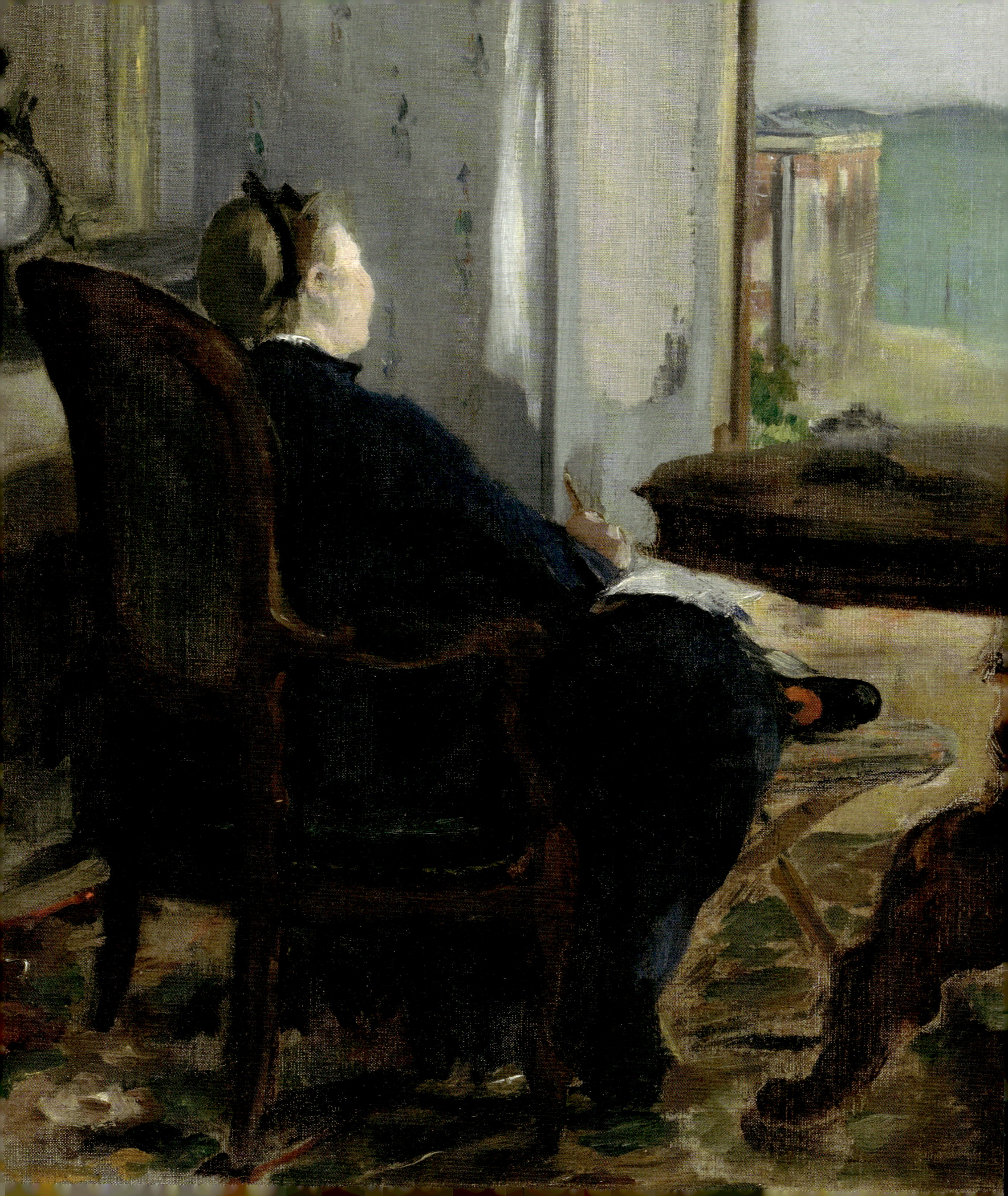

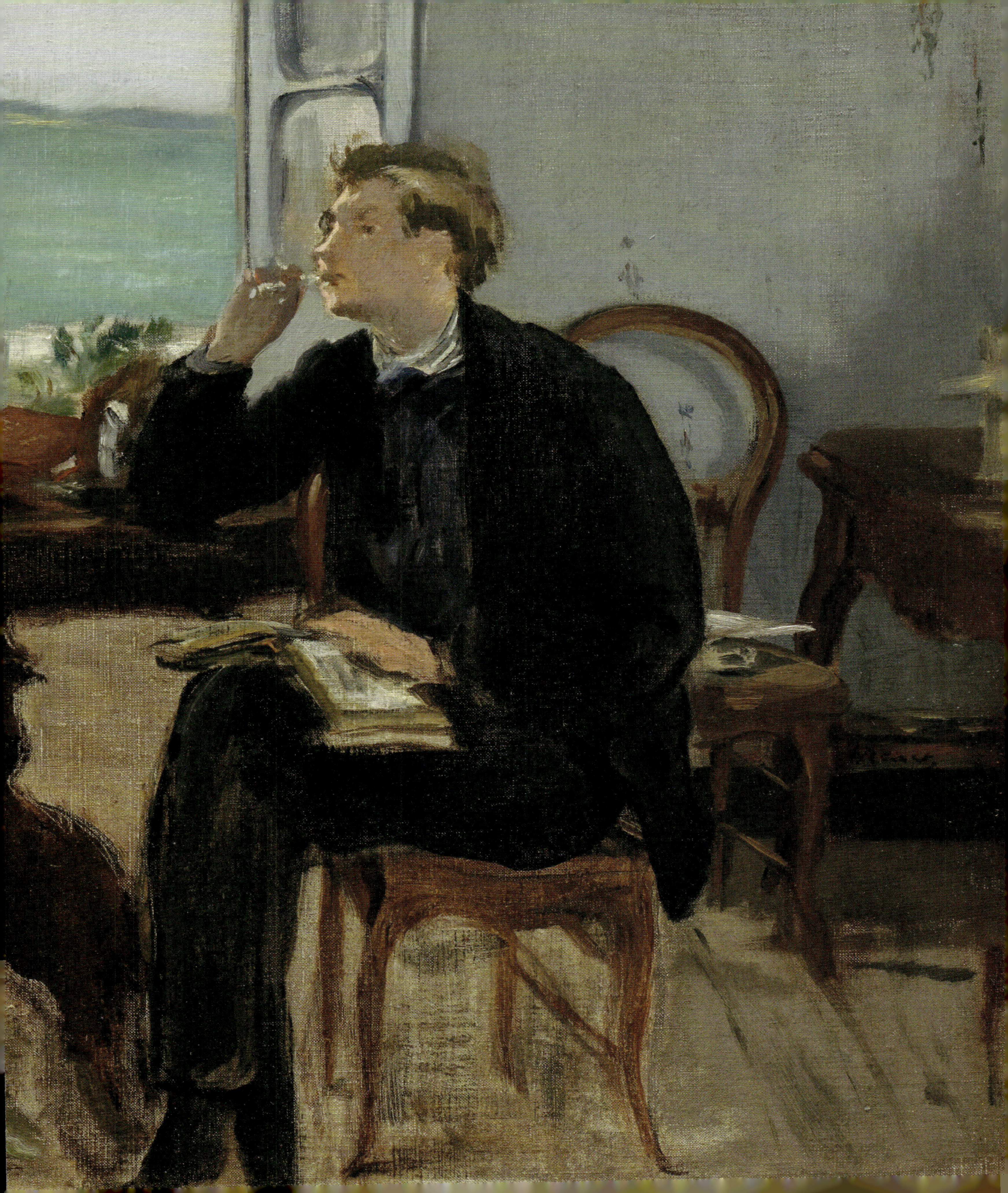

31 ÉDOUARD MANET French, 1832–1883

Moss Roses in a Vase

1882
Oil on canvas
55.9 x 34.6 cm
Signed lower right: Manet.
Acquired by Sterling and Francine Clark, 1923
1955.556

MOSS ROSES IN A VASE is one of a number of small flower pieces completed toward the end of Manet's life, when illness made working on a large scale difficult. Manet is said to have composed these images from bouquets brought by friends and well-wishers visiting the artist in his studio in the rue d'Amsterdam in Paris, where at the time he was able to paint easel pictures more comfortably while seated. In these compositions Manet depicted a variety of blossoms—lilacs, tulips, pansies, pinks, clematis, peonies, as well as roses—that he arranged in glass vases (scholars have identified seven) of various shapes and sizes. Despite his debilitation, he brought to these late works an intensity and verve that make them among his most appealing productions.

Although the Clark's painting relates to Manet's last group of still lifes, it was in all likelihood executed in the late summer of 1882, when the artist and his wife were renting a house in Rueil, outside Paris. Manet, already extremely ill, confined himself to depicting images of the garden as well as small still lifes of fruits or flowers. He likely painted *Moss Roses* from flowers taken from the garden rather than brought by friends. The heavy hourglass-shaped vase is unique in Manet's flower paintings and perhaps belonged to the rented house. Indeed, the composition inverts his usual design in such works, in which a spray of flowers explodes from a small, delicate vase; here, the vase dominates the strongly vertical canvas, and we suspect the artist was most challenged to convey the light refracting through the curving glass and the solid weight of the vase on the tabletop. The bouquet, brilliantly expressed with a painterly virtuosity that suggests no loss of artistic ability, is stuffed somewhat unceremoniously into the mouth of the container. Yet it is this very informality and casualness that give the painting such a striking immediacy, a slice of life recorded with honesty and directness and with a minimum of pretension. The insistent symmetry of the composition is offset by the slight leftward tilt of the vase, which introduces a subtle dynamism, and by the lonely rosebud lying on the tabletop, a poignant metaphor, perhaps, of the artist's trying physical state.

Manet's later still lifes were often painted as gifts for friends or, on occasion, sold. The early provenance of *Moss Roses in a Vase* is not known, and the picture first made an appearance with the dealer Georges Bernheim in the early twentieth century. Sterling Clark purchased it in 1923, describing it as "a wonderfully fine Manet." Although Clark did not collect Manet with the enthusiasm he bestowed on other Impressionists like Renoir, Monet, or Pissarro, he did eventually come to own two fine ink drawings, a small oil depicting the artist's wife and her son in an interior at Arcachon (cat. 30), painted in 1871, and a pastel of the actress Méry Laurent, drawn the same year as *Moss Roses in a Vase*.

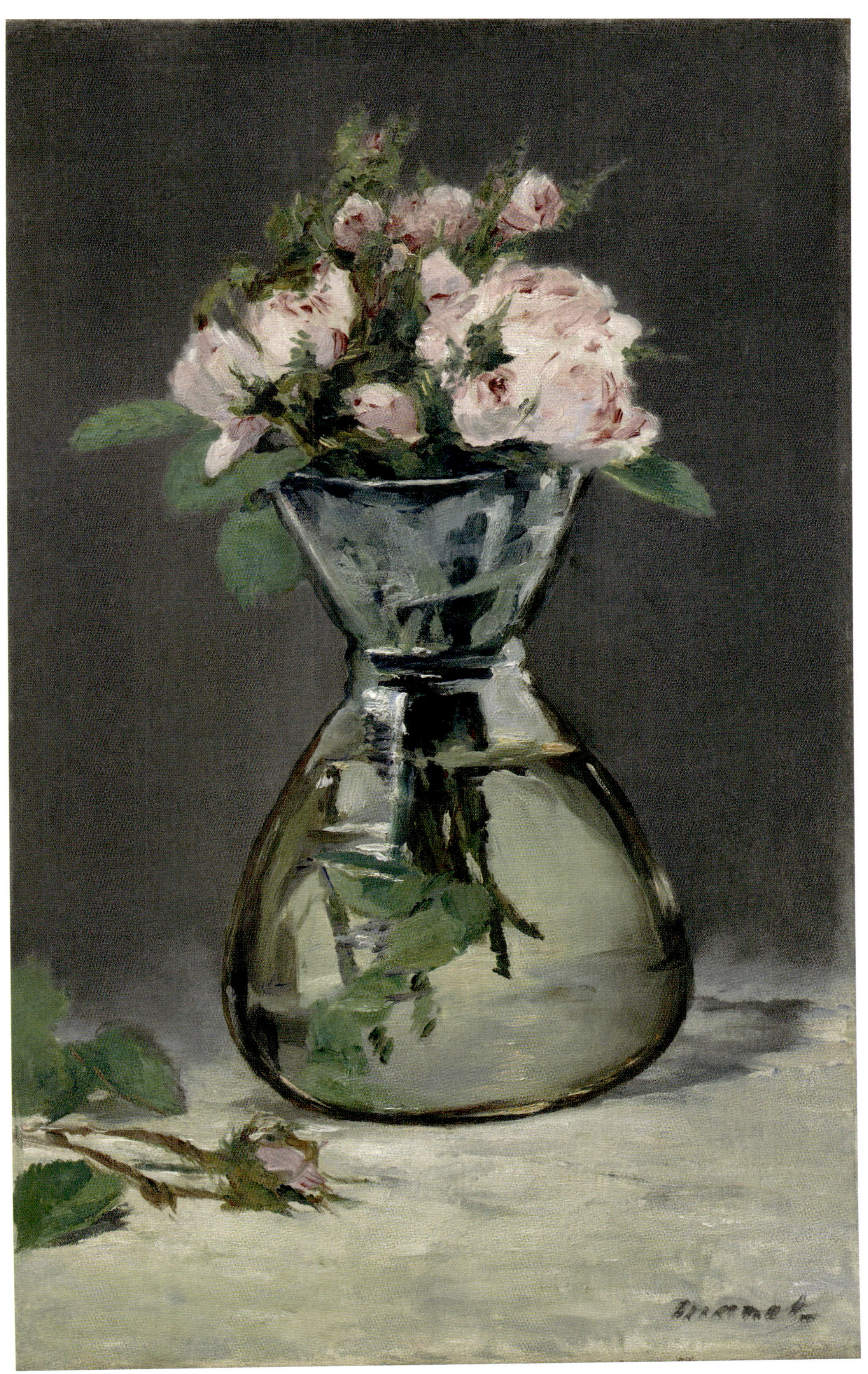

32 HENRI FANTIN-LATOUR French, 1836–1904

Roses in a Bowl and Dish

1885
Oil on canvas
45.9 x 63 cm
Signed and dated upper right: Fantin. 85
Acquired by Sterling and Francine Clark, 1936
1955.734

FANTIN-LATOUR FIRST FOUND SUCCESS as a still-life painter in the 1860s, and throughout the rest of his career flower pieces provided him with financial stability, though he also painted portraits and allegorical subjects. While his early still lifes were often complicated compositions that included fruit, flowers, and tablewares, by the mid-1880s Fantin-Latour increasingly concentrated on isolating flowers as the focus of his paintings. *Roses in a Bowl and Dish* is a superb example of his work from this period, and it showcases the artist's talent in portraying the myriad forms and colors of his subject.

Roses were among Fantin-Latour's favored flowers, as he capitalized on the fashion for cultivated roses in Victorian England, where many of his paintings were sold. The painter and critic Jacques-Émile Blanche singled out the artist's mastery of this subject, writing that "it is in his roses that Fantin has no equal. The rose—so complicated in its design, contours, and color, in its rolls and curls, now fluted like the decoration of a fashionable hat, round and smooth, now like a button or a woman's breast—no one understood them better than Fantin." Indeed, each rose in the Clark's picture seems to have its own distinct identity yet is in harmony with the larger composition.

As was often his practice, the artist has left almost half of the picture surface a thinly painted off-white, through which one can see the weave of the canvas. Seen against this background, the meticulously rendered forms of the roses and their vibrant colors jump out at the viewer, emphasizing the dimensionality and monumental presence of the flowers.

Roses in a Bowl and Dish was first owned by Charles Ricada, who was a friend of the artist and whose portrait Fantin-Latour submitted to the 1889 Salon. Sterling Clark bought the picture in 1936 and often used it as a touchstone for other still-life paintings he was considering. Francine Clark, however, seemed even more enamored than Sterling with Fantin-Latour's oeuvre, describing him as a first-rate master whose work was "as fine as Renoir at times."

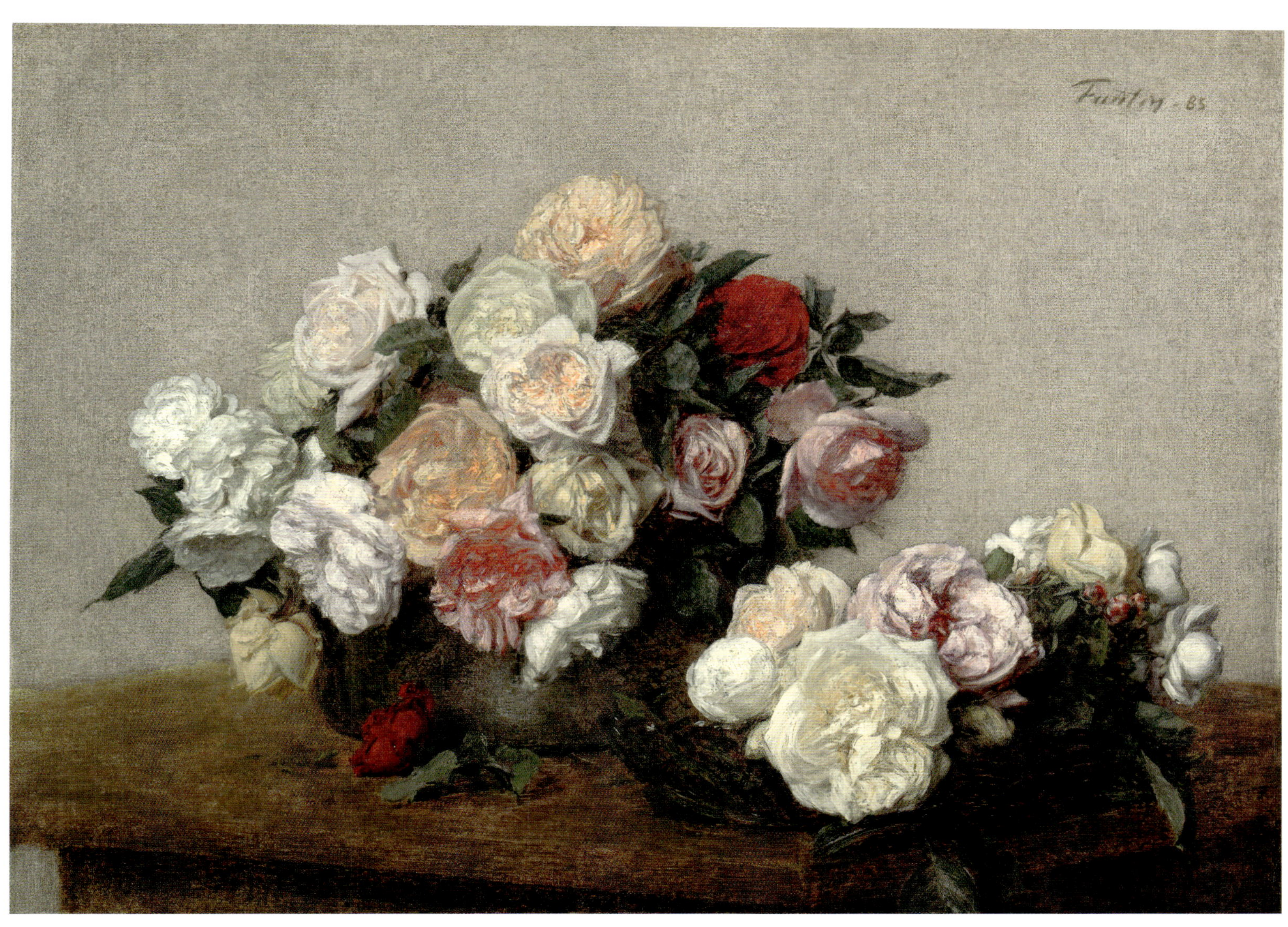
Fantin - 85

33 CAROLUS-DURAN French, 1838–1917

The Artist's Gardener

1893
Oil on canvas
81.6 x 54.8 cm
Signed upper left: Carolus-Duran.; dated and inscribed upper right: St Aygulf, Obre 1893.
Acquired by Sterling and Francine Clark, 1941
1955.40

CAROLUS-DURAN'S SUCCESS AS A PORTRAIT PAINTER was founded on his highly sophisticated portraits of wealthy sitters. The Clark painting, by contrast, portrays a working-class man identified as the artist's gardener when the picture was first exhibited in 1894. The canvas depicts a ruddy man with wild hair, wearing a wrinkled overcoat. The subject stares beyond the viewer in a confident and almost impatient manner, as though he was stopped by the artist and is eager to get back to his work. The loose brushwork and subdued palette, consisting almost entirely of earth tones, add to the feeling that the painting was executed quickly. According to the inscription in the upper right corner, the portrait was made in October 1893 at Saint-Aygulf, a town on the French Riviera where Carolus-Duran owned a sumptuous villa.

Although Carolus-Duran's initial interest in producing paintings such as the present picture likely was fueled by a desire to free himself from the staid format of his acclaimed society portraits, *The Artist's Gardener* was favorably received and quickly bought by the English horticulturist and art collector William Robinson. It exemplifies some of the virtues of Carolus-Duran's work, described by the critic Théodore Duret as "clear cut, absolute, [and] frank . . . the impression emerging from this virile art is a singular one of vitality and power."

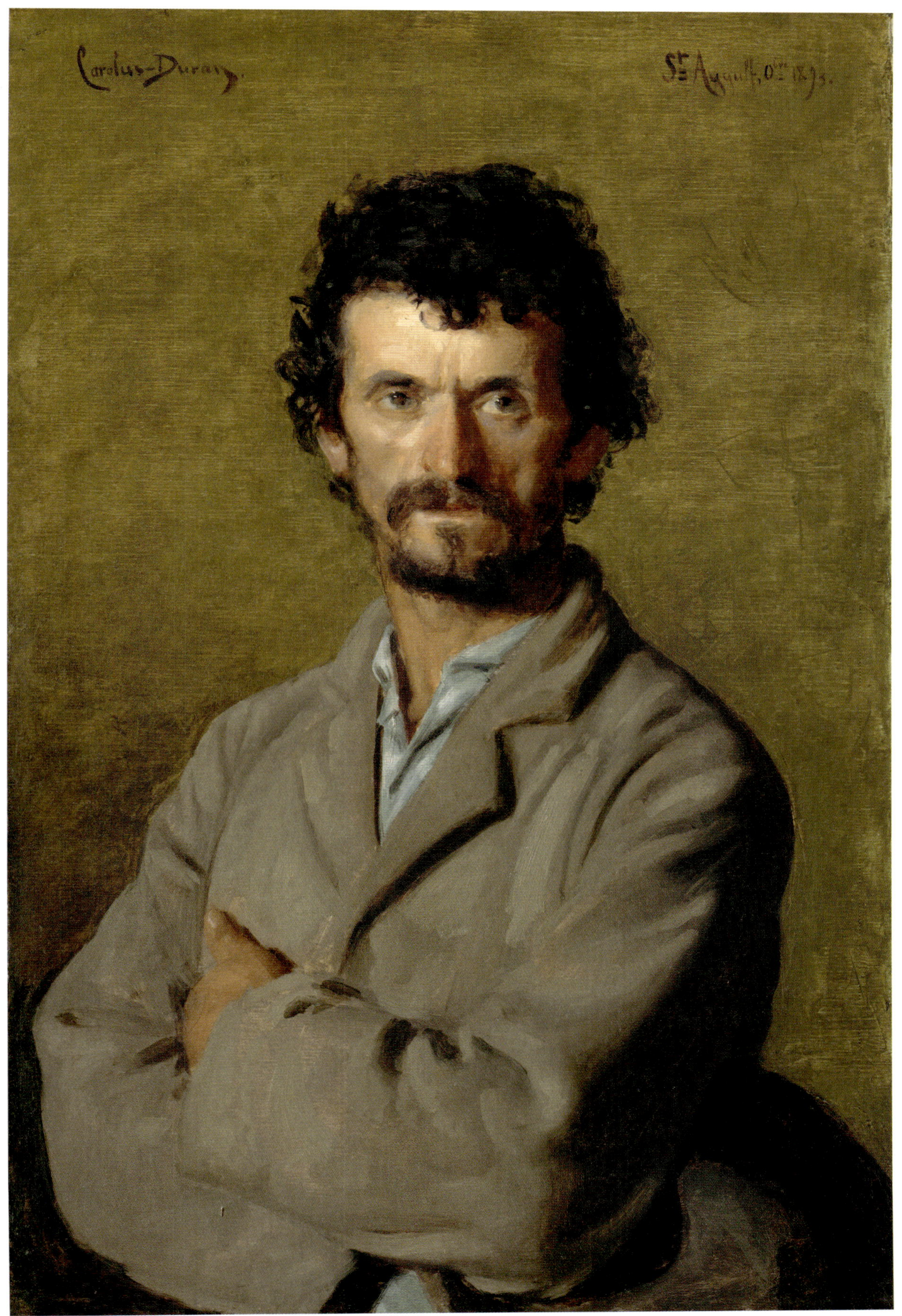
Carolus-Duran

34 EDGAR DEGAS French, 1834–1917

Self-Portrait

c. 1857–58
Oil on paper mounted on canvas
26 x 19.1 cm
Acquired by Sterling and Francine Clark, 1948
1955.544

BETWEEN 1854 AND 1864 DEGAS PAINTED, drew, and etched about forty self-portraits. This was a period in which the young artist was voraciously studying the works of the Old Masters, traveling through Italy, and honing his painterly craft. Almost none of these portraits were sold to the public and most of them stayed in the artist's studio until his death in 1917. Degas seems to have been drawn to self-portraiture as a subject through which he could experiment with different approaches, emulating artists as varied as Raphael, Rembrandt, Ingres, and Courbet.

Like many of Degas's self-portraits, this example is small and intimate. Its tightly cropped composition focuses the viewer's attention on the artist's face, and the outward gaze combined with the play of shadows seems to invite a close scrutiny of a soul-searching young man. Portrayed with a striking bohemian hat, orange cravat, and incipient beard, the subject is the epitome of an artist who is coming into his own. Degas executed this painting when he was about twenty-three years old and traveling through Italy for the first time. *Self-Portrait* is thus situated at a crucial moment in the artist's development. Having trained briefly in the academic tradition in Paris, Degas began to create his own style during his Italian sojourn. It is perhaps telling that Degas executed this and many other small works of this period in oil on paper. He may have chosen the medium, associated with student sketches and preparatory studies for larger subjects, because he viewed *Self-Portrait* more as a painterly exercise than a finished work.

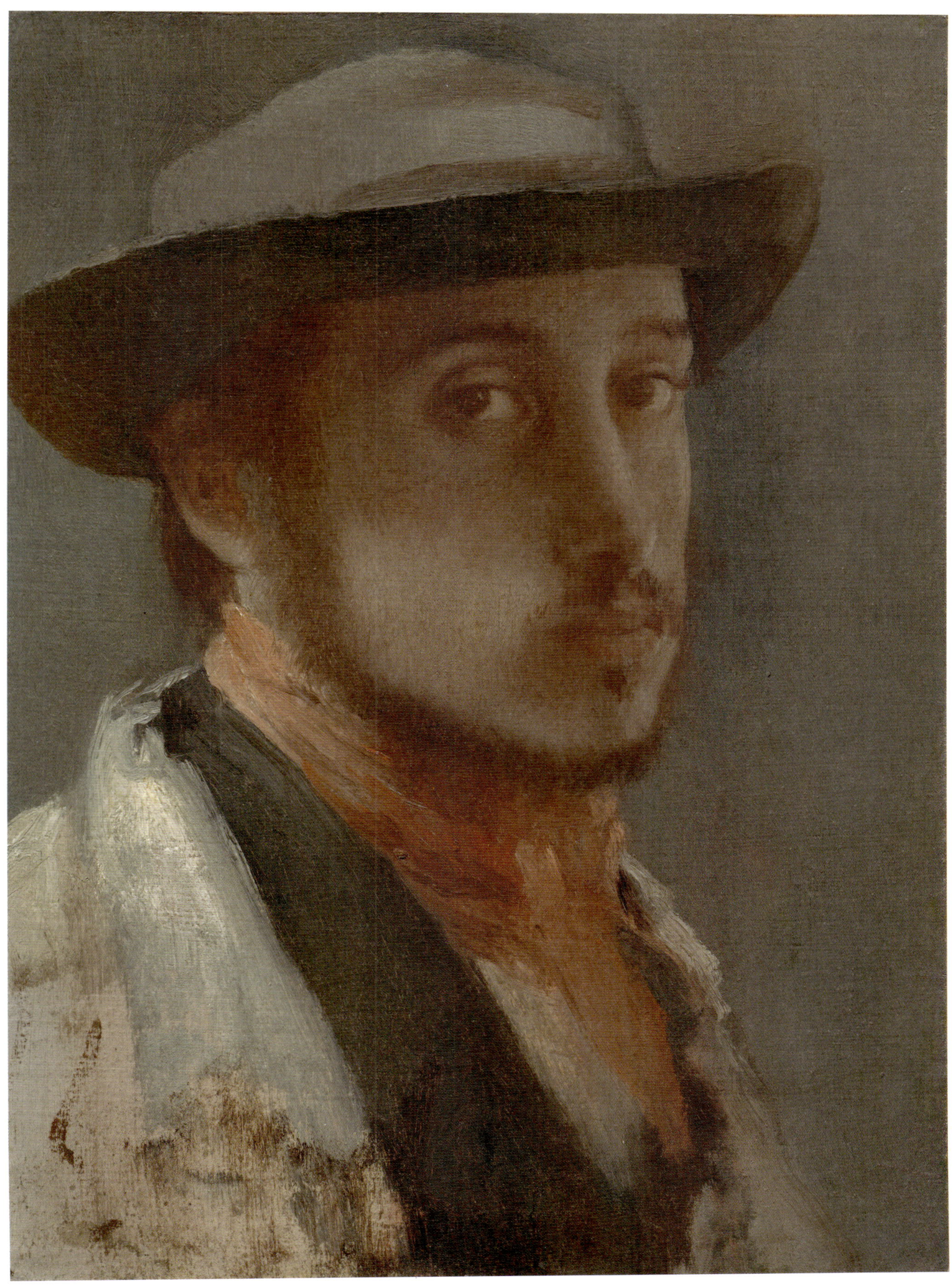

35 EDGAR DEGAS French, 1834–1917

Portrait of a Man

c. 1877
Oil on canvas
79.1 x 59.1 cm
Stamped lower left: Degas
Acquired by Sterling Clark, 1919
1955.44

STERLING CLARK PURCHASED *PORTRAIT OF A MAN* at the fourth Degas atelier sale in July 1919. The subject of the portrait has never been confirmed, but speculation has included both the poet Paul Verlaine and the novelist Edmond Duranty. As Degas rarely accepted commissions, it is likely that the subject was a friend or acquaintance.

Portrait of a Man is from an ambitious group of portraits, made in the 1860s and 1870s, in which Degas explored often radical approaches to the depiction of his contemporaries. In this picture, for instance, the sitter turns obliquely from the viewer, precluding eye contact. The self-absorption of the man suggests that we have intruded on a private moment of intense concentration. The background depicting what appears to be a stormy sea and an unidentified book in front of the sitter add to the sense that there is a hidden narrative in this picture.

In contrast to the almost furtive detachment of the sitter, Degas's delicate use of washes of paint and attention to modeling leave no doubt that this is a very closely observed individual. The artist's superb draftsmanship is displayed in details such as the sitter's hands and ear. While Degas has left the picture in various states of finish, the canvas retains an overall harmony in its warm tonality. The loosely brushed background sets off the worked-up passages in the sitter's face, which include a wide range of flesh tones. The extreme spareness of the background focuses our view and heightens the gravity of the subject.

Portrait of a Man was neither exhibited nor sold during Degas's lifetime and, lacking a signature, may have been regarded as unfinished by the artist. Degas did, however, sign other canvases in similar states of finish and exhibit them as completed works. The picture's unknown provenance from the time before it appeared in the July 1919 atelier sale makes securing the date when it was painted problematic, and proposed dates have ranged from the mid-1870s through the early 1880s.

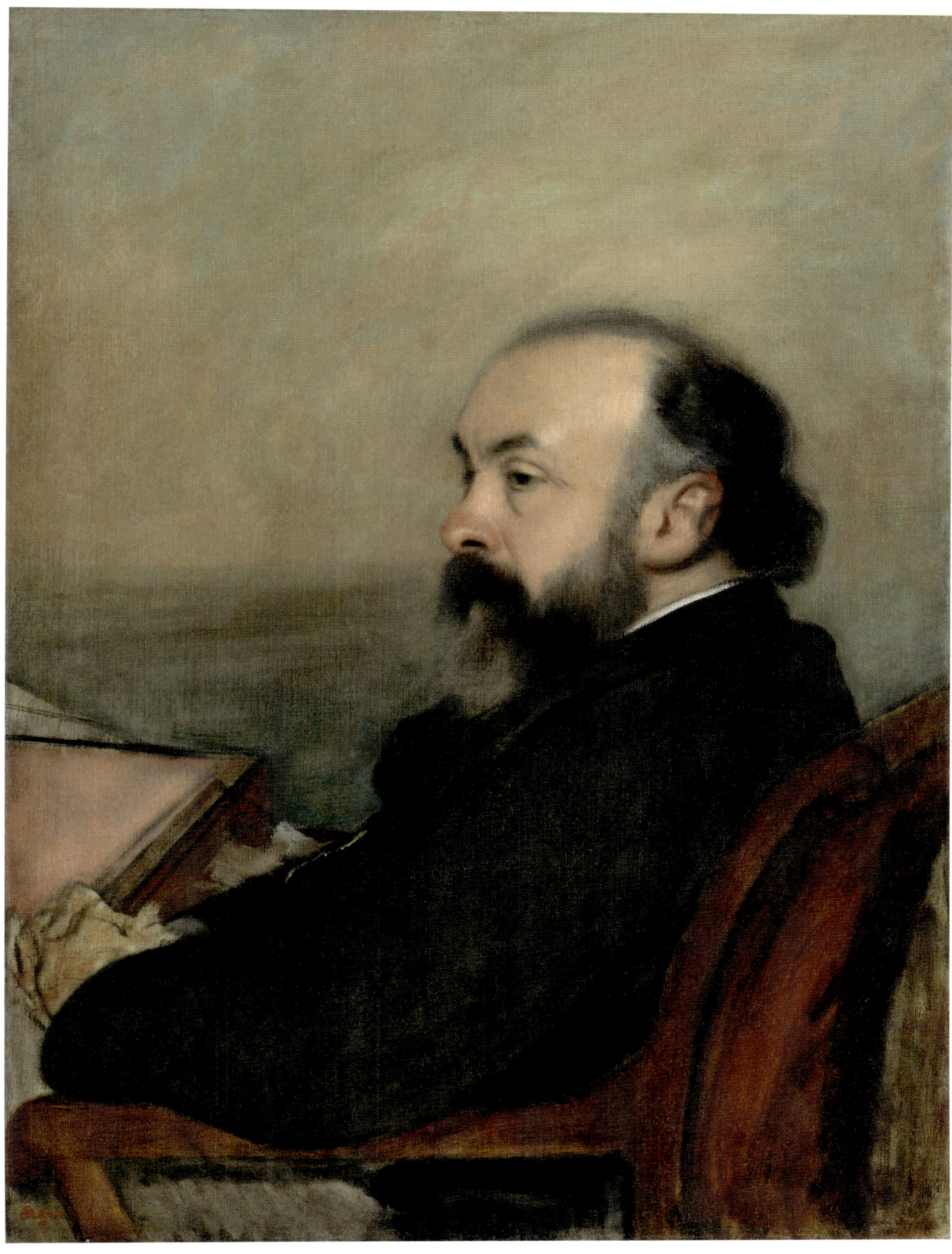

36 EDGAR DEGAS French, 1834–1917

Dancers in the Classroom

c. 1880
Oil on canvas
39.4 x 88.4 cm
Signed upper right: degas
Acquired by Sterling and Francine Clark, 1924
1955.562

DANCERS IN THE CLASSROOM IS ONE OF A SERIES OF PAINTINGS by Degas of unusual dimension—long horizontal works with a width that is more than twice the height. All of these paintings, which range in date from the late 1870s to the early 1890s, depict ballerinas posing or resting in a large practice room. While the ballet and its dancers was by far the most important subject for Degas throughout his career, this series of paintings also showcases Degas's exploration of wide-angle interior spaces. The wide, frieze-like composition of these canvases and use of a high and oblique viewpoint were likely inspired by Japanese *surimono* prints.

Degas catches the physical grace of the ballerinas as well as the psychological conditions—the strain and exhaustion—of the competitive atmosphere of the dance studio. In *Dancers in the Classroom,* the dancers, tired from their exertion, remain in their own isolated worlds, oblivious to one another and to the viewer. Degas enlivens this artfully composed scene with bright passages of tutus, sashes, and a colorful fan that play off the muted hues of the studio walls and floor.

As with most of the pictures in the series, Degas never formally exhibited *Dancers in the Classroom*, yet it is evident that he worked tirelessly to resolve the composition to his satisfaction. He reworked many of the figures a number of times, most significantly in the position of the outstretched leg of the girl adjusting her stocking, which was tried in at least nine different variations. The depth of Degas's concern for the spatial relationships in these paintings is demonstrated by his decision, in the midst of working on *Dancers in the Classroom*, to remove the painting from its strainer, fold out the tacking edge at top and bottom by minute amounts (one centimeter at the top, two at bottom), and restretch the painting—gaining slight but evidently critical space for the composition.

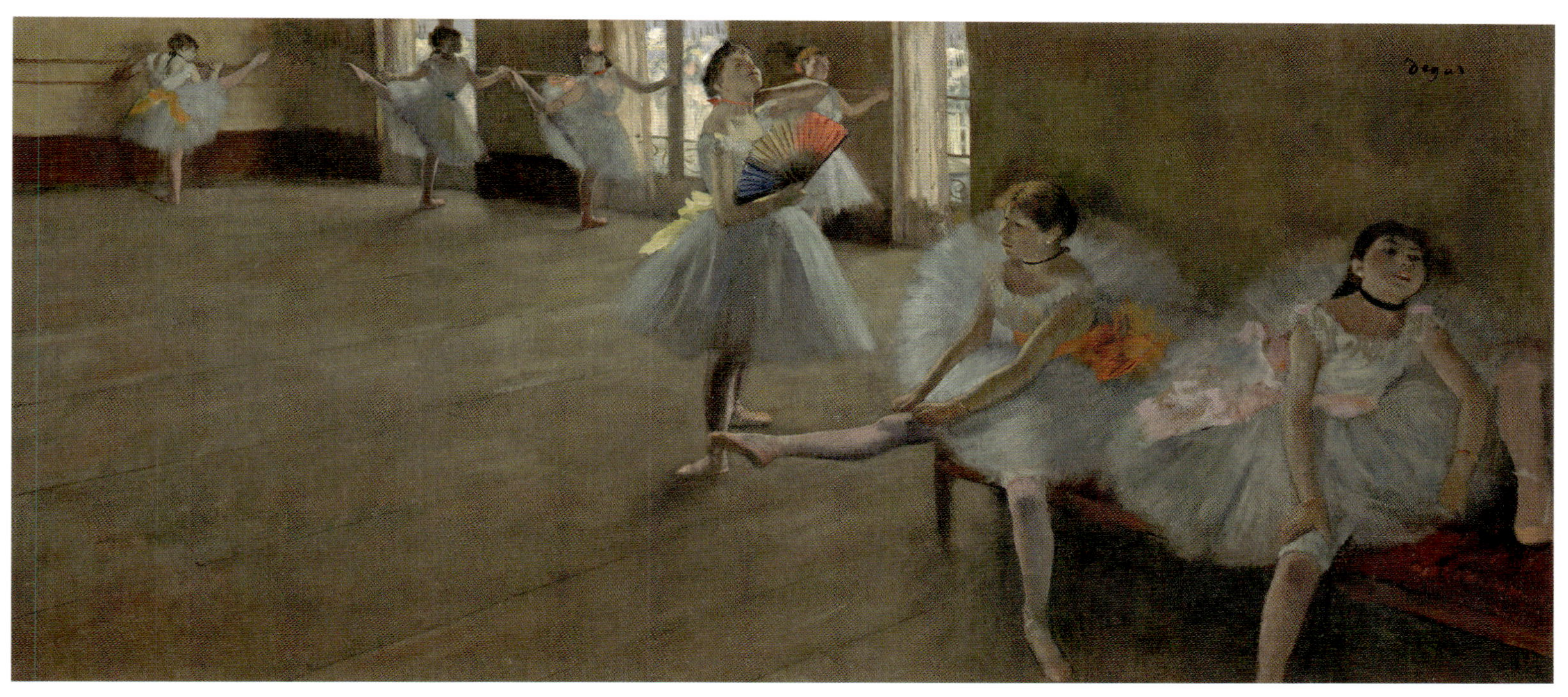
Degas

37 EDGAR DEGAS French, 1834–1917

Before the Race

c. 1882
Oil on panel
26.7 x 34.9 cm
Signed lower right: Degas
Acquired by Sterling and Francine Clark, 1939
1955.557

BEFORE THE RACE IS ONE OF THREE IDENTICALLY TITLED and compositionally linked scenes that Degas made in the early 1880s. He was likely inspired to paint the racetrack because it gave him the opportunity to study the complex forms of horses from many different angles and viewpoints. In *Before the Race*, for instance, the five horses together present an almost 360-degree view of the animal.

Degas's fascination with horses parading probably began in 1860, when he made studies of Benozzo Gozzoli's *Journey of the Magi* frescoes in the Palazzo Medici Riccardi in Florence. Gozzoli's composition has, in fact, been proposed as a source for the two horse-and-jockey tandems on the right of *Before the Race*. Ever eager to learn from past and current artists, Degas studied sources as varied as the Parthenon frieze and contemporary English racing prints. In addition to studying other artists and sketching live horses, he is reported to have had a full-size stuffed horse installed in his studio.

With its dazzling brushwork and play of light, movement, and color, *Before the Race* shares much in common with the plein-air painting of Degas's Impressionist contemporaries. Yet Degas preferred to work up his paintings in the studio. There are close to twenty preparatory drawings that can be linked to *Before the Race*. Degas's particular mode of composition drew on his ability to incorporate and modify ideas from a large cache of drawings and meld them into a harmonious balance. Some vestiges of this process of adapting and shifting drawings can be seen through close scrutiny of the horses' limbs. In fact, discussing this picture with his friends, Degas somewhat embarrassedly admitted that "the legs of the horses . . . are badly placed." In contrast to his meticulously prepared figures in the picture, the landscape of the scene is less detailed, and these different levels of finish add a spontaneous quality to the painting that contributes to its allure.

Before the Race was praised by art dealers and collectors very early on. Upon purchasing the painting, the wealthy artist Henry Lerolle asked Degas to a party where the work would be admired. In 1898, it shows up in the background of a painting by Renoir of Lerolle's daughters at the piano (Musée de l'Orangerie, Paris). There is no doubt that the avid horseman Sterling Clark, who bought the painting in 1939, was attracted to the picture not only by Degas's painterly bravado but also by the equestrian subject matter.

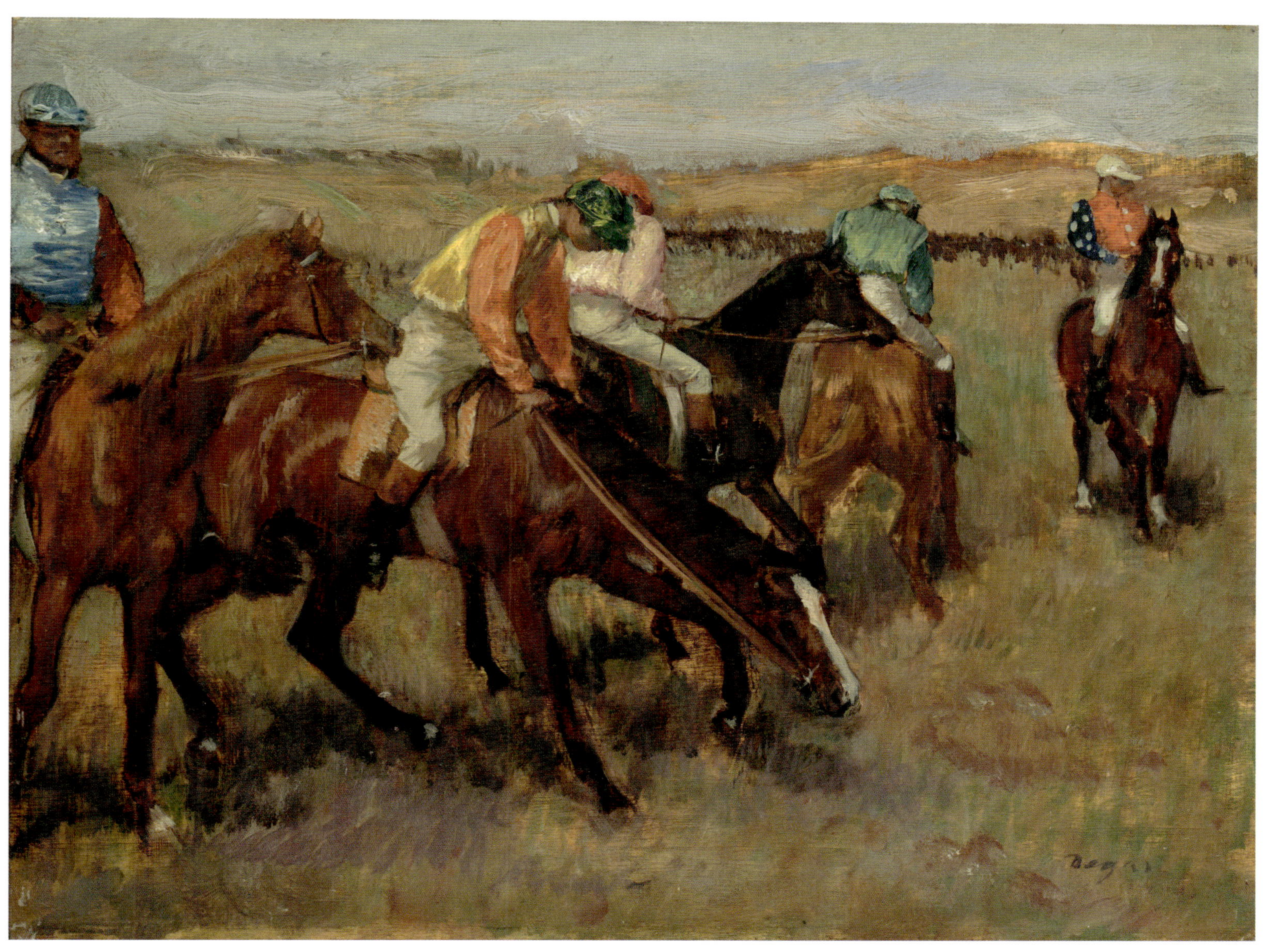
Degas

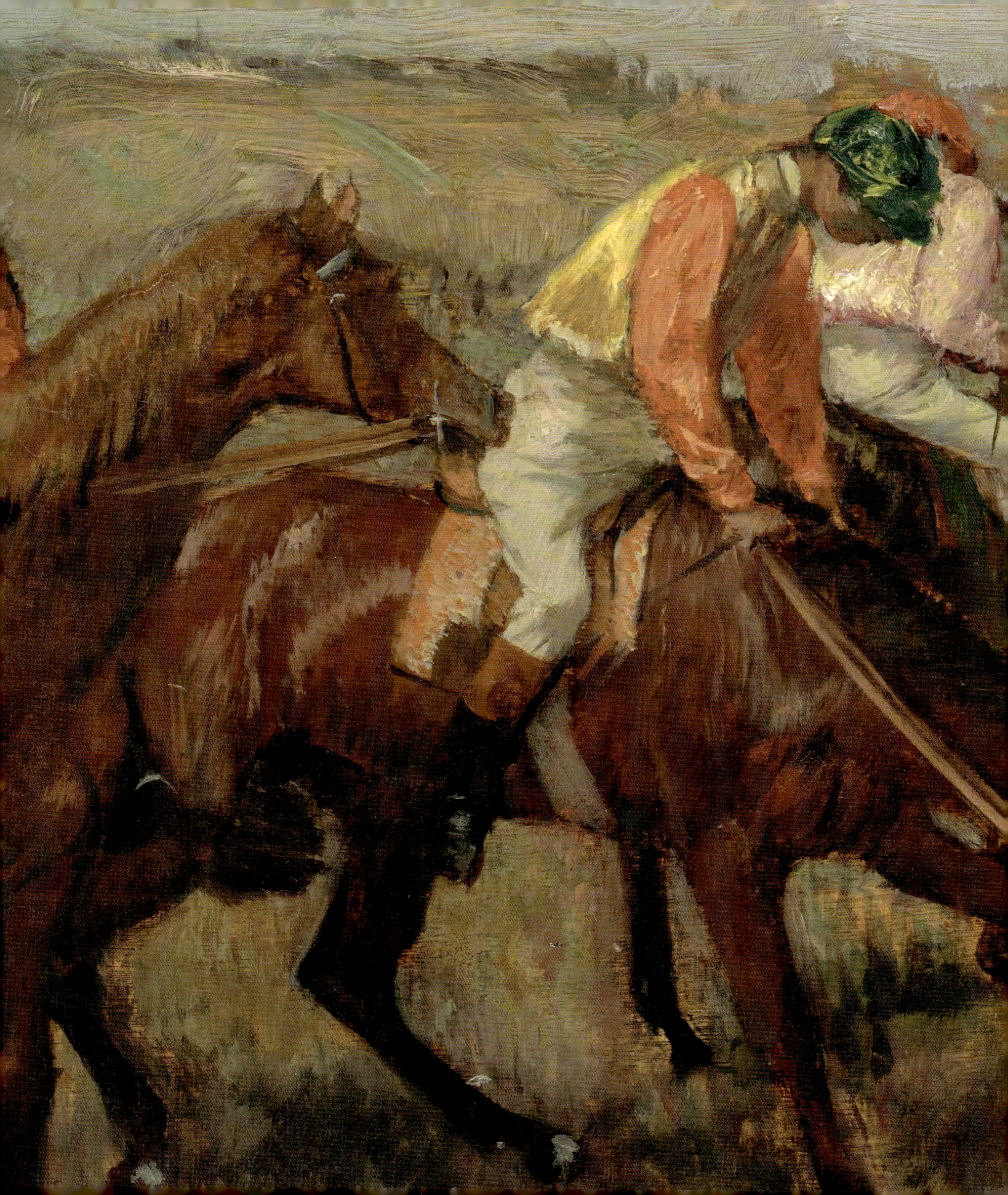

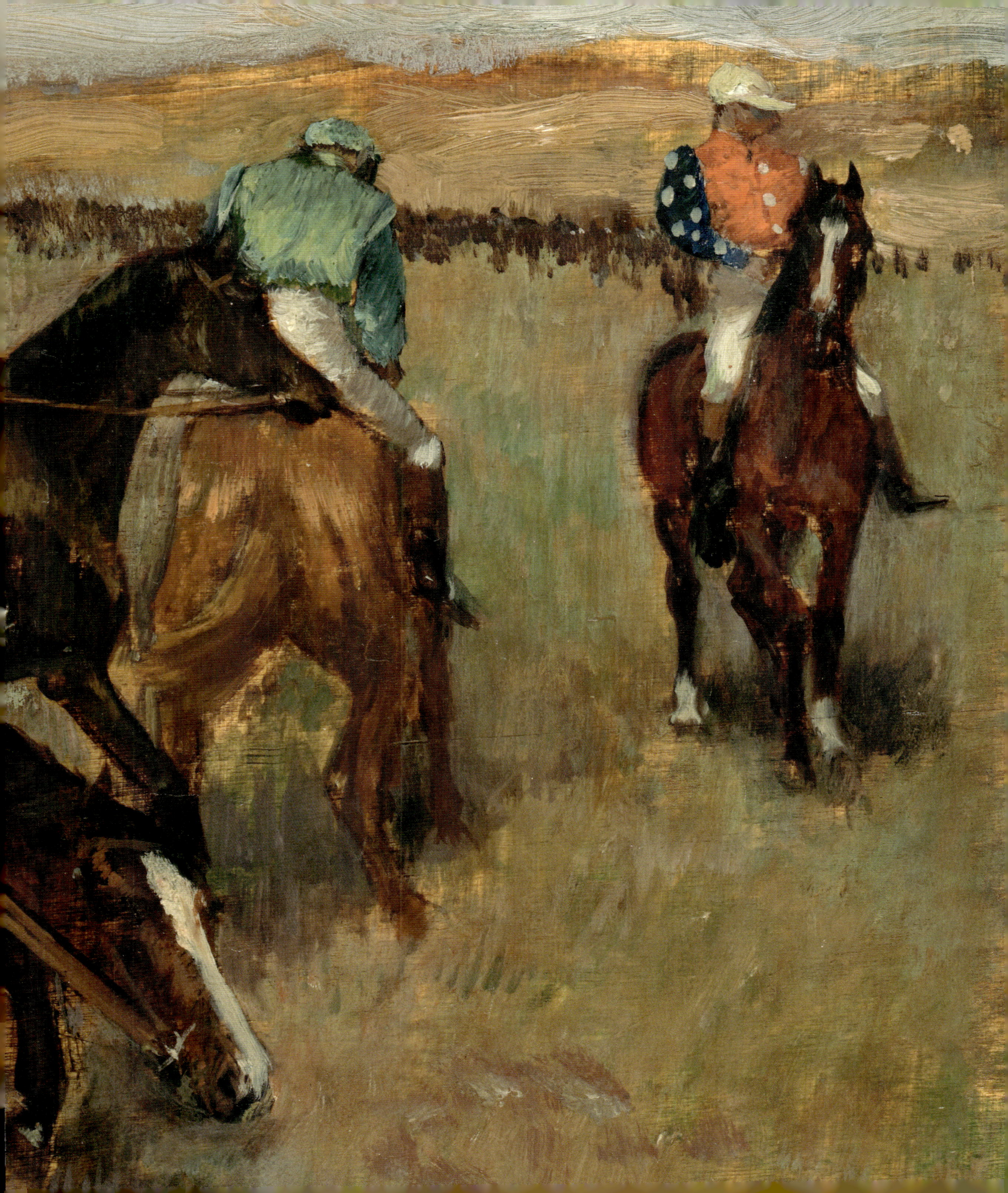

38 **JEAN-LÉON GÉRÔME** French, 1824–1904

The Slave Market

1866
Oil on canvas
84.6 x 63.3 cm
Signed and dated lower right: J. L. GEROME
Acquired by Sterling and Francine Clark, 1930
1955.53

THE SLAVE MARKET IS AMONG GÉRÔME'S most provocative paintings. At the center of the scene stands a nude woman for sale as a slave, surrounded by a group of men. Her prospective buyer holds her head with one hand and probes her teeth with his finger, an act more common to horse-trading. The seller, apparently pleased with the imminent transaction, stands to the right. While indeterminate, the setting is suggestive of a courtyard market in the Near East, probably intended to be identified as Egypt. Gérôme's meticulous technique and attention to details of costume and architecture were such that one critic, upon seeing the painting at the Paris Salon of 1867, remarked, "*The Slave Market* is a scene drawn from life."

That comment notwithstanding, it is unlikely that Gérôme saw such events on his travels through North Africa; while slavery was practiced, there are no reports of open-air slave markets of the type depicted here, and Gérôme sometimes set similar scenes in ancient Rome. Rather, in painting *The Slave Market* the artist was engaging in a tradition of depicting Near Eastern and North African cultures as exotic, mysterious, and even barbaric. The potential eroticism of a full-length female nude being displayed amid fully clothed males—the nude African male slave is half-hidden in the right background—would not have been lost on him or his clients either. The conflicting message of the picture was perhaps captured best by the caricaturist Chaim, who parodied Gérôme's image with the caption "An Arab with a toothache buys a slave to chew his dinner for him."

By placing the scene in an obviously exotic locale, Gérôme has made it possible for the intended European audience to approach the picture without feelings of complicity in the action. This estrangement, moreover, allows the viewer to censure the practice of slave-trading while still enjoying the idea of complete access to the female body, both physical as well as visual. Gérôme's highly refined academic style is masterfully employed in his depiction of the passive female nude surrounded by clothed men. Despite the seeming naturalism and objectivity of the artist's approach to the scene, *The Slave Market* betrays a worldview that is permeated with stereotypes of race and gender and is anything but neutral.

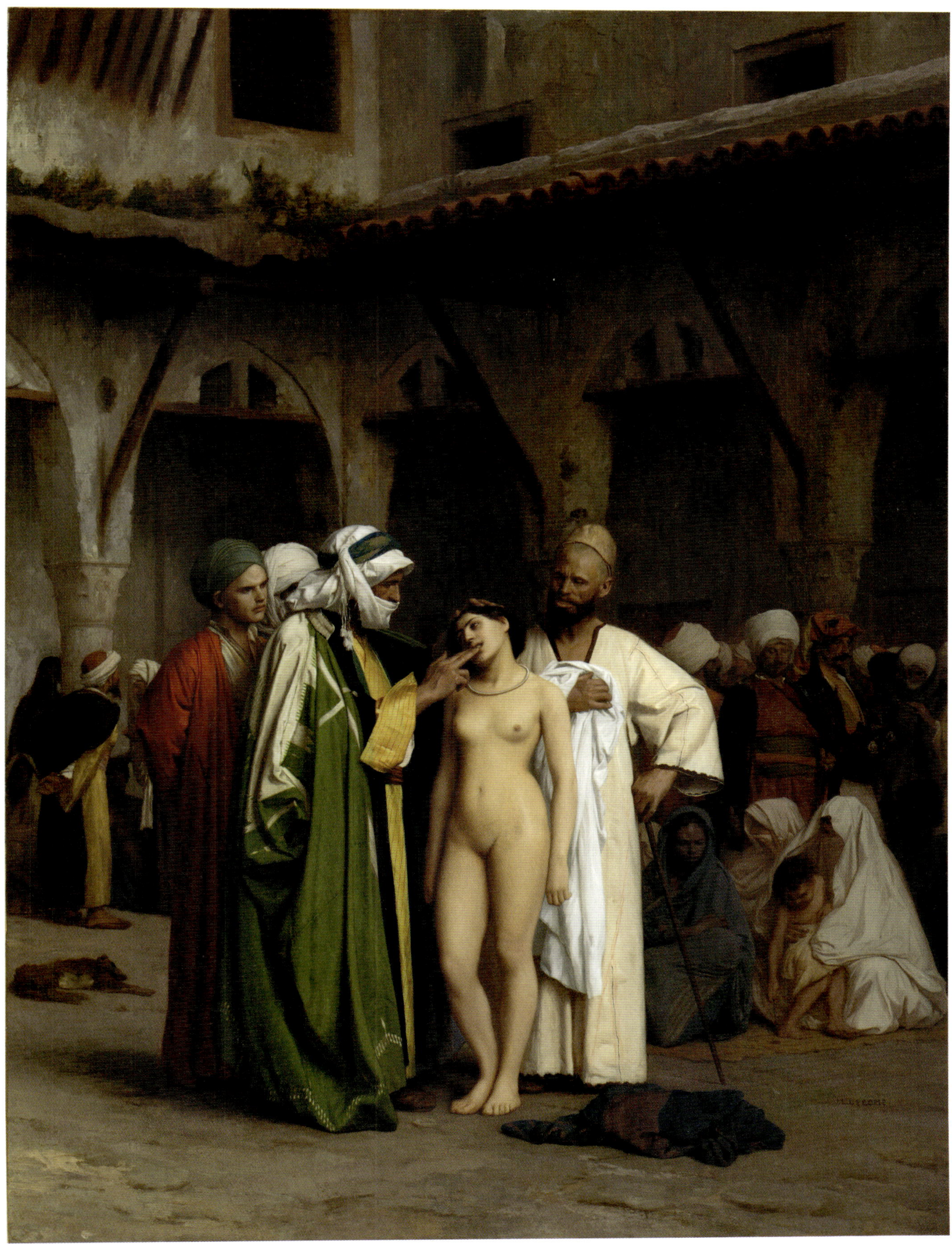

39 JEAN-LÉON GÉRÔME French, 1824–1904

Fellah Women Drawing Water

1870 or 1875
Oil on canvas
67.3 x 100.2 cm
Signed center right: J. L. GEROME.
Acquired by Sterling and Francine Clark, 1942
1955.52

IN 1868 GÉRÔME SPENT FIVE MONTHS TRAVELING IN THE NEAR EAST, one of the longest of his many excursions to the region. In the company of other artists, photographers, and writers, he journeyed through Egypt, Palestine, and Syria. After spending a month in Cairo, the group set off for the region of El Faiyum, south of the city, in a caravan of donkeys and camels. In his account of the trip, the writer Paul Lenoir described seeing groups of fellah, or peasant, women walking from the town to draw water from the river. Gérôme portrays such a scene in the Clark's painting. Several groups of women fill and carry large jugs of water, while others rest in the shade. Two women in the foreground with their backs to the viewer are washing laundry in the river. A mosque's minaret is prominent behind a fortified structure at right in the painting, and in the distance there is the suggestion of a faraway city.

This painting can be linked to two other images—a second, similar version of the canvas (Najd Collection, London) and a photograph taken by Gérôme's brother-in-law, Albert Goupil. Accounts of the trip suggest the artists made only quick sketches in the desert, which is likely given the difficulties of desert travel. Although Gérôme undoubtedly observed something similar to the scene depicted, he drew on firsthand written and visual sources some years later to create this painting in his studio, all the while adding his own embellishments.

Fellah Women Drawing Water is uncharacteristic of Gérôme's work of this period in its focus on the landscape rather than figures or architecture. Although it features a desert background, the painting lacks the overt exoticism of scenes such as *The Snake Charmer* (cat. 40) and *The Slave Market* (cat. 38). In fact, the women in *Fellah Women Drawing Water* resemble the French rural laborers so often depicted in the work of artists such as Jules Breton, their Egyptian identity only hinted at through their clothes.

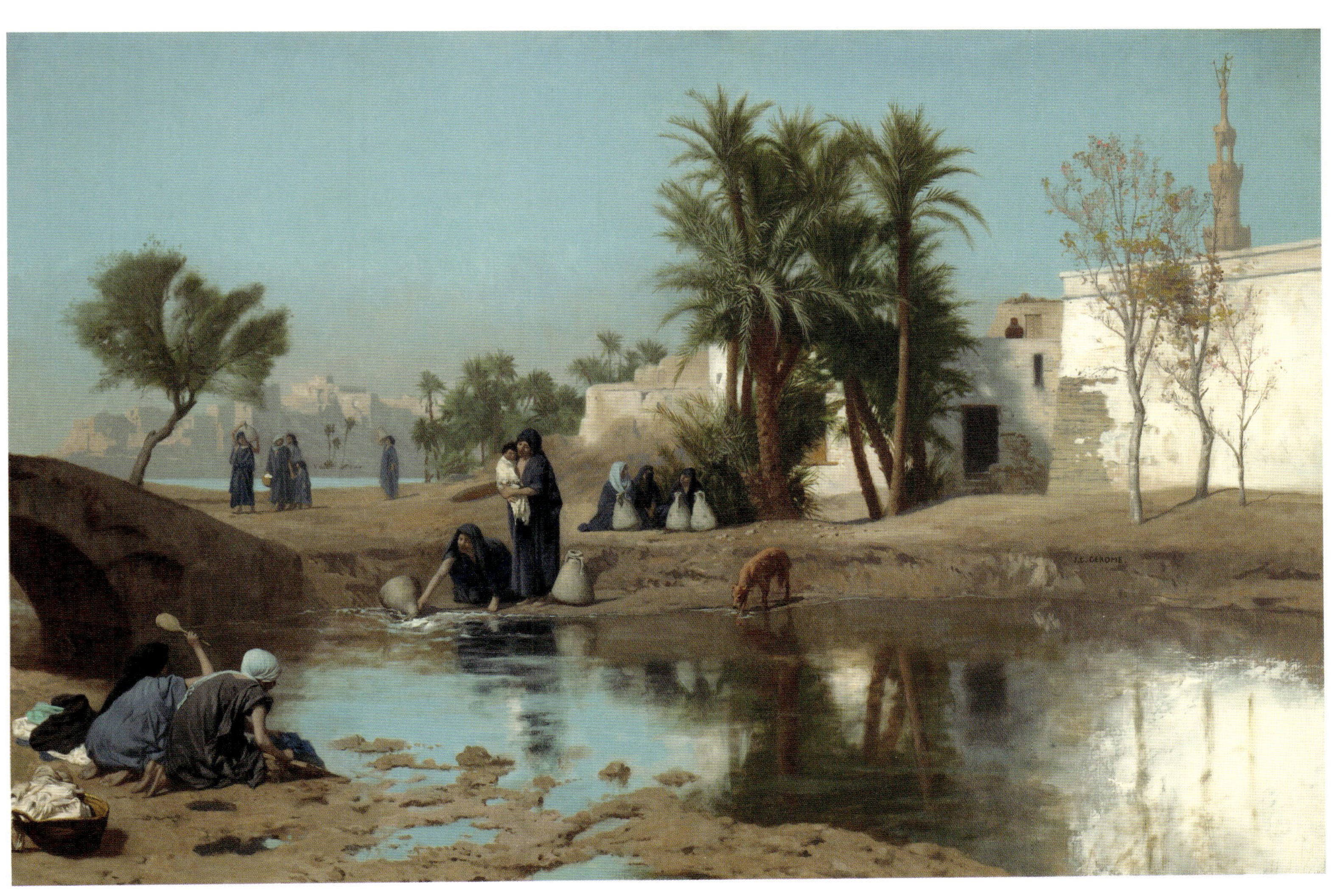

40 JEAN-LÉON GÉRÔME French, 1824–1904

The Snake Charmer

c. 1879
Oil on canvas
82.2 x 121 cm
Signed lower center, left edge: J.L GEROME.
Acquired by Sterling and Francine Clark, 1942
1955.51

GÉRÔME'S METICULOUS DEPICTION OF ARCHITECTURAL DETAILS and costumes in *The Snake Charmer* creates the impression that the painting portrays a specific observed event. Like the majority of Gérôme's work, however, the painting was executed in the studio, incorporating disparate elements from diverse sources, including photography. On close inspection it becomes clear that for all of its mesmerizing exoticism, the painting is rife with historical inaccuracies.

The arch-shaped tile work that Gérôme painted in the background is copied from three panels located in the Ottoman Topkapi Palace in present-day Istanbul. The practice of snake charming, however, was not an Ottoman tradition. It is known that snake charming, complete with a nude young male performing this art, did take place in nineteenth-century Egypt. It is not certain, however, whether Gérôme witnessed such a spectacle while traveling through Egypt or relied on secondhand sources as his inspiration for the present scene. Further complicating the geography of the composition is the floor, which likely mirrors that in the mosque of 'Amr ibn al-'As in Cairo, even though the artist was familiar enough with Islamic practice to know that such a performance would not have been welcome in a sacred space. Similarly, the painting presents a range of ethnic types in the audience and a mish-mash of costumes and weapons (some of which the artist used as props in other paintings). Gérôme included highly detailed elements such as the Qur'anic verses in the frieze running along the back wall to accentuate the exotic and heighten the distance between his subjects and his European audience. Indeed, it seems that the true subject of the painting is not any particular event but the idea of the foreign and strange.

Despite the factual inconsistencies of his paintings, Gérôme assembled various details into finely wrought and compelling scenes that were praised by the artist's contemporaries. This fact is underscored by the high price that *The Snake Charmer* commanded when it was completed, as well as its inclusion in the 1893 World's Columbian Exposition in Chicago. The painting was owned by Sterling Clark's parents for a time in the late nineteenth and early twentieth centuries, and Clark had fond memories of it hanging in his childhood home. When he saw the painting on the market in 1942, he bought it without hesitation at a bargain price of five hundred dollars. While it is unknown what feelings, if any, Sterling had about the specific subject, both his regard for Gérôme's painterly skill and familial nostalgia for the picture led him to write in his diary that it was "a masterpiece for that kind of painting." In recent decades *The Snake Charmer* has become an icon of Orientalist imagery.

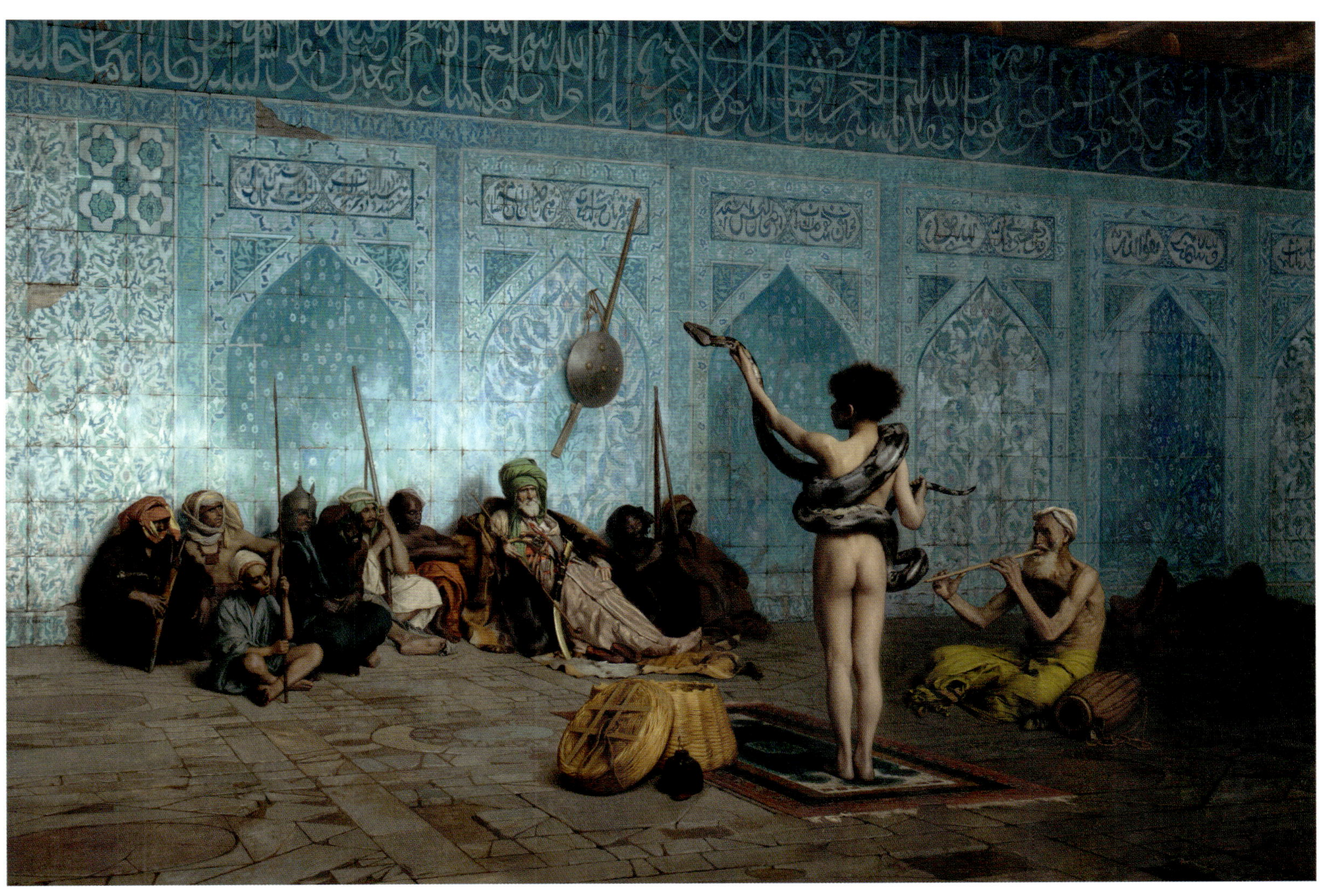

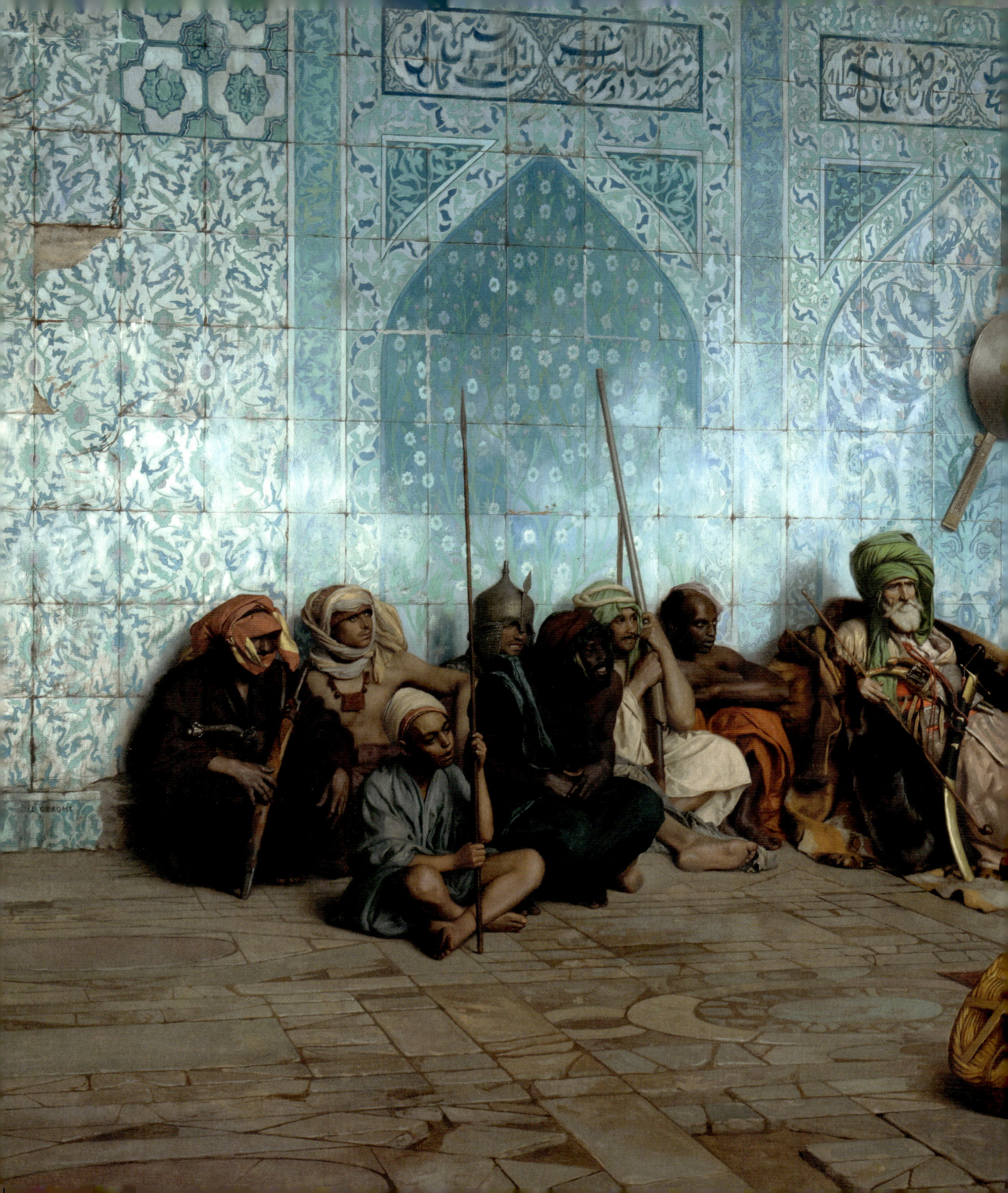

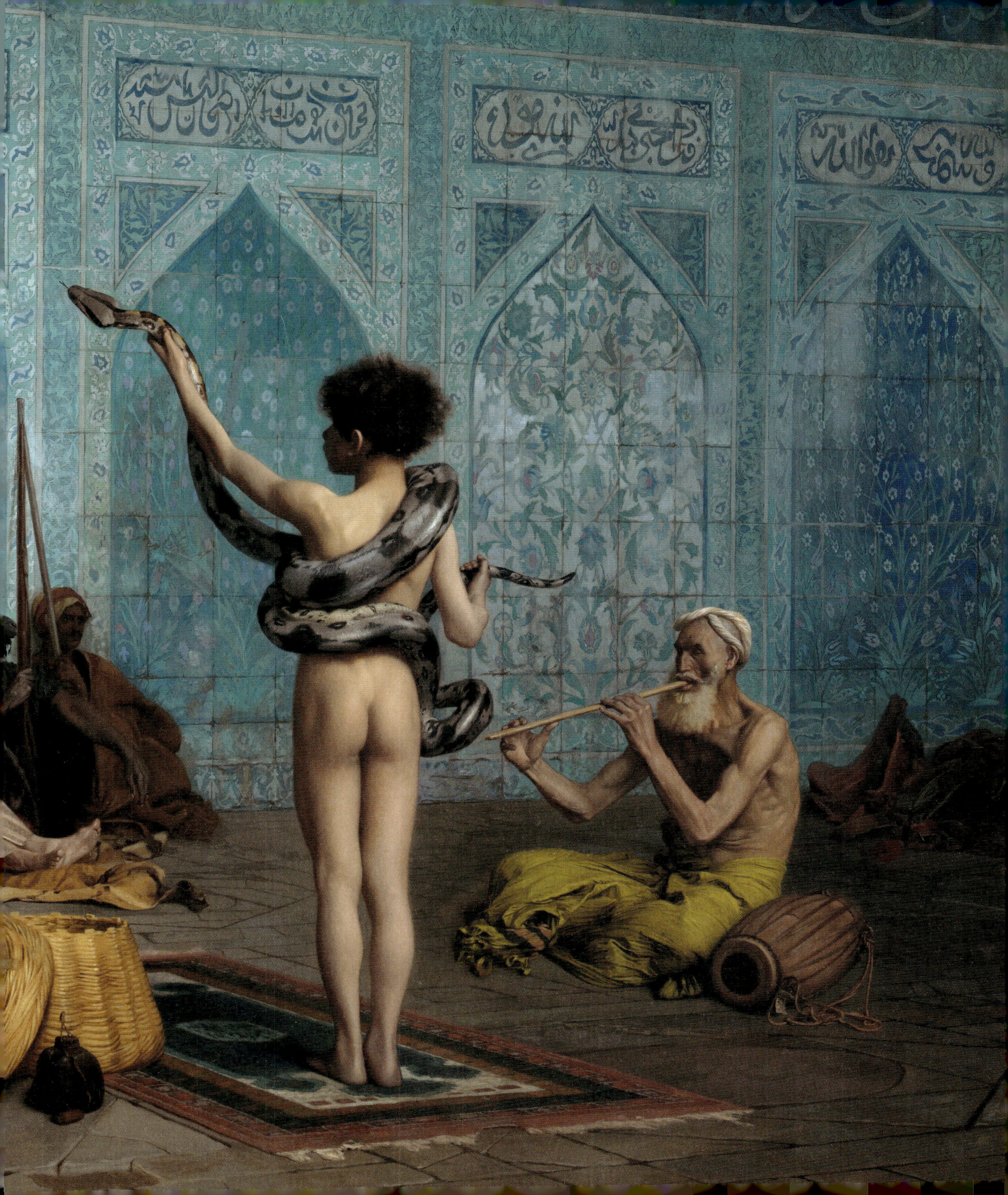

41 WILLIAM-ADOLPHE BOUGUEREAU French, 1825–1905

Seated Nude

1884
Oil on canvas
116.5 x 89.8 cm
Signed and dated upper right: W—BOUGUEREAU—1884
Acquired by Sterling and Francine Clark, 1938
1955.659

ONE OF THE LEADING ACADEMIC PAINTERS IN FRANCE, Bouguereau is best known for his images of the female figure. As in much of his work, the focus of *Seated Nude* is the skill with which Bouguereau renders the tone of the sitter's skin and the precision with which he captures the model's difficult pose. The soft flesh of the bather is accentuated by its juxtaposition with the background of hard rock, and the position of the sitter is portrayed with consummate skill and anatomical accuracy. Contemporaries marveled at Bouguereau's draftsmanship, and the American artist Carroll Beckwith went so far as to praise Bouguereau's depiction of hands and feet as "marvels of grace and proportion." Indeed, in *Seated Nude*, the artist has chosen exceedingly challenging positions for both the hands and feet, and rendered them flawlessly.

At the time he executed *Seated Nude*, Bouguereau was working on a larger horizontal scene of a group of bathers, yet it is unlikely that the Clark picture is related to it in any way other than its theme. Depictions of bathers were among his favored subjects, as they were for any artist trained in the academic tradition. The specific pose of *Seated Nude* brings to mind Hippolyte Flandrin's *Nude Youth Seated on a Rock* of 1835–36 (Musée du Louvre, Paris), an icon of early nineteenth-century French painting that Bouguereau would have known well. The Clark picture could almost be seen as an updating of the earlier painting, with the sex of the figure changed but with the same pose and setting. The youth in Flandrin's painting is shown sitting on a rock overlooking the sea, with arms wrapped around his drawn-up knees. Bouguereau has softened the composition and created a more intimate picture by portraying a female body and turning the sitter's gaze toward the viewer. He also complicated the sitter's pose by crossing the legs and intertwining the hands—perhaps in a display of painterly one-upmanship. Other details, such as the beautifully drawn and painted blue fabric that wraps around the model's head and spills down her back, or the convincingly rendered reflection of her foot in the water, could be seen as virtuosic displays of painterly skill. It is likely that such craftsmanship was what attracted Sterling Clark, who continually praised artists' command of materials and technique.

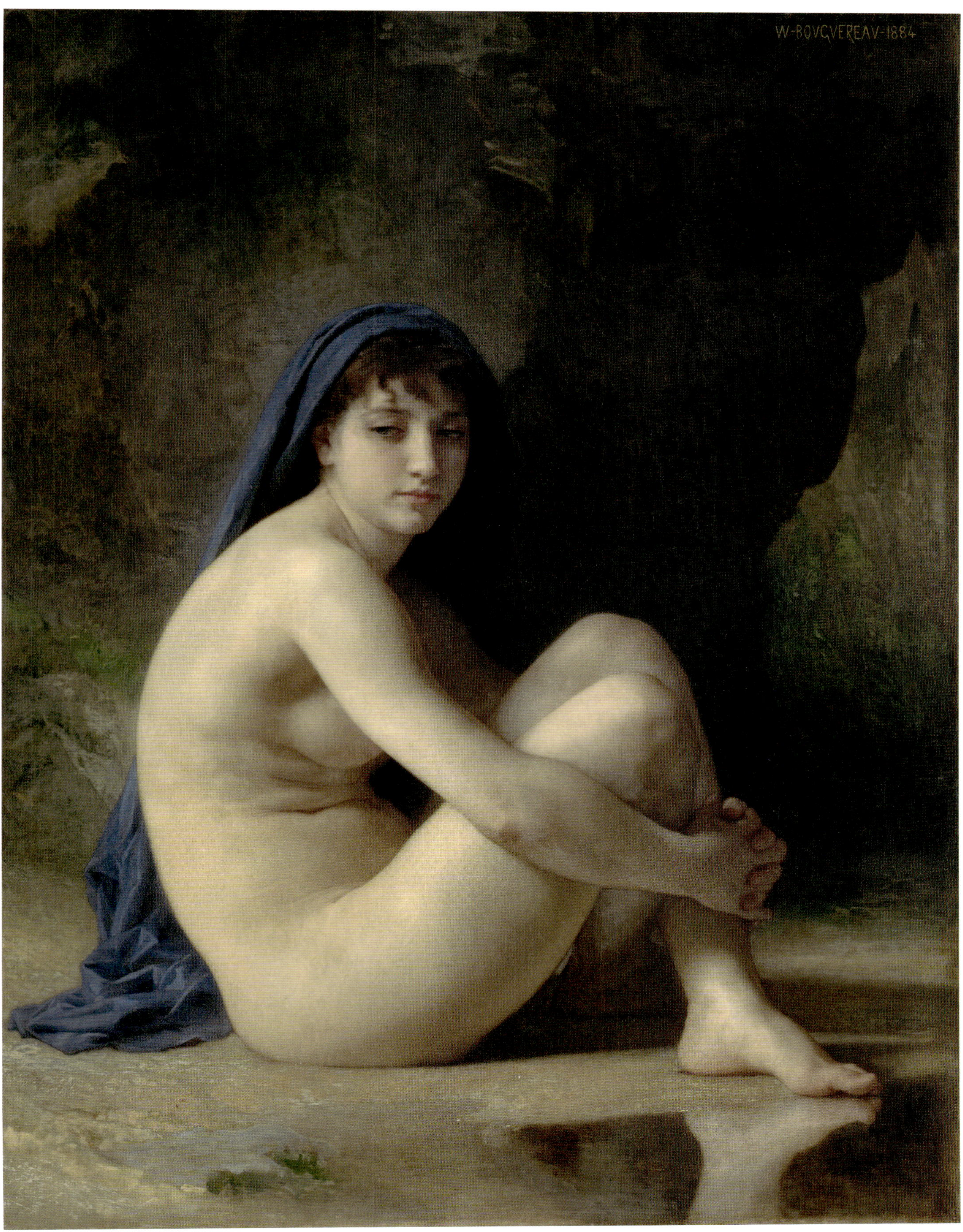
W-BOVGVEREAV-1884

42 ALFRED STEVENS Belgian (active in France), 1823–1906

A Duchess (The Blue Dress)

c. 1866
Oil on panel
31.4 x 26 cm
Signed lower right: Alfred Stevens.
Acquired by Sterling and Francine Clark, 1920
1955.865

A DUCHESS WAS FIRST EXHIBITED at the Paris Exposition Universelle of 1867, along with seventeen other pictures by Stevens. It garnered favorable reviews, solidifying the artist's reputation as the leading painter of fashionable genre scenes.

In *A Duchess*, a young woman wearing a stylish blue velvet dress contemplates a portrait hanging on a wall opposite her. It is unlikely that Stevens intended to portray a specific woman in the painting; rather, the artist was more concerned with generally capturing the world and character of a wealthy, if not necessarily aristocratic, circle.

Throughout *A Duchess* Stevens focuses on the detailed rendering of individual objects, and his particularly bravura handling of the dress attests to his skill as a painter. Indeed, in one review from 1867 Stevens's work was described as "simply a matter of painting." Beyond this display of craft, however, he infuses the image with layers of meaning that create a vague narrative. For instance, while the subject stares intently at the portrait on the wall, hinting at an aristocratic lineage, she is surrounded by objects typical of the nineteenth-century nouveau riche. Particularly notable in this regard is the color of her dress, most likely created using a newly discovered chemical dye, and the Japanese screen and tablecloth, which reflect the craze at that time for all things Japanese. Indeed, it seems that Stevens has playfully placed the screen in such a way that the bald figure depicted on it and positioned directly behind his main subject, the woman in the blue dress, apes her intent gaze. Further complicating the interpretation of this scene is the fact that the painting itself would have been a high-priced indicator of wealth and was meant to hang in a room not unlike the one portrayed here.

In *A Duchess* Stevens both included Japanese objects, such as the screen behind the woman, and adopted the abrupt spatial transitions seen so often in Japanese graphic work, using the screen to enhance the effect of the shallow, ambiguous space and to heighten the contrast between the deep recession of the room and the woman in the foreground. At the same time, the meticulous technique, with richly colored paint applied in delicate glazes on a wooden panel, recall the genre paintings of seventeenth-century Dutch masters, artists who were being rediscovered in France during these years.

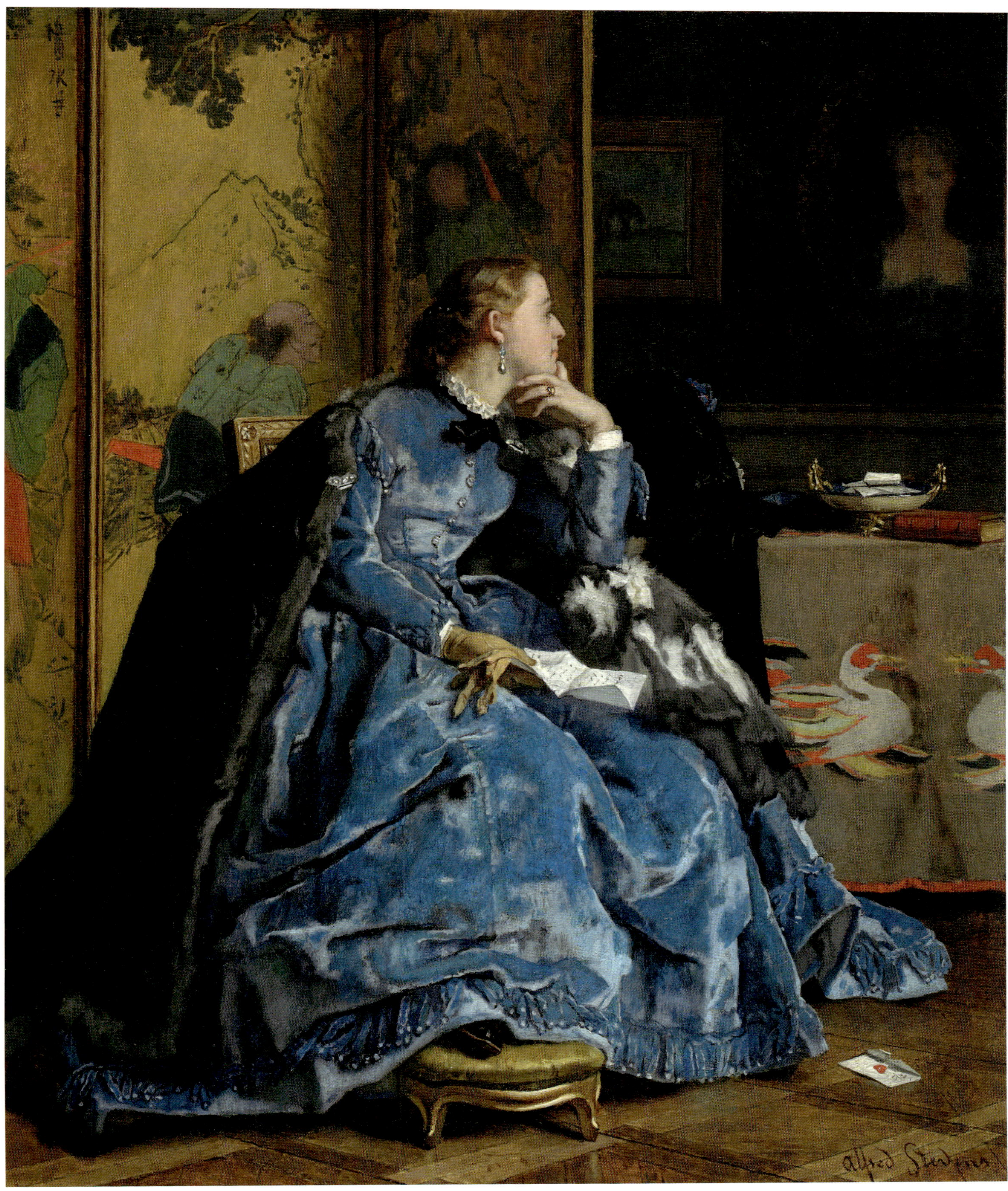
Alfred Stevens

43 ALFRED STEVENS Belgian (active in France), 1823–1906

Memories and Regrets

c. 1874
Oil on canvas
61.4 x 46.4 cm
Signed lower left: AStevens. [AS monogram]
Acquired by Sterling and Francine Clark, 1933
1955.860

AS WITH MANY OF STEVENS'S PICTURES FROM THE 1870S, *Memories and Regrets* entices the viewer to create a narrative surrounding the picture without elucidating the story's particulars. A woman sits in a chair looking down toward a letter in her right hand. A gown, fan, and parasol are piled on her left, yet the woman is dressed only in undergarments. An air of melancholy is enhanced not only by the woman's downcast face but also by her slumped posture and the listless manner in which she holds the letter. It is apparent that despite the trappings of a comfortable life—evident in the fancy bureau adorned by brushes, perfume bottles, and a jar with Japanese decoration—the woman is far from satisfied.

Piecing together the various details of the painting, one can surmise that the woman has recently returned from a night out. The slightly open drawer suggests that the letter she holds has been read many times before and that it pertains to a heart-wrenching relationship from the past. The artist leaves visual clues to the possible scenario, but it is up to the viewer to imagine the specific circumstances that may be motivating the woman's sadness. In addition to creating a modern tableau suggesting lost love, Stevens includes details that link the picture to deeper traditions. The mirror and other luxury items on the dresser are characteristic elements in *vanitas* imagery of seventeenth-century Dutch genre painting. Furthermore, the model's pose is clearly reminiscent of generic images of melancholy and can be linked to such iconic works as Albrecht Dürer's *Melencolia I*.

On a stylistic level, *Memories and Regrets* is notable for its broad handling of paint. It is on the whole more loosely brushed than is usual for Stevens, who was renowned for his tight and meticulous brushwork, as in the Clark's *A Duchess* (cat. 42). One turn-of-the-century critic effusively praised the painting as "a rare and perhaps unique canvas in Stevens's oeuvre through the breadth of its treatment and the softness of its touch." It is largely due to these qualities that *Memories and Regrets* has been compared to contemporary works by Degas and Manet. Indeed, it has long been suggested, although never definitively proven, that Stevens's model for the picture was Victorine Meurent, who famously posed for Manet's *Olympia* (Musée d'Orsay, Paris) about twelve years earlier.

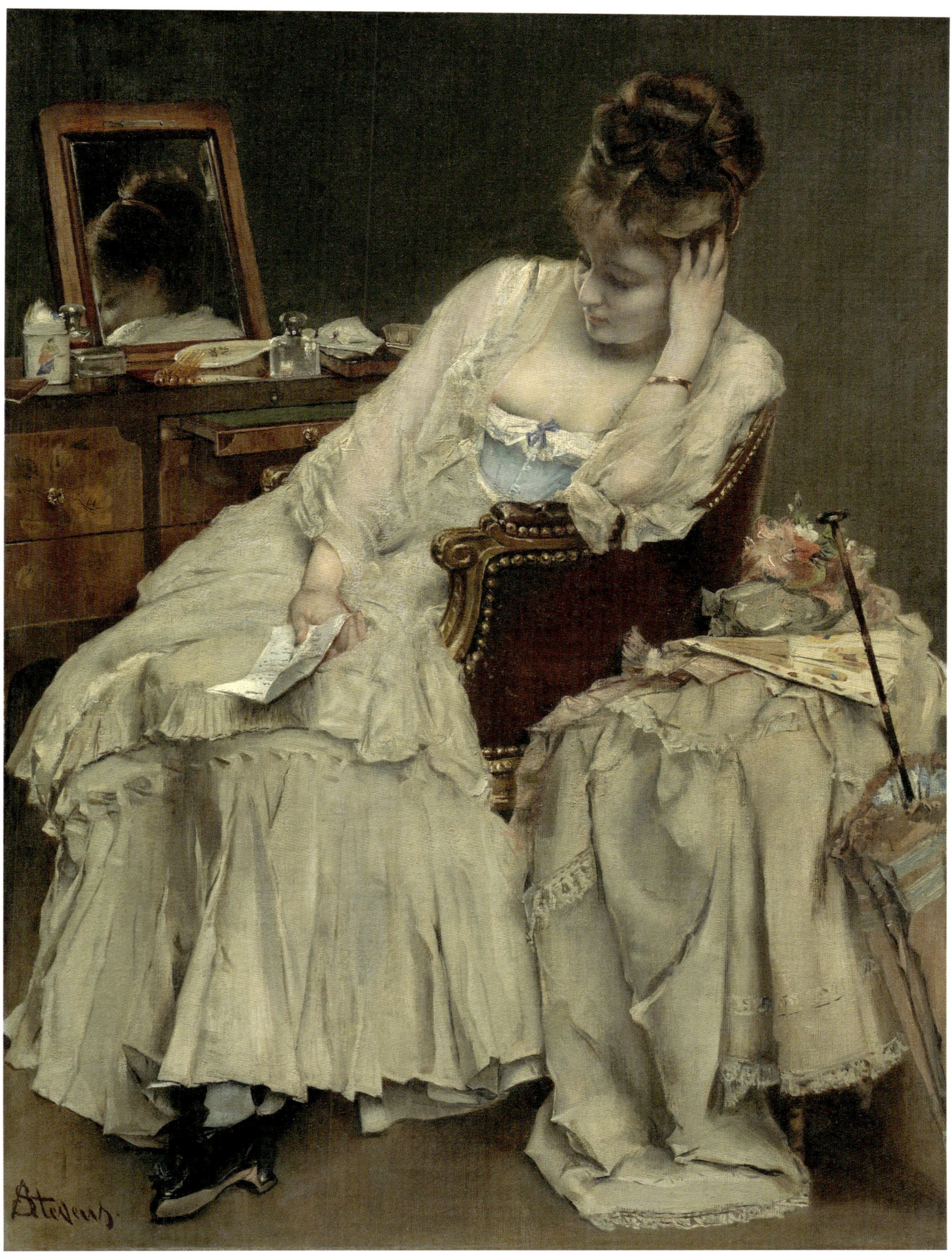
Stevens

44 GIOVANNI BOLDINI Italian (active in France), 1842–1931

Crossing the Street

1873–75
Oil on panel
46.2 x 37.8 cm
Signed and dated lower left: Boldini / 75
Acquired by Sterling and Francine Clark, 1925
1955.650

BOLDINI SETTLED IN HIS PARIS STUDIO on the place Pigalle in early 1872, and his first depictions of the city were inspired by the scenes just outside his door. He became enamored with capturing the fast-paced life of modern Paris, venturing throughout the city, painting the bustling Parisian society amid the backdrop of boulevards and squares.

As described by a critic of the time, *Crossing the Street* shows "a corner of the *Place Pigalle*, with a dandy leaning out of the window of a hackney coach to look at a *cocotte* passing by, raising the hem of her petticoat and holding a bunch of flowers." Glancing slightly to the right, the woman is beautiful and sophisticated in her stylish ruffled dress, holding a vibrant bouquet of pink flowers. The fact that she is unaccompanied and has apparently just emerged from the lingerie shop across the street lends her a certain allure.

The visual pleasure of the work is enhanced through Boldini's characteristically dazzling paint effects. The gray cobblestone street has a luminescence that spills over into the whole scene. The blue shawl of the older woman whose back is to the viewer adds a bright touch of color. The carefully painted shutters and striped awnings add picturesque details to the top half of the canvas. Throughout the picture, Boldini's quick brushstrokes give a sense of movement, which is accentuated by the horses and carriages in the background and the black dog that runs across the street. For all of its seeming spontaneity, *Crossing the Street* was started in 1873, but Boldini did not finish it until two years later, in 1875.

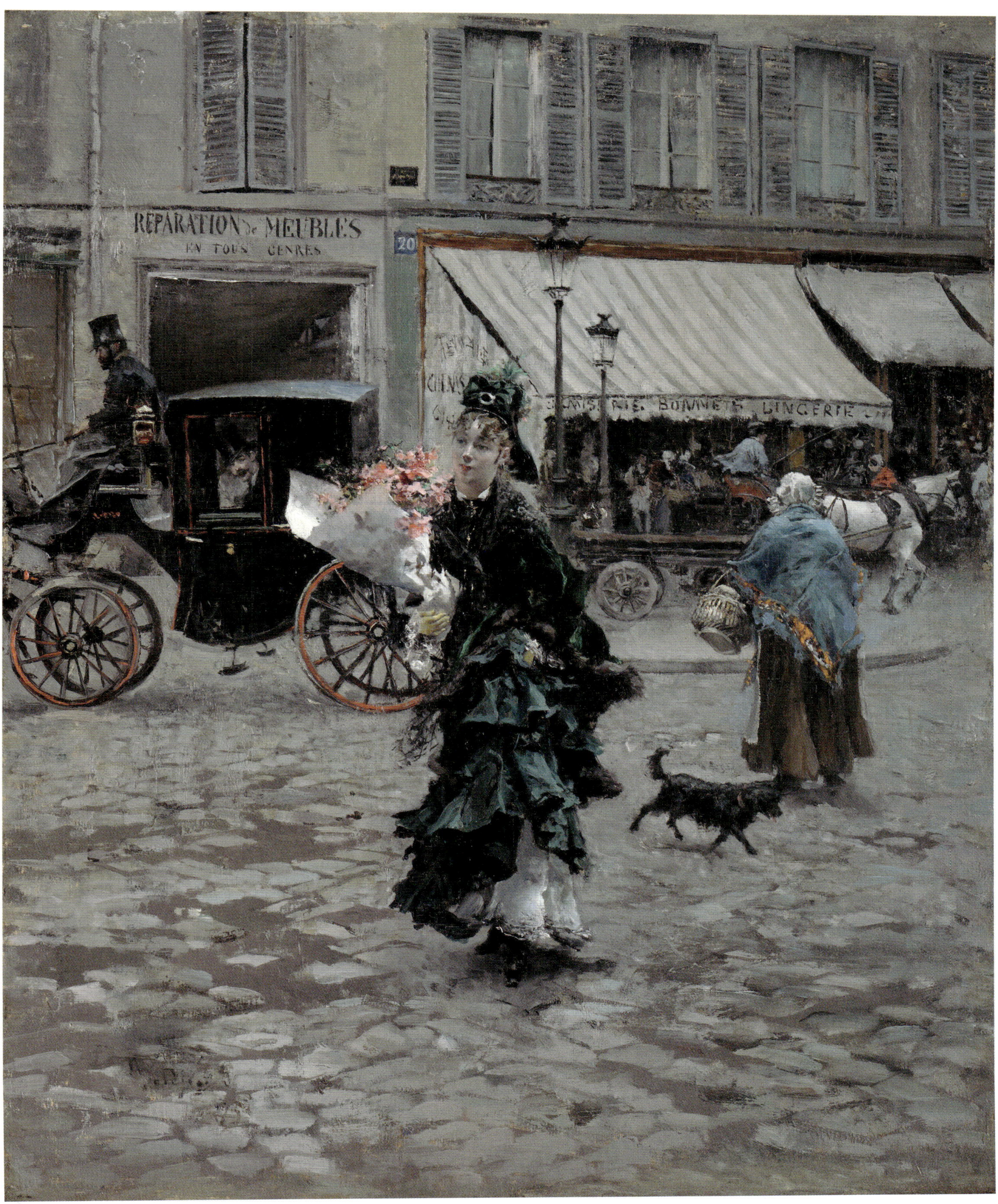

REPARATION de MEUBLES
EN TOUS GENRES
20
BONNETS LINGERIE

45 GIOVANNI BOLDINI Italian (active in France), 1842–1931

Young Woman Crocheting

1875
Oil on canvas
36.2 x 27.4 cm
Signed and dated lower left: Boldini / 75
Acquired by Sterling and Francine Clark, 1941
1955.648

YOUNG WOMAN CROCHETING IS JUST THE SORT OF SMALL-SCALE, beautifully painted genre scene that established Boldini's early reputation soon after his arrival in Paris from his native Italy in 1871. It was only much later, in the 1890s and first decades of the twentieth century, that he became famous for his fashionable portraits of Parisian society figures. The Clark picture ostensibly depicts members of a bourgeois family at ease in their home, the young woman focused on her needlework, the boy examining a fencing foil amid the clutter of their sitting room. In fact, the crumpled carpet, the silk-upholstered divan, the bass viol, and other objects are common to Boldini's early interiors and were no doubt studio props; the young woman seated among a profusion of pillows is Berthe, one of the artist's favorite models during the 1870s. Rather than representing an actual household, the painting was certainly made in the artist's studio. Nevertheless, the intention was to summon up the sense of a quiet afternoon of urban idyll, with the attractive blonde woman occupying her time in a productive pursuit and the young adolescent boy admiring a grown man's weapon. The painting's title, whether original to Boldini or not, nicely encapsulates the scene.

Boldini earned a successful living painting these sorts of pictures for the art market, often working through Goupil, one of the most prominent dealers in Paris. His repertoire was wide; sometimes he placed scenes outside in gardens or in the streets of the capital, as in the Clark's *Crossing the Street* (cat. 44), and occasionally he clothed his figures in seventeenth- or eighteenth-century costumes. In such images he was following on the success of French genre painters, especially Jean-Louis-Ernest Meissonier, who had won accolades for his small-scale interiors. What Boldini brought to this artistic category was a brighter palette and a looser, flickering handling of paint, beautifully evident in *Young Woman Crocheting* in, for example, the range of colors in the carpet or the flashing brushwork in the folds of the woman's dress. These elements show the influence of the younger generation of Impressionist painters who were just making themselves known to the public in the mid-1870s.

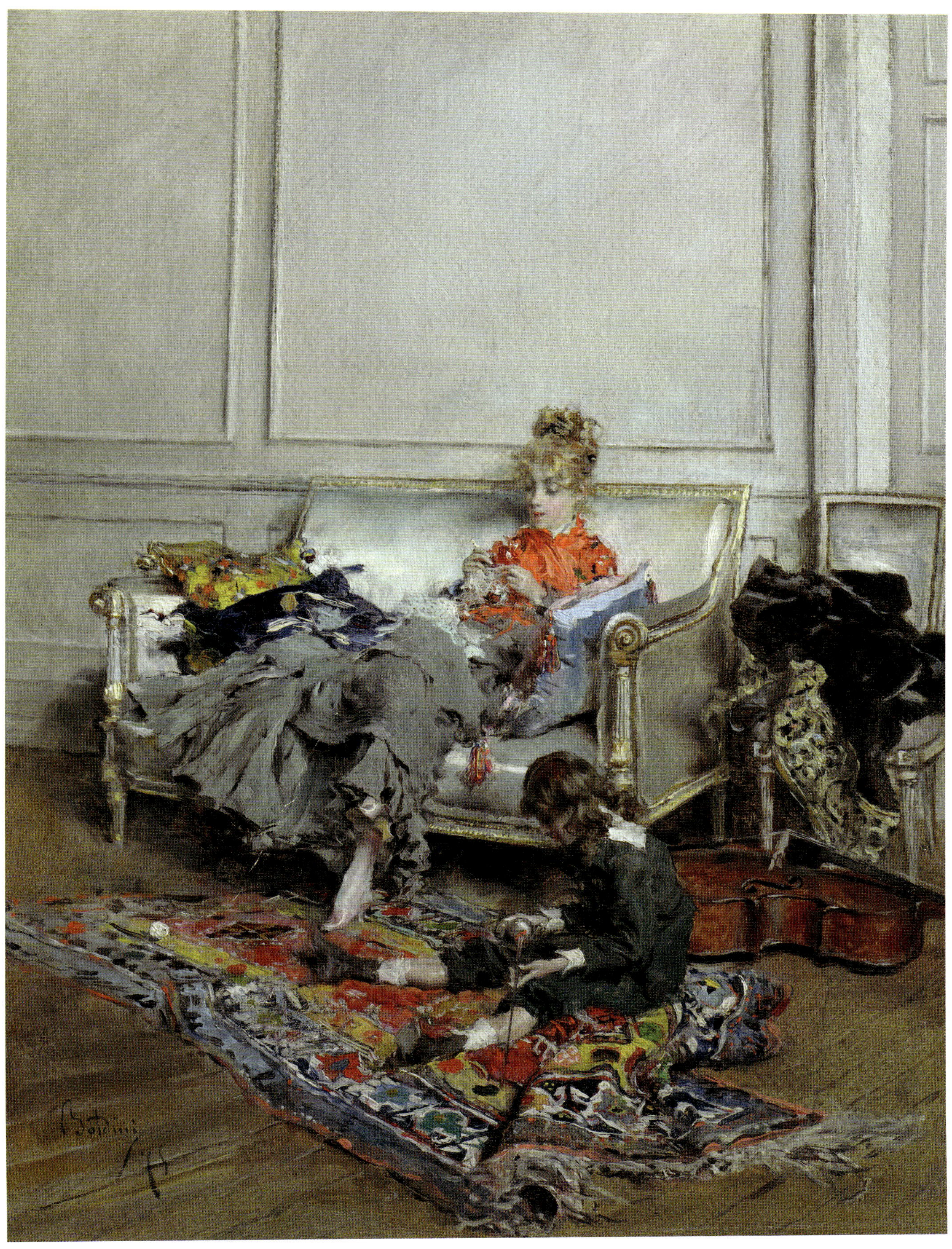

46 JAMES TISSOT French, 1836–1902

Chrysanthemums

c. 1874–76
Oil on canvas
118.4 x 76.2 cm
Signed bottom, left of center: J. J. Tissot
Acquired by the Clark in honor of David S. Brooke (Institute Director, 1977–94), 1994
1994.2

IN 1871 TISSOT MOVED TO LONDON in the aftermath of the Franco-Prussian War, under suspicion of aiding the Paris Commune. Already having developed a reputation in Paris as a society painter, Tissot quickly became a part of London's vibrant art scene. He achieved critical acclaim in 1872 for a series of historical genre paintings that he exhibited at the Royal Academy. Soon thereafter, however, he began focusing on the modern life of fashionable women in paintings such as *Chrysanthemums*.

Like so many of his London paintings, *Chrysanthemums* provides an intimate view into contemporary domestic life. A beautiful young woman in a conservatory has rolled up her sleeves and is busy adjusting the placement of the pot of flowers in front of her. She looks up as if caught unawares, and we have the sense that a private moment has been breached by our presence. Tissot portrays her face slightly out of focus and hides her eyes in dark shadows, as if to accentuate her guarded demeanor. The effect of these passages is heightened by the almost photographic clarity with which the artist renders some of the flowers surrounding the figure. Although the woman adds an alluring human presence, she is almost overwhelmed by the brilliantly blooming flowers that surround and almost subsume her. Her squatting position within a sea of plants and her yellow, white, and black clothing make her seem all but a flower herself.

The eponymous chrysanthemums that Tissot took such pains to depict were reaching a peak of fashionable popularity in late nineteenth-century England. The flower was celebrated not only for its vibrant blooms but also for its hardiness and tolerance of air pollution in crowded cities. The chrysanthemum gained further acclaim when it became the centerpiece of popular exhibitions at public city garden conservatories in London.

It is likely that the picture was staged inside Tissot's own glass conservatory (one of the glass panels is clearly visible in the top left corner of the picture) attached to his studio in Saint John's Wood. Increasingly popular in England after the repeal of the glass tax in 1849, conservatories became associated with not only nurturing plants but also the "cultivation" of proper Victorian women. It was observed that "the hothouse became suitable as a metaphor for privileged women because respectable femininity was defined as dependency, delicacy and fragility—highly decorative but always in need of protection." Tissot would have been aware of these associations when he depicted the gardener in *Chrysanthemums*.

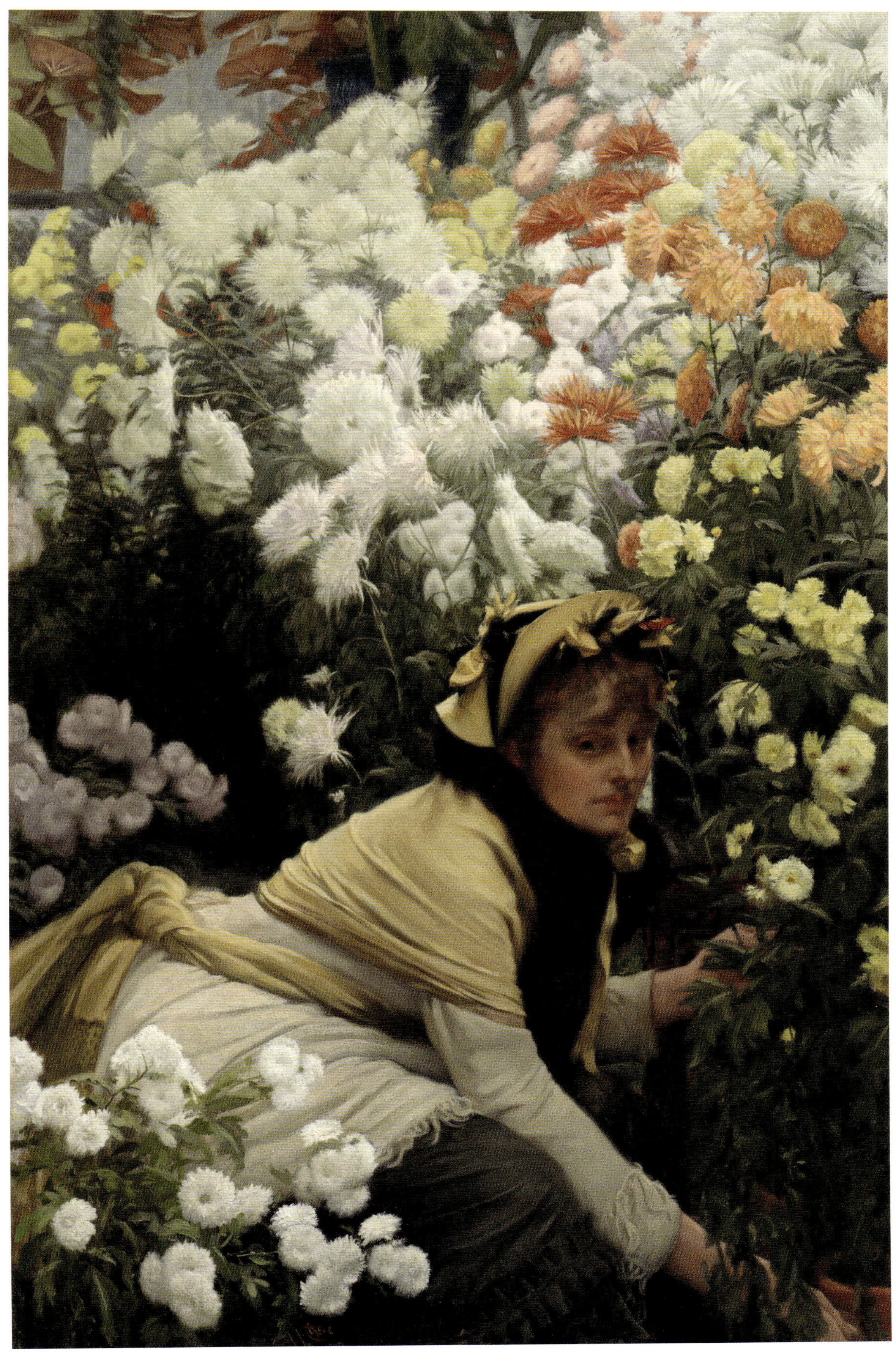

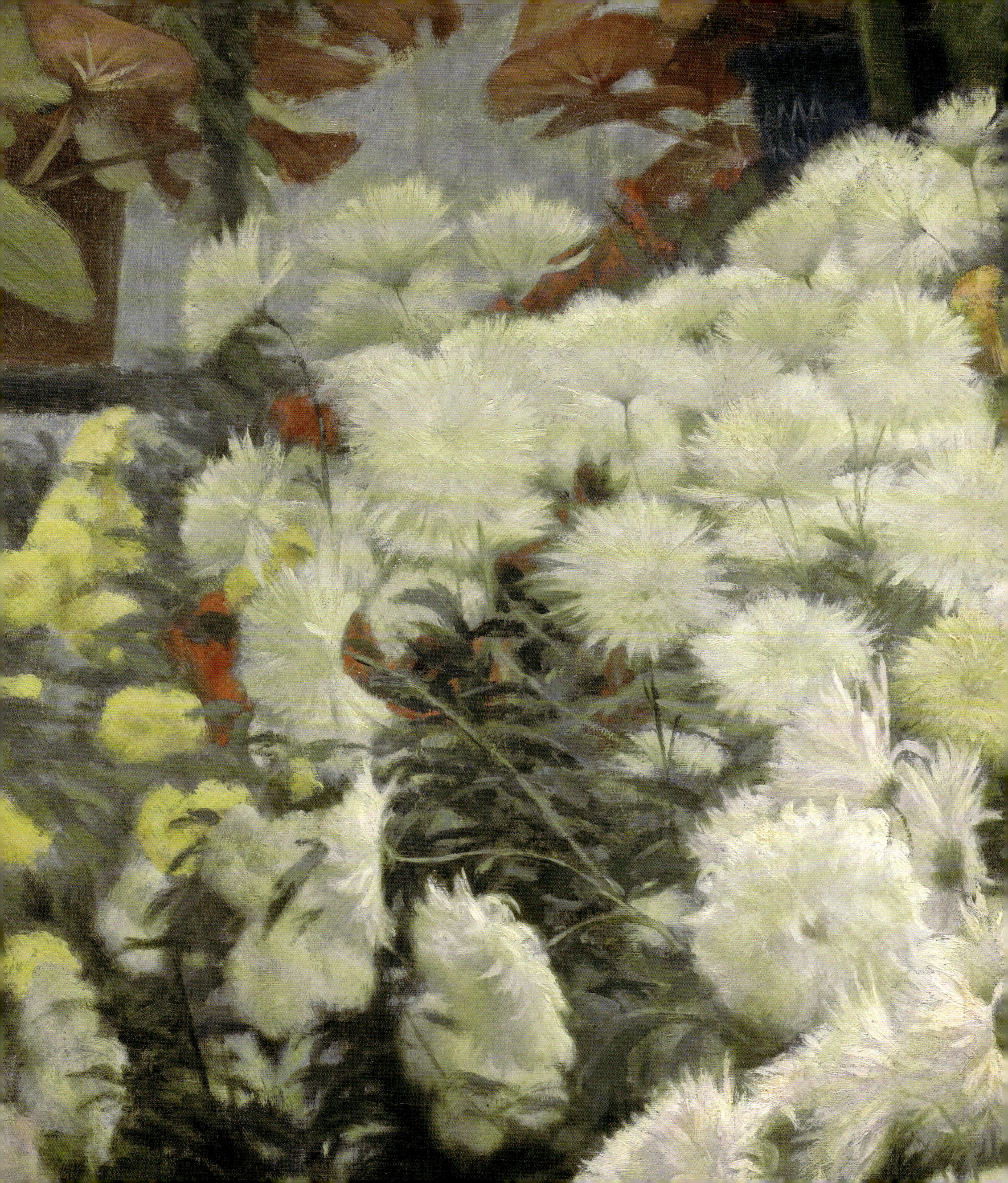

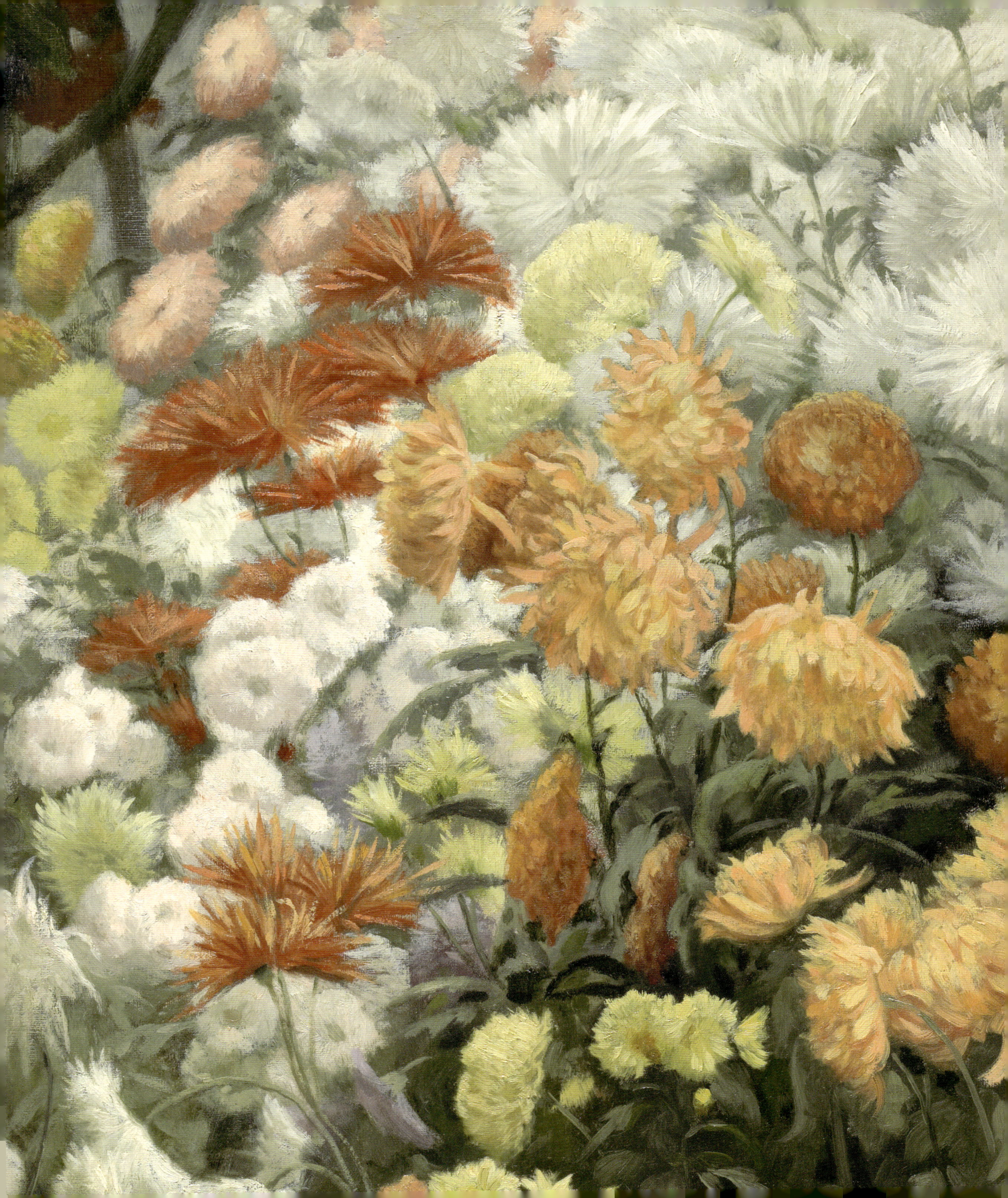

47 PIERRE-AUGUSTE RENOIR French, 1841–1919

Self-Portrait

c. 1875
Oil on canvas
39.1 x 31.6 cm
Signed lower right: Renoir.
Acquired by Sterling and Francine Clark, 1939
1955.584

THIS VIBRANT SELF-PORTRAIT DEPICTS THE ARTIST in his mid-thirties, smartly dressed, with a blue-striped starched collar and a blue *lavallière* necktie. The attention to sartorial matters, however, is compellingly juxtaposed with unkempt facial hair and a nervously alert expression. The wide eyes, vigorous brushwork, and slightly furrowed brow give this work a psychological intensity not always expected of Renoir. The artist's bold expression is further accentuated by the off-center gaze and the textural use of bright paint throughout the face, which becomes even more prominent set against the dark and thinly painted background. Much more than a simple likeness, the portrait is an expressive statement of Renoir's audacious personality and artistic vision.

Renoir included the work in the second Impressionist group exhibition in 1876, but he had mixed feelings about its success as a painting. He referred to the canvas as a "paltry sketch" and supposedly threw it in a trash bin, from where it was allegedly retrieved by the collector Victor Chocquet. In fact, even after receiving a large sum of money for its sale, Renoir remained more bemused by the vagaries of the art-buying public than proud of his accomplishment, commenting that he was "sorry that it was no better than it was." Perhaps Renoir's hesitation to embrace *Self-Portrait* stems from its experimental nature. It is markedly different from his other portraits of the time, which are typically executed with a soft and gentle handling.

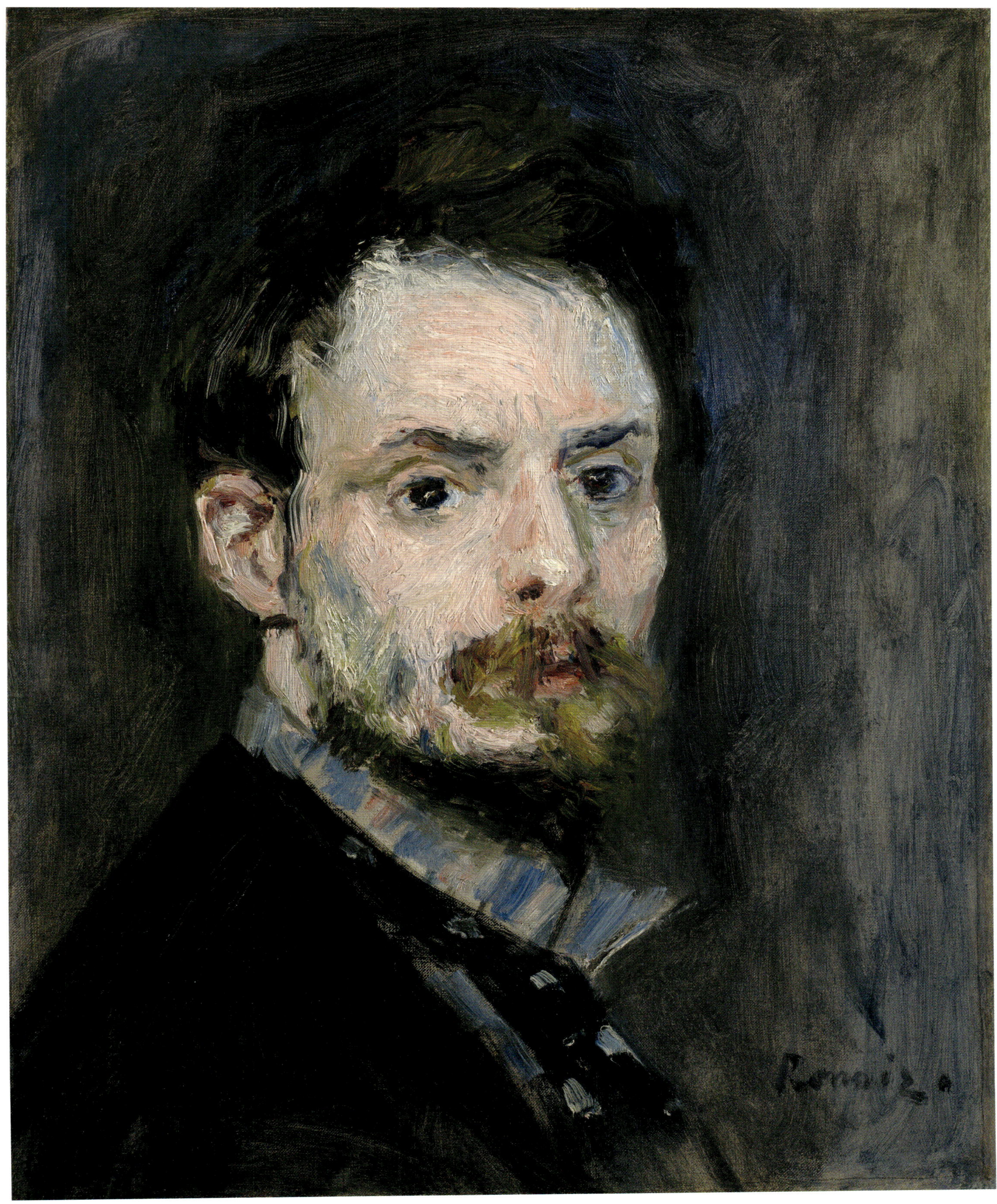
Renoir

48 PIERRE-AUGUSTE RENOIR French, 1841–1919

Portrait of a Young Woman (L'Ingénue)

c. 1874
Oil on canvas
55.7 x 46.4 cm
Signed upper right: Renoir.
Acquired by Sterling and Francine Clark, 1940
1955.606

EXECUTED AROUND THE TIME OF THE FIRST Impressionist exhibition in 1874, *Portrait of a Young Woman* reveals Renoir's sensitivity to color and innate talent for deft brushwork. Thinly painted brushstrokes are punctuated by virtuosic dabs of dense color; the contrast between the rich blues of the scarf and bonnet and the delicately rendered skin tones provides visual intrigue. Similarly, Renoir added volume and character to the girl's dark blonde hair by depicting it in a wide range of hues, including blues, reds, greens, oranges, and yellows. The deep blues of her eyes and the red of her lips provide central pivots to the whole composition.

Like many of Renoir's paintings of young women from the mid-1870s, the Clark's picture is somewhere between a portrait and a character study. The sitter has been identified as the actress Henriette Henriot, who modeled frequently for Renoir during this period. At the time, Henriot was struggling to achieve recognition on the stage, although in the early 1890s she would become the leading actress in André Antoine's productions. The artist thus felt no compunction to modify her features to conform to his ideal of feminine beauty. He shows her fashionably dressed and set against a nondescript background. She gently holds her scarf with one hand and raises a finger to her lip with the other, as if in anticipation. Her gaze is intent on something or someone outside the picture frame. Given the sitter's youth and somewhat anxious expression, the painting early on acquired the title *The Ingenue*, a label that Renoir surely would not have sanctioned. Nevertheless, as a depiction of an expression or character, rendered with a quick and lively brush, *Portrait of a Young Woman* was an obvious heir to the "fantasy portraits" produced by such late-eighteenth-century French artists as Jean-Honoré Fragonard and Jean-Baptiste Greuze, whose works were enjoying a newfound fame in the 1870s.

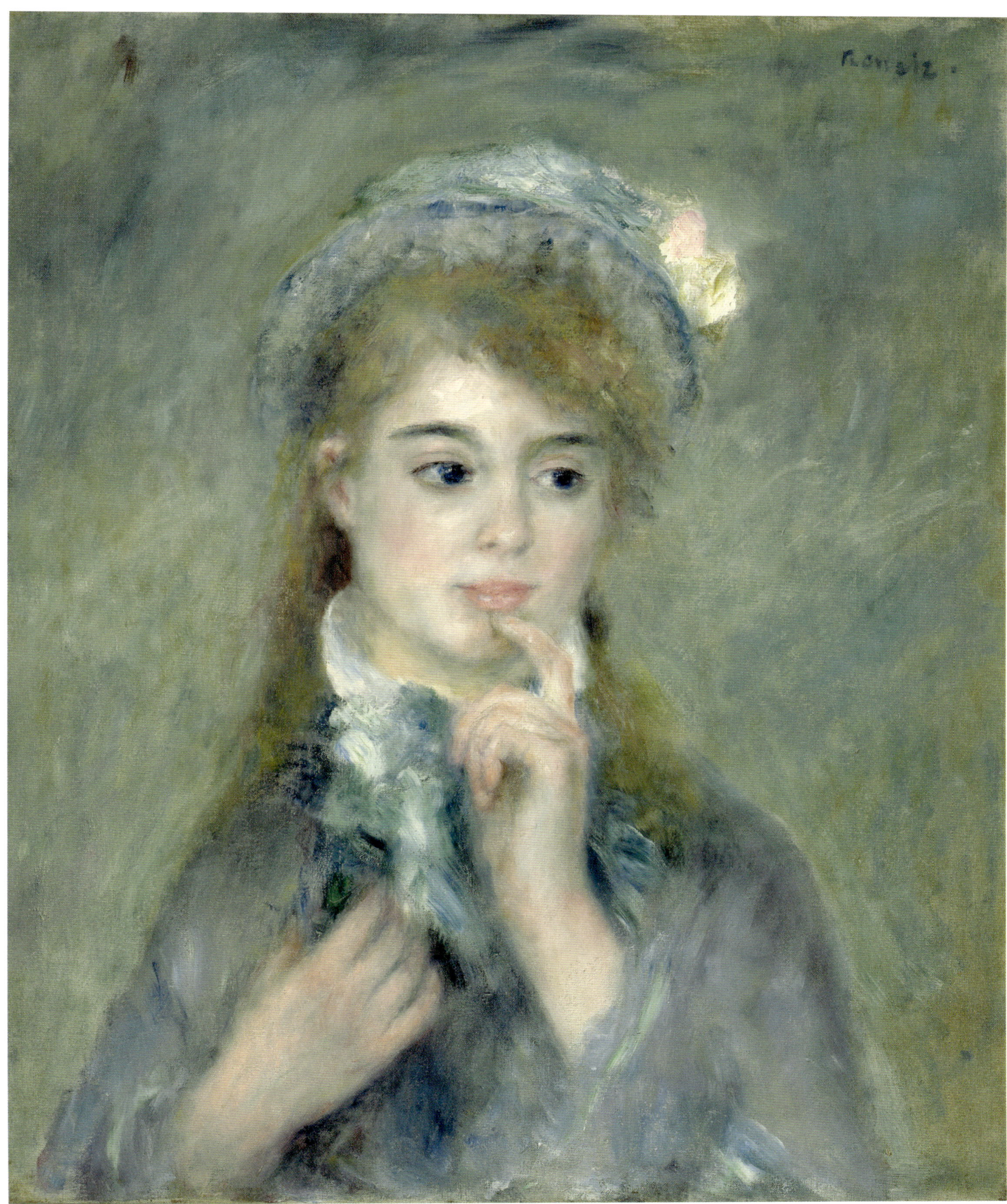
Renoir.

49 PIERRE-AUGUSTE RENOIR French, 1841–1919

Portrait of Madame Monet (Madame Claude Monet Reading)

c. 1874
Oil on canvas
61.6 x 50.3 cm
Signed lower left: A. Renoir.
Acquired by Sterling and Francine Clark, 1933
1955.612

RENOIR PAINTED THIS PORTRAIT OF CAMILLE MONET, Claude Monet's first wife, while staying with the artist and his family at Argenteuil, about seven miles northwest of Paris, where he was a frequent guest in the 1870s. The three round Japanese *uchiwa* fans on the wall may have been a gift from Renoir, as it was customary at the time to bring a housewarming present of three fans. He depicted Camille in a quiet moment, seated on a sumptuous divan and reading a book. While ostensibly a portrait (it was titled *Portrait of Mme M . . .* when first exhibited in 1904), the picture comes across more as a genre scene—we are hard-pressed to recognize Camille's features amid the myriad daubs of paint—or, indeed, as an exploration of broken color and bold compositional design. The artist seems to lose himself in the busy pattern of the divan and its juxtaposition with the equally rich fabrics of the sitter's Turkish caftan. The dress's blue fabric both sets off the central figure and creates a visual link with the wall behind the couch, while its front panels echo the pinks and greens of the divan. Small flecks of paint not only provide a textural element to the picture's surface but also add a vibrancy to an otherwise everyday scene.

Little is known of Camille Monet; she is said to have been a quiet and modest woman who usually deferred to her husband. She is most familiar through her frequent presence in paintings by Monet and his circle of friends. Renoir himself portrayed Camille on a number of occasions, and at least two other times in the same Turkish caftan that she wears in the Clark's painting. In this case Renoir was not concerned with defining her features or expression with much precision; he appears to have been more interested depicting a generalized image of a woman reading. This theme would have provoked some contemporary viewers who saw the burgeoning market for fiction aimed at women as a threat to their supposedly impressionable nature. While *Portrait of Madame Monet* resists an explicit interpretation relating to this debate, for the late-nineteenth-century viewer the portrayal of a woman absorbed in her reading would have had a distinctly modern feel.

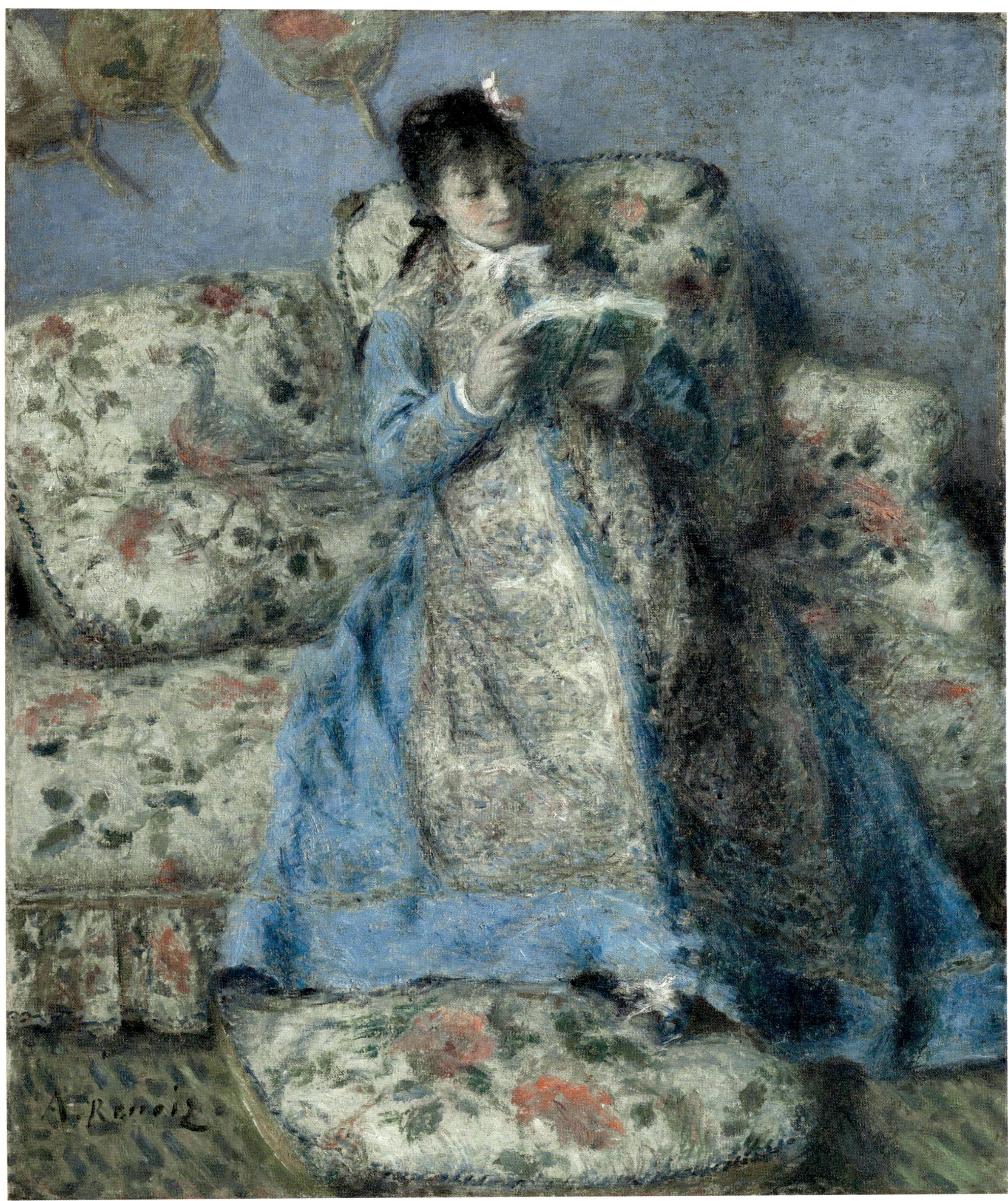
A. Renoir

50 PIERRE-AUGUSTE RENOIR French, 1841–1919

Girl Crocheting

c. 1875
Oil on canvas
73.5 x 60.3 cm
Signed lower right: Renoir.
Acquired by Sterling Clark, 1916
1955.603

POSED IN A DOMESTIC INTERIOR, a young woman sits quietly, her attention focused on her crocheting. Her long red-blonde hair hangs loose, and she is humbly dressed in a plain skirt and a shift that has slipped from her shoulder, baring her skin to the light. Her dress suggests that she is a servant; the fireplace behind her, and the glass and vase placed on its mantel, would appear to belong to a bourgeois household. The young girl is most likely Nini Lopez, who posed for many of Renoir's paintings in the mid-1870s. She was described as having "an admirable head of golden-blonde hair" and was "the ideal model, punctual, serious, discreet." However, the picture should in no way be considered a conventional portrait but rather a type of genre scene that Renoir was making one of his specialties in the 1870s. By that time, images of women sewing had become popular in French genre painting, though more typically focused on the peasantry. Renoir modernized the subject by placing the figure in a bourgeois interior. He invites the spectator to imagine that we are viewing her unawares within this private space, which heightens the sexual charge of her undress. Moreover, the painting marks the extreme point of Renoir's rejection of conventional notions of tonal modeling. Lighting, space, and even, to an extent, the figure's contour are achieved wholly through modulations of color. The sitter's bright, sun-drenched hair and flesh are painted with a thick impasto of varied hues.

Girl Crocheting has a special place in the Clark's collection of Renoirs, as it is the first of the thirty-nine paintings by the artist that Sterling and Francine Clark would own. Sterling bought the painting in 1916, although at the time he was unsure whether he would keep it. In order to protect himself against a loss, Clark requested a guarantee from the dealer to buy back the picture at its purchase price within five years if he should decide to return it. As it turns out, not only did he keep it but it would become indicative of his taste for the next forty years.

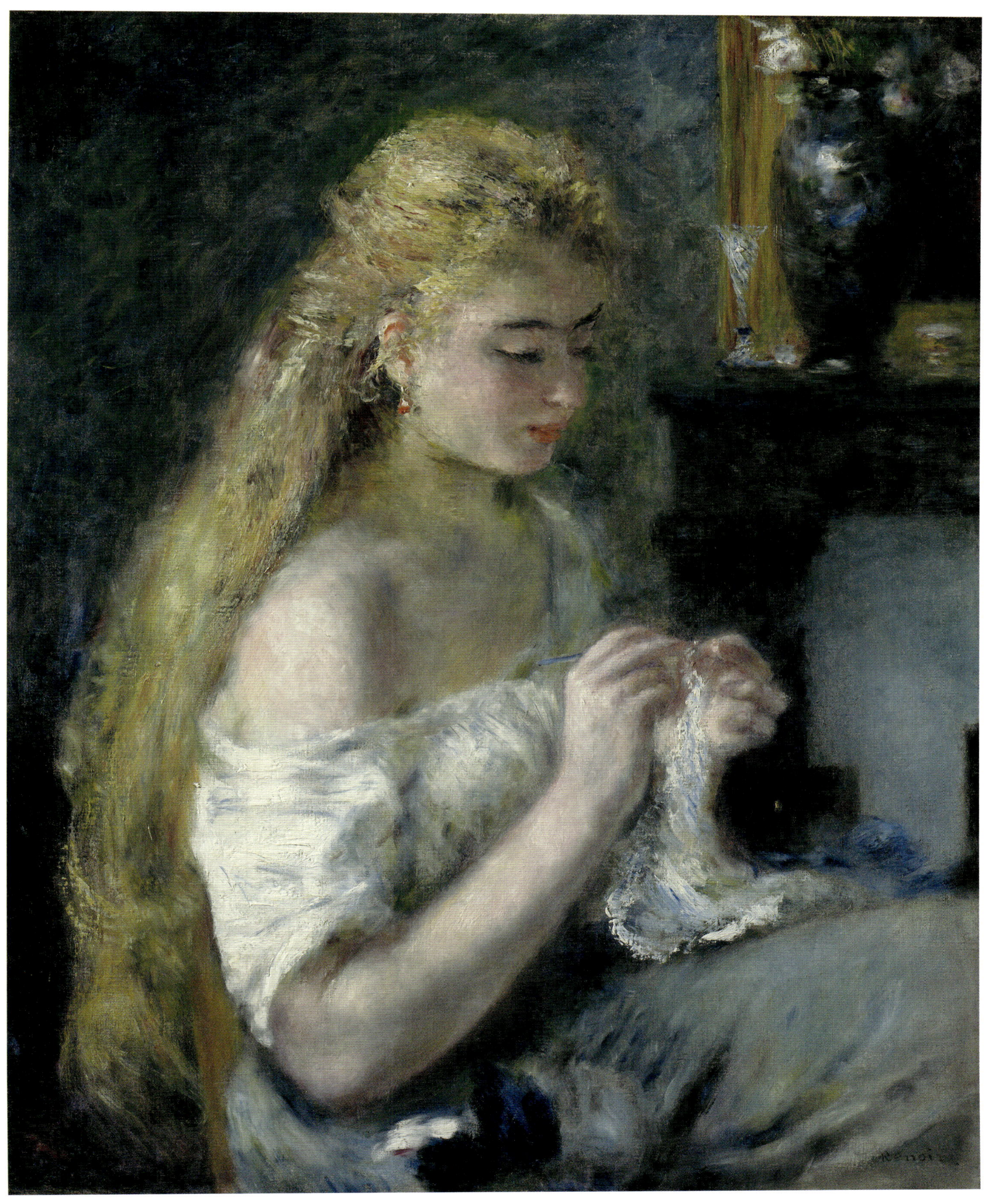

51 PIERRE-AUGUSTE RENOIR French, 1841–1919

Bridge at Chatou

c. 1875
Oil on canvas
51.1 x 65.4 cm
Signed lower right: Renoir.
Acquired by Sterling and Francine Clark, 1925
1955.591

IN 1875 RENOIR BEGAN PAINTING AT THE RESTAURANT FOURNAISE, which would become the setting for some of his most ambitious and famous pictures. Situated on an island in the Seine nine miles west of Paris, alongside the village of Chatou, the restaurant offered Renoir an unparalleled view of this particular expanse of the river and the bridge that crossed it. This bridge was often described as the boundary between the rough factory culture on the outskirts of Paris and the bucolic countryside. In this light, it is noteworthy that in *Bridge at Chatou* Renoir portrays the bank of the river filled with loosely defined buildings and with no indication of the natural beauty so near at hand. It is, in fact, one of Renoir's most urbanized landscapes.

Quickly painted in bright colors, *Bridge at Chatou* typifies Renoir's style in the mid-1870s, when he was much less concerned with accurate delineation of forms than in describing the effects of light and the sense of varied color through deft brushwork. Particularly notable is Renoir's juxtaposition of intense blues and yellows, which is repeated many times throughout the picture. It is likely that the composition was inspired at least in part by Monet's paintings of the bridge at Argenteuil, which were executed in 1874. In both Monet's work and *Bridge at Chatou*, the bridge begins on the right-hand side of the canvas and is portrayed at an angle that leads the viewer into the composition. As was his wont, Renoir took considerably fewer pains than Monet to accurately render the reflections in the water, which are merely suggested in the present picture.

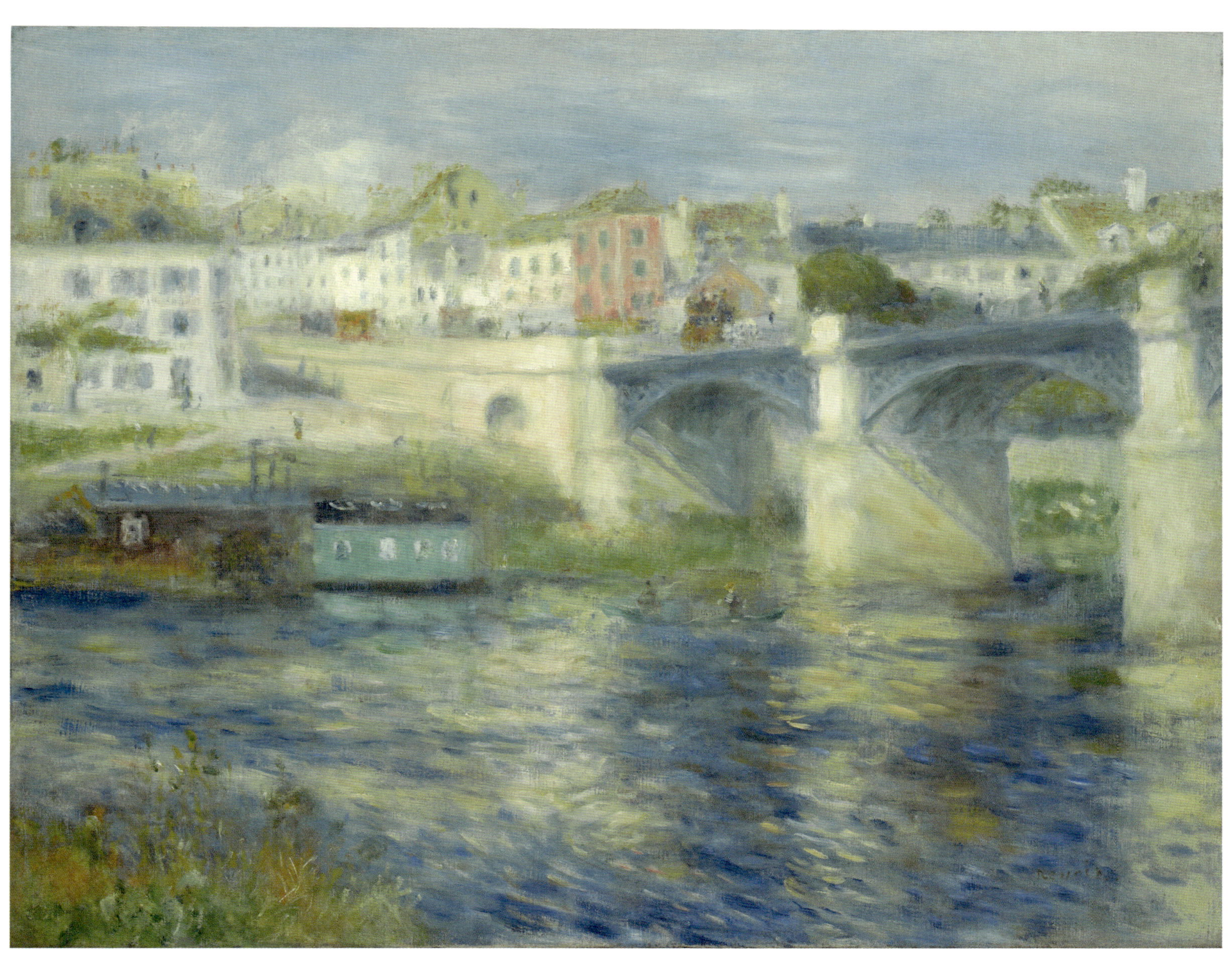

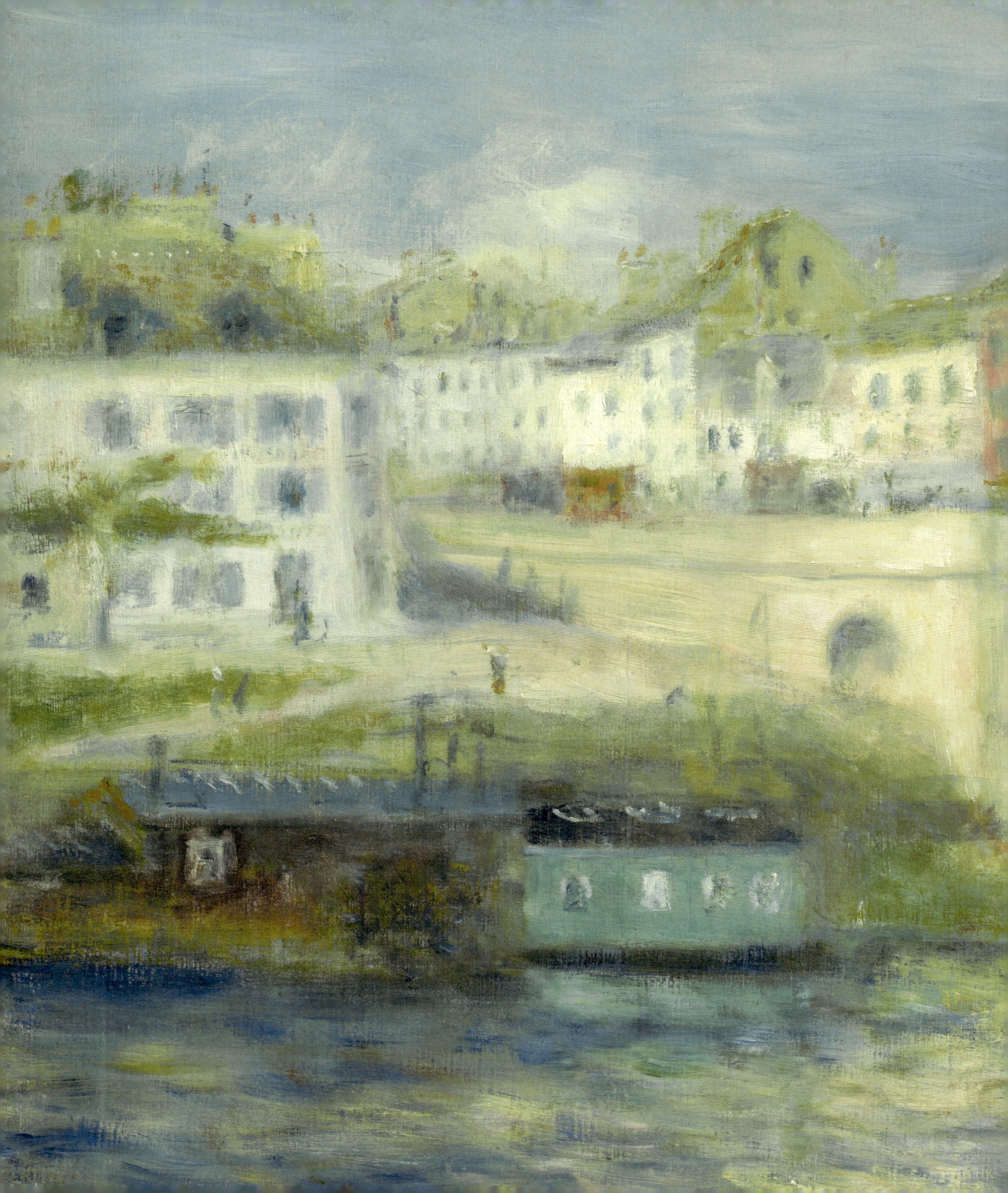

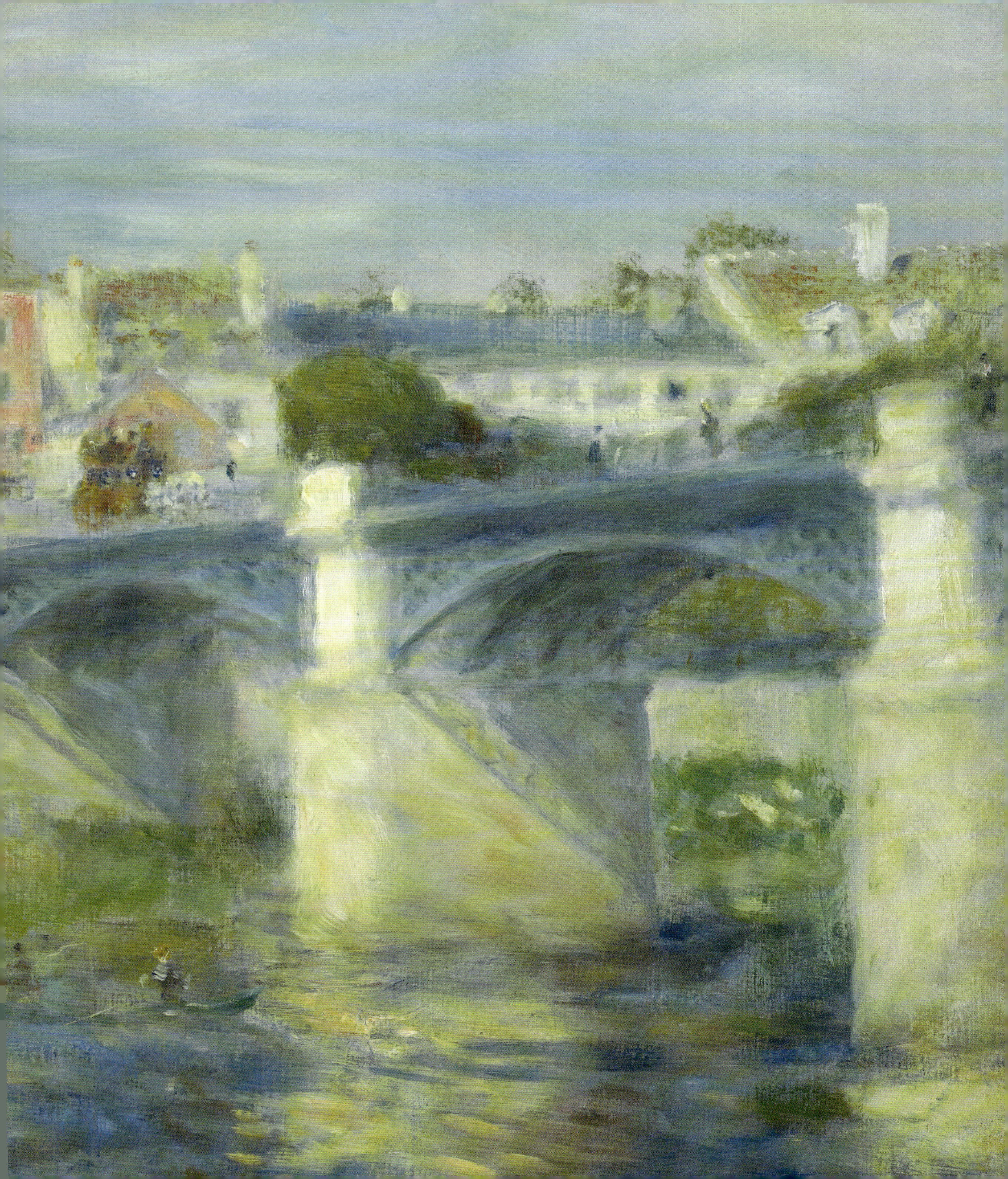

52 PIERRE-AUGUSTE RENOIR French, 1841–1919

Père Fournaise

1875
Oil on canvas
56.2 x 47 cm
Signed and dated right center: Renoir. 75.
Acquired by Sterling and Francine Clark, 1939
1955.55

ALPHONSE FOURNAISE WAS THE PROPRIETOR OF A RESTAURANT and boat-rental business on an island in the river Seine at Chatou, nine miles west of Paris. Renoir was a regular customer at the establishment from the 1860s onward, and it is the site of some of his most famous paintings, including *Luncheon of the Boating Party* (Phillips Collection, Washington, D.C.). Renoir himself described the restaurant as a place where there were "plenty of pretty girls to paint." Renoir and Fournaise became good friends, with the restaurateur sometimes accepting paintings in lieu of payment for meals. The present portrait was commissioned by Fournaise in part to thank Renoir for bringing new clients to the establishment.

Renoir portrays Fournaise in a casual moment, with a beer in front of him and a pipe in his mouth. He is wearing a dark waistcoat over a loose white shirt with a carefully pinned cravat and a dark cap. His gaze is to the left, and one can imagine that the second beer in the foreground belongs to a conversation companion. The painting gives the sense of a man comfortably enjoying convivial company.

The loose and informal brushwork seems appropriate to the leisurely subject. The composition revolves around the warm flesh tones of Fournaise's face and wrist, which are enlivened by intense touches of red. Renoir softened the dark waistcoat by brushing a light layer of yellow over the blue while the paint was still wet. The sitter's sparkling blue eyes are rendered in a sequence of delicate flecks of paint. The background, which now tends toward a drab brown, was originally a more purplish red hue, further enlivening the scene. It is one of a number of instances in which Renoir used a pigment that has faded and changed tonality over time.

Late in his life, Renoir singled out his portrait of Fournaise as an example of the public's changing attitudes toward his work. He commented that the painting, which at first was thought of as "the height of vulgarity, suddenly became distinguished in its handling when I began to fetch high prices at the auctions." Somewhat bitterly, he reminisced that "the same people who now talk with the greatest conviction about the refined treatment of the portrait of Père Fournaise wouldn't have shelled out five louis [a hundred francs] for a portrait, at a time when five louis would have been so useful to me." Years later, Sterling Clark had no such reservation about the painting when he first saw it, noting in his diary that it was a "fine picture" and that there was "no question about its quality."

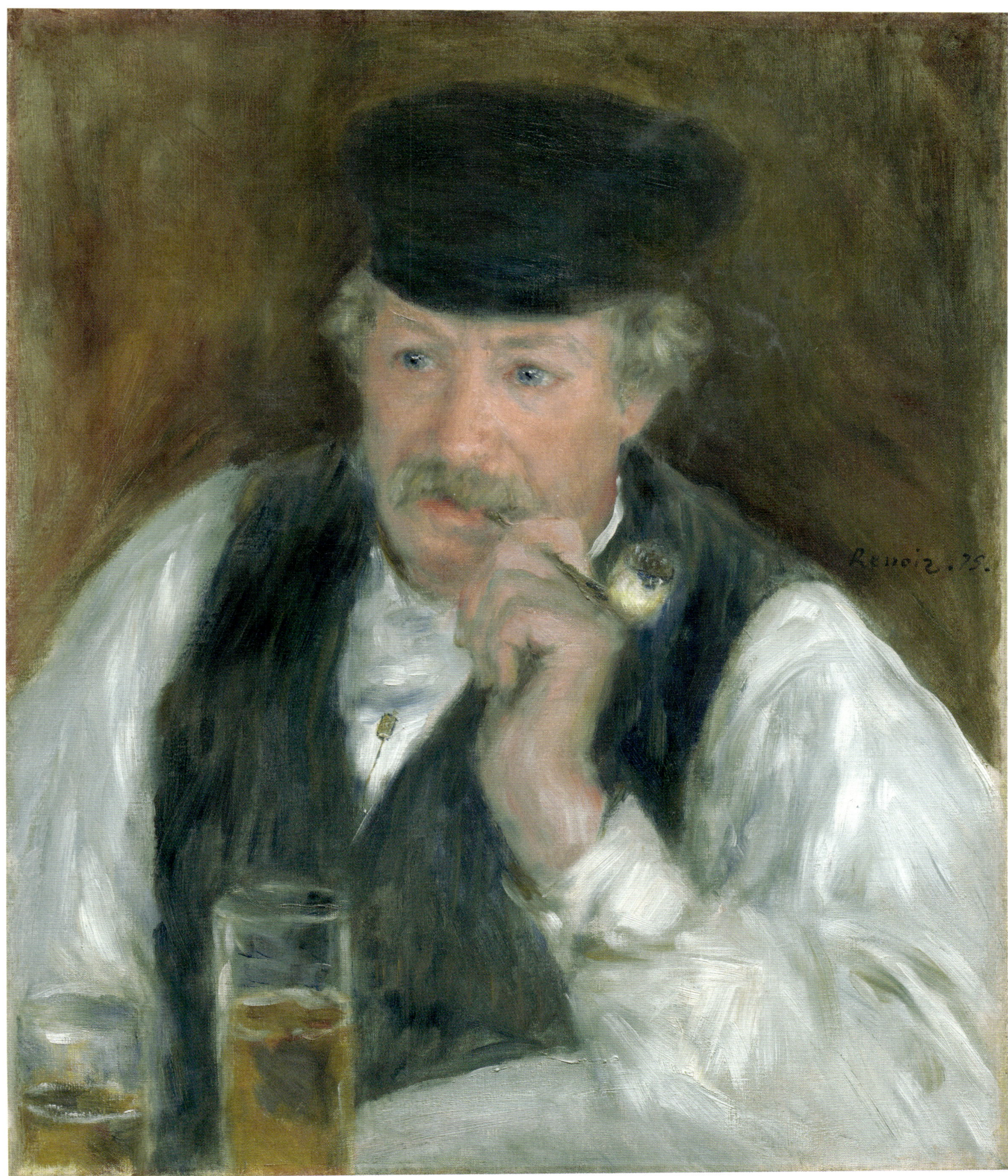
Renoir. 75.

53 PIERRE-AUGUSTE RENOIR French, 1841–1919

Girl with a Fan

c. 1879
Oil on canvas
65.4 x 54 cm
Signed lower left: Renoir.
Acquired by Sterling and Francine Clark, 1939
1955.595

LIKE SO MANY OF RENOIR'S PAINTINGS OF YOUNG WOMEN, *Girl with a Fan* defies easy categorization. The model is Jeanne Samary, a well-known actress at the Comédie-Française who specialized in the roles of coquettish servant girls. Renoir frequently used her as a model between 1877 and 1881, explicitly painting her portrait three times. Although Renoir neither conceived nor exhibited the present painting as a conventional portrait, he seems to be toying with the boundaries between portraiture and genre painting. He has consciously generalized the model's features to conform more closely to the ideal of a beautiful young woman but has in all other respects infused the painting with Samary's identity. Photographs and engravings of Samary's dressing room show a wall with bold stripes and chairs with scroll-like decorations that match the one on which this model sits. They also reveal that the ceiling of the dressing room was adorned with Japanese fans of the type she is seen holding. It is doubtful that these individualizing attributes would have been known to a broader public, but the first owner of the painting, Samary's husband, Marie-Joseph-Paul Lagarde, would certainly have recognized their significance.

Regardless of its status as a portrait or genre painting, *Girl with a Fan* is an alluring picture that stands out among Renoir's many images of pretty young girls. In addition to the fan, the enclosed space and the asymmetry of the composition suggest that Renoir was experimenting with Japanese pictorial devices. While he did not share the passion for Japanese art that was so meaningful for his friends Edgar Degas and Claude Monet, he undoubtedly saw the display of Japanese art at the Exposition Universelle of 1878, and the imagery would have been fresh in his mind when he painted this picture. He placed the head of the young girl near the center of the composition, tightly surrounding her with the bouquet of bright chrysanthemums, the backdrop of striped wallpaper, and the fan, held close to her cheek and perfectly parallel to the picture plane. Rather than create visual confusion, these pictorial conceits emphasize the girl's three-dimensional volume. Accessorized with a fashionable hat, Japanese fan, and a shiny earring, the alluring young lady is an archetype of a Parisian society girl, who seems to float in front of an enigmatic background.

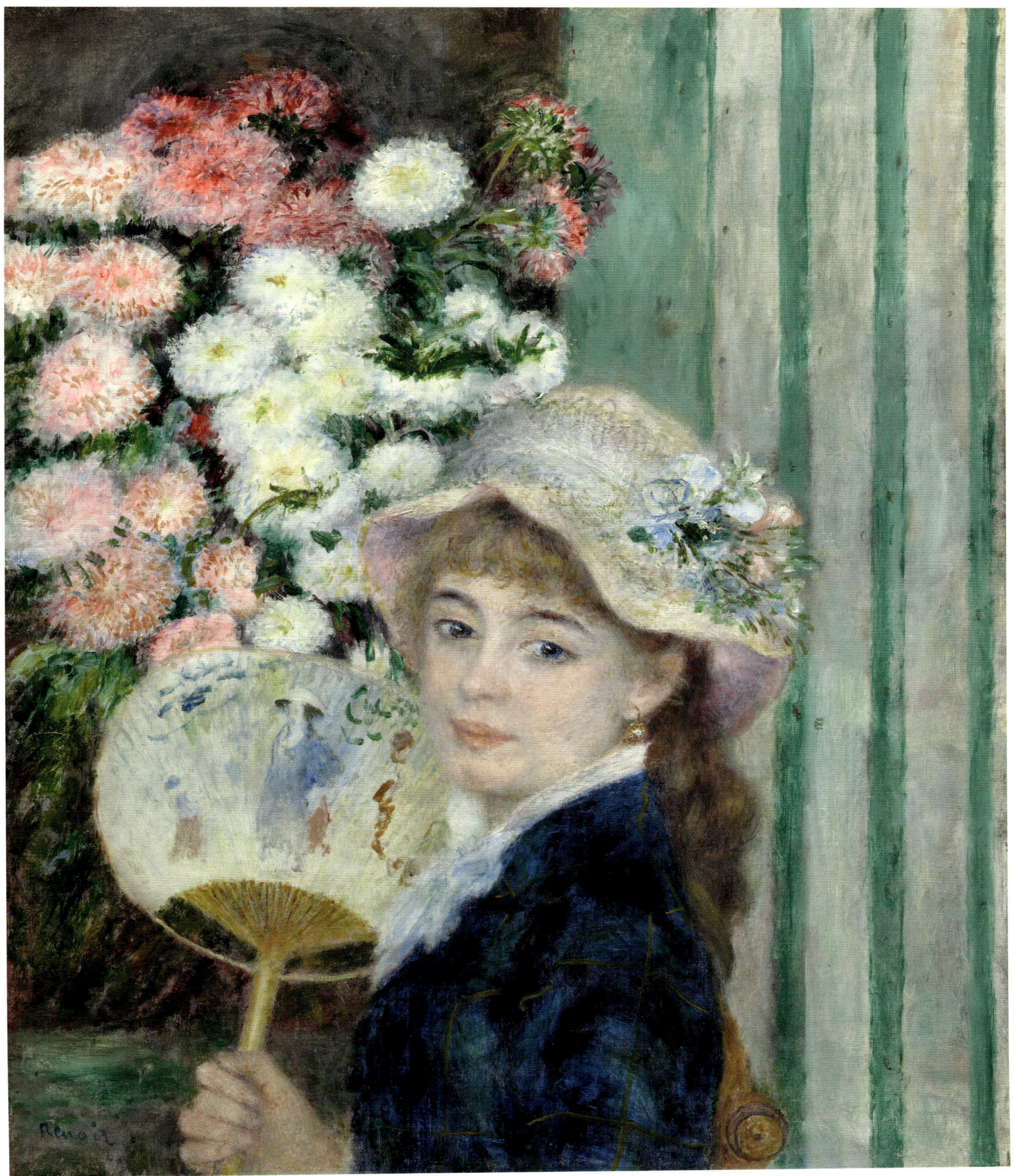
Renoir.

54 PIERRE-AUGUSTE RENOIR French, 1841–1919

Thérèse Berard

1879
Oil on canvas
55.9 x 46.8 cm
Signed and dated upper right: Renoir. 79.
Acquired by Sterling and Francine Clark, 1946
1955.593

PAUL BERARD WAS A PROTESTANT BANKER who was a close friend and patron of Renoir's. In 1879 Berard invited Renoir for the first time to his Château de Wargemont, northeast of Dieppe. It was during this inaugural visit (Renoir would return often in the following years) that he executed this portrait of Thérèse, Berard's niece. It is one of many portraits of Berard family children that Renoir would eventually paint, including *Sketch of Heads (The Berard Children)* in the Clark collection. The artist also painted landscapes in the area around Wargemont, as well as still lifes and wall panels that would decorate the Berard household.

In the portrait, a thirteen-year-old Thérèse Berard stares obliquely away from the viewer in a demure and somewhat melancholy manner. Her long hair hangs loose over her shoulders. Renoir lavished considerable attention not only on her downcast eyes but also on the dress's elaborate lace collar. The outfit, while typically worn by children in the countryside, was not to the sitter's liking. In fact, family tradition has it that Thérèse was never fond of the portrait because of the attire she was depicted wearing. Renoir, for his part, not only took great pains to capture the character of the dress but also used its color as a jumping-off point for the darker purplish hue of the background; the painting becomes a subtle orchestration of blues and purples.

For all its bold use of a limited color range, *Thérèse Berard* is nonetheless conventional in its pose and expression. Renoir himself commented that when painting a portrait it was above all "necessary for a mother to recognize her daughter," and to please his new patrons he may have downplayed any experimentation. Contrary to his normal working methods, for this portrait Renoir drew the entire image in graphite on the primed canvas before beginning to paint. He then applied relatively thin layers of color rather than his usual thick brushstrokes, perhaps in an attempt to create an accurate likeness and a more acceptable painting surface.

Sterling Clark adored the painting, describing it in his diaries as a "real treasure . . . in bluish tones and white mostly—one of the best portraits I have ever seen by Renoir—pleasant subject, alive, beautiful coloring, and well drawn."

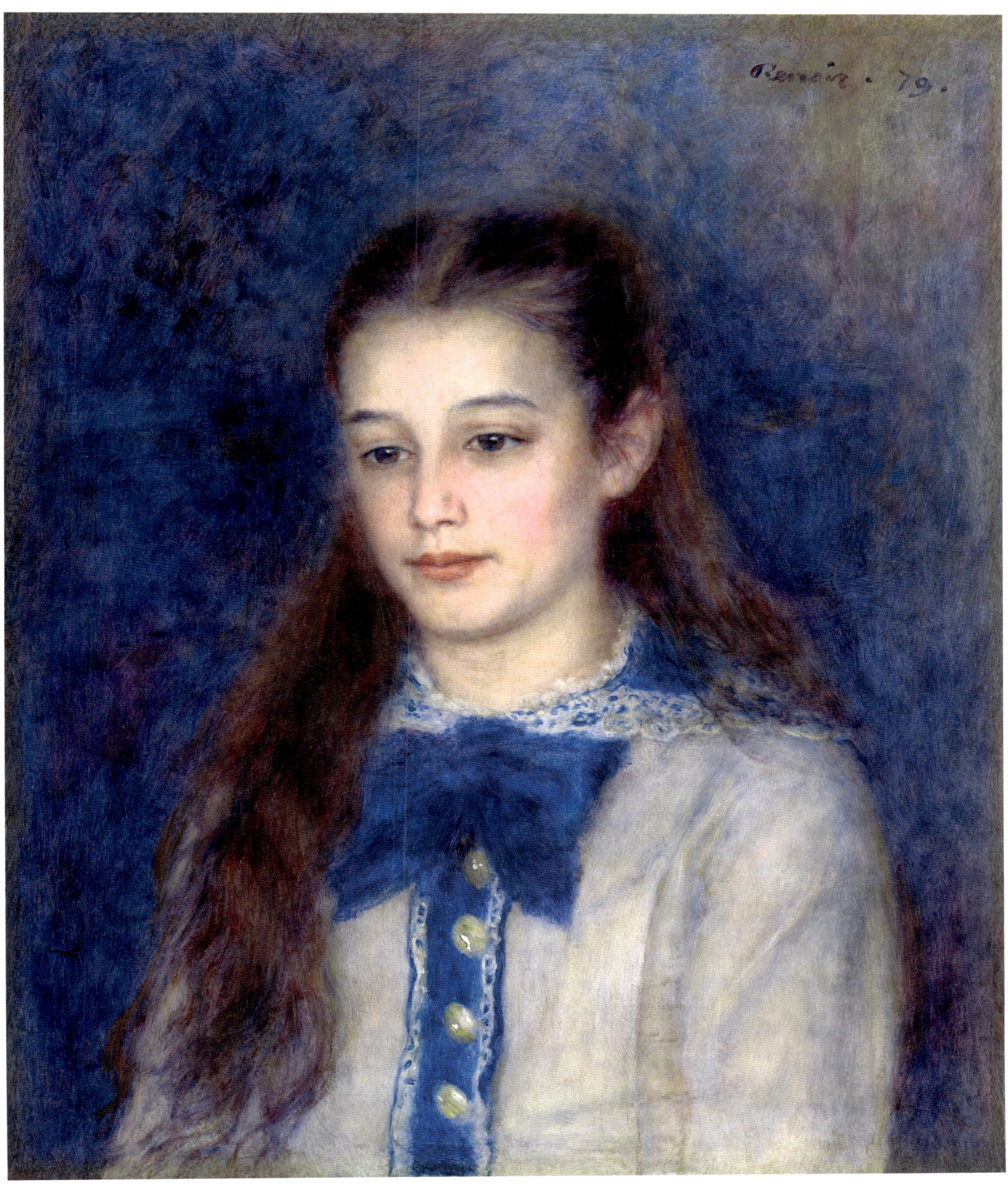
Renoir . 79.

55 PIERRE-AUGUSTE RENOIR French, 1841–1919

Sleeping Girl

1880
Oil on canvas
120.3 x 91.9 cm
Signed and dated lower right: Renoir. 80.
Acquired by Sterling and Francine Clark, 1926
1955.598

SLEEPING GIRL WAS FIRST EXHIBITED AT THE SALON OF 1880, where it received unfavorable reviews, perhaps due to its being hung in an obscure and unflattering location. Subsequently, Renoir's dealer Paul Durand-Ruel submitted it to the seventh Impressionist exhibition in 1882. Although the canvas never achieved the critical acclaim Renoir had hoped for, it became a favorite of Durand-Ruel's, and the dealer installed it as a centerpiece of the *petit salon* of his private residence. He also chose an etching of the painting to adorn the catalogue frontispiece of a major retrospective that was organized in 1892.

The model for the painting has been identified as Angèle, a young girl from the Montmartre neighborhood of Paris who was known for her many lovers, irregular lifestyle, and colorful slang. She is shown here asleep on a red chair wearing a blue dress, striped peasant stockings, and a white shift that slips off her shoulders. While the dress and stockings are typical attire for working-class women, the feathered hat and bourgeois armchair on casters are obvious props supplied by the artist. The erotic undertones that permeate the canvas—the open posture of the sitter, her bare shoulder, the cat that sits on her lap—were not lost on the critics and caricaturists who derided the painting when it was first exhibited.

It has been suggested that Renoir simply caught the model during a weary moment after a night of carousing, and this hypothesis is given some credence by evidence from X-ray photographs, which suggest that there was originally a bottle of wine next to the sitter's right leg. But it is also true that Renoir was painting a well-established genre of the female model in a casual pose. In such a situation, the sitter becomes more human and natural, and the role of the artist and viewer becomes less aesthetic and more voyeuristic.

Close inspection reveals that Renoir spent much energy in choosing certain elements of the final composition. There are indications that the indeterminate background originally might have been a more defined space, with perhaps a door in the left background. The biggest change, however, is evident in the model's chair, which initially was much larger and possibly made of wicker. In the end, Renoir created an image that has a clear and vivid presence. The contrasting blue and red tonalities are complemented by the artist's deft brushwork. The white shift, rendered in a freely brushed impasto to heighten its contrast with the flesh tones behind it, is a particularly exquisite example of Renoir's painterly craft. Indeed, Sterling Clark described *Sleeping Girl* as "a really magnificent piece of painting, color, and art."

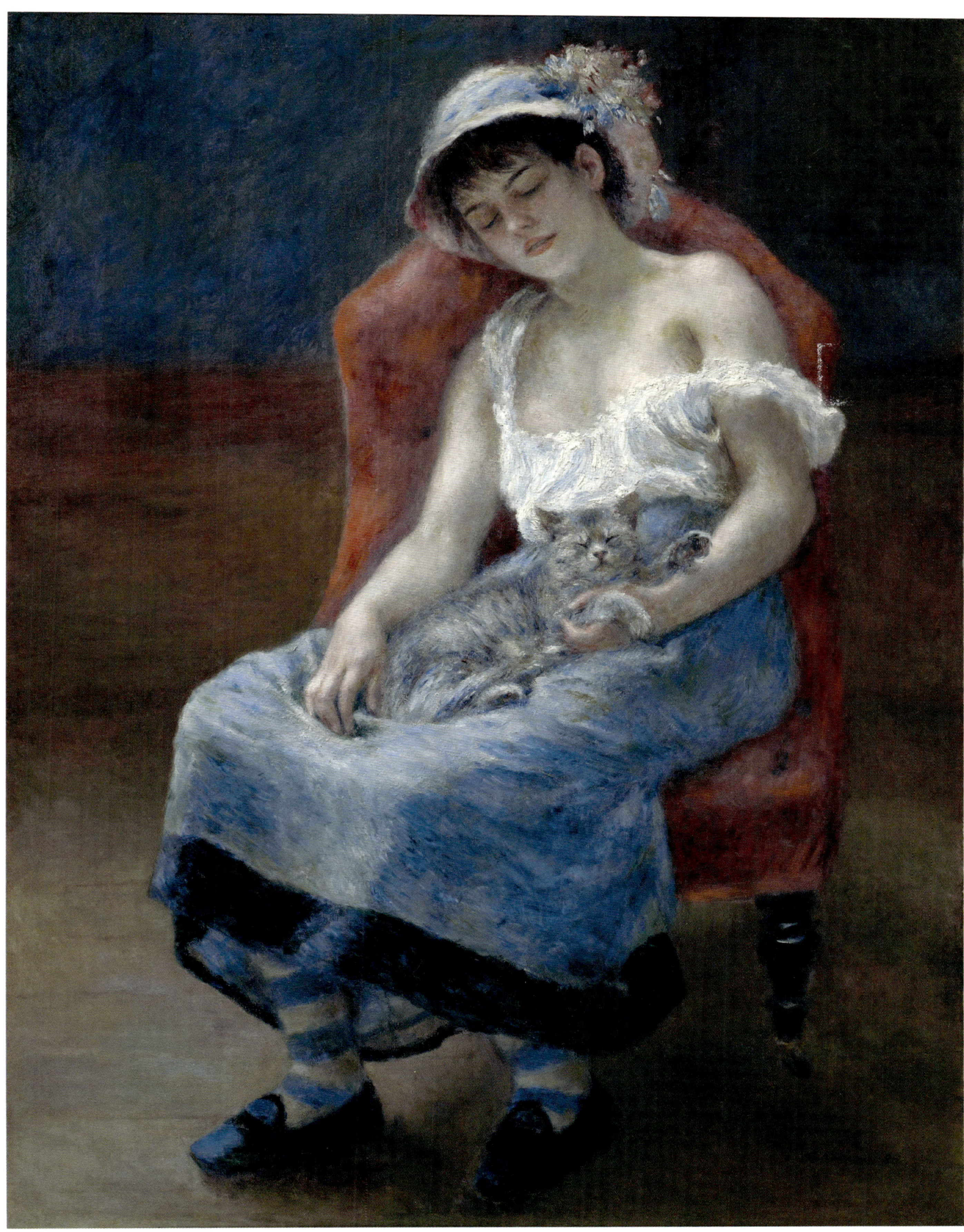

56 PIERRE-AUGUSTE RENOIR French, 1841–1919

A Box at the Theater (At the Concert)

1880
Oil on canvas
99.4 x 80.7 cm
Signed and dated upper left: Renoir. 80.; signed center left: Renoir.
Acquired by Sterling and Francine Clark, 1928
1955.594

THIS PAINTING IS THE LAST AND ARGUABLY MOST AMBITIOUS of Renoir's depictions of elegantly dressed figures seated in theater boxes. In this example, marked by warm colors and rich brushwork, the woman on the left, resplendent in a full-length black evening gown, looks directly at the viewer. Her younger companion, dressed more simply, turns away shyly, revealing her long and luxurious black hair. They hold a musical score and a bouquet of flowers and seem lost in reverie, hardly conscious of even each other's presence or of the performance. Without the dark red curtain and the fluted pilaster, it would be difficult to locate this scene in a theater at all.

According to Renoir's dealer Paul Durand-Ruel, *A Box at the Theater* was originally commissioned as a portrait of the daughters of Edmond Turquet, the French Under-Secretary of State for Fine Arts, but Turquet was unhappy with the result and rejected the canvas. Rather than destroy the painting, Renoir decided to rework the composition and generalize the features of the sitters to turn it into a genre painting. Whether or not this story is true, there is no question that Renoir made striking changes to the picture over time. Most dramatically, he removed a third, male figure that he had originally included in the upper right corner, now covered with a fringed velvet curtain; hints of this figure are still visible to the naked eye. Renoir also altered certain facial features and changed the hairstyle of the woman on the left (she was likely originally wearing an elaborate headdress). Furthermore, it is not clear whether the girl holding the bouquet was part of the initial painting. If she was added later, this might explain some of the spatial awkwardness between her and the older sitter's elbow.

The picture was first shown at the seventh Impressionist exhibition in 1882 with the title *Une loge à l'Opéra*, though the background details suggest a theater rather than the recently opened Palais Garnier. There was some division among critics, with one remarking that it was "crudely drawn," and "where two elegant women converse about everything except what is taking place on the stage." Another wrote that the painting "contains a young girl in black whose eyes and smile are deliciously lively." Sterling Clark, who purchased it in 1928, greatly admired the canvas, writing that "the woman is lovely, the coloring, facture and composition great."

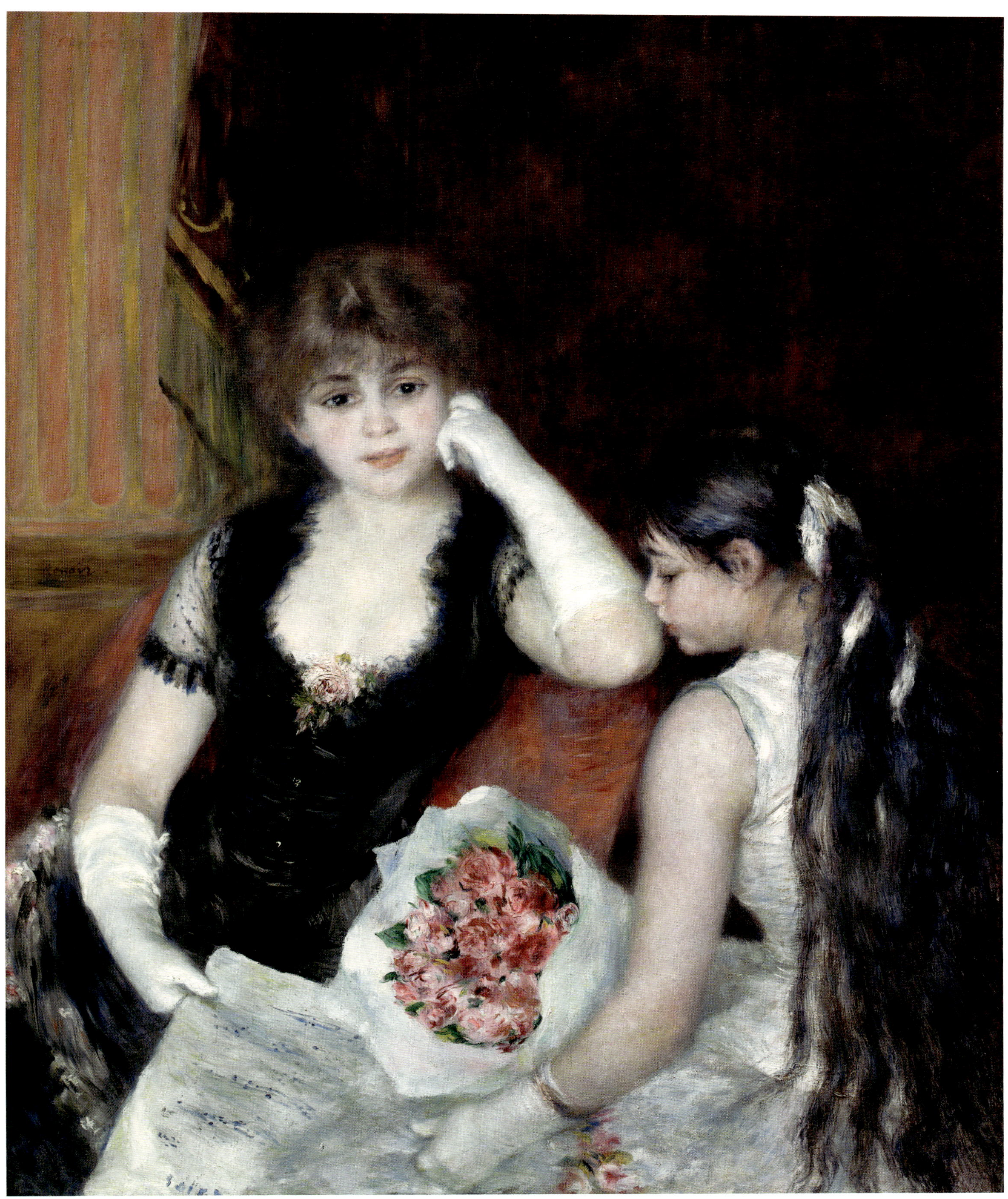

57 PIERRE-AUGUSTE RENOIR French, 1841–1919

Peonies

c. 1880
Oil on canvas
55.3 x 65.7 cm
Signed lower right: Renoir.
Acquired by Sterling and Francine Clark, 1942
1955.585

RENOIR ONCE TOLD A FRIEND THAT "painting flowers rests my brain. I don't feel the same tension as when I am face-to-face with a model. When I paint flowers, I place my colors and experiment with values boldly, without worrying about spoiling a canvas." Painted about 1880, *Peonies* embodies these experimental qualities and is especially notable for its sense of immediacy and direct painterly improvisation. The sumptuous bouquet fills the composition, with some of the flowers overflowing the confines of the canvas. The vibrant reds and pinks of the blooms jump out against the deep blue background. Even though this is presumably an indoor subject, the dazzling colors of the peonies are indicative of the bright palette Renoir developed for his sun-filled outdoor scenes. The undefined and thinly painted vase provides a textural contrast to the thickly impastoed flowers, giving the peonies added weight and presence. Renoir employed a varied touch throughout, with the lavish forms of the blooms punctuated by the linear strokes of the crisp green leaves. It is clear that the ebullient effects of color and brushwork are as much at the center of this painting as the eponymous flowers.

Peonies were first introduced into European nurseries in the 1860s and quickly became a familiar presence in domestic French horticulture. Their blooms were praised most of all for adding vibrant patches of varied color to the garden landscape. Surprisingly, although the flowers in *Peonies* appear to be close at hand, they are not rendered with the botanical detail such a view would ostensibly afford. Renoir instead emphasizes the general lushness and density of the flowers—the very effect a patch of peonies in a garden might have. He seems to be portraying an up-close examination of the general character of a group of blooms rather than describing individual flowers.

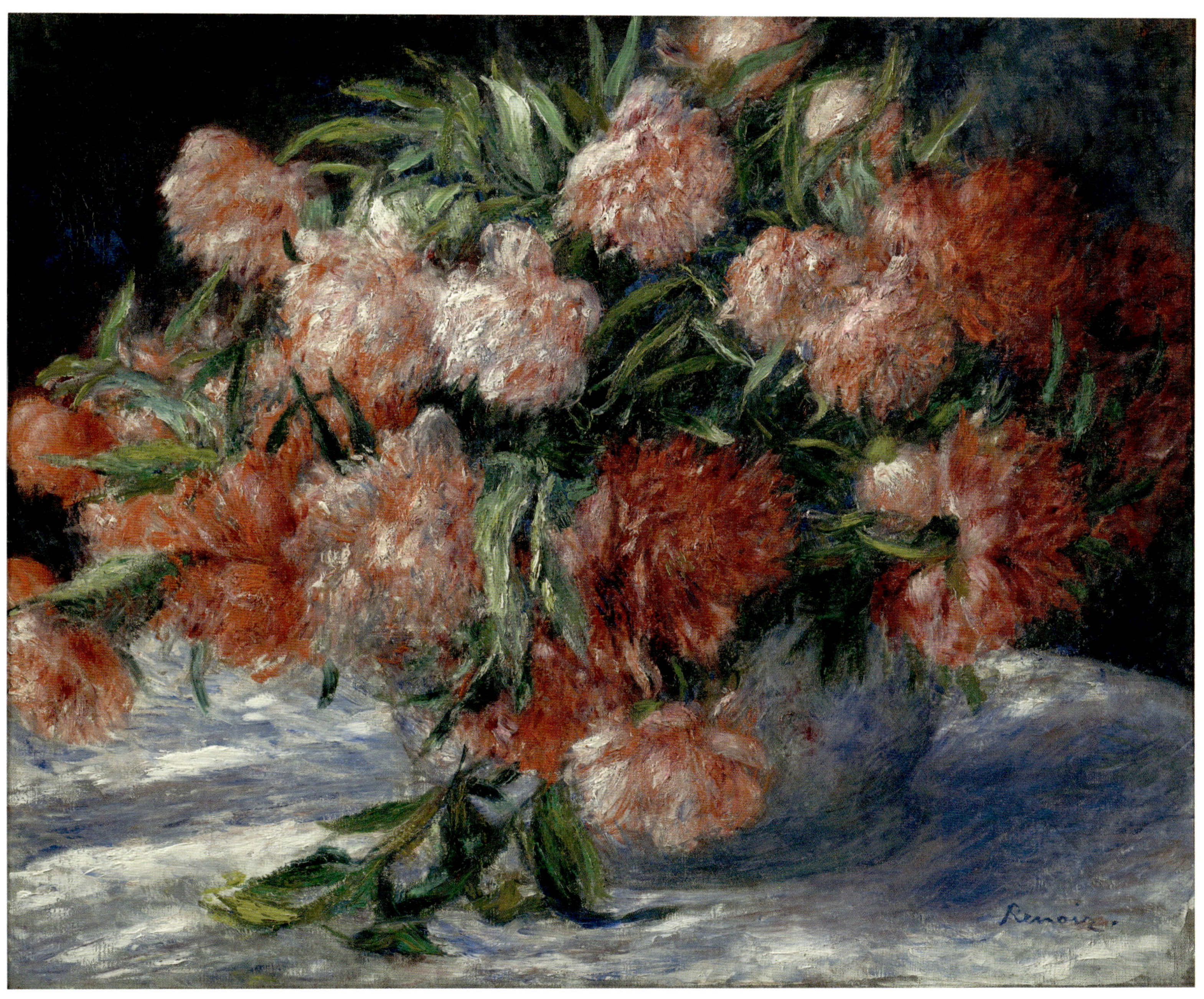
Renoir.

58 PIERRE-AUGUSTE RENOIR French, 1841–1919

Sunset

1879 or 1881
Oil on canvas
45.7 x 61 cm
Signed lower right: Renoir
Acquired by Sterling and Francine Clark, 1941
1955.602

A RAPID SKETCH FULL OF DRAMATIC LIGHT EFFECTS, *Sunset* is unusual in Renoir's oeuvre in that it has no indication of a geographical location. It is unclear exactly when the canvas was painted, although it likely dates from either 1879 or 1881. In its audacious technique and vantage point, *Sunset* is very close to *Seascape* (Art Institute of Chicago), a more finished picture made in 1879. By the same token, a letter from July 1881 reports that Renoir was busy painting on the Normandy coast and created an "effect of sunset painted in ten minutes," which may very well allude to this work.

In creating this atmospheric picture, Renoir has animated the water's surface by highlighting the effect of the sun's light on the ocean waves. The motion of the water itself is not the focus here; the diagonal brushstrokes convey movement, but Renoir seems less concerned with the quality of the water than with what is occurring on the surface. The sea is heavily worked up, with superimposed layers of color creating a liquid effect. The sky, in contrast, is painted in broad, rapid swaths. Despite the differences in the brushwork, Renoir achieved an overall coherence in the picture through his use of color. The contrasts of blue and orange in the sky and the same colors, scattered in smaller strokes across the sea below, create both variety and unity. The boat, though tiny and painted only in two seemingly casual dabs of darker blue, creates a central pivot around which the play of color in the rest of the composition revolves. Although the canvas is painted in a sketchy manner, the fact that Renoir signed it indicates that he felt it was a finished and complete picture.

Sunset is sometimes compared to Monet's *Impression, Sunrise* (Musée Marmottan Monet, Paris), which was shown in the first Impressionist group exhibition in 1874 and whose title led to the label "Impressionism." While there is no doubt that Renoir was aware of Monet's canvas—and was perhaps responding to it in *Sunset*—the two paintings differ in many aspects. Most notably, Renoir's canvas is much less finished than Monet's. Unlike Monet, Renoir does not appear concerned with accurately rendering watery details or precise reflections; rather, he seems more intent on capturing the feeling of the sunset and its myriad effects on the texture of the sea—a true "impression"—while Monet is much more meticulous in his articulation of the watery light.

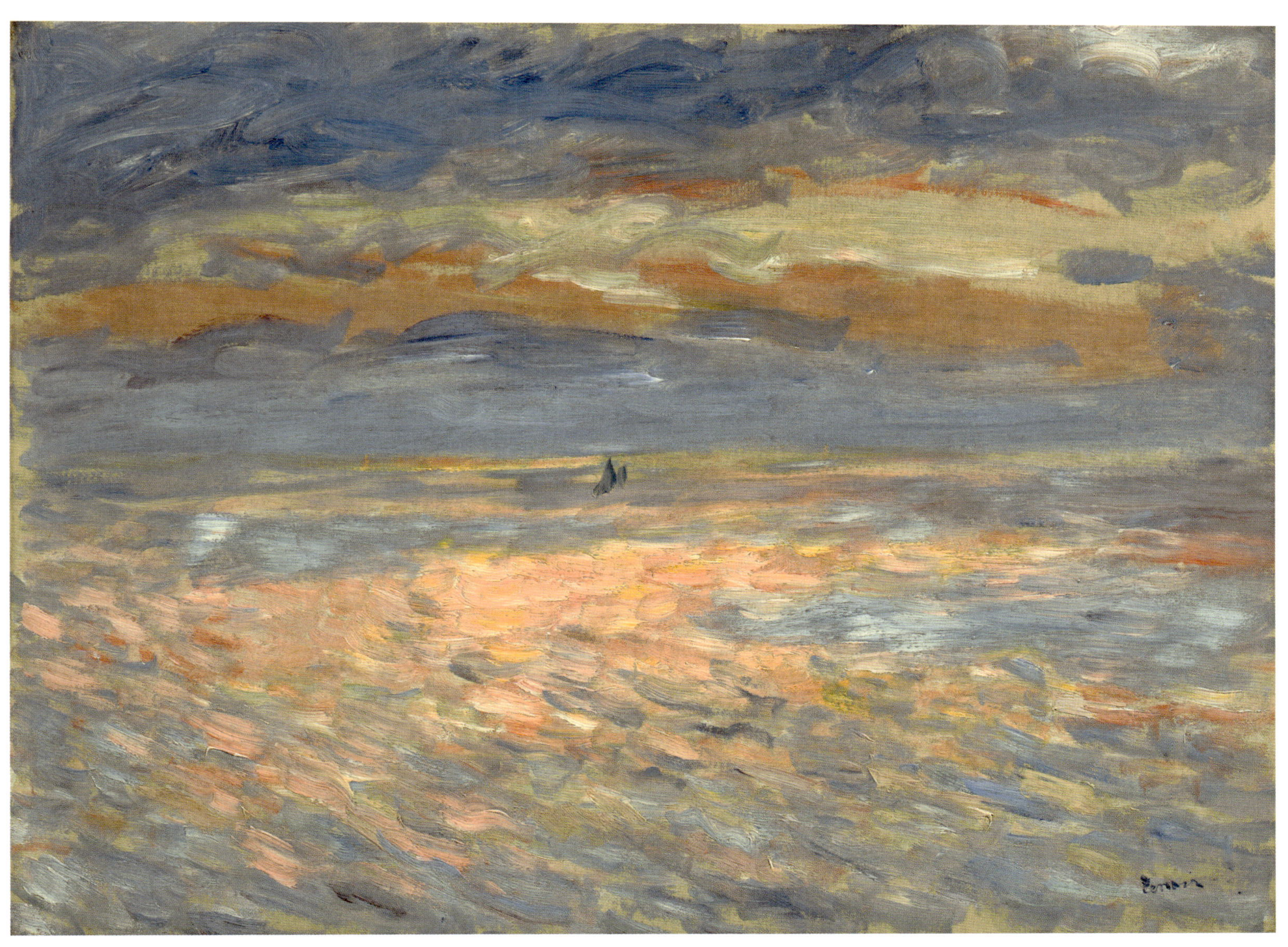

59 PIERRE-AUGUSTE RENOIR French, 1841–1919

Venice, the Doge's Palace

1881
Oil on canvas
54.5 x 65.7 cm
Signed and dated lower right: Renoir. 81.
Acquired by Sterling and Francine Clark, 1933
1955.596

GAINING THE FINANCIAL MEANS TO TRAVEL ABROAD for the first time in 1881, Renoir set off at once for Italy to study works by the Old Masters, especially those of Raphael. His first stop on this pilgrimage was Venice, where the artist was drawn to masterpieces by Titian, Veronese, and Canaletto. The paintings Renoir executed there focused on the main tourist attractions, which he depicted in his usual Impressionist style. In *Venice, the Doge's Palace* Renoir chose the most famous buildings of the city for his subject. He sarcastically wrote to a friend that he "painted the Doge's Palace seen from San Giorgio; that has never been done before, I think. There were at least six of us queuing up to paint it."

While most of his paintings from his stay in Venice are more like sketches than finished works, *Venice, the Doge's Palace* is one of two that he worked into a more complete state (the other is a view of the Grand Canal now in the Museum of Fine Arts, Boston). Despite employing an Impressionist scheme of variegated color and working to capture ephemeral light effects, Renoir rendered the buildings with a remarkable degree of accuracy, such as the precise details of the thirty-four arches of the palace. The creamy, sunlit façades reflect some of the rich blues of the sky, and the loosely painted gondolas and bright sails punctuate the foreground, adding touches of vibrant color amid the predominantly light palette of the canvas. Similarly, the gold orb and cross on top of the San Marco basilica add visual interest to the skyline.

Venice, the Doge's Palace was most likely included in the seventh Impressionist group exhibition, which was organized by Paul Durand-Ruel, Renoir's dealer. It was received very unfavorably, with one critic writing that it represented "the most outrageous series of ferocious daubs that a calumniator of Venice could possibly imagine." In retrospect, *Venice, the Doge's Palace* stands at a crossroads in Renoir's development as a painter, as it was in the months following its execution that, through his direct acquaintance with works by the Old Masters, he began to incorporate more precise draftsmanship into his painting and became increasingly concerned about articulating the volume of solid objects.

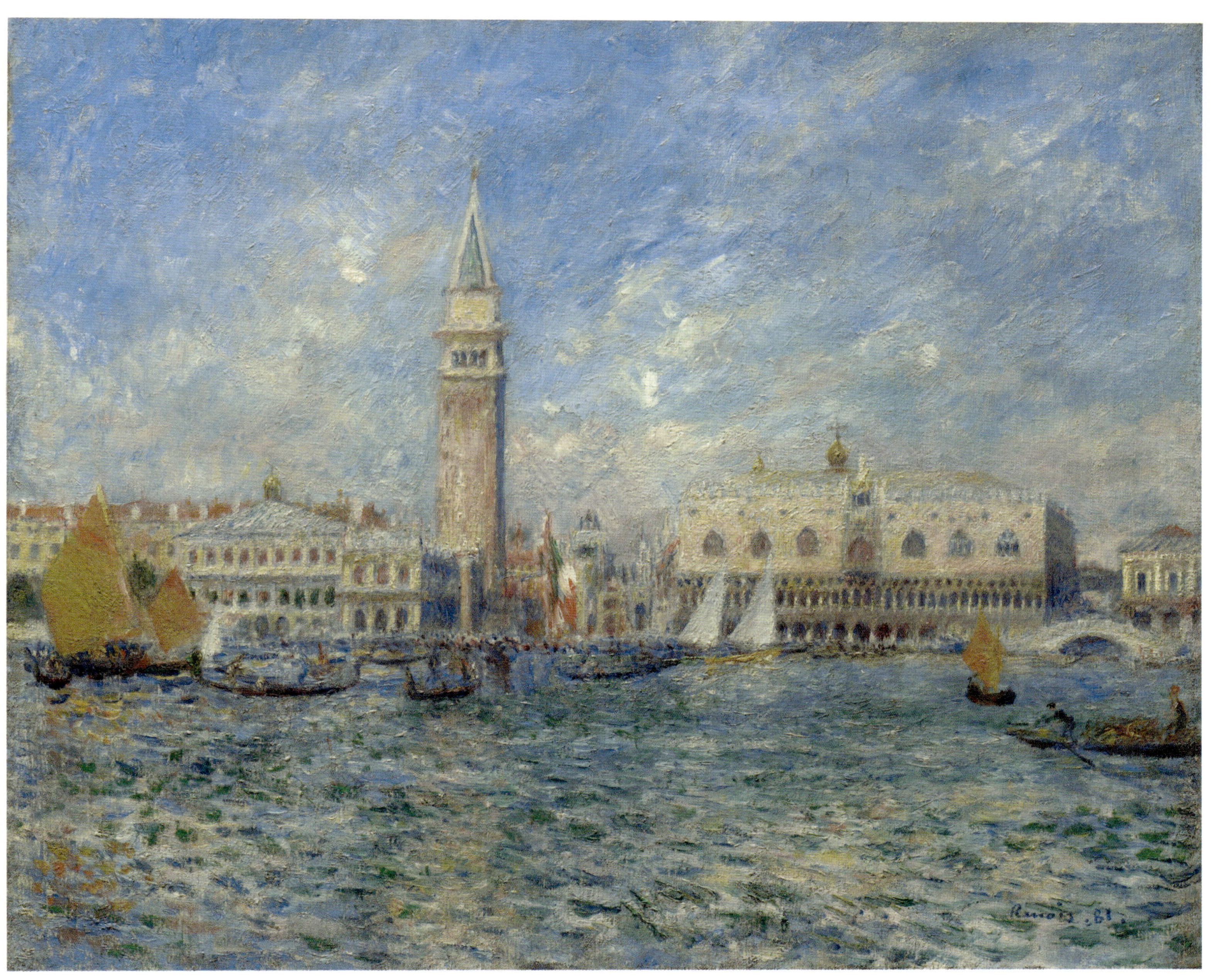

60 PIERRE-AUGUSTE RENOIR French, 1841–1919

Bay of Naples, Evening

1881
Oil on canvas
57.9 x 80.8 cm
Signed and dated lower left: Renoir. 81.
Acquired by Sterling and Francine Clark, 1933
1955.587

RENOIR PAINTED *BAY OF NAPLES, EVENING* IN NOVEMBER 1881 during his trip to Italy and Algeria. The view looks eastward across the bay toward Mount Vesuvius. In the foreground the Strada del Piliero and Porto Grande are alive with the hustle and bustle of seaside life, while the serene background is awash in sun-drenched glory. Mount Vesuvius, prominent in the distance but seen through a veil of humid atmosphere, emits a wisp of smoke. Renoir infused the scene with local flavor, such as the bay full of typical Neapolitan boats, the woman carrying a burden on her head, and a donkey loaded with supplies.

Unlike the slightly earlier *Venice, the Doge's Palace* (cat. 59), this canvas is thinly painted; the brushwork, while still prominent, is less emphatic. These changes were perhaps inspired by Renoir's experience of the ancient frescoes of Pompeii and Herculaneum, though he also may have been responding to the humid atmosphere of the locale. His technique of parallel diagonal brushstrokes, which lends a sense of structure and texture to the scene, also seems to have been developed in Naples, as can be seen in *Onions* (cat. 61) as well. Yet for all its innovation, *Bay of Naples, Evening* showcases Renoir's traditional penchant for creating harmonious color effects. He gives the bright palette a warm tonality by using red and orange streaks that recur through the mountains, water, and the boardwalk. This integrated color scheme unifies the three zones of the painting and also helps create a pleasant sense of balance throughout the canvas.

Renoir painted two views of the Bay of Naples from this same vantage point: the Clark picture, which captures the bay in the glow of the warm evening sun, and a second, now in the Metropolitan Museum of Art, New York, depicting the scene in the cool morning light. The practice of painting similar views in different temporal and atmospheric conditions, while prevalent in the work of Monet, is unusual in Renoir's oeuvre. It is likely that Renoir was inspired by his friend's example in conceiving these two views of the bay.

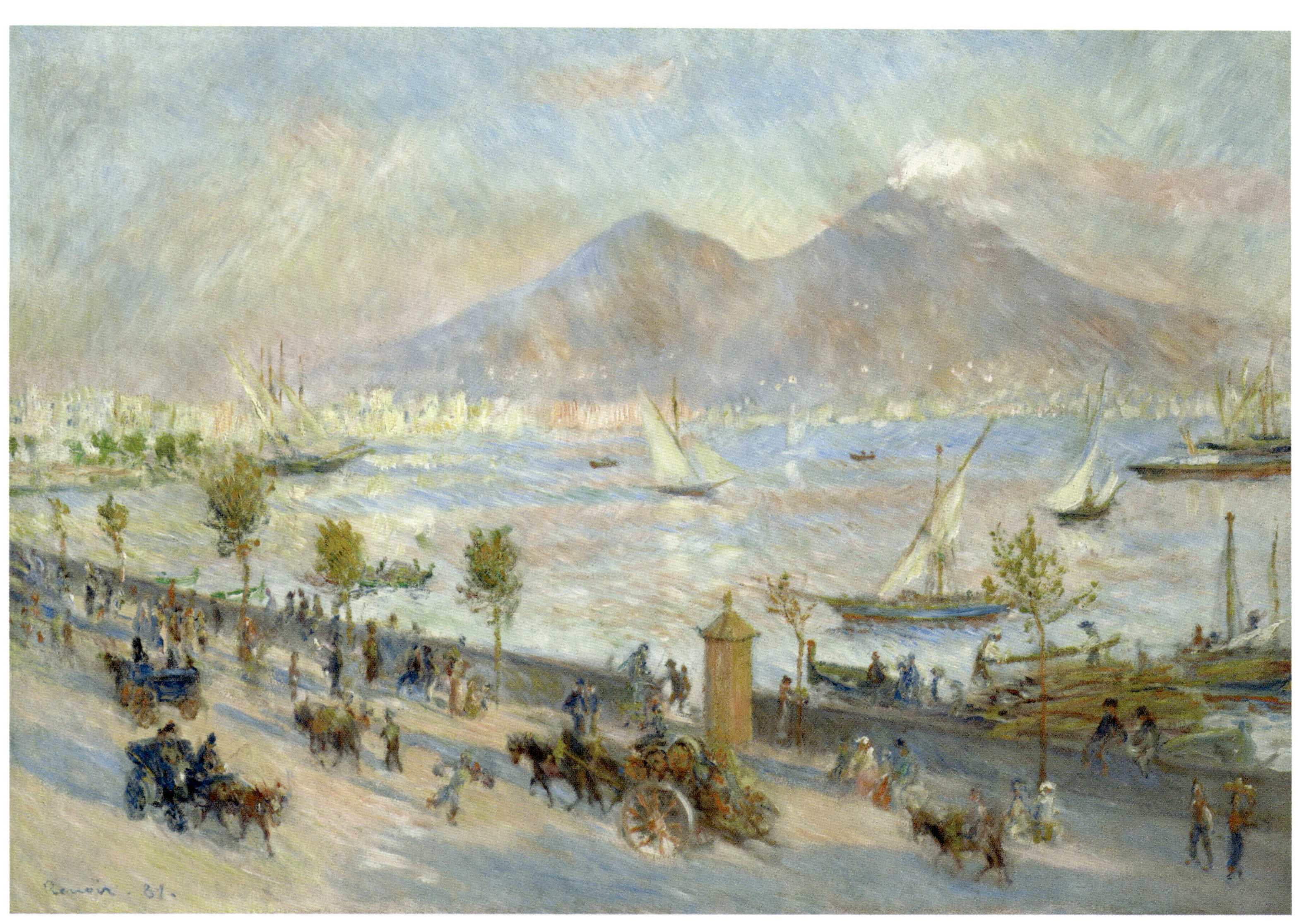

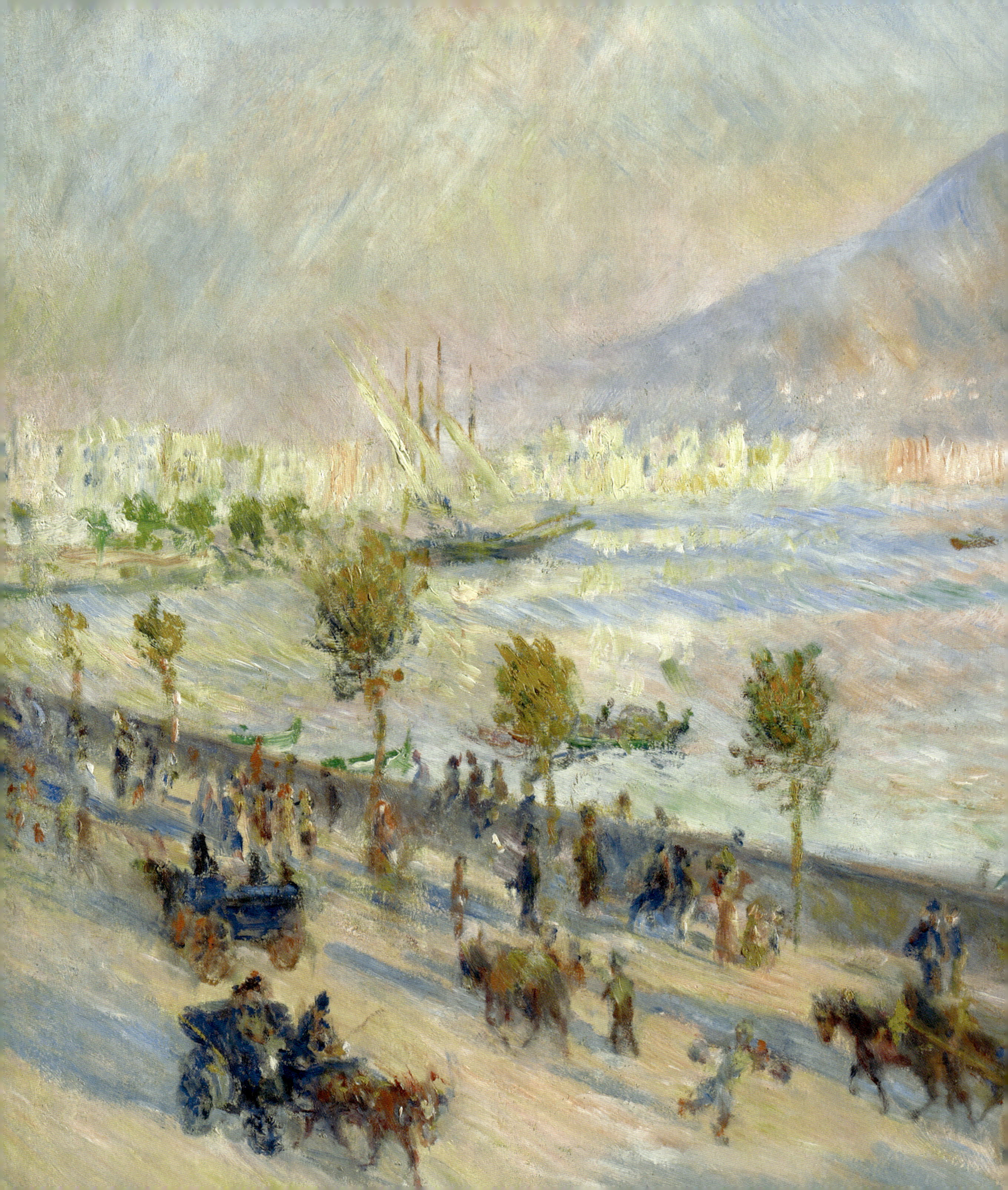

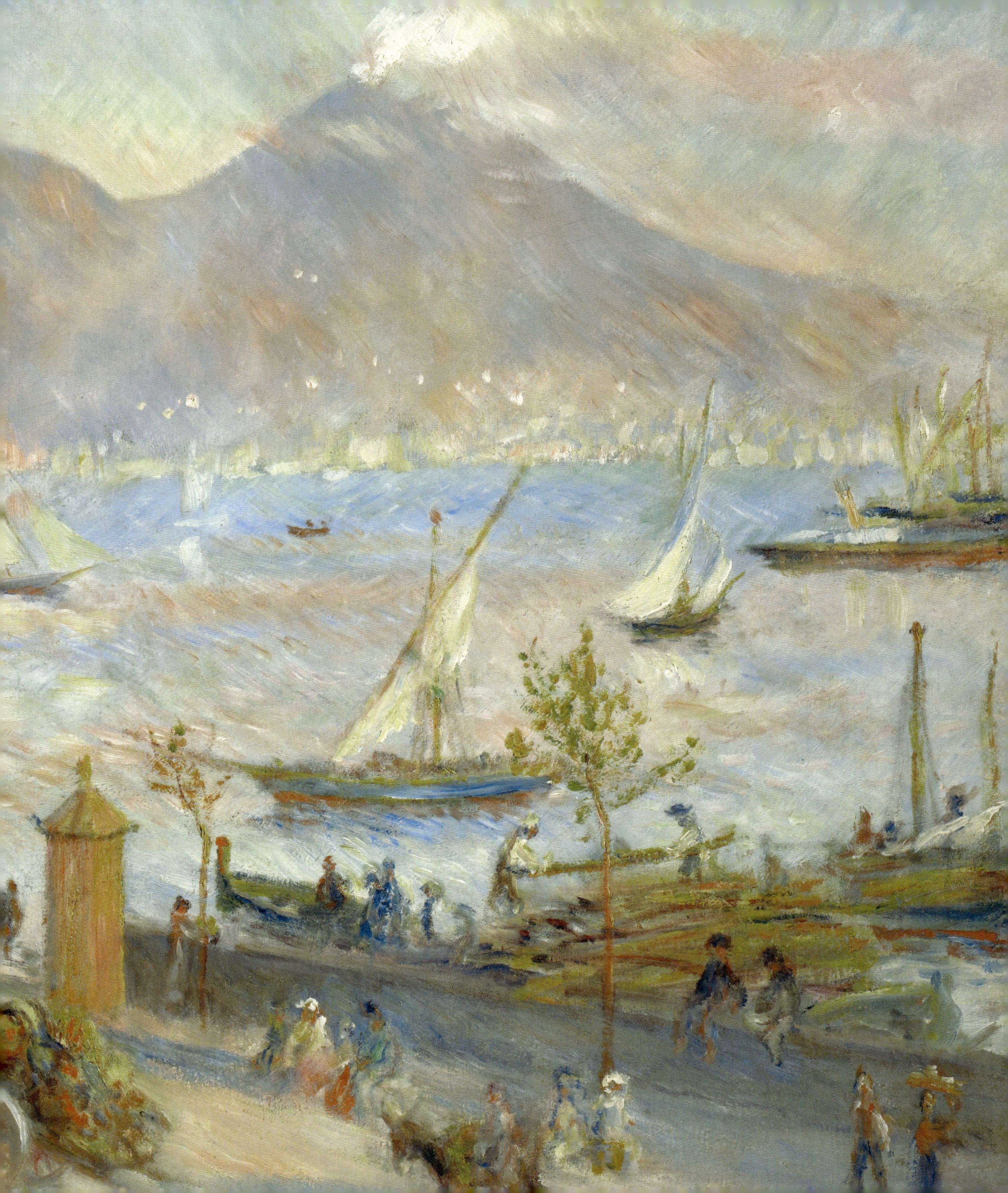

61 PIERRE-AUGUSTE RENOIR French, 1841–1919

Onions

1881
Oil on canvas
39.1 x 60.6 cm
Signed, dated, and inscribed lower left: Renoir. Naples. 81.
Acquired by Sterling and Francine Clark, 1922
1955.588

EARLY IN 1881, THE ART DEALER PAUL DURAND-RUEL began to buy Renoir's paintings on a regular basis, giving the forty-year-old artist the financial freedom to take an extended tour of Italy. It was during this trip that *Onions* was painted, in late November on a visit to Naples. While traveling throughout Italy, Renoir studied the work of the Old Masters and honed his skill for rendering solid forms. Indeed, the rounded forms of the onions and garlic are heightened by Renoir's striking use of parallel diagonal brushstrokes in the background. This type of brushwork is characteristic of the development of Renoir's style throughout this period. Compared with *Blonde Bather* (cat. 62), clearly based in theme and style on the grand tradition of painting, *Onions* is far less ambitious, if nevertheless more straightforwardly appealing to modern taste.

Renoir endows the onions and garlic with a liveliness and remarkable sense of texture. Loosely arranged across a table, positioned on and off a crumpled white cloth with a red and blue border, the onions are enlivened by their precarious placement, subtle colors, reflections, and curves. The free brushwork and intimate composition put this work squarely within Impressionist practice. The rhythm of the composition is dynamic, with the echoing shapes of the onions and garlic, set at different angles, creating an appearance of animation that is supported by the brushwork and the overall tonality of the canvas. The picture balances the warm reds, yellows, and pinks of the onions with softer, cooler hues in the background.

In contrast to Renoir's elaborate still life of peonies executed about 1880 (cat. 57), *Onions* is deliberately relaxed and informal. Whether this is indicative of the artist's feeling of freedom from economic constraints, a commentary contrasting the Italian way of life to the artifice of Parisian culture, or simply the artist's caprice is not known. Sterling Clark reiterated on many occasions that it was his favorite among his collection of Renoir's works, and he often used it as a yardstick for judging other pictures.

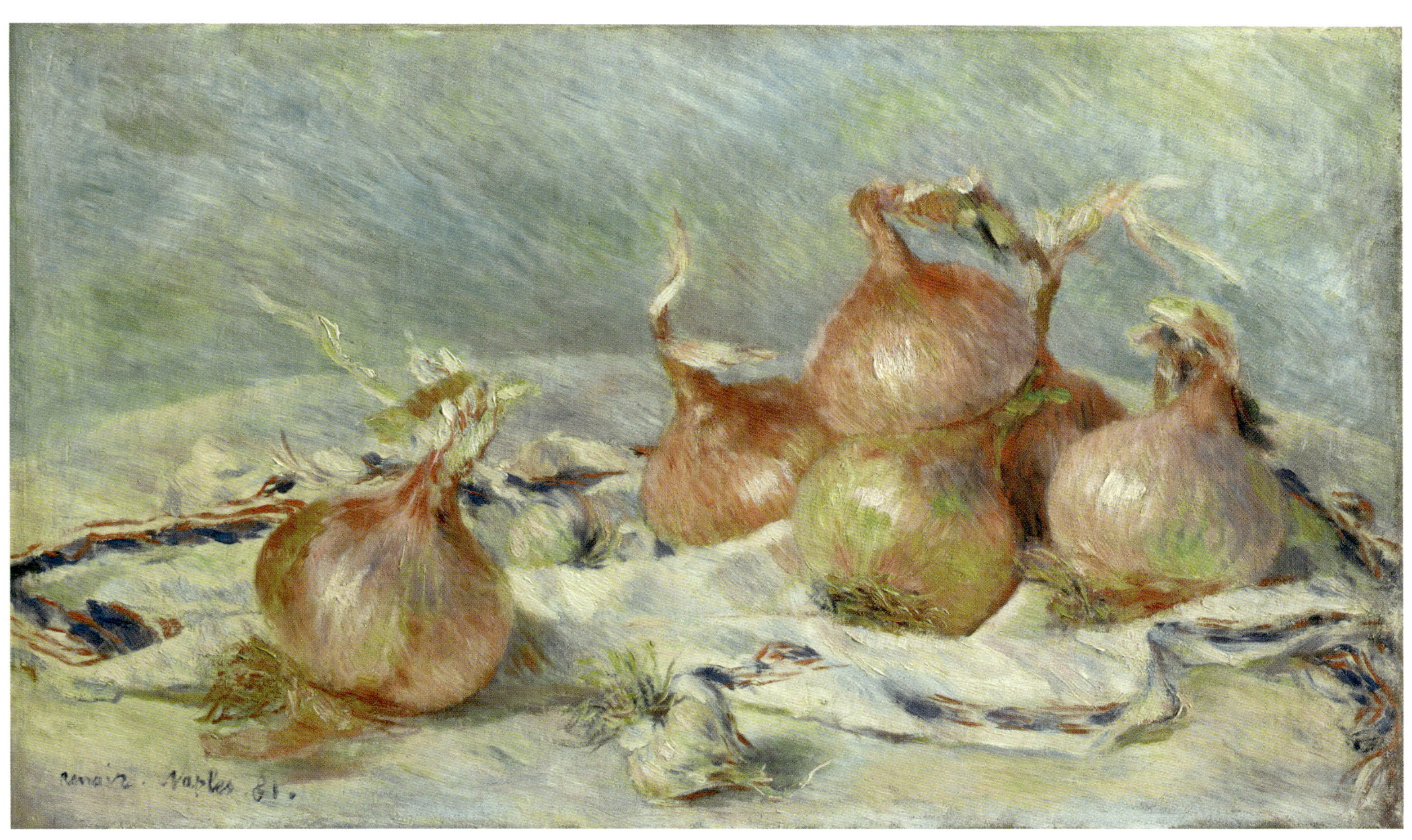
renoir. Naples 81.

62 PIERRE-AUGUSTE RENOIR French, 1841–1919

Blonde Bather

1881
Oil on canvas
81.6 x 65.4 cm
Signed, dated, and inscribed top right: à Monsieur H. Vever / Renoir 81 [partially overpainted] / Renoir. 81.
Acquired by Sterling and Francine Clark, 1926
1955.609

BLONDE BATHER MARKS A TURNING POINT in Renoir's art and is among the most significant pictures he brought back from his trip to Italy in 1881–82. Renoir claimed to have painted it from a boat in the Bay of Naples—that is, in a manner typical of Impressionist practice, though this would appear unlikely. The seascape, loosely based on the coast near Capri, seems more like a backdrop, and the model, almost certainly the artist's mistress and future wife, Aline Charigot, is posed as if on the shore or even in the studio. Yet the picture does capture the brilliance of full sunlight falling over the ample forms of the "bather," who sits before the viewer like a modern Venus rising from the sea, her reddish-blonde hair blown back by the breeze.

Created when Renoir was experiencing works of antiquity and the Old Masters as never before, the picture demonstrates the artist's burgeoning interest in boldly defining his figures and eschewing modern trappings for a more timeless image. Renoir later remarked that Raphael's frescoes in Rome had especially impressed him: "Raphael broke with the schools of his time, dedicated himself to the antique, to grandeur and eternal beauty." *Blonde Bather* has often been compared to Raphael's fresco of Galatea in the Villa Farnesina, as well as the ancient wall paintings at Pompeii. In fact, when Renoir first returned from Italy and showed the picture to his friends and patrons, they were said to have been shocked, afraid that the artist would no longer paint in the style they were accustomed to before his sojourn.

Later in life Aline would say that she had been very thin during their Italian trip. If true, the ample forms of the *Blonde Bather* may reflect Renoir's attempt to monumentalize the figure to grand proportions, not unlike the nudes that appear in paintings by Titian or Rembrandt, artists he admired in addition to Raphael. For all its innovation, however, the painting does not wholly split from Renoir's Impressionist style. In particular, the modeling of the flesh, with soft blues and reds used to suggest shadows, and the varied color in the model's hair are typical of Impressionism, as is the loosely painted and colorful background. The painting as a whole maintains Renoir's masterful and idiosyncratic way of melding form and color.

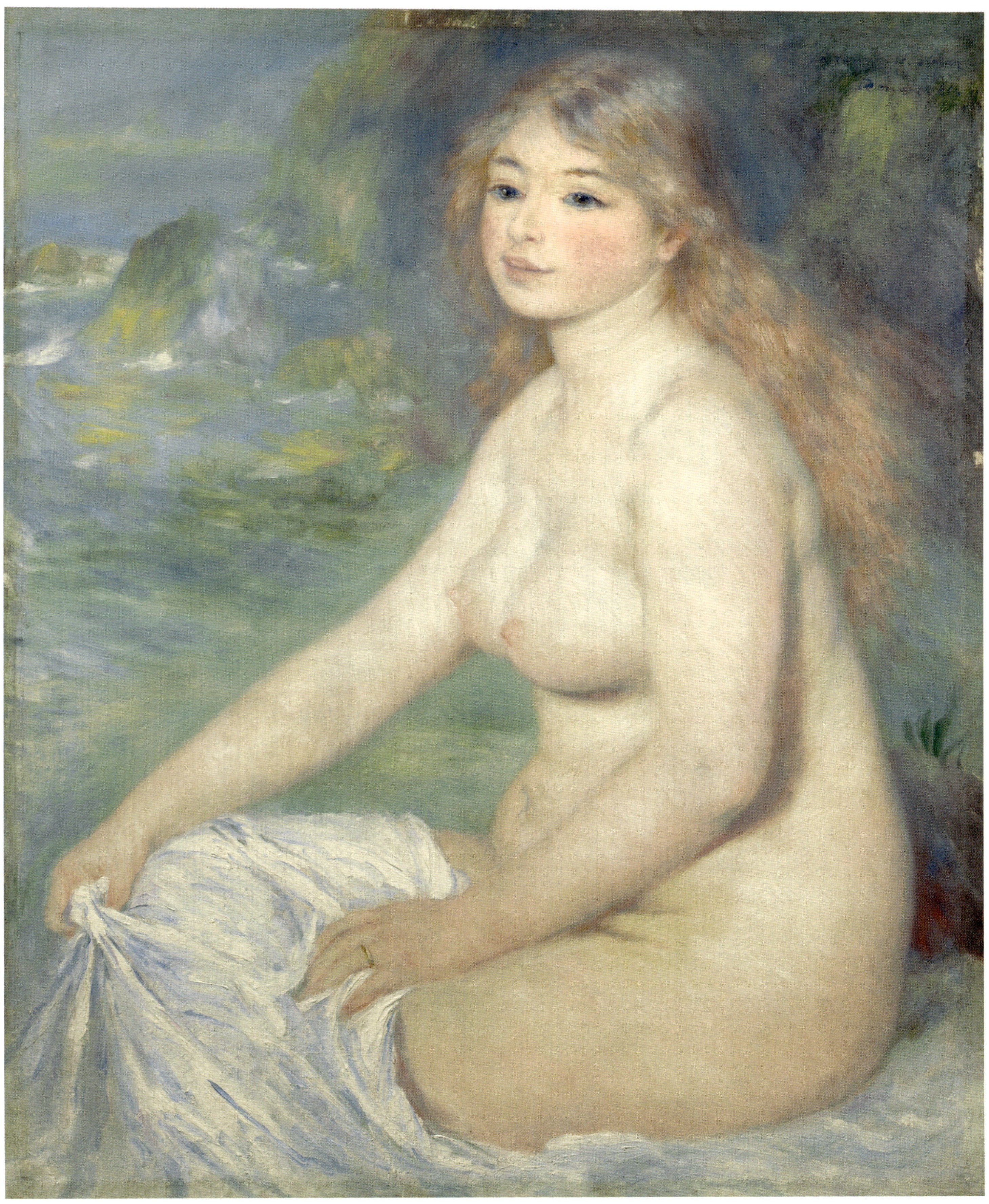

63 PIERRE-AUGUSTE RENOIR French, 1841–1919

Child with a Bird (Mademoiselle Fleury in Algerian Costume)

1882
Oil on canvas
126.4 x 78.1 cm
Signed and dated lower right: Renoir 82.
Acquired by Sterling and Francine Clark, 1937
1955.586

LATE IN HIS LIFE RENOIR REMINISCED about his trip to Algeria in 1882, recalling in particular "a life-sized portrait of a young girl named Mlle. Fleury, dressed in Algerian costume, in the setting of an Arab house, holding a bird." Although Renoir explicitly states the model's name in his remembrance, it is somewhat ambiguous whether the work should be seen as a portrait or a genre painting. Sterling Clark believed the painting portrayed the daughter of the governor general of Algeria, but there was no Governor General Fleury at the time the canvas was executed. In fact, the exact identity of the girl in the painting has not been determined. Further complicating the picture's status is that when first exhibited in 1883 it was titled *L'Enfant à l'oiseau*, with no mention of the identity of the model. As with so many of Renoir's works, *Child with a Bird* seems to be both a portrait and a genre painting at the same time.

As a genre painting, the canvas draws on several different traditions. It is clearly related to pictures of European models wearing exotic costumes, of which Renoir himself was fond. *Child with a Bird* is distanced from this genre, however, in that it was painted in an Algerian house and only the model's blonde hair and fair complexion distinguish it from a representation of an "exotic" subject. The motif of a coquettish woman shown holding a bird—in this case, one traditionally described as a falcon but that has been identified as a common kestrel—was not unusual in European art. Conventionally, these images play on the relationship of the caged or controlled bird with the position and status of the woman portrayed.

Renoir fills the work with a palpable luminosity. Orange and blue tones play off each other throughout the canvas, which is highlighted by the bright reds in the sash and the intense greens in the scarf. The picture was for the most part thinly painted, with Renoir employing a rich impasto to such areas as the figure's costume. Sterling Clark was undoubtedly drawn to the deft brushwork and the harmony of color throughout the painting, although he was slightly more reticent about the figure, at one point describing the girl as "dwarfish." When he decided to buy the painting in 1937, however, he wrote in his diary that it "looked fine and the child less dwarfish than I remembered."

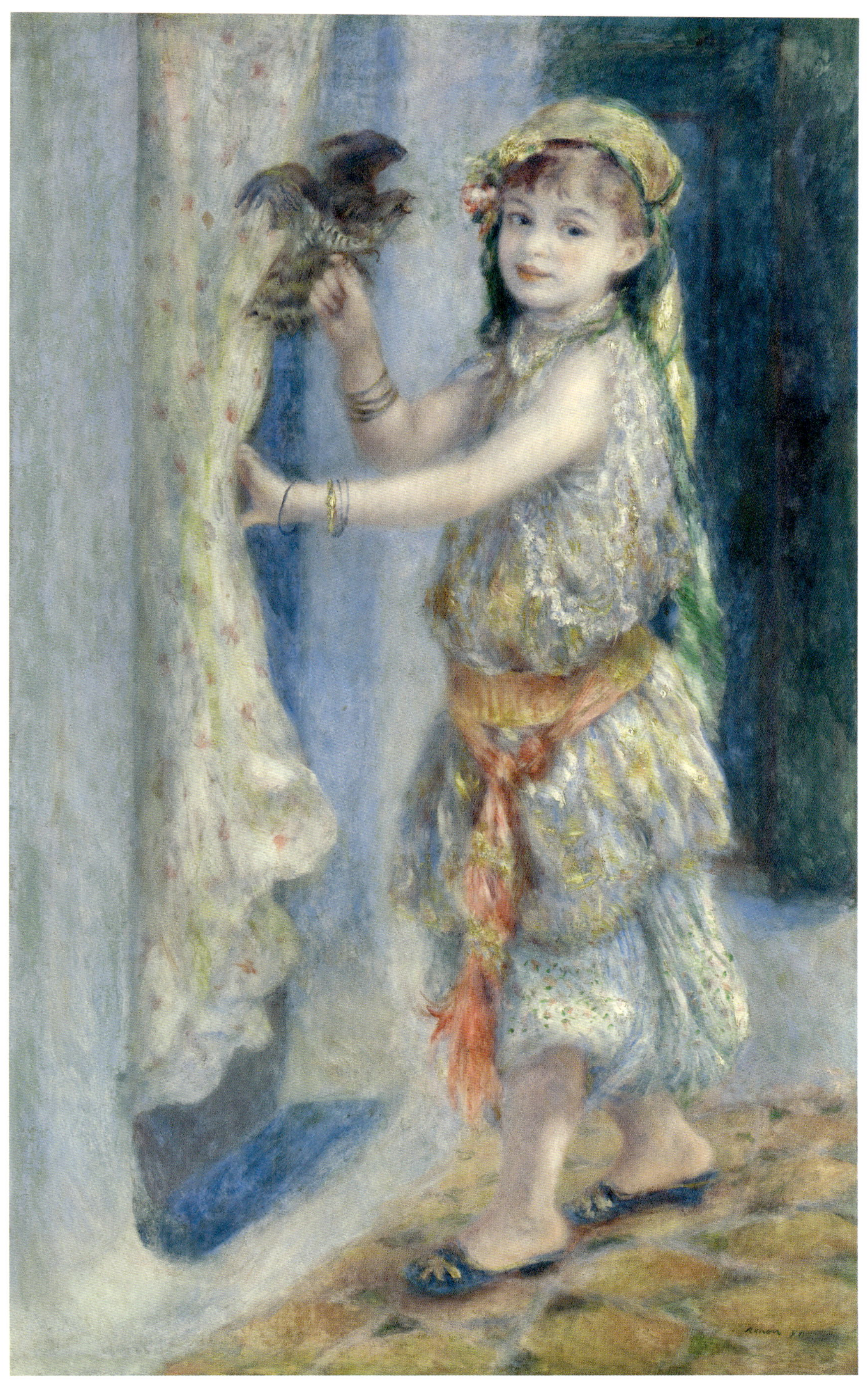

64 PIERRE-AUGUSTE RENOIR French, 1841–1919

Marie-Thérèse Durand-Ruel Sewing

1882
Oil on canvas
64.9 x 54 cm
Signed and dated lower left: Renoir. 82.
Acquired by Sterling and Francine Clark, 1935
1955.613

BEGINNING IN THE 1880S, Paul Durand-Ruel began to purchase Impressionist paintings, especially those by Renoir, in substantial quantities. He would remain Renoir's principal dealer until the end of the artist's life, in the process becoming a close personal friend. In 1882 Durand-Ruel commissioned Renoir to paint portraits of all five of his children, perhaps inspired by the portraits the artist had been making of the banker Paul Berard's children. Durand-Ruel invited Renoir to a house he had rented in Dieppe, on the Normandy coast, for the month of August. It was in the garden of this house that Renoir executed the present portrait of Marie-Thérèse, Durand-Ruel's eldest daughter. The painter Jacques-Émile Blanche, who visited the house, remembered that "the Durand-Ruel children posed for [Renoir] in a garden . . . beneath the moving leaves of the chestnut trees; the sun dappled their cheeks with reflections incompatible with the beautiful 'flat modeling' of studio lighting."

Marie-Thérèse Durand-Ruel Sewing corroborates Blanche's account. Renoir captures the tonal effects of sunlight throughout the painting. The sitter's hair, for instance, is rendered in varying shades of yellows and browns that are accentuated by the blue reflections of her dress and the purples of the bow tying back her tresses. Sterling Clark was particularly struck by the artist's depiction of the red hat, which is painted in hues ranging from bright yellow to deep red. The colorful flowers and foliage behind the sitter infuse the scene with the gaiety of a summer garden in full bloom. Despite the vivacity of this painting, Durand-Ruel was apparently unhappy with the result, as indicated in one of Renoir's letters: "I think that Durand is not very pleased with his portraits," he wrote, continuing, "don't talk to me anymore about portraits in sunlight. A nice dark background, that's the right thing."

The general subject of a young girl engrossed in a domestic activity was a theme Renoir returned to again and again over his career. *Marie-Thérèse Durand-Ruel Sewing* is significant in that it displays some of the newer techniques Renoir began incorporating into his painting after his trip to Italy in 1881. In particular, the defined profile of the sitter, enhanced by its contrast with the darker colors behind it, is telling of the artist's heightened ambition to set his figures apart from their surroundings.

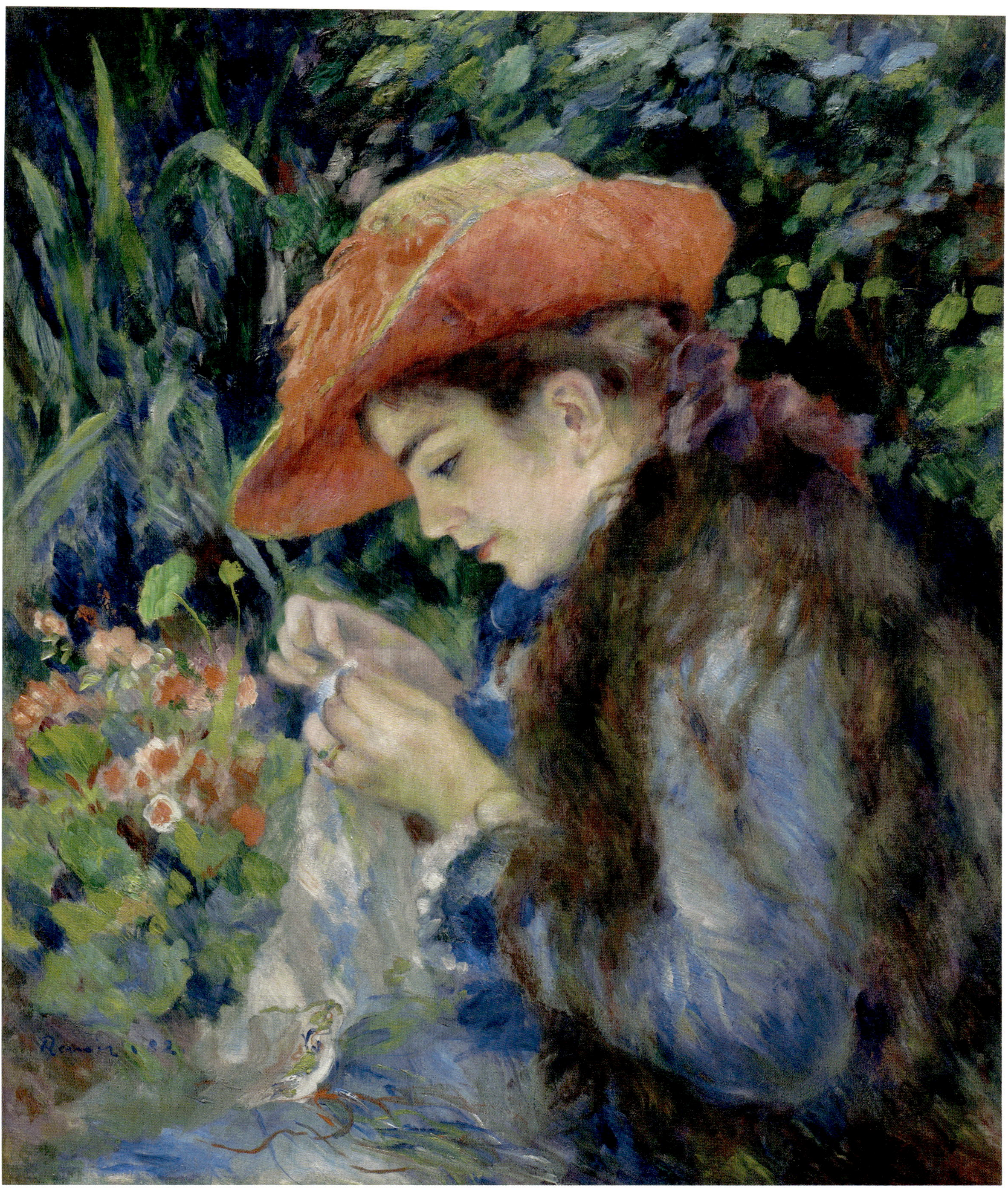

65 PIERRE-AUGUSTE RENOIR French, 1841–1919

Apples in a Dish

1883
Oil on canvas
54.1 x 65.3 cm
Signed and dated lower left: Renoir. 83.
Acquired by Sterling and Francine Clark, 1951
1955.599

APPLES IN A DISH WAS PAINTED JUST TWO YEARS after *Onions* (cat. 61), yet the two still lifes could not be more different. In contrast to the cascading, informal arrangement of the onions, the apples are shown formally stacked and viewed frontally. It is likely that this change in approach was inspired by Renoir's friend and colleague Paul Cézanne, whom Renoir visited in 1882. In general, Renoir tended to use still-life subjects as vehicles for experimentation, and it is often in paintings such as *Apples in a Dish* that we are able to catch the artist as he pushes himself in new directions.

Throughout the canvas, warm and cool colors play against each other, creating a lively and variegated surface. There is an insistent diversity of tones that is at odds with Renoir's usual penchant to craft a composition around a single dominant color relationship. The vibrant and varied hues of the apples are set off by the intense blue of the fruit bowl, whose white edges and feet punctuate the colorful surfaces. Greens, yellows, reds, and blues are juxtaposed in myriad combinations. One has the sense that Renoir is consciously working to expand his palette, yet the overall painting maintains a striking harmony.

For all of its experimental nature, however, Renoir signed and dated *Apples in a Dish*, indicating that he considered it a finished work in its own right. Perhaps more perplexing than the eclectic tonal structure of *Apples in a Dish* is the presence of a rotting apple on the table in the foreground of the canvas. This is not a motif that can be traced with any regularity in nineteenth-century still-life paintings, and is at odds with Renoir's general avoidance of signs of decay and age in his works.

While his thoughts on the painting are unrecorded, *Apples in a Dish* holds a special place as the last Renoir picture Sterling Clark purchased. Clark acquired the work in 1951, when his plans for a permanent museum to house his collection were becoming more concrete. He bought both the present painting and Alfred Sisley's *Apples and Grapes in a Basket* (cat. 18) within months of each other, and he likely viewed the two pictures as a complementary pair.

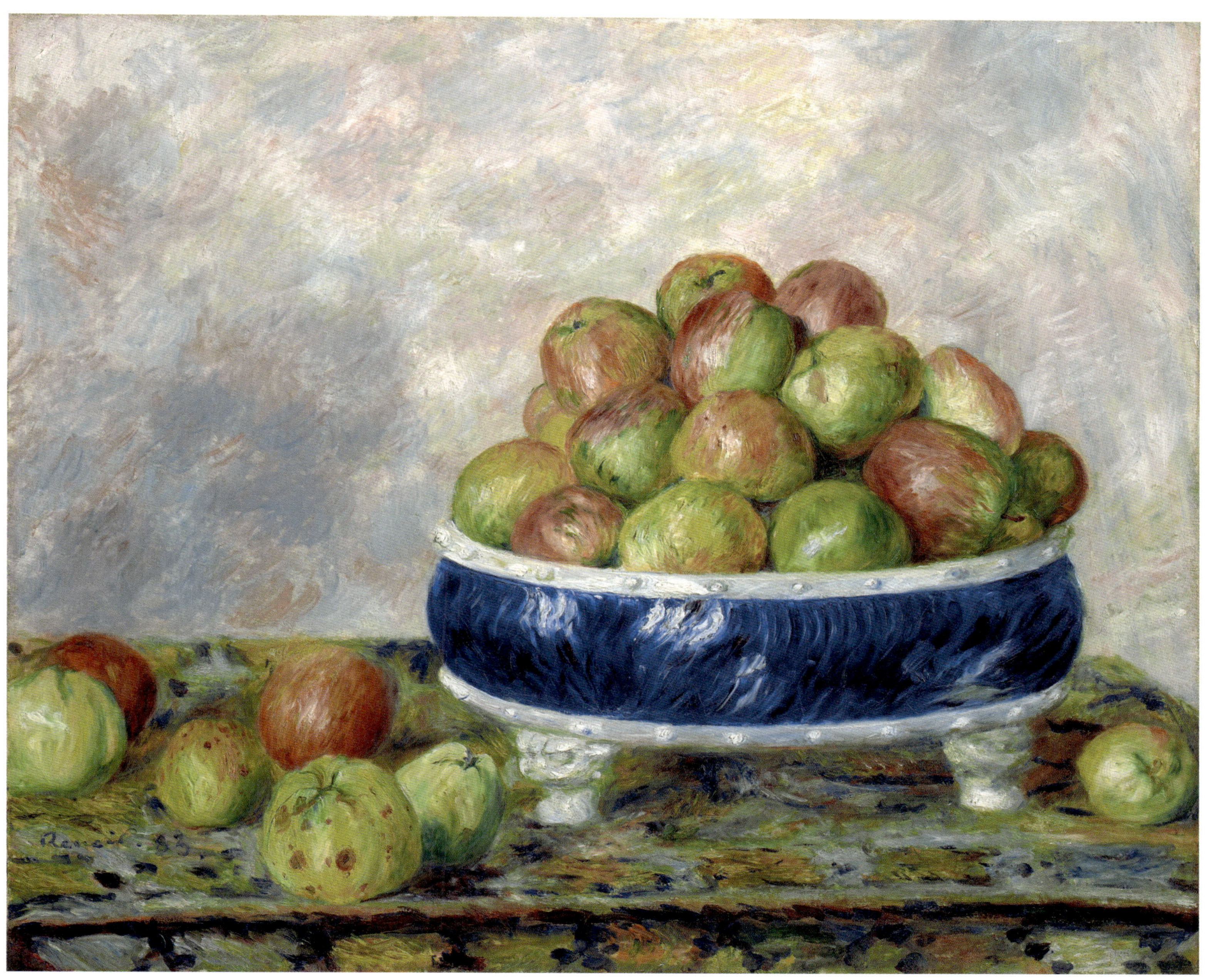

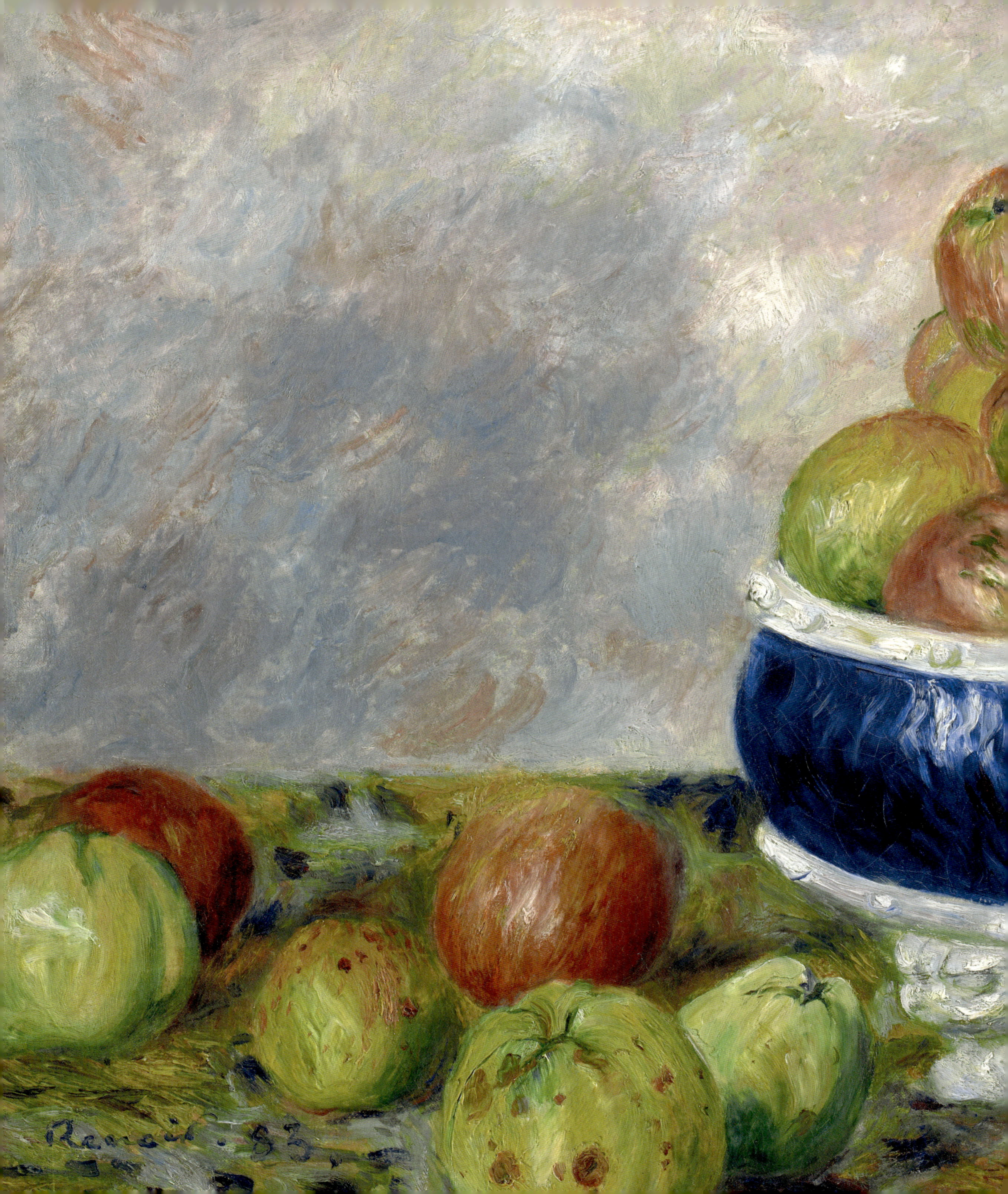
Renoir. 83.

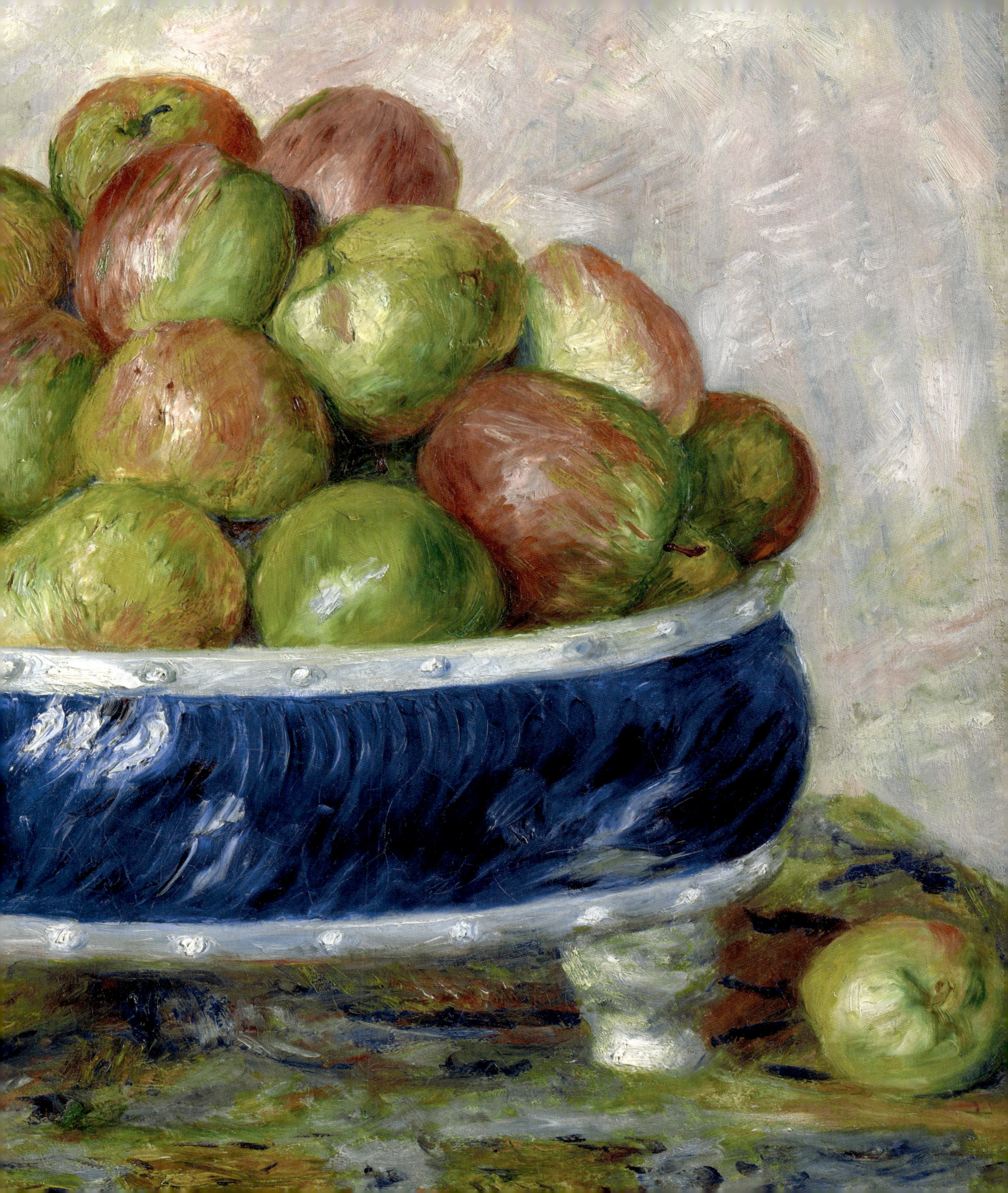

66 **PIERRE-AUGUSTE RENOIR** French, 1841–1919

The Letter

c. 1895–1900
Oil on canvas
64.9 x 81.1 cm
Signed lower right: Renoir.
Acquired by Sterling and Francine Clark, 1937
1955.583

THE LETTER IS ONE OF RENOIR'S MANY GENRE PAINTINGS that depict two women without giving any clues about their relationship. Seated side by side and leaning into each other, they concentrate on a letter that the nearer figure is writing, an open ink pot close at hand. Renoir hints at their position and status: the decorative panel and wallpaper in the background, as well as their clothes, suggest the young women are members of the bourgeoisie; the letter writer is no doubt well educated. Despite this, Renoir used Gabrielle Renard, his wife's distant cousin, as the model for the figure on the left. Renard, who would become one of Renoir's favorite models, was a housekeeper and decidedly not a bourgeoise. This is one of many instances in his work where Renoir created a specific role and identity for a model that was distinct from her actual status. Yet this role-playing points to no specific narrative. The two models' actions and facial expressions give little hint at their states of mind or the contents of the letter. The viewer is left to imagine a scenario on his or her own, giving the picture a certain timeless appeal.

A similar fiction is probably at work in the elaborate hat worn by the woman on the right. Ringed with red poppies, it is typical of the props Renoir used in such settings. Even though such ornate hats were out of fashion by the 1880s, Renoir continued to include them in genre scenes like this one, sometimes against the advice of his dealer Paul Durand-Ruel.

The color scheme in *The Letter* is characteristic of Renoir's work from the 1890s, when he was experimenting with the use of black and abandoning some of the Impressionist color devices, such as using blue for modeling. Here, variations in color suggest three-dimensionality, and contrasting tones are often set next to each other. By these standards, *The Letter* was an unlikely acquisition for Sterling Clark, who by and large preferred the artist's earlier work and often had harsh words for Renoir's later output.

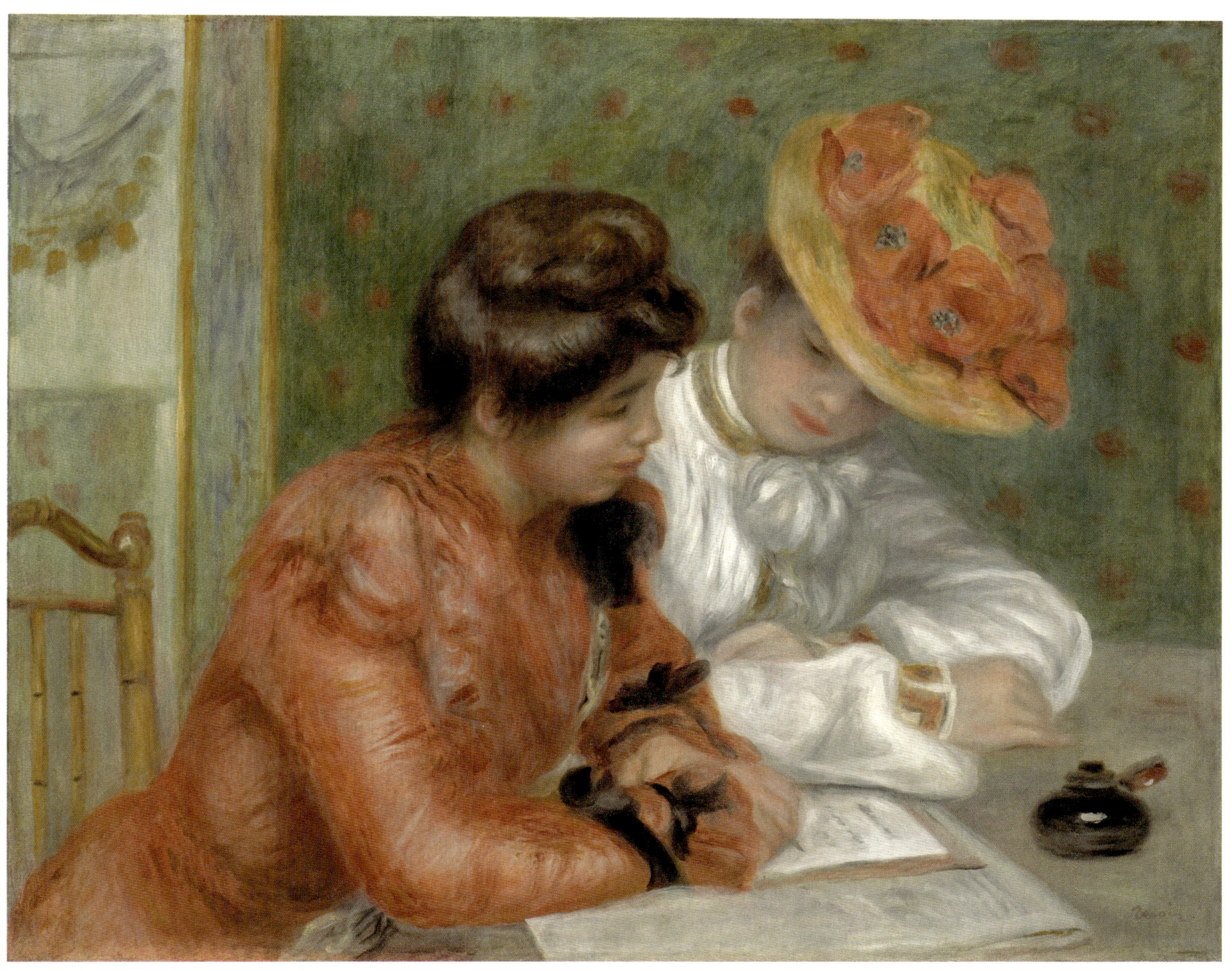

67 PIERRE-AUGUSTE RENOIR French, 1841–1919

Self-Portrait

1899
Oil on canvas
41.4 x 33.7 cm
Signed upper left: Renoir.
Acquired by Sterling and Francine Clark, 1937
1955.611

BY THE TIME RENOIR PAINTED THIS SELF-PORTRAIT he was a well-established and successful artist, and he depicts himself as a mature and confident man. The flowered wallpaper in the background and the subject's respectable bourgeois clothes suggest a man who is used to comfortable living. It is possible, however, that some of this appearance is due to modifications suggested by Julie Manet (Berthe Morisot's daughter and Édouard Manet's niece). It was likely this portrait she was referring to when she wrote that "[Renoir] is finishing a self-portrait that is very nice, but he had made himself look rather harsh and wrinkled, we insisted that he suppress some wrinkles, and now it's more like him." In fact, Renoir's health was beginning to fail in the late 1890s, and the arthritis that would cripple him in later years began to show itself in the form of rheumatic attacks. In contrast to the energetic, almost wild eyes in his self-portrait of about 1875 (cat. 47), Renoir here shows himself with large, open eyes that betray a world-weariness and exude a feeling of empathy. He himself commented that this portrait "catches those calf's eyes."

In the end, Renoir has subtly drawn attention away from the creases and marks of age on his face by incorporating them into the brush pattern that is used throughout the canvas. It is this brushwork that gives the painting vitality despite its restricted and subdued color scheme of beiges, browns, and blues. Renoir's depiction of light playing off his cheeks and beard is particularly deft, contributing vibrant highlights to the composition.

Renoir never exhibited this painting and it stayed in his studio until his death in 1919. Shortly afterward, his son Pierre sold the painting to Paul Durand-Ruel, from whom Sterling Clark bought it in 1937.

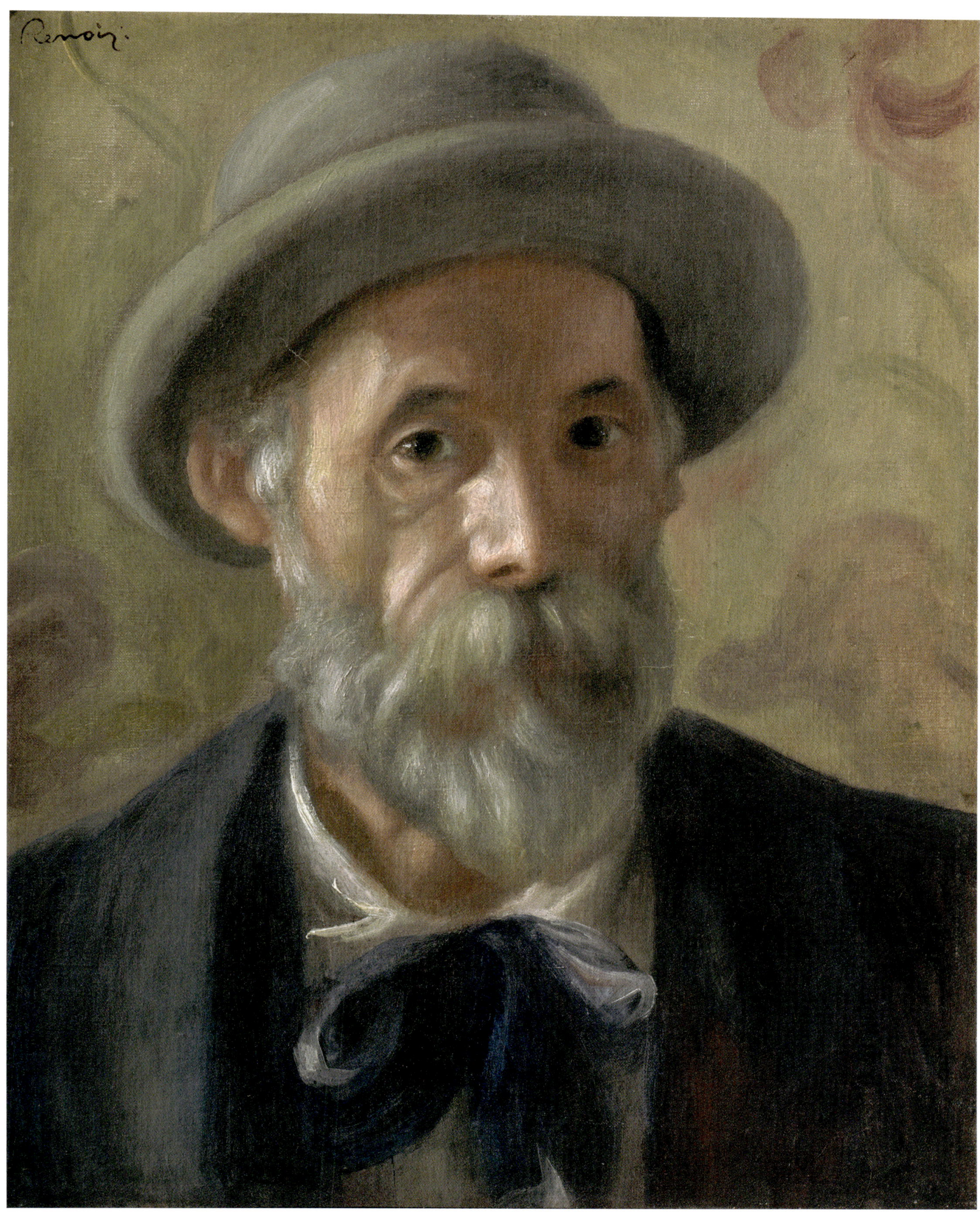
Renoir.

68 BERTHE MORISOT French, 1841–1895

Dahlias

c. 1876
Oil on canvas
45.7 x 55.9 cm
Studio stamp lower right: Berthe Morisot
Acquired by the Clark, 1974
1974.28

DAHLIAS IS ONE OF THE FEW STILL-LIFE PAINTINGS Morisot executed in the 1870s, a period in which she was garnering much attention for her intimate depictions of feminine domesticity. Her reluctance to embrace still-life subjects might have stemmed from a resistance to the traditional notion that female artists were expected to produce paintings of flowers, fruit, and decorative objects.

In this case she was perhaps inspired by the still-life experiments of her brother-in-law Édouard Manet (see cat. 31) or the flower paintings of Monet and Renoir (see cat. 57). *Dahlias* shows both a painterly confidence and a desire to subvert the conventions of the scene. Morisot places the vase, a large ceramic tureen-like container, to the left of center. Portrayed from a slightly elevated viewpoint, the vase and the table it sits on seem a little off-kilter, giving the picture a subtle visual dynamism. It is the vase that dominates the composition, so much so that the flower blooms nearly run out of space at the top of the canvas. Morisot underlines this fact by painting the vase in sumptuous and richly dense layers of white paint, drawing the viewer's attention and creating the effect of reflected sunlight.

The asymmetrical placement of the vase is echoed by the arrangement of secondary objects: a shadowy form at the lower left resembles a fan, but it lies there unexplained, while a tiny portrait in an oval frame is almost obscured behind the flowers at top right. The overall feeling is one of interruption and tantalizing defiance that is characteristic of many of Morisot's domestic scenes. What, for example, might we find if we had the key to unlock the drawer, whose keyhole stares out so prominently at the bottom of the canvas?

Morisot never exhibited *Dahlias* and did not sign the painting. It was, however, selected by Monet, Renoir, Degas, and the poet Stéphane Mallarmé to be included in the memorial exhibition that followed Morisot's untimely death in 1895. Mallarmé in particular praised Morisot's ability as a painter of still-life subjects, making sure to include other examples as well that were completed later in the artist's career. *Dahlias* remained with Morisot's family; her daughter Julie owned it until her death in 1966 and lent the work to numerous exhibitions. The Clark acquired the painting in 1974.

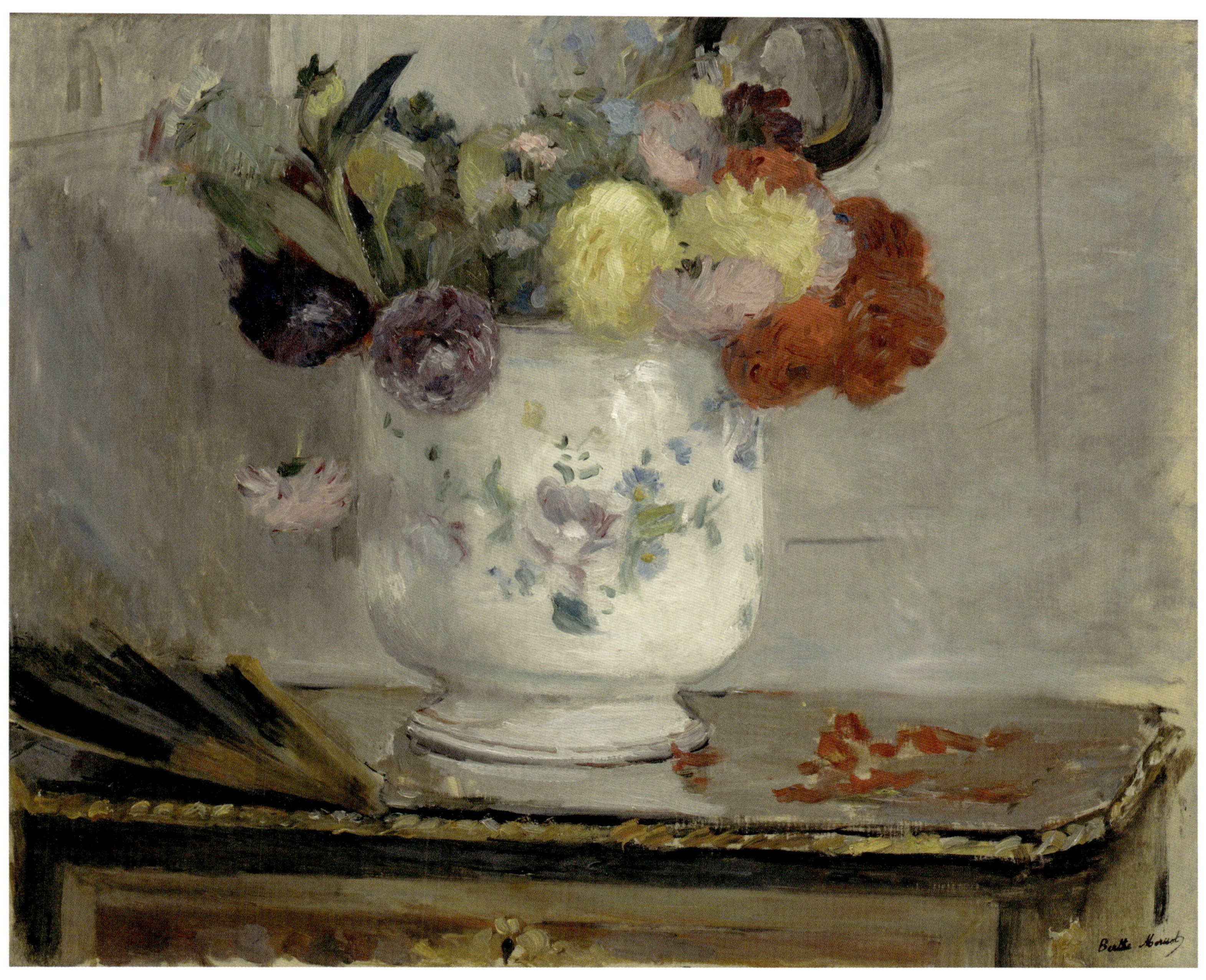
Berthe Morisot

69 BERTHE MORISOT French, 1841–1895

The Bath

1885–86
Oil on canvas
92.1 x 73.3 cm
Signed lower right: Berthe Morisot / Berthe Morisot
Acquired by Sterling and Francine Clark, 1949
1955.926

THE MODEL FOR *THE BATH* WAS MOST LIKELY ISABELLE LAMBERT, a seventeen-year-old girl whom Morisot had painted on several occasions in 1885 and 1886. She is shown in a white shift, reaching up to tie her hair with a black ribbon. She has already tied a blue choker around her neck and applied rouge to her cheeks and lips. With a hairbrush on her lap and a perfume vaporizer within reach, there is no doubt that she is getting herself ready to go out into the world. Like many pictures by Morisot and her fellow woman Impressionist Mary Cassatt, the canvas depicts an intimate moment in the domestic life of a respectable young lady, here captured with a combined delicacy and painterly boldness that places the work among Morisot's most successful compositions.

The Bath was first shown at the eighth Impressionist exhibition in 1886, where it appeared alongside an eclectic mix of work that included paintings by the Neo-Impressionists Georges Seurat and Paul Signac, as well as fantasy drawings by Odilon Redon. Morisot's slashing brushwork, clear colors, and areas of exposed canvas, however, are more typical of earlier Impressionist paintings. Despite the seemingly quick approach to the final picture, Morisot made careful preparatory pastel studies of the head and arms, the trickiest part of the composition. In fact, the varying levels of finish—from the carefully worked hands and face to the mere suggestion of a wall behind the model—add to the painting's allure. In praising *The Bath*, one critic of the 1886 exhibition even quoted the eighteenth-century critic Denis Diderot, a particularly astute reference given that Morisot's fascination with the Rococo painters Jean-Honoré Fragonard and François Boucher was at its peak during this period.

Morisot herself seems to have been very fond of the painting, keeping it until her death, when it then passed to her friend and fellow Impressionist Claude Monet. It stayed in Monet's family until the 1940s.

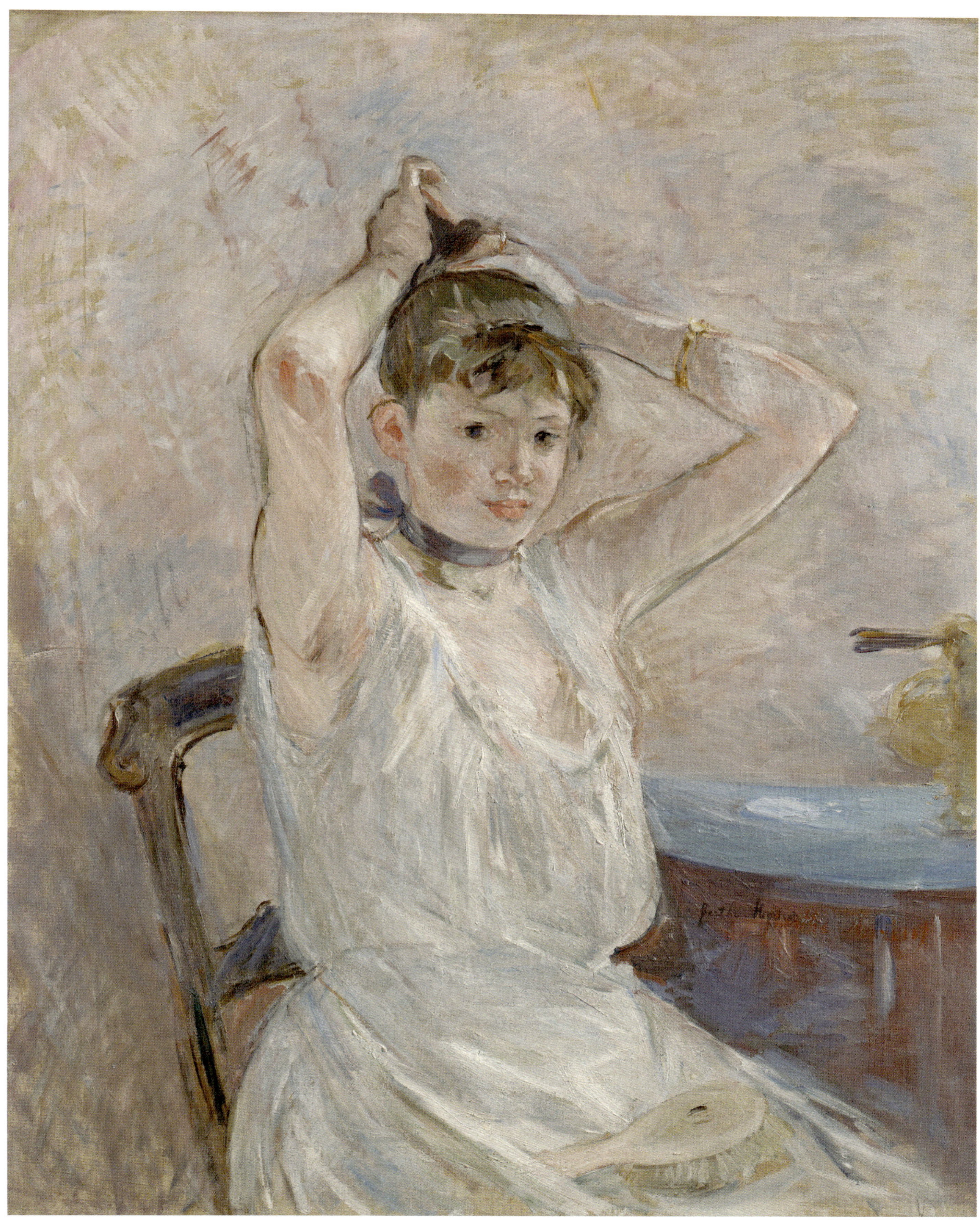

70 HENRI DE TOULOUSE-LAUTREC French, 1864–1901

Carmen

1884
Oil on canvas
52.9 x 40.8 cm
Acquired by Sterling and Francine Clark, 1951
1955.525

CARMEN IS AN EARLY WORK painted just as Toulouse-Lautrec was moving away from his academic training and developing an avant-garde style. The straightforward pose and the generally somber palette are somewhat conventional for a portrait, but there is already more than a hint of the audacity and boldness of the artist's later work in the confrontational expression of the model and the bright yellows and reds of her face and hair.

The model for the painting, Carmen Gaudin, was first seen by Toulouse-Lautrec on the avenue Clichy in the Montmartre neighborhood of Paris in the spring of 1884. Both Toulouse-Lautrec and his colleague Henri Rachou were struck by Gaudin's facial features and bright red hair, causing the former to exclaim, "Isn't she fantastic! And how tough she looks! If only I could get her to pose for me, that would be wonderful!" Although not a model by profession, Gaudin agreed to pose after being approached by Rachou. She also sat in more formal settings for Toulouse-Lautrec's teacher Fernand Cormon and the society painter Alfred Stevens. Toulouse-Lautrec became so enamored of her as a subject that he eventually used her as the model for at least twelve paintings over the next seven years, describing her in a letter to his mother as a "woman whose hair is all gold." In the Clark's painting she comes across as somewhat defiant and uncomfortable, refusing to meet the artist's gaze and hiding beneath her bangs. Significantly, Gaudin was the first of many women Toulouse-Lautrec encountered on the streets of Montmartre and recruited as models, a practice that infused his paintings with both a sense of specificity and modernity.

Carmen was first owned by Rachou, to whom Toulouse-Lautrec perhaps gave the canvas as a gift in memory of their first encounter with Gaudin. It later passed into the collection of Arthur Huc, a journalist in Toulouse, and Sterling Clark purchased it in 1951. It is one of three paintings by Toulouse-Lautrec that Clark owned, along with many of the artist's drawings and prints.

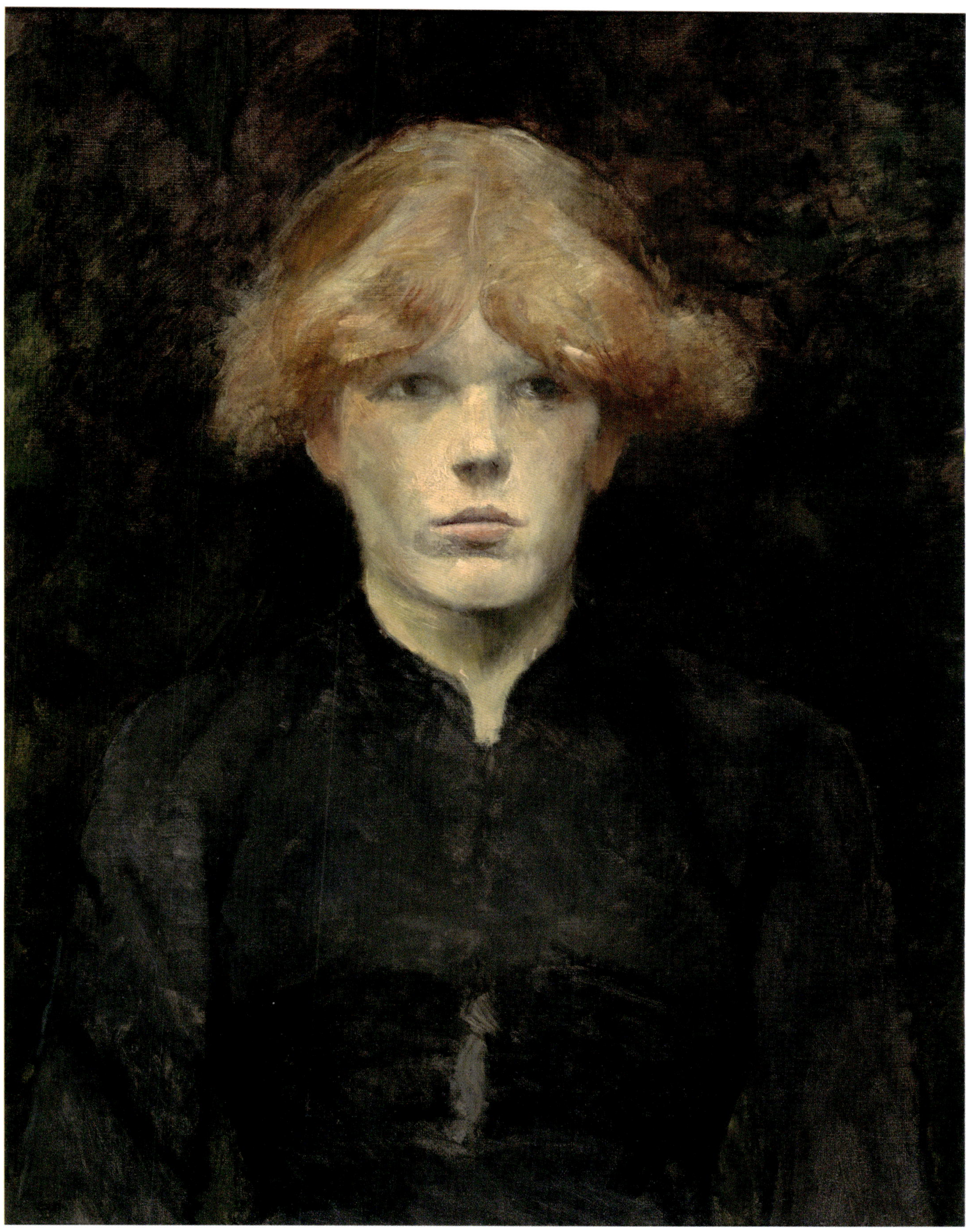

71 HENRI DE TOULOUSE-LAUTREC French, 1864–1901

Waiting

c. 1888
Oil on canvas
56.2 x 47 cm
Signed upper right: HTLautrec [HTL monogram]
Acquired by Sterling and Francine Clark, 1952
1955.564

WELL KNOWN FOR HIS VIBRANT AND THEATRICAL DEPICTIONS of dancers in *café-concert* spaces and dance halls, Toulouse-Lautrec created in *Waiting* a much more subdued and pensive scene. The artist chose an unusual viewpoint, above and behind the figure, hiding her features and emphasizing her slumped pose and downcast gaze as she rests her elbow on the table. There is the sense that the viewer is intruding on an intimate private moment. Toulouse-Lautrec depicted numerous women sitting alone at a table with a glass close at hand in the mid- to late 1880s, the period when he was increasingly involved with making posters for the popular entertainments in his Montmartre neighborhood. His growing participation in this milieu was spurred in part by Aristide Bruant, a singer and songwriter who opened a cabaret called Le Mirliton on the boulevard Rochechouart in the mid-1880s. Toulouse-Lautrec even created two paintings specifically to decorate Bruant's cabaret.

With few clear attributes, the sitter in *Waiting* remains unidentified; she could be the same Carmen Gaudin who posed for the Clark's painting *Carmen* (cat. 70). Regardless of her identity, the work conveys a melancholic aura through the woman's isolation and her downward gaze. At first glance, she appears to be seated at a café table, perhaps waiting for someone or simply passing the time lost in thought. Upon closer inspection, however, one sees the corner of a canvas visible at the upper left, indicating that this scene takes place in the artist's studio. In the late 1880s Toulouse-Lautrec had a growing interest in portraying the appearances and attitudes of women who frequented Montmartre cafés, even as he remained within the controlled confines of his own studio, and this picture is a clear example of this concern.

Toulouse-Lautrec drew much of the composition of this work with charcoal on the canvas, then applied paint in very thin layers. The fluid washes and visible passages of charcoal underdrawing add to the painting's allure, accentuating the somber and meditative mood. Even with the highlights of the contrasting yellow and green of the table and glass, and a few touches of blue on the canvas in the background, it is a relatively restrained palette compared with that of Toulouse-Lautrec's later works.

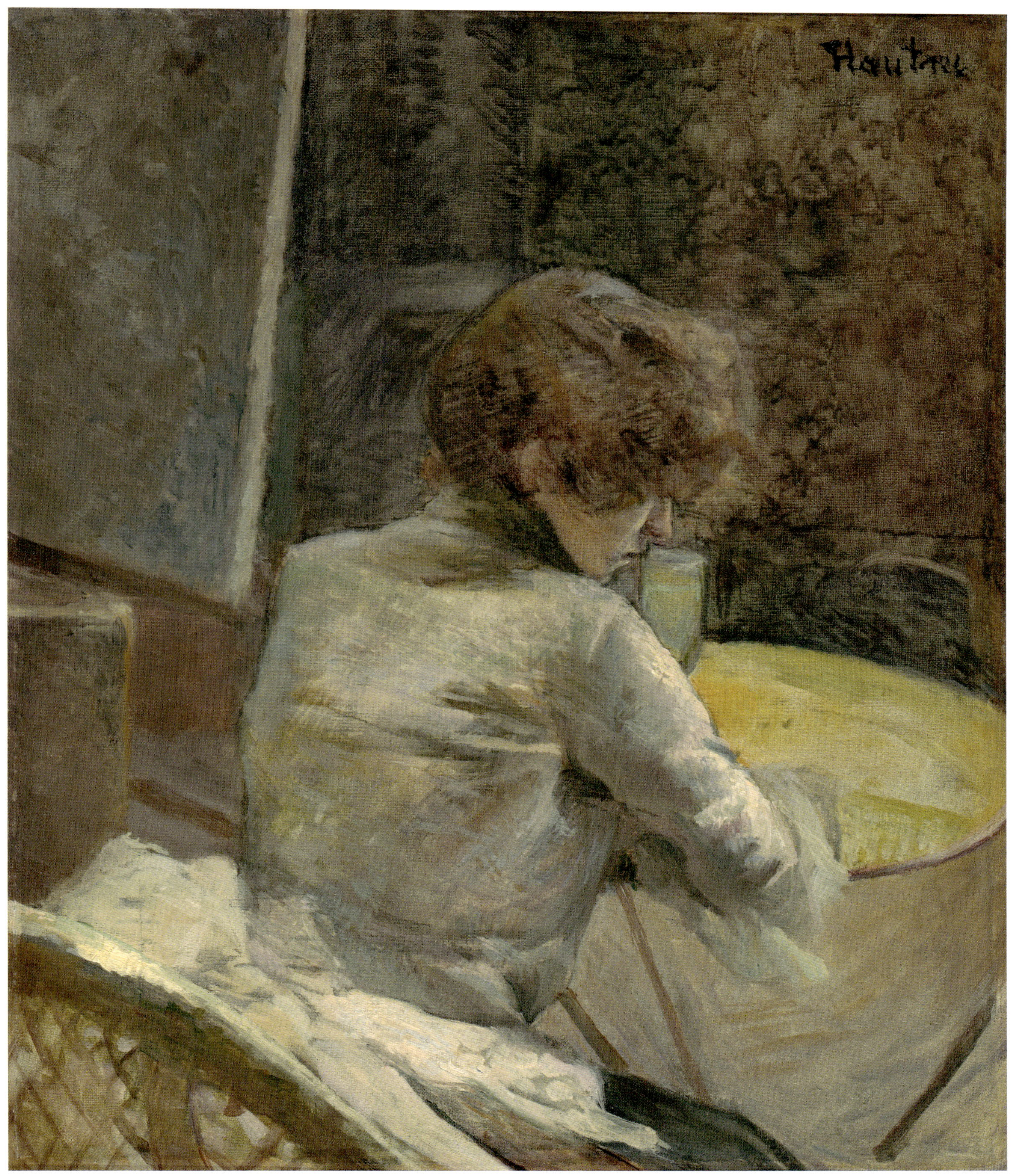

72 PIERRE BONNARD French, 1867–1947

Women with a Dog

1891
Oil on canvas
41 x 32.4 cm
Signed and dated lower right: PBonnard [PB in monogram] / 1891
Acquired by the Clark, 1979
1979.23

WOMEN WITH A DOG WAS PAINTED when Bonnard was twenty-four and closely allied with the group of young artists who named themselves the Nabis, after the Hebrew word for prophet. The decorative aesthetic the Nabis followed drew in large part from the work of Paul Gauguin and from the simplified forms and flattened pictorial space of Japanese prints. While Bonnard had achieved early fame for his graphic work (receiving public recognition for a color lithograph advertising poster from 1891), *Women with a Dog* exemplifies his decorative, nonperspectival style on canvas. The insistent flatness of the central figure's checked dress situates her directly at the surface of the image, and the distance between this woman and the background figures is suggested through the latters' smaller size and higher placement. Bonnard borrowed these spatial techniques from Japanese woodblock prints, which he would have been familiar with from an exhibition of Japanese works that was held in 1890 at the École des Beaux-Arts, where Bonnard was studying at the time.

Women with a Dog demonstrates the kind of decorative painting Bonnard experimented with early in his career. Busy and densely patterned, the canvas is reminiscent of the much larger murals and folding screens the Nabis created to decorate collectors' rooms. As in many of his paintings, Bonnard used members of his family as models. The woman at the left is his sister Andrée Bonnard Terrasse, and the one on the right is his cousin Berthe Schaedlin. Bonnard made preparatory drawings for the composition and continued to modify *Women with a Dog* throughout the painting process. His working technique is seen in the passages of pen that outline the major figures, as well as the graphite marks on the main figure's arm. These marks are not only vestigial remains of a preliminary stage but are also significant contributions to the integrity of the composition.

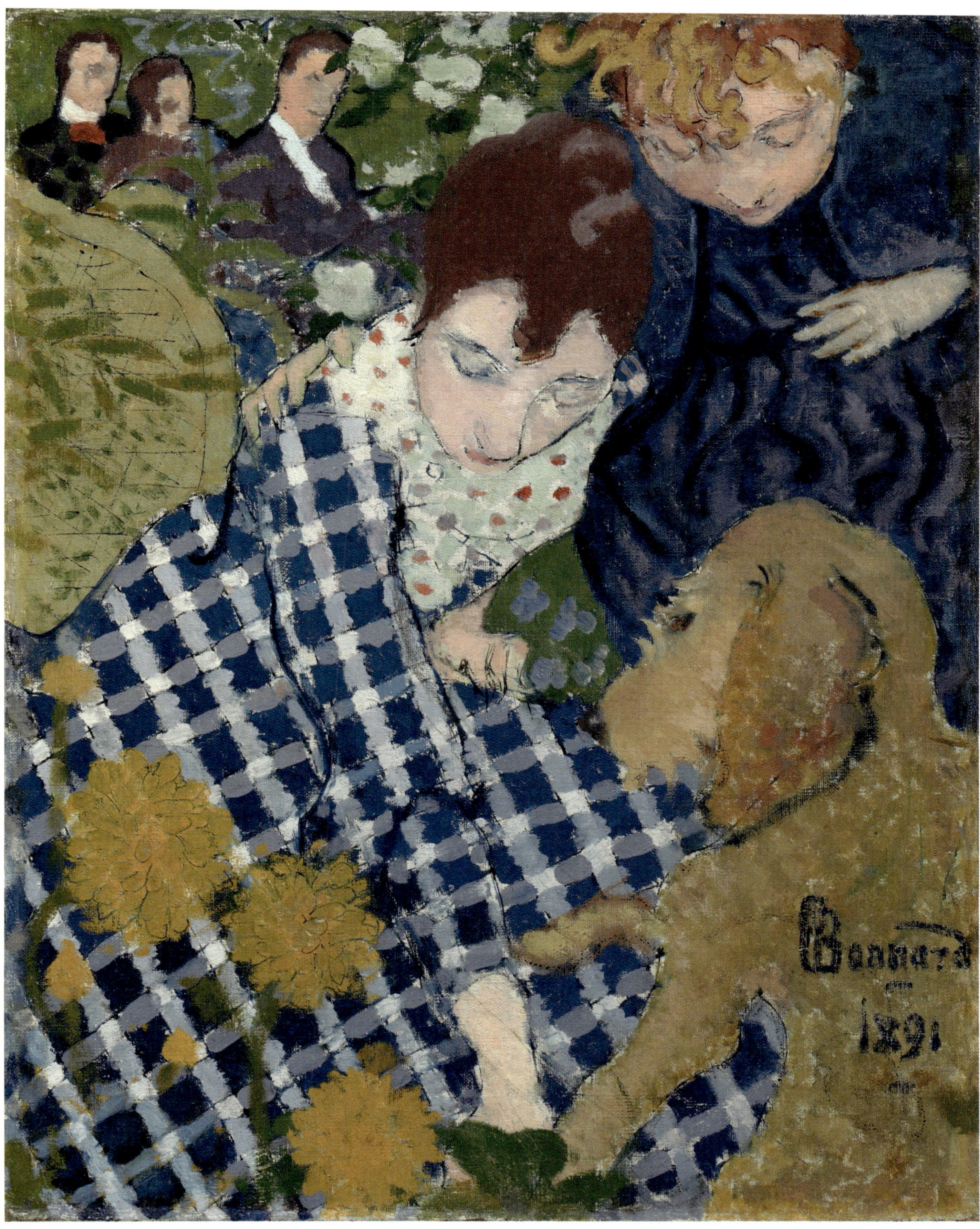
Bonnard
1891

73 PAUL GAUGUIN French, 1848–1903

Young Christian Girl

1894
Oil on canvas
65.3 x 46.7 cm
Signed and dated lower right: P. Gauguin 94.
Acquired by the Clark in honor of Harding F. Bancroft (Institute Trustee, 1970–87; President, 1977–87), 1986
1986.22

YOUNG CHRISTIAN GIRL WAS PAINTED IN 1894 while Gauguin was spending several months in the small village of Pont-Aven in Brittany. It is part of a group of works by Gauguin that focus on the life and faith of Breton peasants. While his other paintings from this period show Breton women in traditional black dresses and starched white hats, the figure in *Young Christian Girl* wears a bright yellow dress and a black hat. Gauguin spent much of his artistic life in the South Seas, moving there permanently in 1895, and the tropical culture he encountered there had a significant influence on his oeuvre. The yellow dress, in fact, was likely modeled on the clothing given by Christian missionaries to South Sea islanders. More than simply adding a tropical flavor to the painting, however, the bright dress plays off the other vibrant colors in the picture, from the russet trees in the upper right corner to the glowing orange hills and the bright blue sky. Gauguin revels in deftly juxtaposing these hues, which stand out even more boldly in the absence of a traditional perspective to the landscape.

The painterly technique of *Young Christian Girl* is matched by the picture's compelling subject. The dissatisfaction with Paris and urban sprawl that initially led Gauguin to travel to the South Seas also drew him to rural areas where the modern way of life had not yet taken hold. Breton peasants lived relatively simple lives at the end of the nineteenth century; they worked in the fields during the week and went to church on Sundays. The young girl in Gauguin's painting is devoted to her faith; she stands in the open air, hands joined, a cross around her neck, her eyes downcast or closed, concentrating on her prayers. There is a deep serenity and sense of purpose to the figure, which is aided by the lilac-hued shapes that fan out around the girl's shoulders, suggestive of an angel's wings.

For all of its intense color and indebtedness to the Impressionists and Van Gogh, *Young Christian Girl* looks both forward toward bolder experiments in abstraction and farther backward toward Old Master portraits of people praying. In fact, on the very trip through Europe when Gauguin painted *Young Christian Girl*, he was intently studying the work of fifteenth-century Netherlandish artists such as Hans Memling.

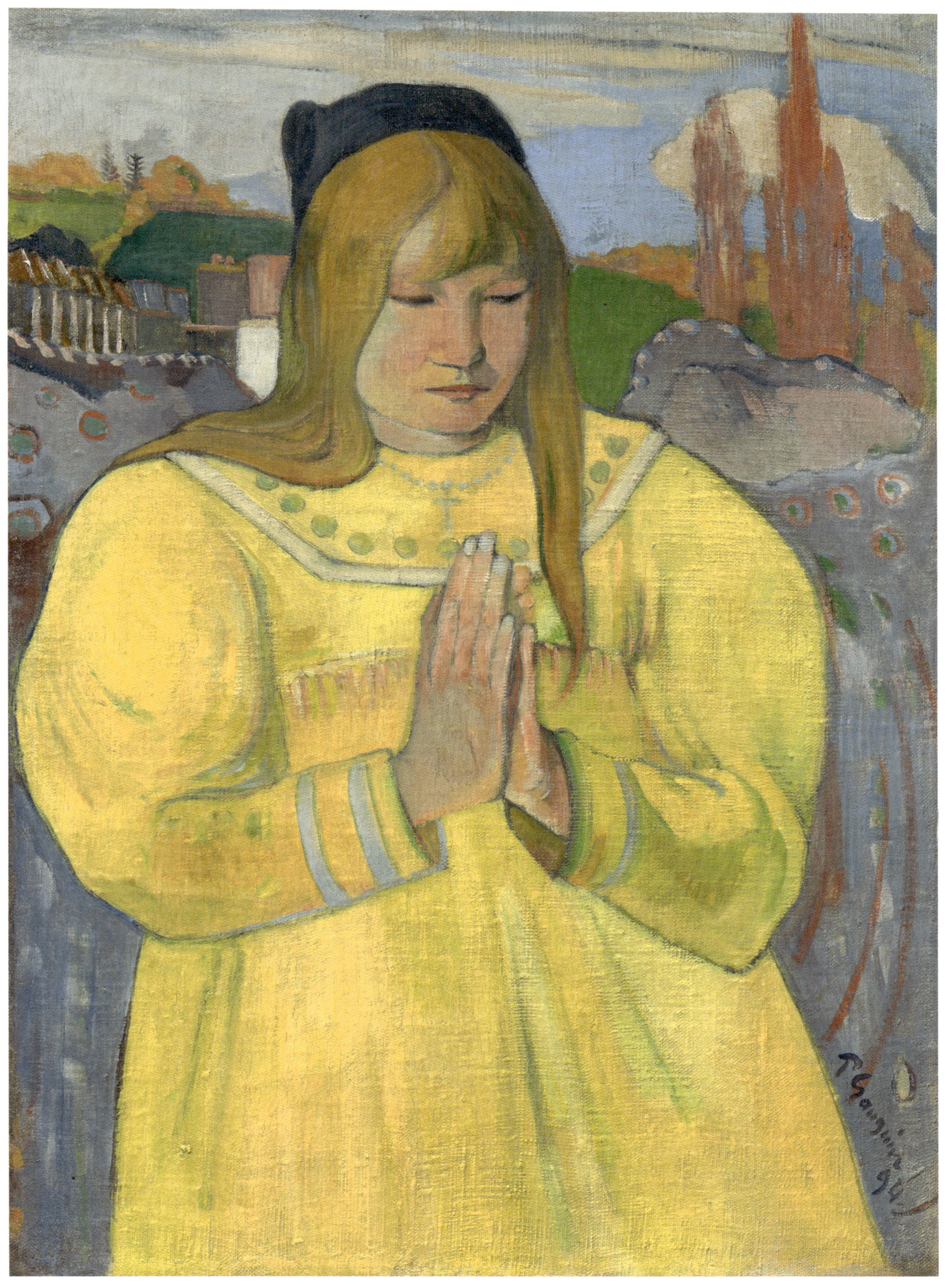

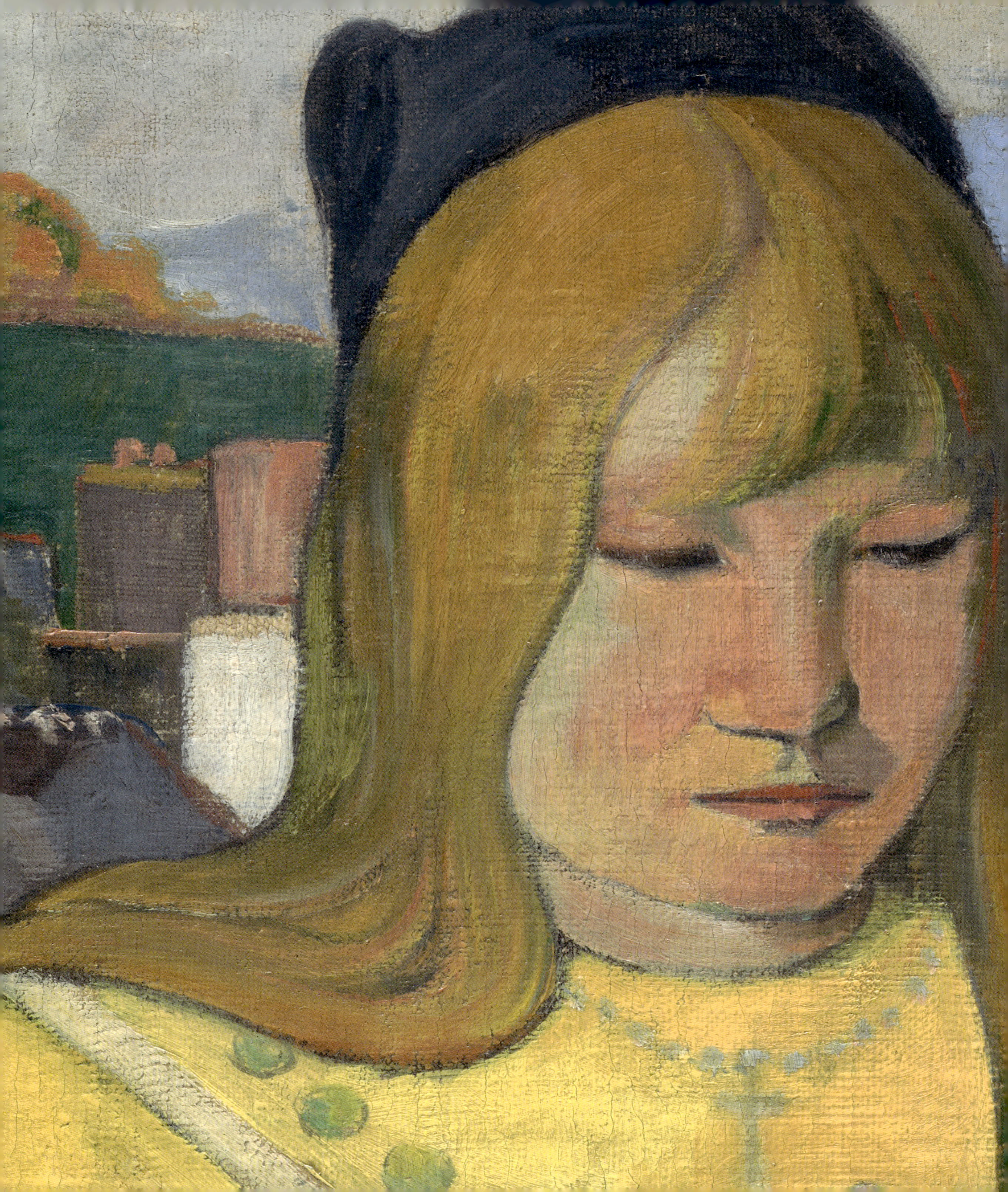

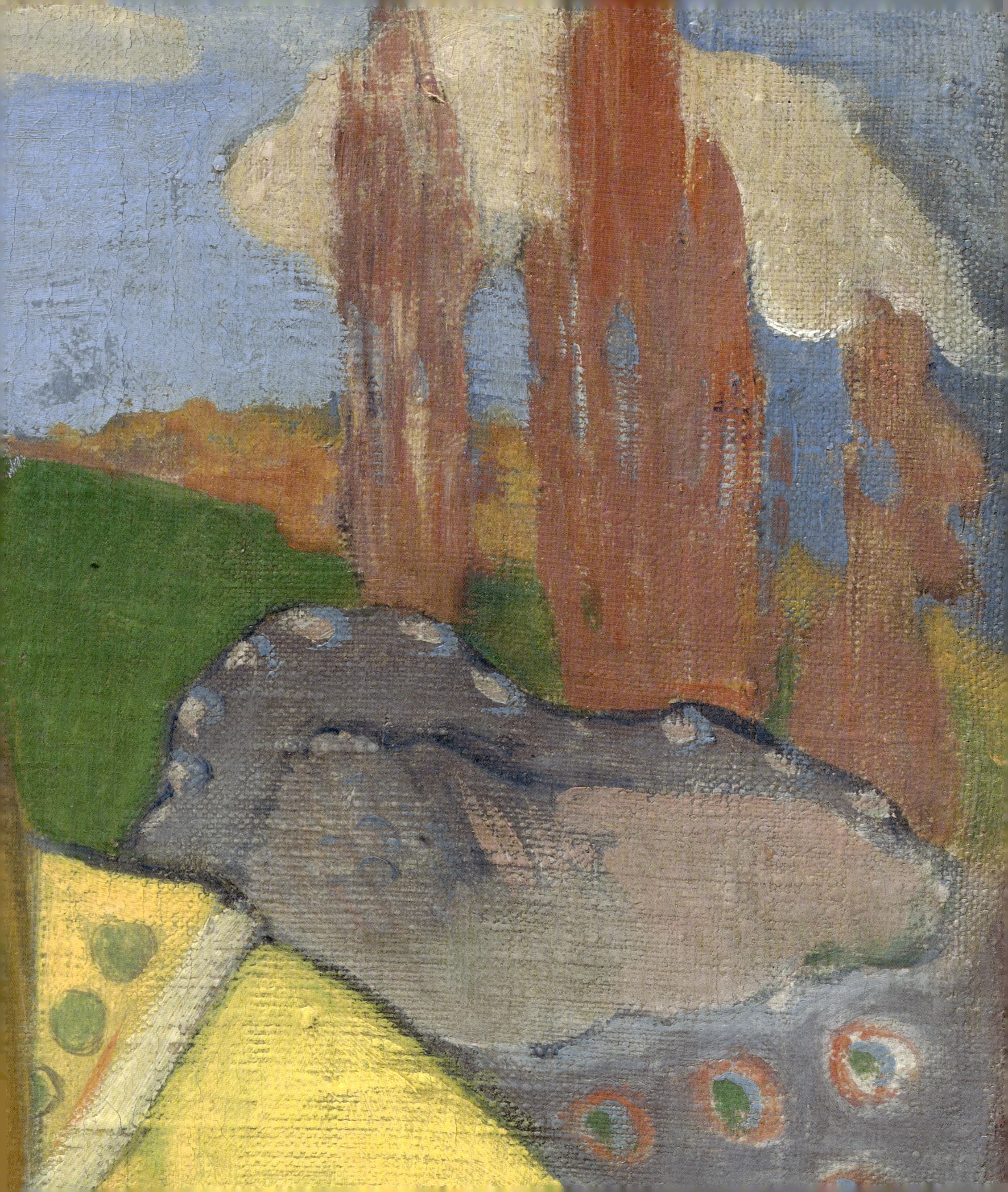

FURTHER READING

Cahill, Timothy. *Art in Nature: The Clark Inside and Out.* Williamstown, Mass.: Sterling and Francine Clark Art Institute, 2005.

Conforti, Michael, et al. *The Clark Brothers Collect: Impressionist and Early Modern Paintings.* Exh. cat. Williamstown, Mass.: Sterling and Francine Clark Art Institute, 2006.

Conrads, Margaret C. *American Paintings and Sculpture at the Sterling and Francine Clark Art Institute.* New York: Hudson Hills, 1990.

Gibson, Sarah Scott, et al. *Book Illustrations from Six Centuries in the Library of the Sterling and Francine Clark Art Institute.* Williamstown, Mass.: Sterling and Francine Clark Art Institute, 1990.

Haverkamp-Begemann, Egbert, et al. *Drawings from the Clark Art Institute: A Catalogue Raisonné of the Robert Sterling Clark Collection of European and American Drawings, Sixteenth through Nineteenth Centuries, at the Sterling and Francine Clark Art Institute, Williamstown.* 2 vols. New Haven and London: Yale University Press, 1964.

House, John. *The Genius of Renoir: Paintings from the Clark.* Exh. cat. Williamstown, Mass.: Sterling and Francine Clark Art Institute; Madrid: Museo Nacional del Prado, 2010.

"Sterling and Francine Clark Art Institute." Special issue, *Magazine Antiques* 152 (Oct. 1997).

Wees, Beth Carver. *English, Irish & Scottish Silver at the Sterling and Francine Clark Art Institute.* New York: Hudson Hills, 1997.

INDEX

CREDITS

PHOTOGRAPHY CREDITS

Permission to reproduce images is provided by courtesy of the owners listed in the captions. Additional photography credits are as follows:

ADDITIONAL CREDITS

The entries in this book draw heavily on research that will be published in the Clark's forthcoming catalogue of nineteenth-century European paintings. In particular, we are indebted to the following scholars: Alexis Goodin, John House, Richard Kendall, Sarah Lees, Kelly Pask, Kathryn Price, and Fronia Wissman.